VIZ GRAPHIC NOVEL
◆◆◆◆◆◆◆◆◆◆◆◆◆◆◆◆

NO NEED FOR TENCHI!™

DREAM A LITTLE SCHEME

STORY AND ART BY
HITOSHI OKUDA

CONTENTS

This volume contains NO NEED FOR TENCHI! PART SIX
in its entirety.

**STORY AND ART BY
HITOSHI OKUDA**

**ENGLISH ADAPTATION BY
FRED BURKE**

Translation/Lillian Olsen
Touch-Up Art & Lettering/Dan Nakrosis
Cover Design/Hidemi Sahara
Editor/Carl Gustav Horn
Director of Sales & Marketing/Dallas Middaugh

Editor-in-Chief/Hyoe Narita
Publisher/Seiji Horibuchi

Printed in Canada

Published by Viz Communications, Inc.
P.O. Box 77010 · San Francisco, CA 94107

10 9 8 7 6 5 4
First Printing, September 1998
Fourth Printing, November 2001

Get your free Viz Shop-by-Mail Catalog!
(800) 394-3042 or Fax (415) 546-7086

NO NEED FOR TENCHI! GRAPHIC NOVELS TO DATE

NO NEED FOR TENCHI!	DREAM A LITTLE SCHE
SWORD PLAY	TENCHI IN LOVE
MAGICAL GIRL PRETTY SAMMY	CHEF OF IRON
SAMURAI SPACE OPERA	THE QUEST FOR MORE
UNREAL GENIUS	MOTHER PLANET

Tales of Tenchi #1
BREAKDOWN

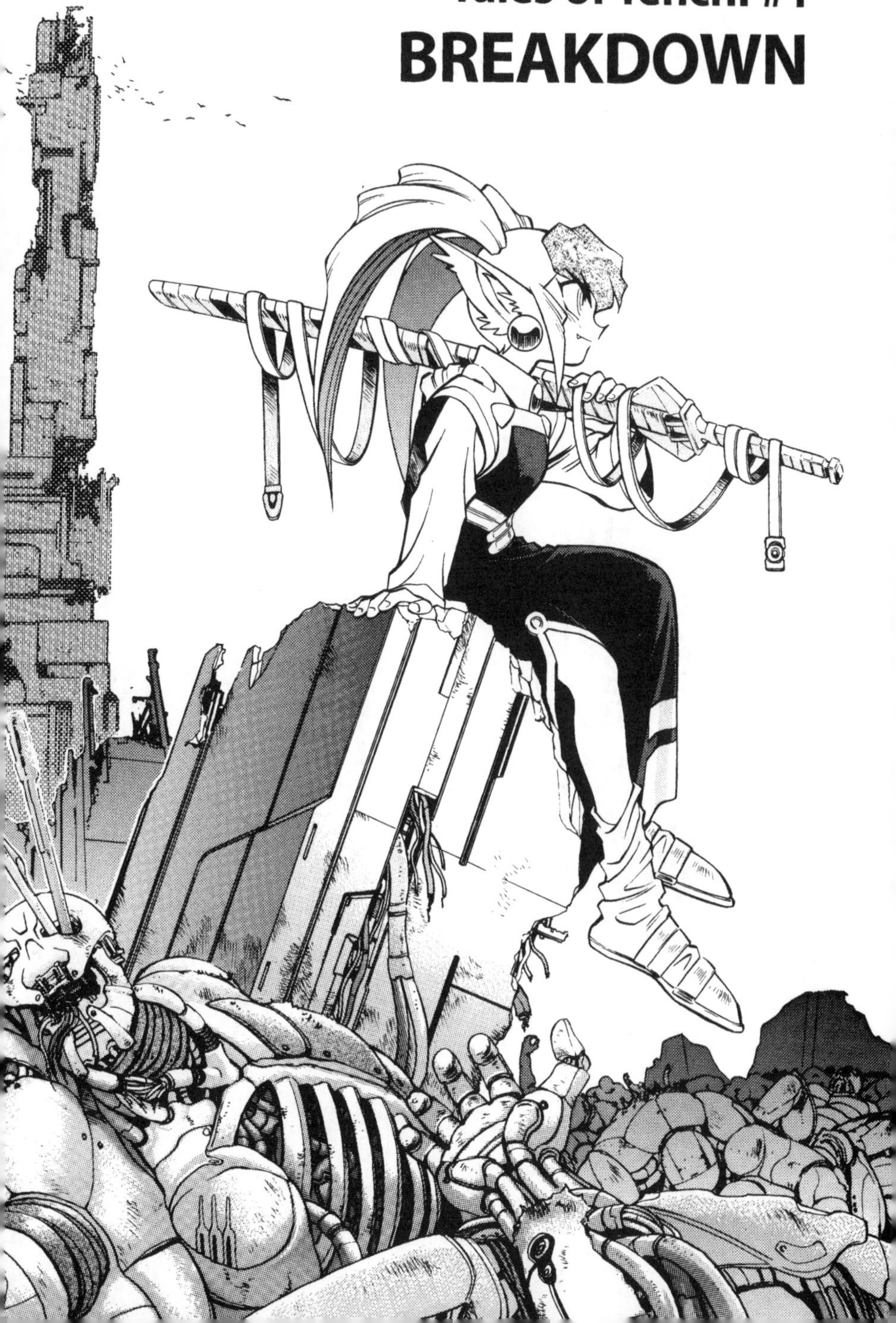

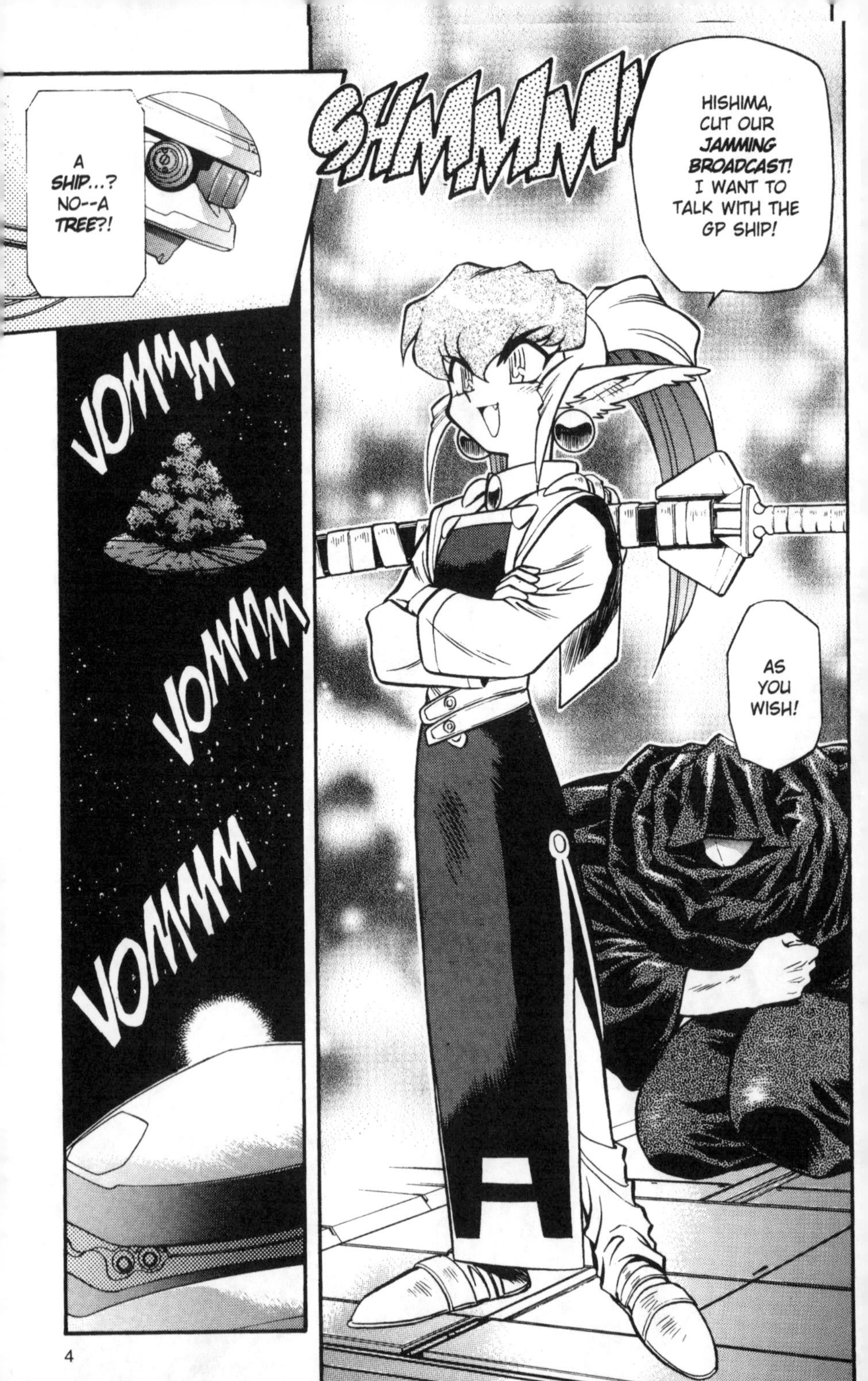
A SHIP...? NO--A TREE?!
VOMMM
VOMMM
VOMMM
SHMMMM
HISHIMA, CUT OUR JAMMING BROADCAST! I WANT TO TALK WITH THE GP SHIP!
AS YOU WISH!

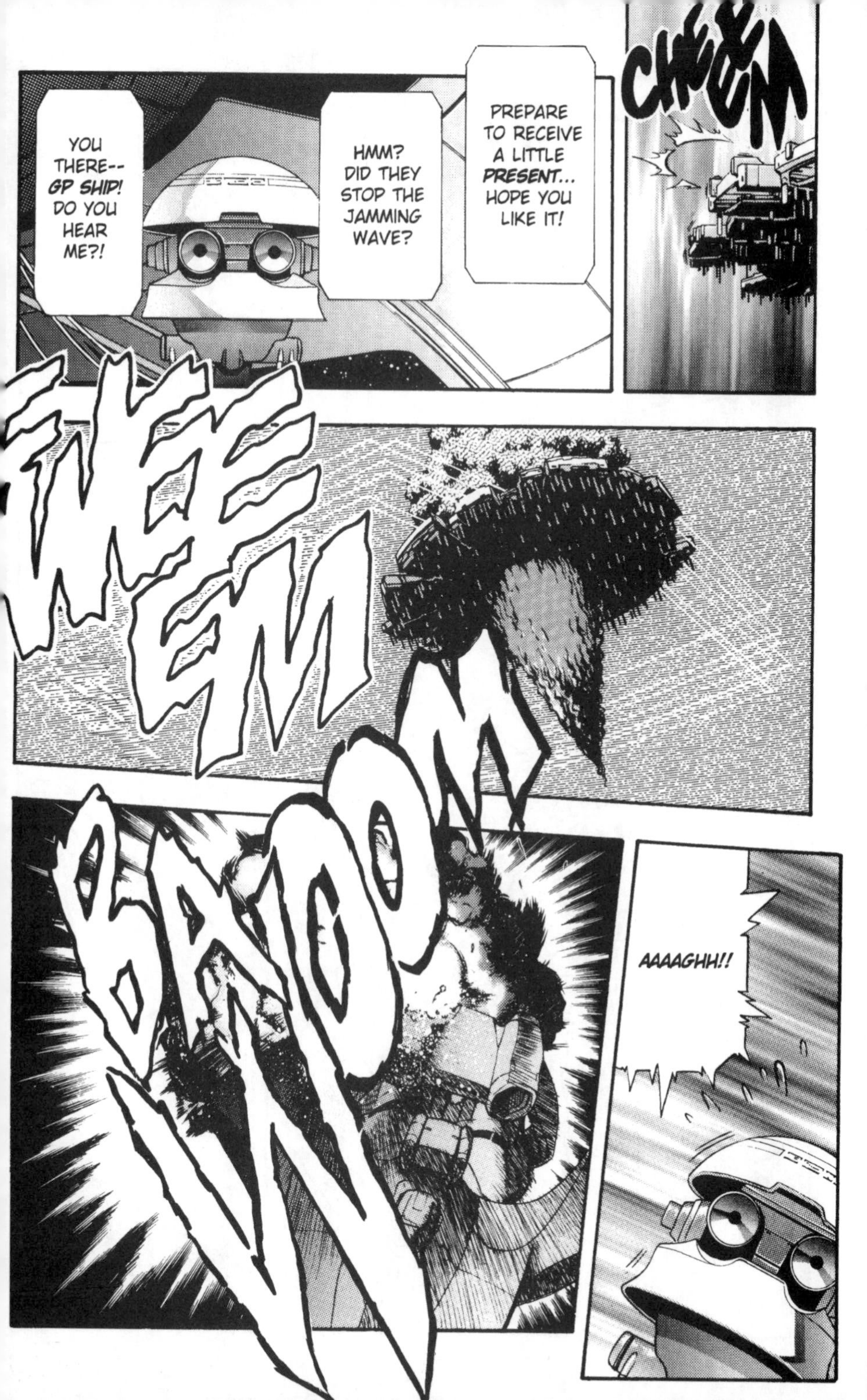

YOU THERE-- GP SHIP! DO YOU HEAR ME?!
HMM? DID THEY STOP THE JAMMING WAVE?
PREPARE TO RECEIVE A LITTLE PRESENT... HOPE YOU LIKE IT!
CHEEN
AAAAGHH!!

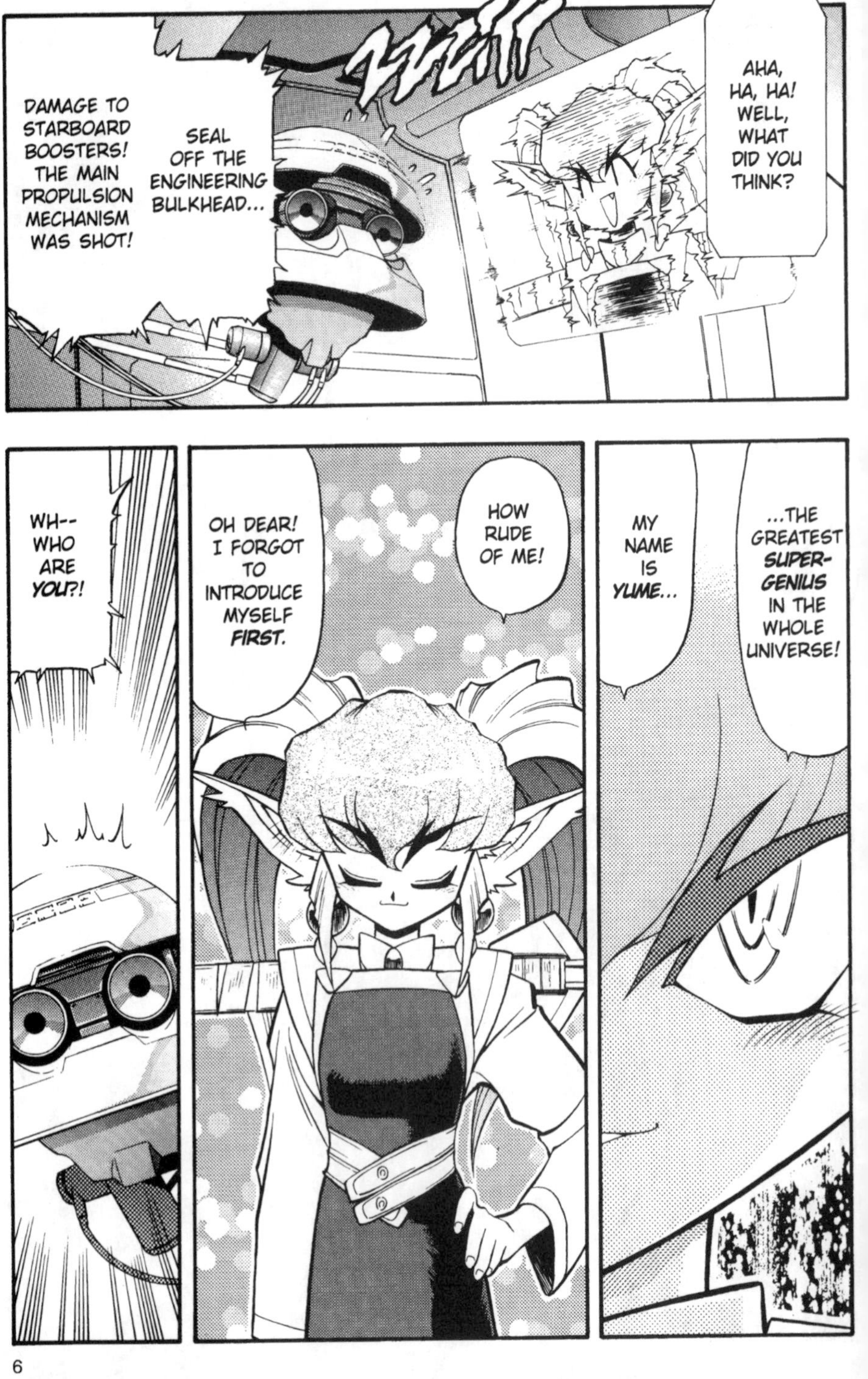
DAMAGE TO STARBOARD BOOSTERS! THE MAIN PROPULSION MECHANISM WAS SHOT!
SEAL OFF THE ENGINEERING BULKHEAD...
AHA, HA, HA! WELL, WHAT DID YOU THINK?
WH-- WHO ARE YOU?!
OH DEAR! I FORGOT TO INTRODUCE MYSELF FIRST.
HOW RUDE OF ME!
MY NAME IS YUME...
...THE GREATEST SUPER-GENIUS IN THE WHOLE UNIVERSE!

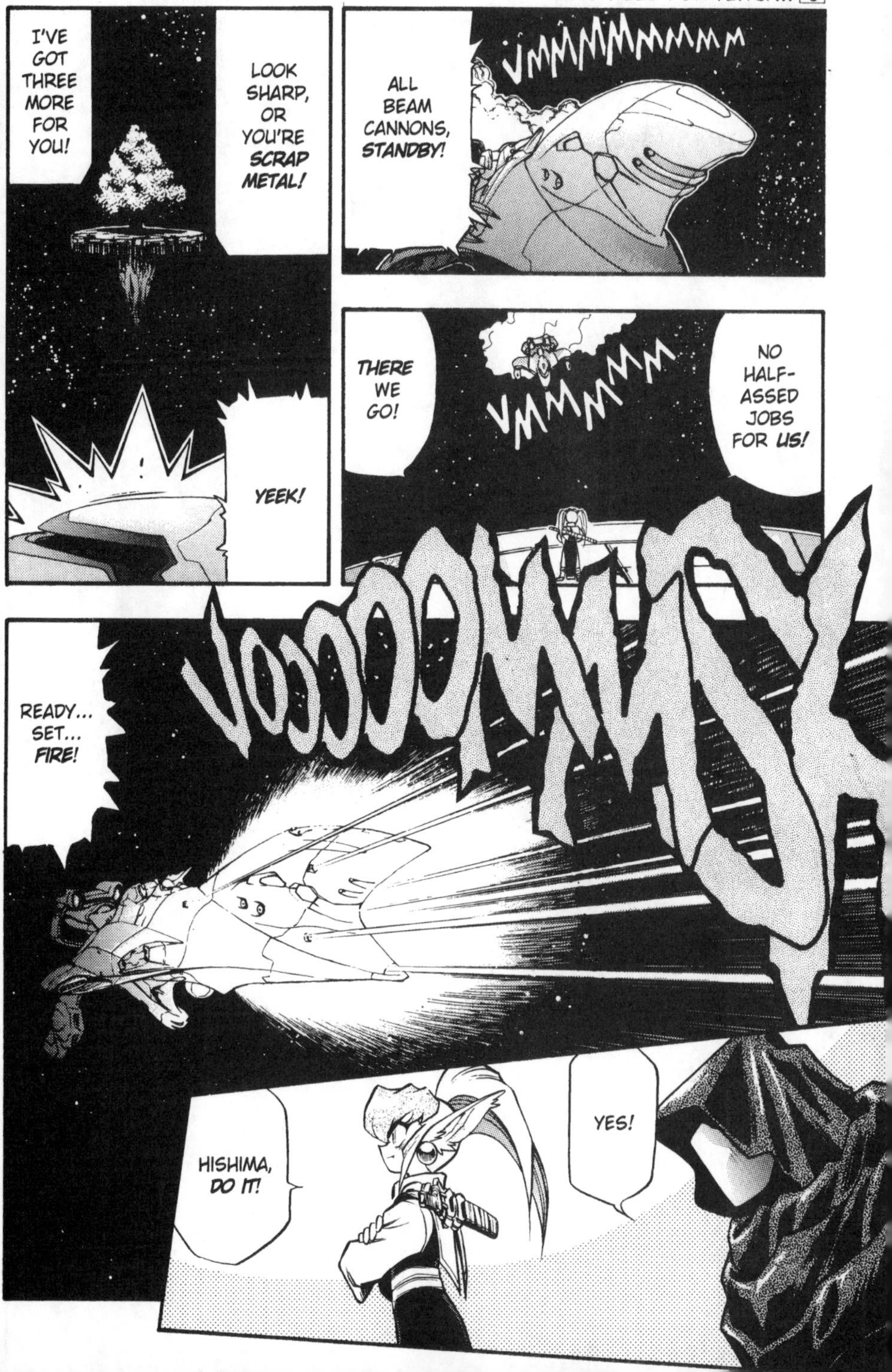
I'VE GOT THREE MORE FOR YOU!
LOOK SHARP, OR YOU'RE SCRAP METAL!
YEEK!
ALL BEAM CANNONS, STANDBY!
THERE WE GO!
NO HALF-ASSED JOBS FOR US!
READY... SET... FIRE!
HISHIMA, DO IT!
YES!

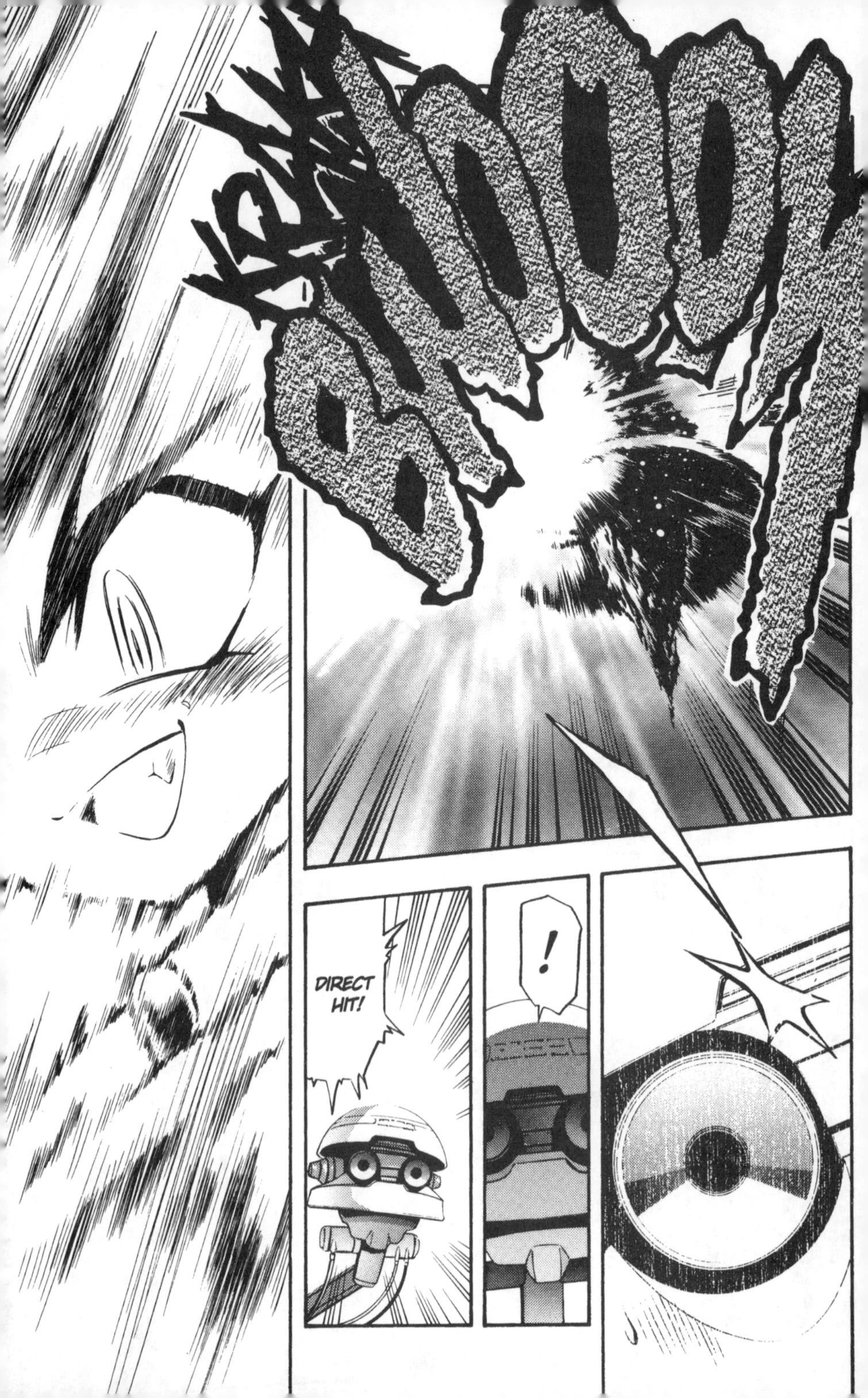
DIRECT HIT!
!

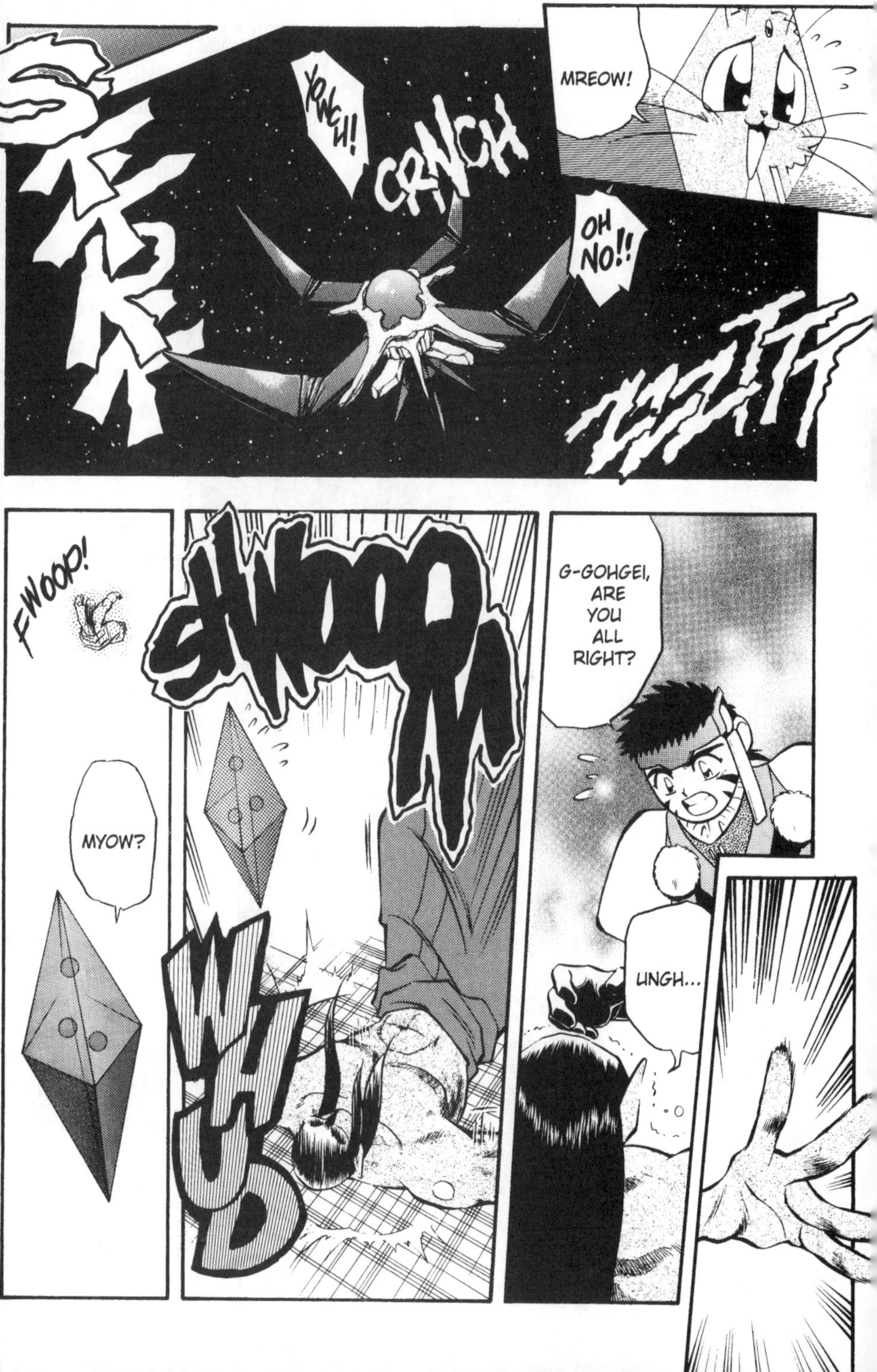
YOWCH!
CRNCH
OH NO!!
MREOW!
FWOOP!
MYOW?
SHWOOM
WHUD
G-GOHGEI, ARE YOU ALL RIGHT?
UNGH...

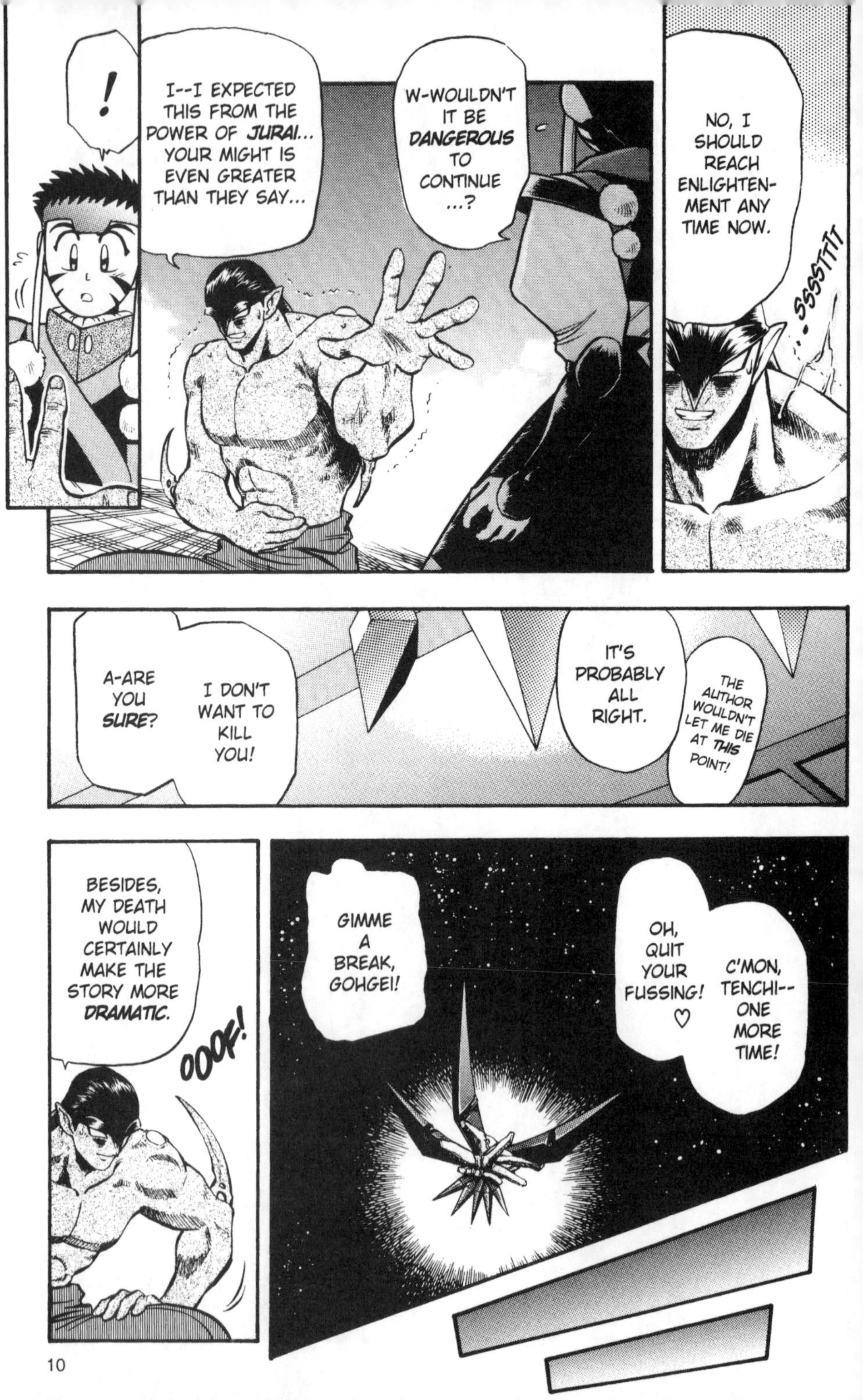
!
I--I EXPECTED THIS FROM THE POWER OF **JURAI**... YOUR MIGHT IS EVEN GREATER THAN THEY SAY...
W-WOULDN'T IT BE **DANGEROUS** TO CONTINUE ...?
NO, I SHOULD REACH ENLIGHTEN-MENT ANY TIME NOW.
..SSSSTTTT
A-ARE YOU **SURE**?
I DON'T WANT TO KILL YOU!
IT'S PROBABLY ALL RIGHT.
THE AUTHOR WOULDN'T LET ME DIE AT **THIS** POINT!
BESIDES, MY DEATH WOULD CERTAINLY MAKE THE STORY MORE **DRAMATIC**.
OOOF!
GIMME A BREAK, GOHGEI!
OH, QUIT YOUR FUSSING! ♡
C'MON, TENCHI-- ONE MORE TIME!

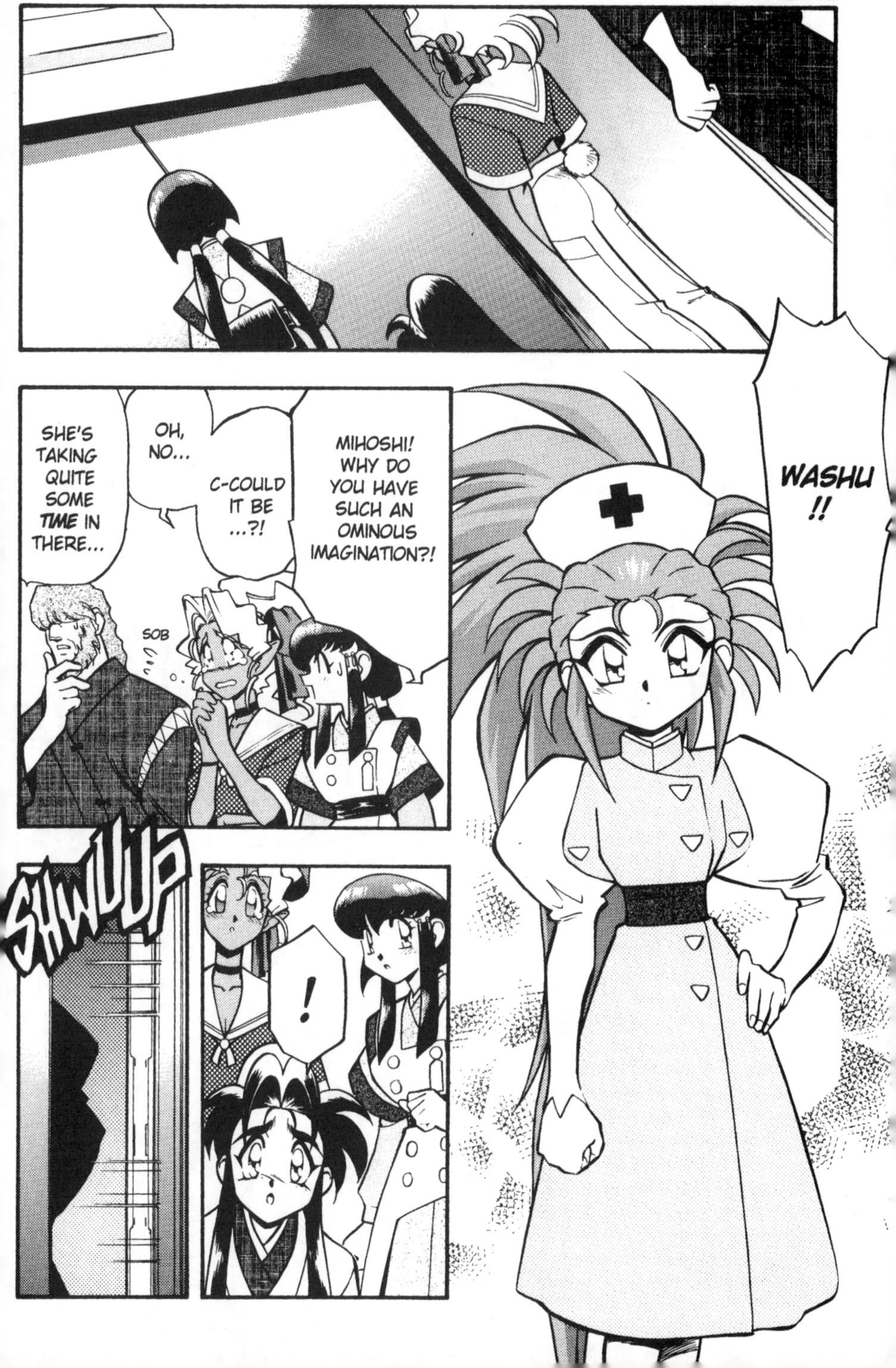
SHE'S TAKING QUITE SOME TIME IN THERE...
OH, NO...
C-COULD IT BE ...?!
MIHOSHI! WHY DO YOU HAVE SUCH AN OMINOUS IMAGINATION?!
SOB
SHWUUP
!
WASHU !!

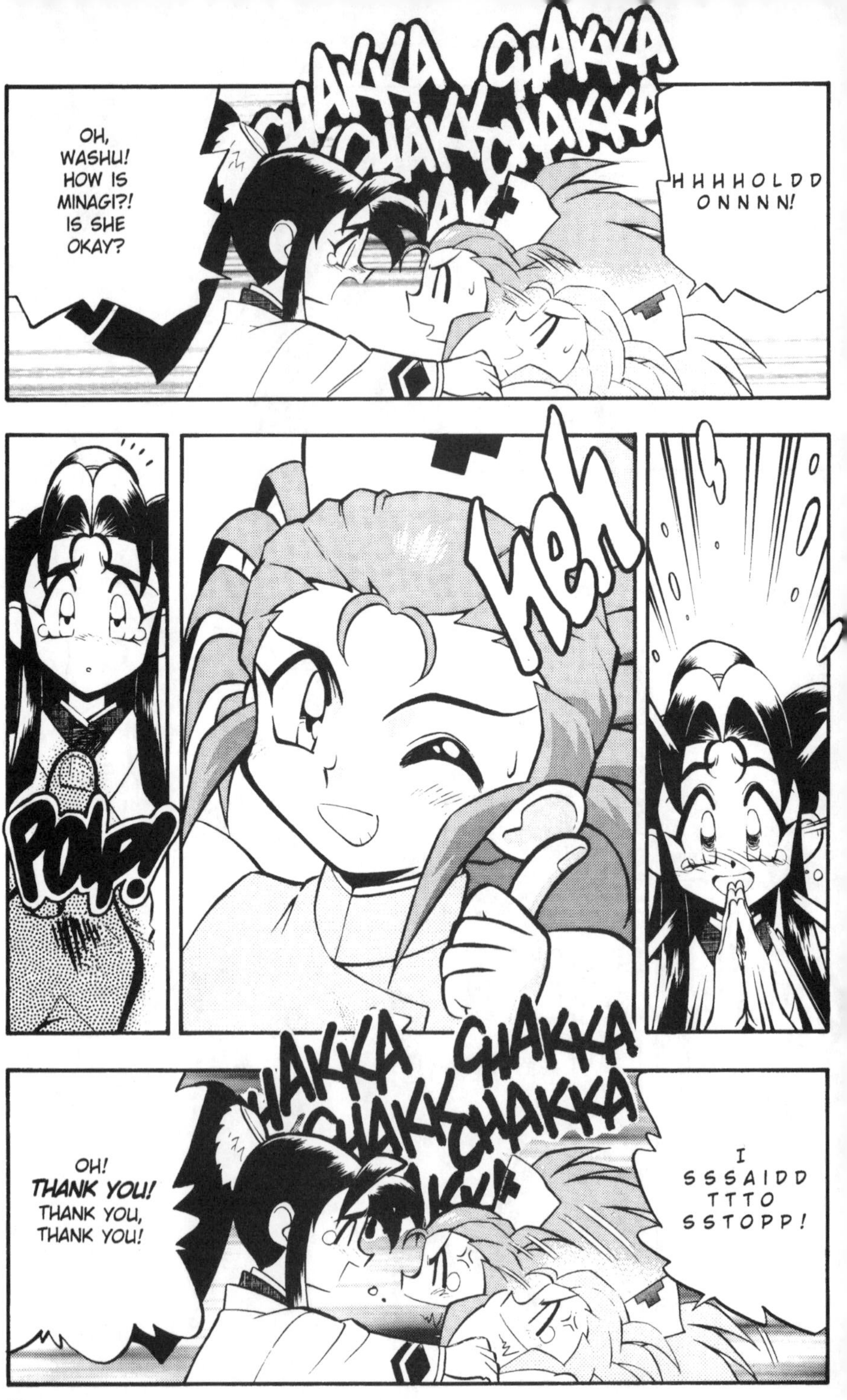
CHAKKA CHAKKA CHAKKCHAKKA
OH, WASHU! HOW IS MINAGI?! IS SHE OKAY?
HHHHOLDD ONNNN!
POW!
heh
OH! THANK YOU! THANK YOU, THANK YOU!
CHAKKA CHAKKA CHAKKCHAKKA
I SSSAIDD TTTO SSTOPP!

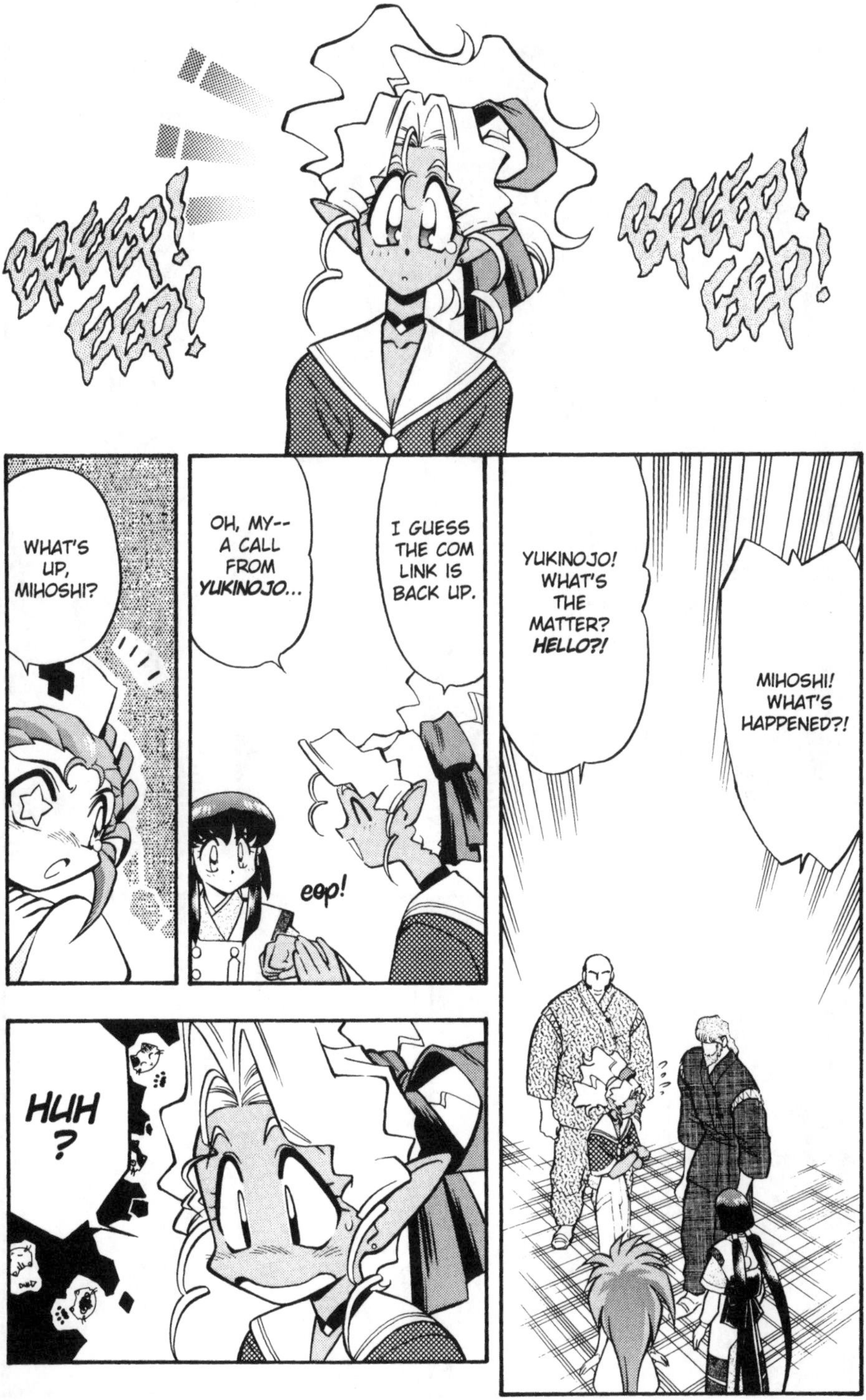
BREEP! EEP!
BREEP! EEP!
WHAT'S UP, MIHOSHI?
OH, MY-- A CALL FROM YUKINOJO...
I GUESS THE COM LINK IS BACK UP.
eep!
HUH?
YUKINOJO! WHAT'S THE MATTER? HELLO?!
MIHOSHI! WHAT'S HAPPENED?!

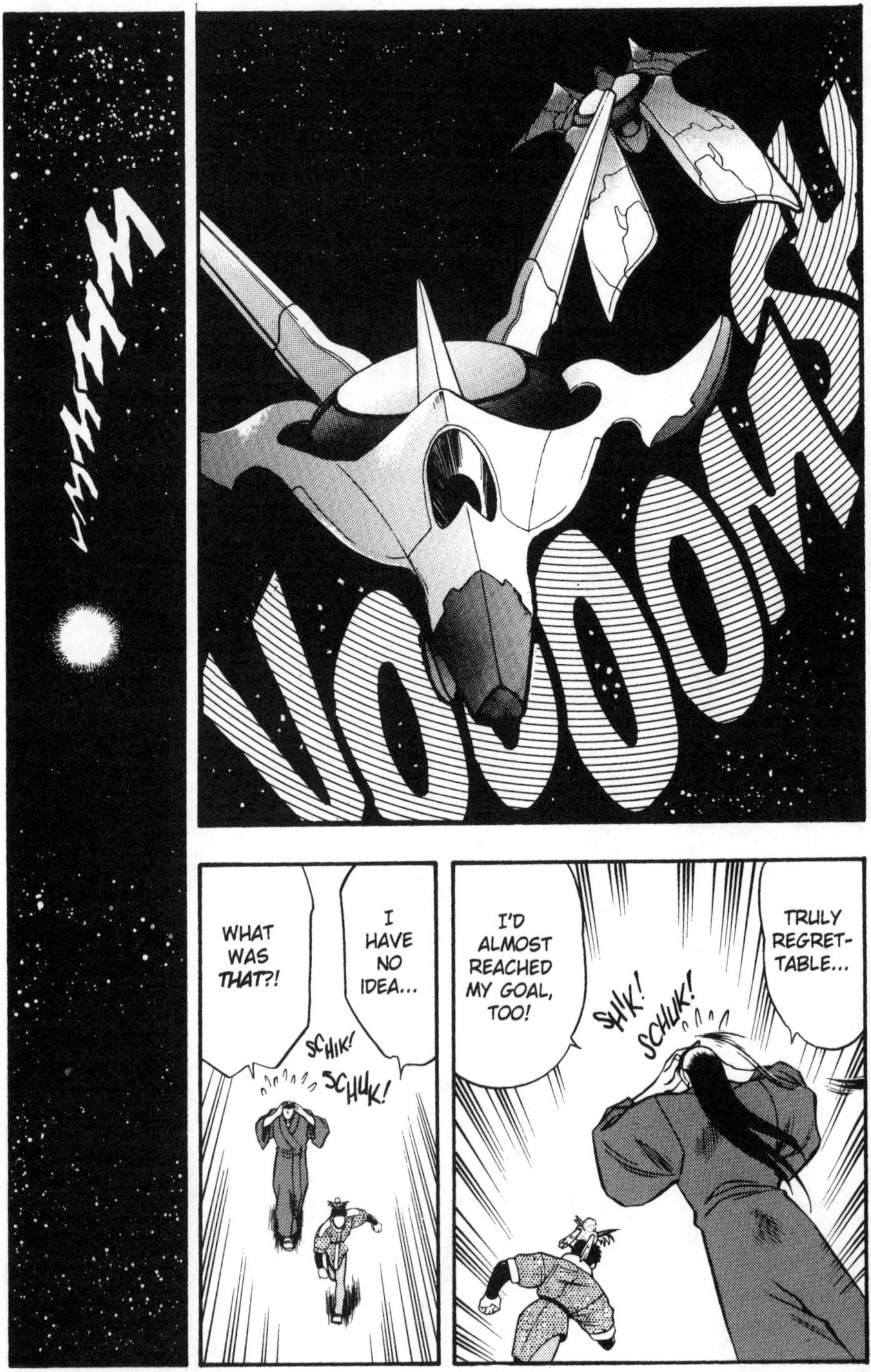
VOOOOM!
WHAT WAS THAT?!
I HAVE NO IDEA...
SCHIK!
SCHUK!
I'D ALMOST REACHED MY GOAL, TOO!
SHIK!
SCHUK!
TRULY REGRET-TABLE...

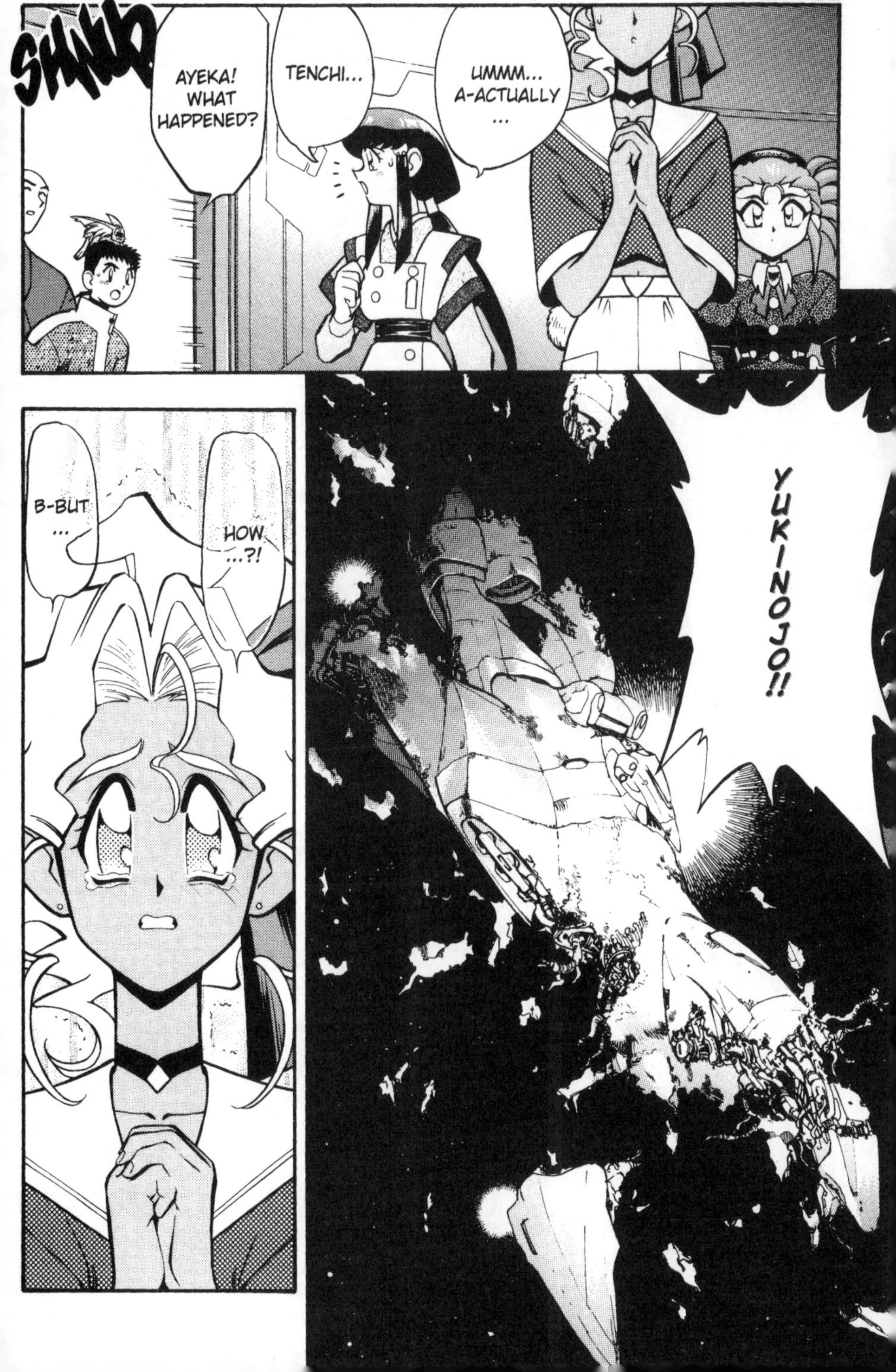
AYEKA! WHAT HAPPENED?
TENCHI...
UMMM... A-ACTUALLY ...
B-BUT ...
HOW ...?!
YUKINOJO!!

WHAT COULD HAVE DONE *THAT*...?

THE CUL-MINATION OF *YEARS* OF META-TECH-NOLOGY...

...*NOTHING* SHOULD SO EASILY BEAT THAT SHIP-- *NOTHING!*

WHICH MEANS IT MUST HAVE RECEIVED AN ABSURDLY CRUSHING BLOW...

GOHGEI...

I'M HAVING ANOTHER ONE OF MY *REALLY* BAD FEELINGS...

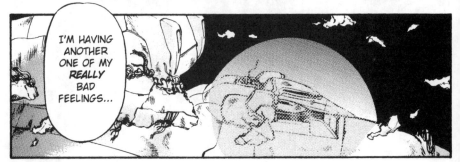

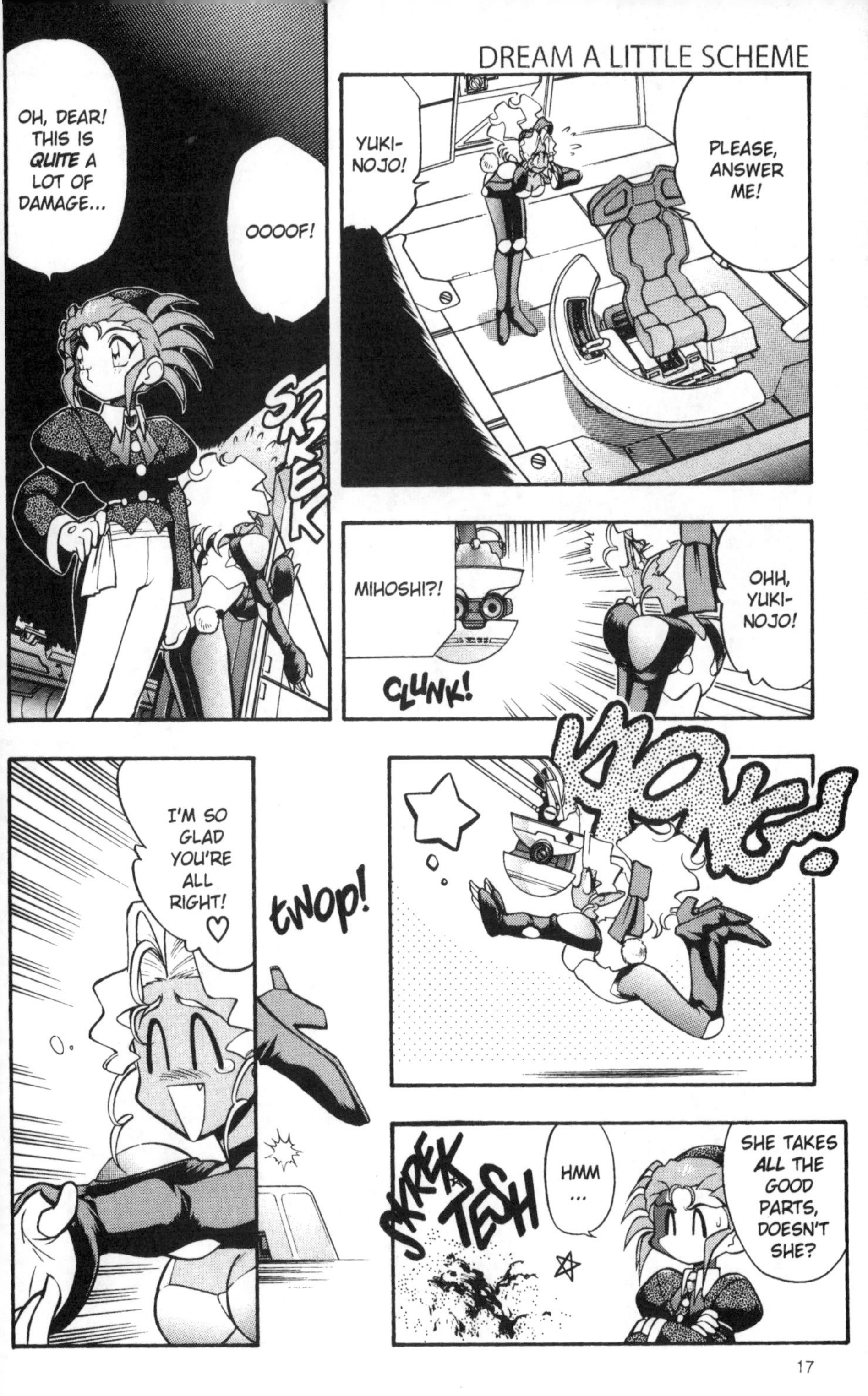
OH, DEAR! THIS IS QUITE A LOT OF DAMAGE...
OOOOF!
SKREEK
YUKI-NOJO!
PLEASE, ANSWER ME!
MIHOSHI?!
CLUNK!
OHH, YUKI-NOJO!
I'M SO GLAD YOU'RE ALL RIGHT! ♡
twop!
WHOMP!
SKREEK TESH
HMM ...
SHE TAKES ALL THE GOOD PARTS, DOESN'T SHE?

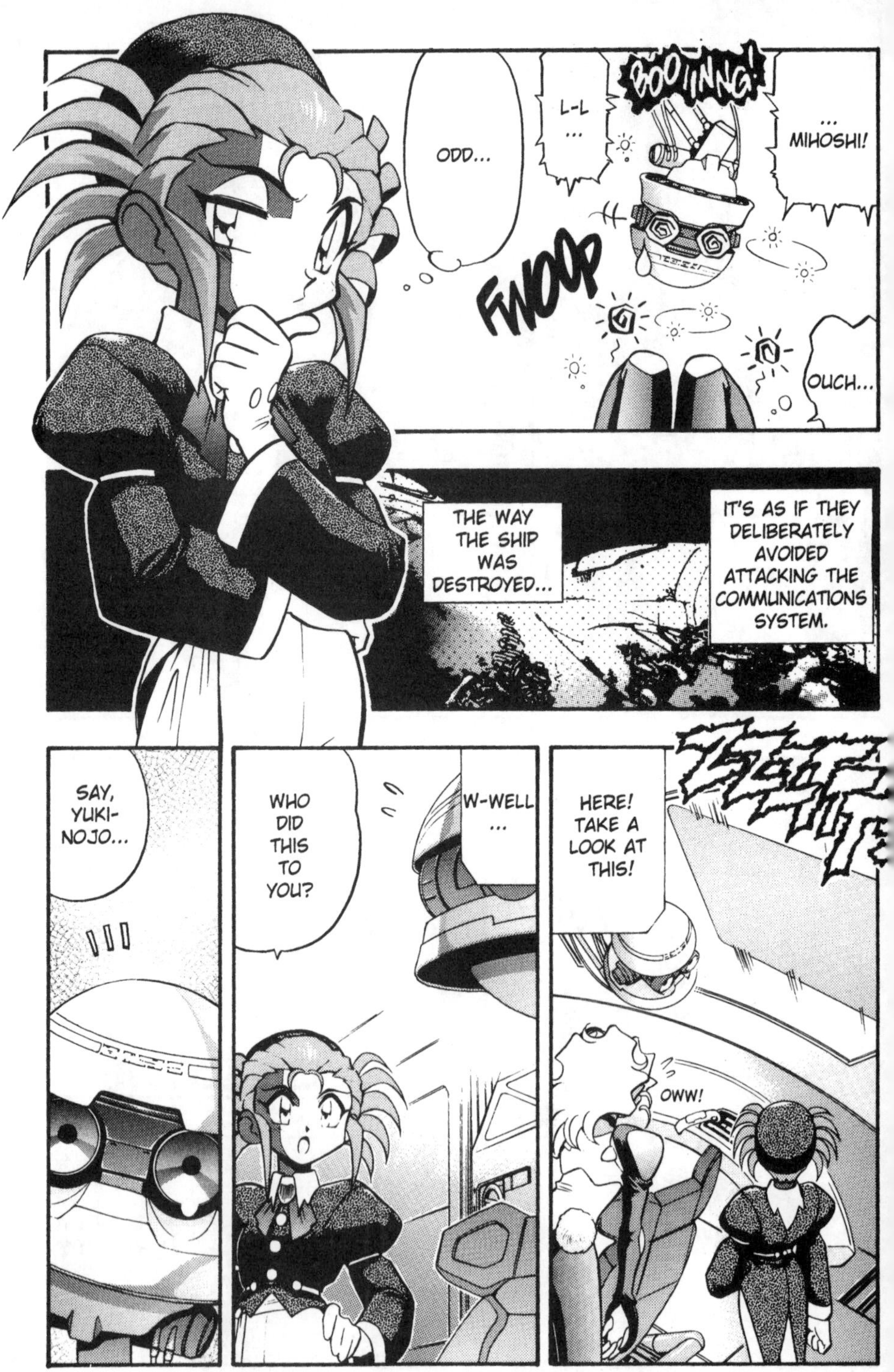
ODD...
L-L ...
BOOIINNG!
... MIHOSHI!
FWOOP
OUCH...
THE WAY THE SHIP WAS DESTROYED...
IT'S AS IF THEY DELIBERATELY AVOIDED ATTACKING THE COMMUNICATIONS SYSTEM.
SAY, YUKI-NOJO...
WHO DID THIS TO YOU?
W-WELL ...
HERE! TAKE A LOOK AT THIS!
OWW!

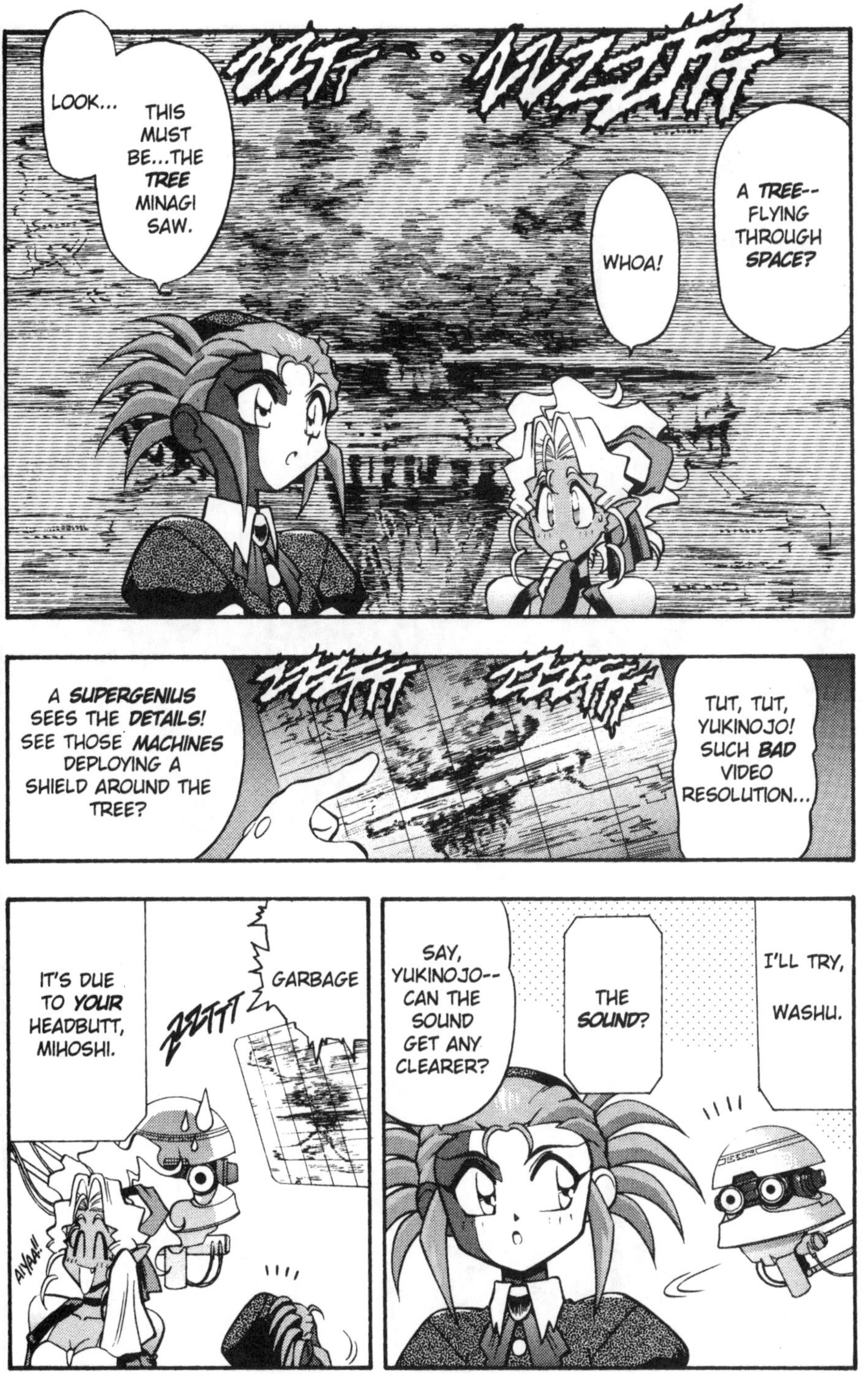

LOOK...
THIS MUST BE...THE TREE MINAGI SAW.
WHOA!
A TREE--FLYING THROUGH SPACE?
A SUPERGENIUS SEES THE DETAILS! SEE THOSE MACHINES DEPLOYING A SHIELD AROUND THE TREE?
TUT, TUT, YUKINOJO! SUCH BAD VIDEO RESOLUTION...
IT'S DUE TO YOUR HEADBUTT, MIHOSHI.
GARBAGE
AIYAA!!
SAY, YUKINOJO--CAN THE SOUND GET ANY CLEARER?
THE SOUND?
I'LL TRY,
WASHU.

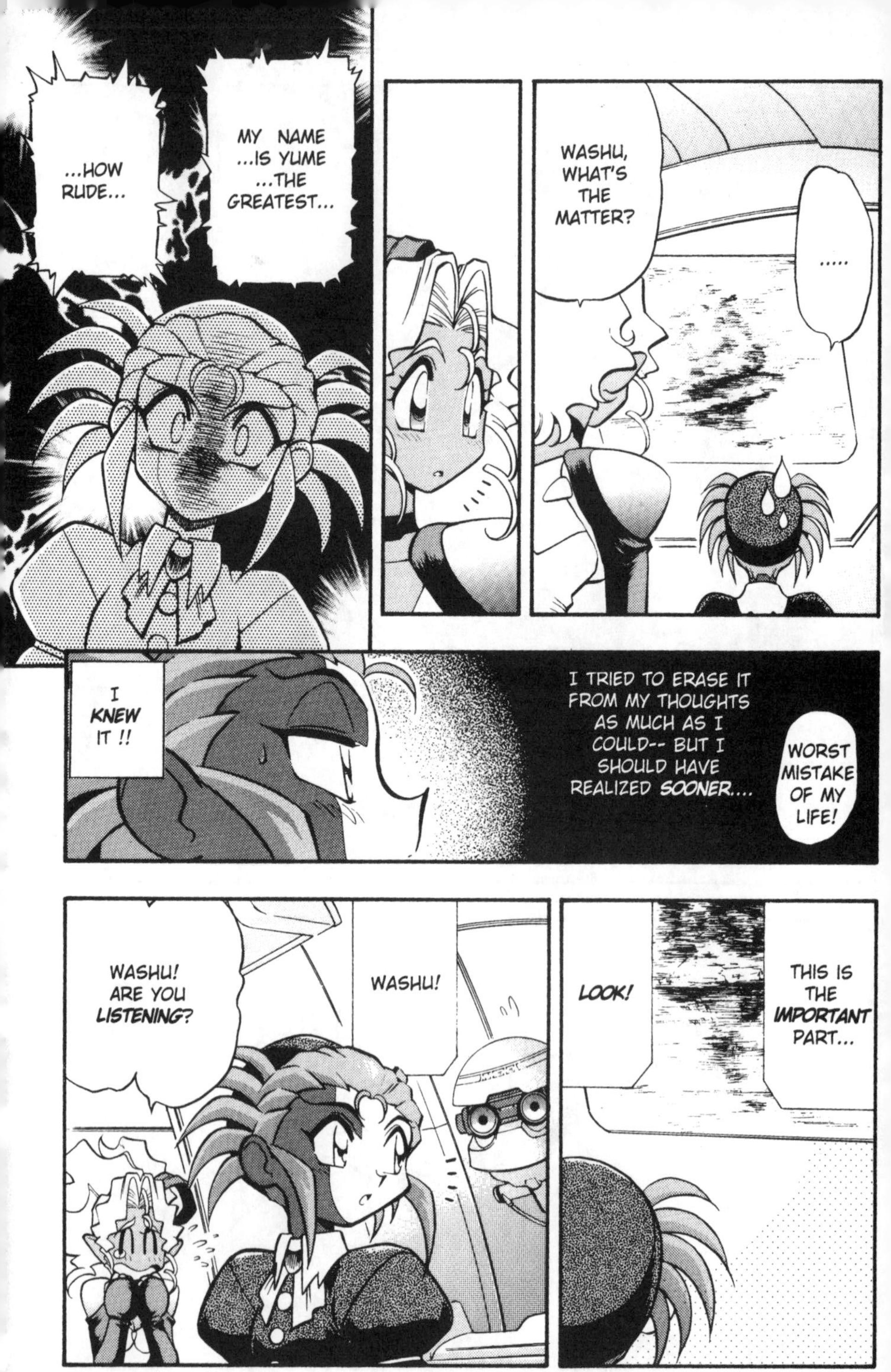
...HOW RUDE...
MY NAME ...IS YUME ...THE GREATEST...
WASHU, WHAT'S THE MATTER?
.....
I KNEW IT !!
I TRIED TO ERASE IT FROM MY THOUGHTS AS MUCH AS I COULD-- BUT I SHOULD HAVE REALIZED SOONER....
WORST MISTAKE OF MY LIFE!
WASHU! ARE YOU LISTENING?
WASHU!
LOOK!
THIS IS THE IMPORTANT PART...

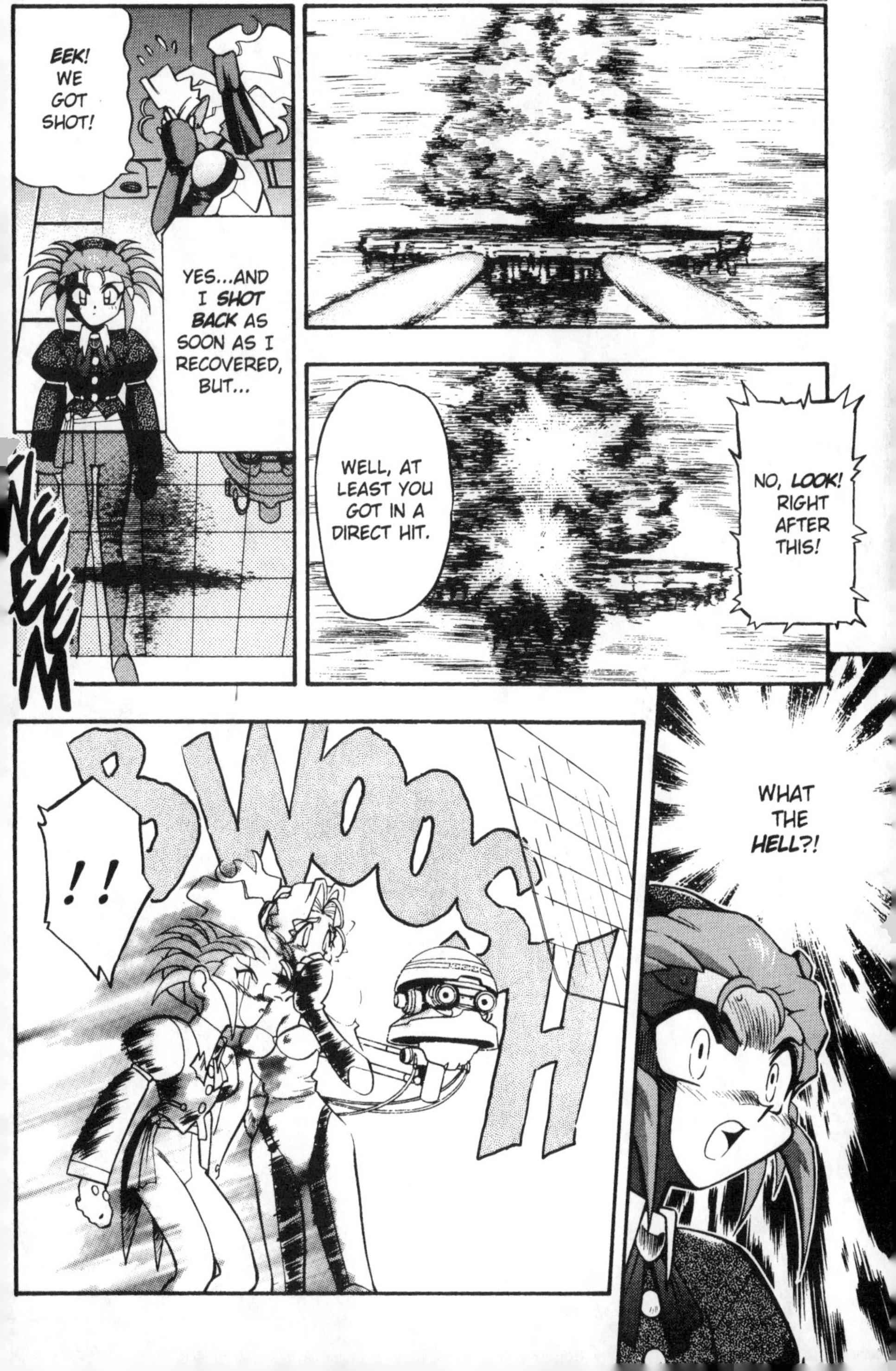
EEK! WE GOT SHOT!
YES...AND I SHOT BACK AS SOON AS I RECOVERED, BUT...
WELL, AT LEAST YOU GOT IN A DIRECT HIT.
NO, LOOK! RIGHT AFTER THIS!
!!
WHAT THE HELL?!

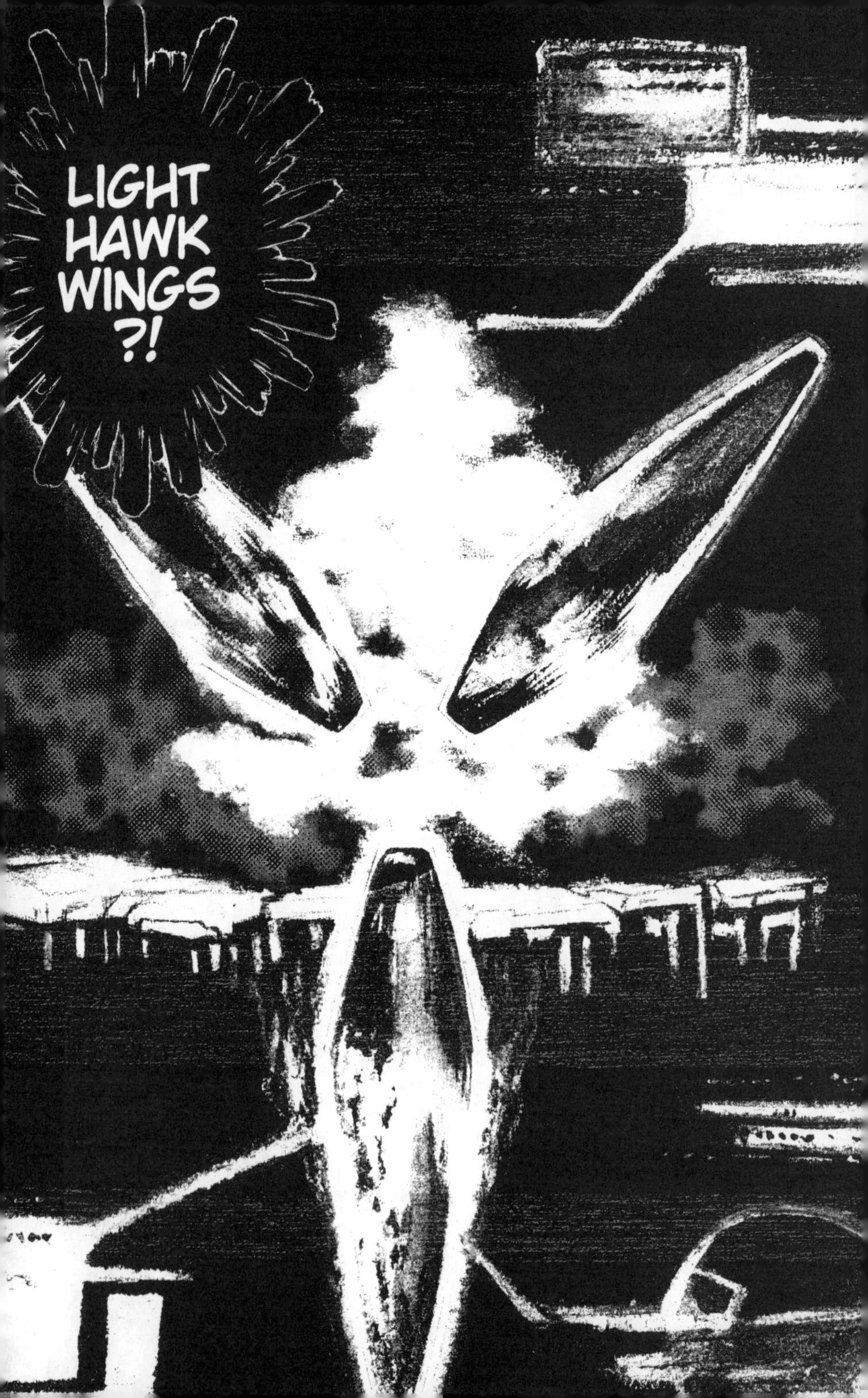
LIGHT HAWK WINGS ?!

Tales of Tenchi #2

DISTURBING THE PEACE

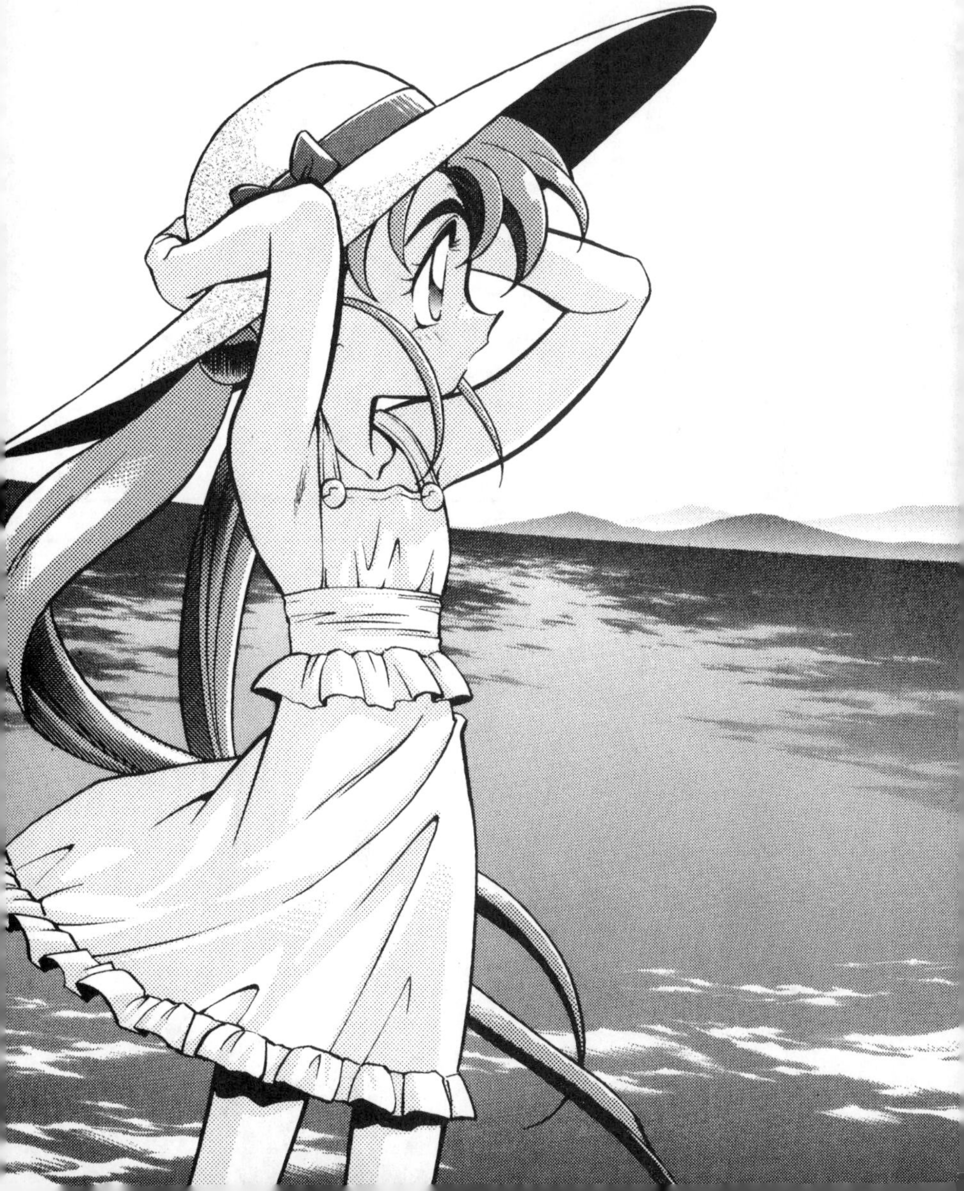

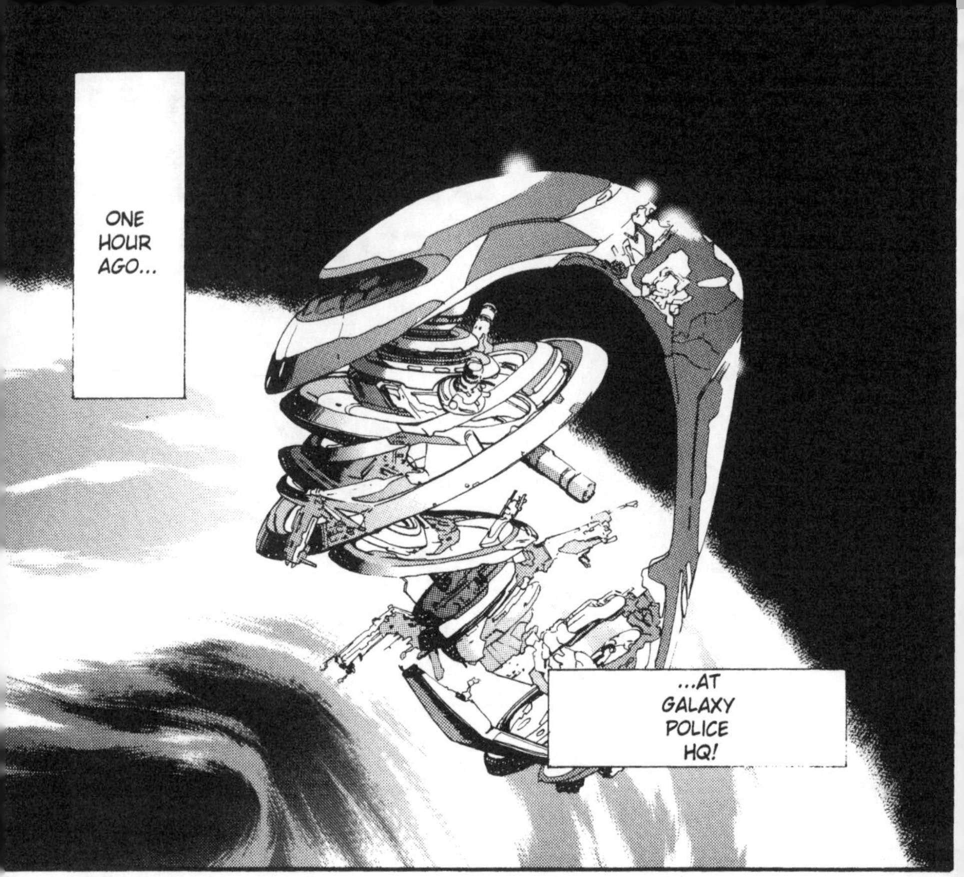
ONE HOUR AGO...
...AT GALAXY POLICE HQ!
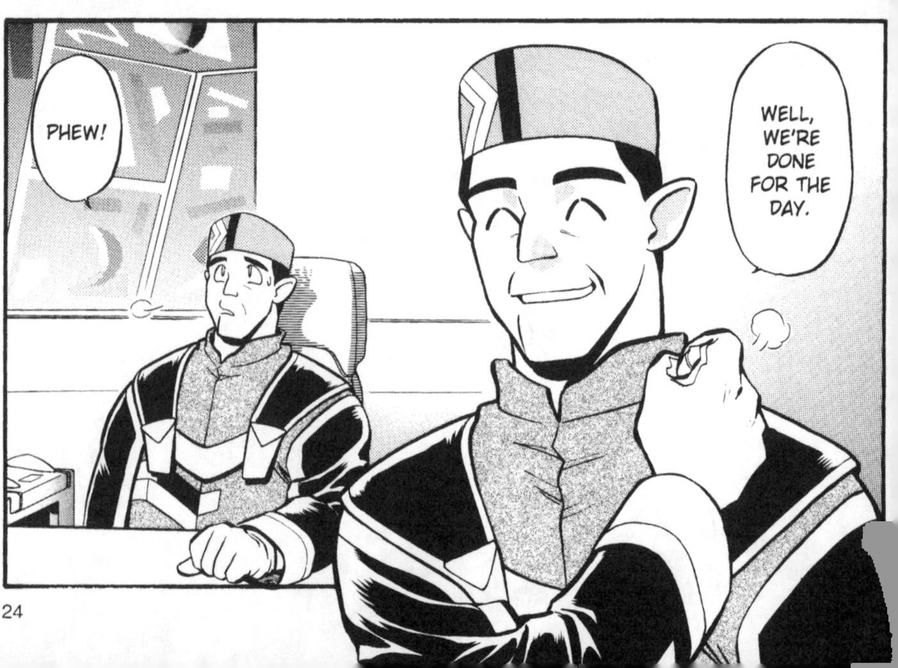
PHEW!
WELL, WE'RE DONE FOR THE DAY.

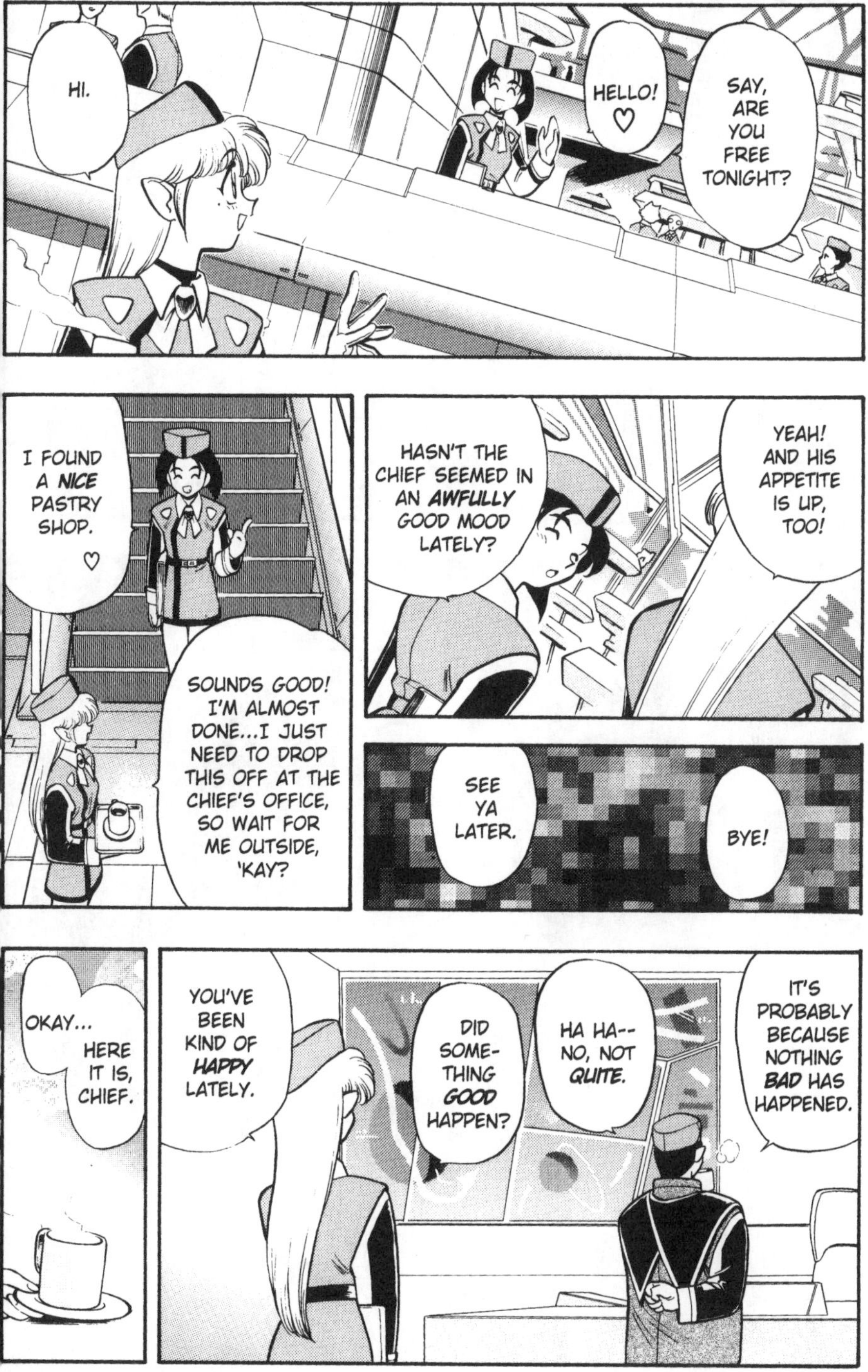
HI.
HELLO! ♡
SAY, ARE YOU FREE TONIGHT?
I FOUND A NICE PASTRY SHOP. ♡
SOUNDS GOOD! I'M ALMOST DONE...I JUST NEED TO DROP THIS OFF AT THE CHIEF'S OFFICE, SO WAIT FOR ME OUTSIDE, 'KAY?
HASN'T THE CHIEF SEEMED IN AN AWFULLY GOOD MOOD LATELY?
YEAH! AND HIS APPETITE IS UP, TOO!
SEE YA LATER.
BYE!
OKAY... HERE IT IS, CHIEF.
YOU'VE BEEN KIND OF HAPPY LATELY.
DID SOMETHING GOOD HAPPEN?
HA HA-- NO, NOT QUITE.
IT'S PROBABLY BECAUSE NOTHING BAD HAS HAPPENED.

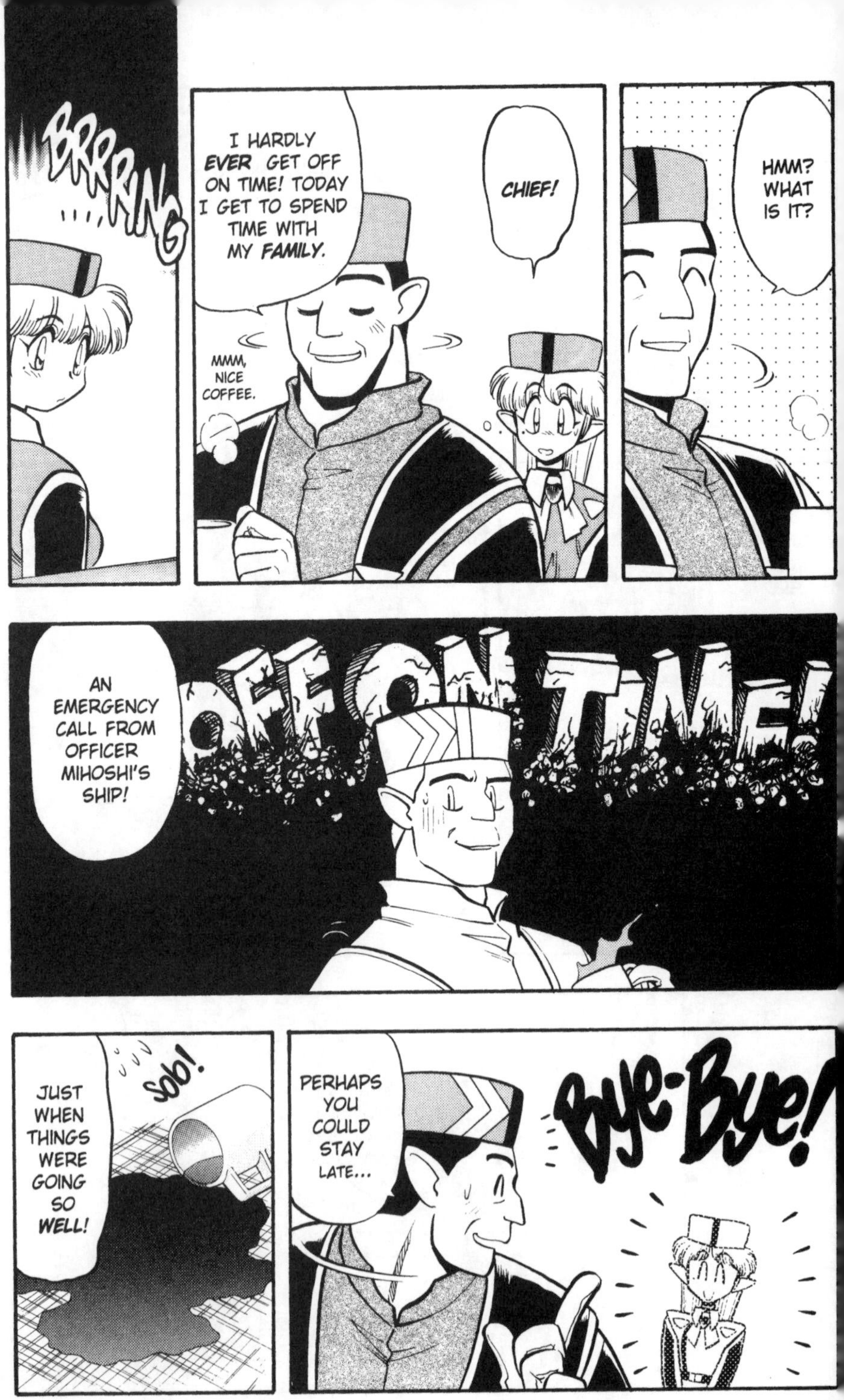
BRRRING
I HARDLY EVER GET OFF ON TIME! TODAY I GET TO SPEND TIME WITH MY FAMILY.
MMM, NICE COFFEE.
CHIEF!
HMM? WHAT IS IT?
AN EMERGENCY CALL FROM OFFICER MIHOSHI'S SHIP!
OFF ON TIME!
JUST WHEN THINGS WERE GOING SO WELL!
SOB!
PERHAPS YOU COULD STAY LATE...
BYE-BYE!

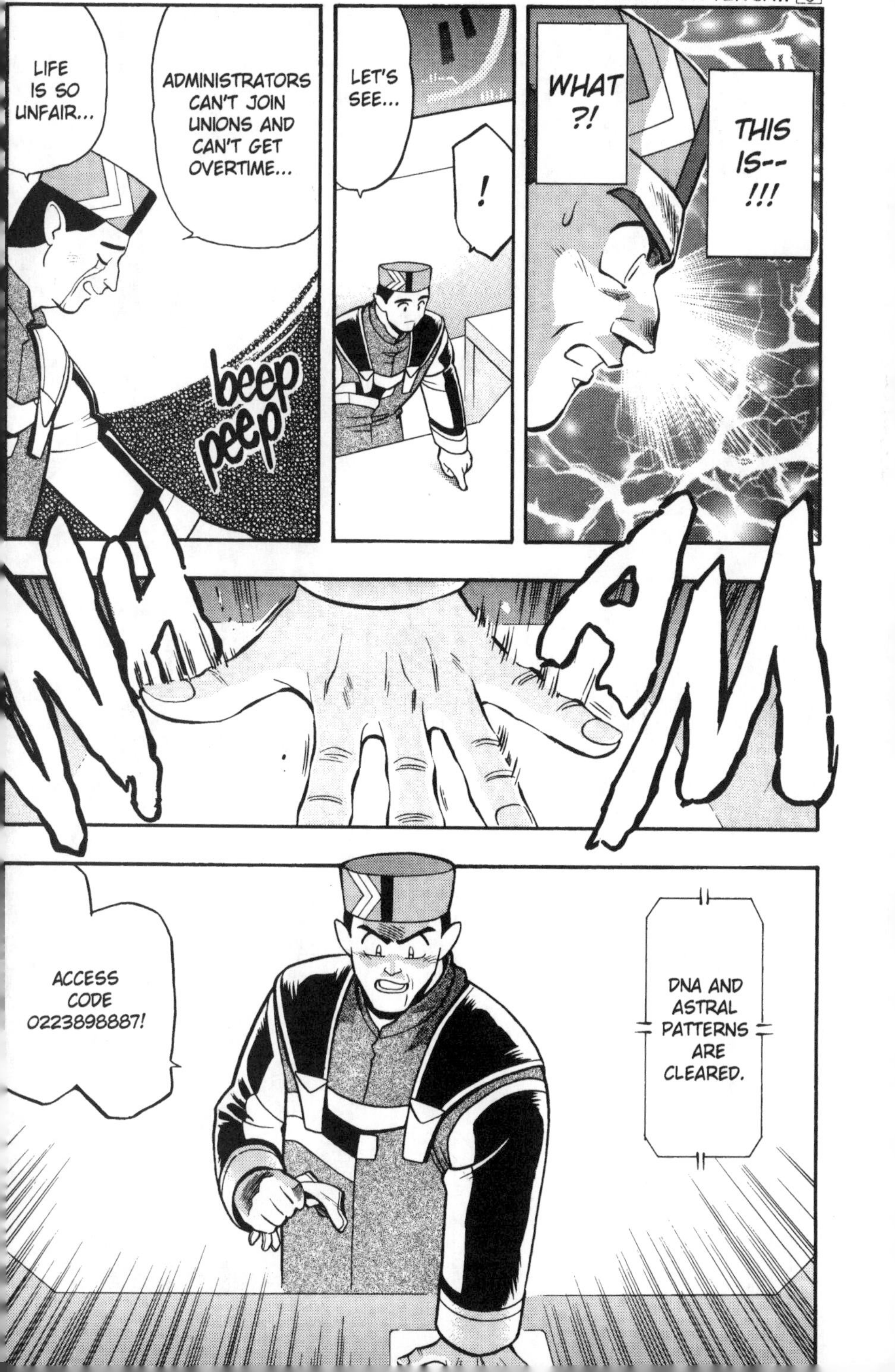
LIFE IS SO UNFAIR...
ADMINISTRATORS CAN'T JOIN UNIONS AND CAN'T GET OVERTIME...
beep peep
LET'S SEE...
!
WHAT ?!
THIS IS-- !!!
WHAM
ACCESS CODE 0223898887!
DNA AND ASTRAL PATTERNS ARE CLEARED.

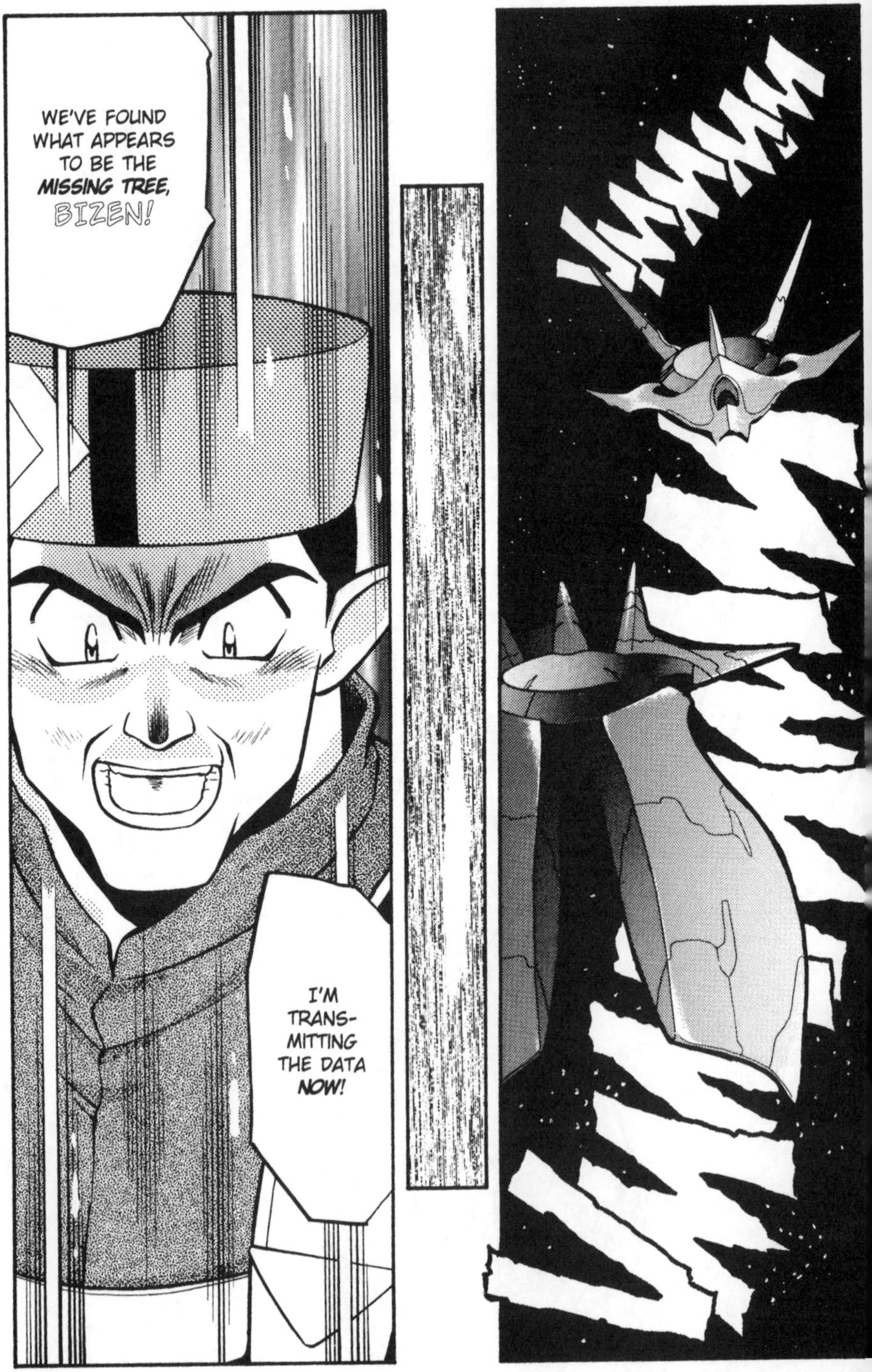
WE'VE FOUND WHAT APPEARS TO BE THE MISSING TREE, BIZEN!
I'M TRANS-MITTING THE DATA NOW!

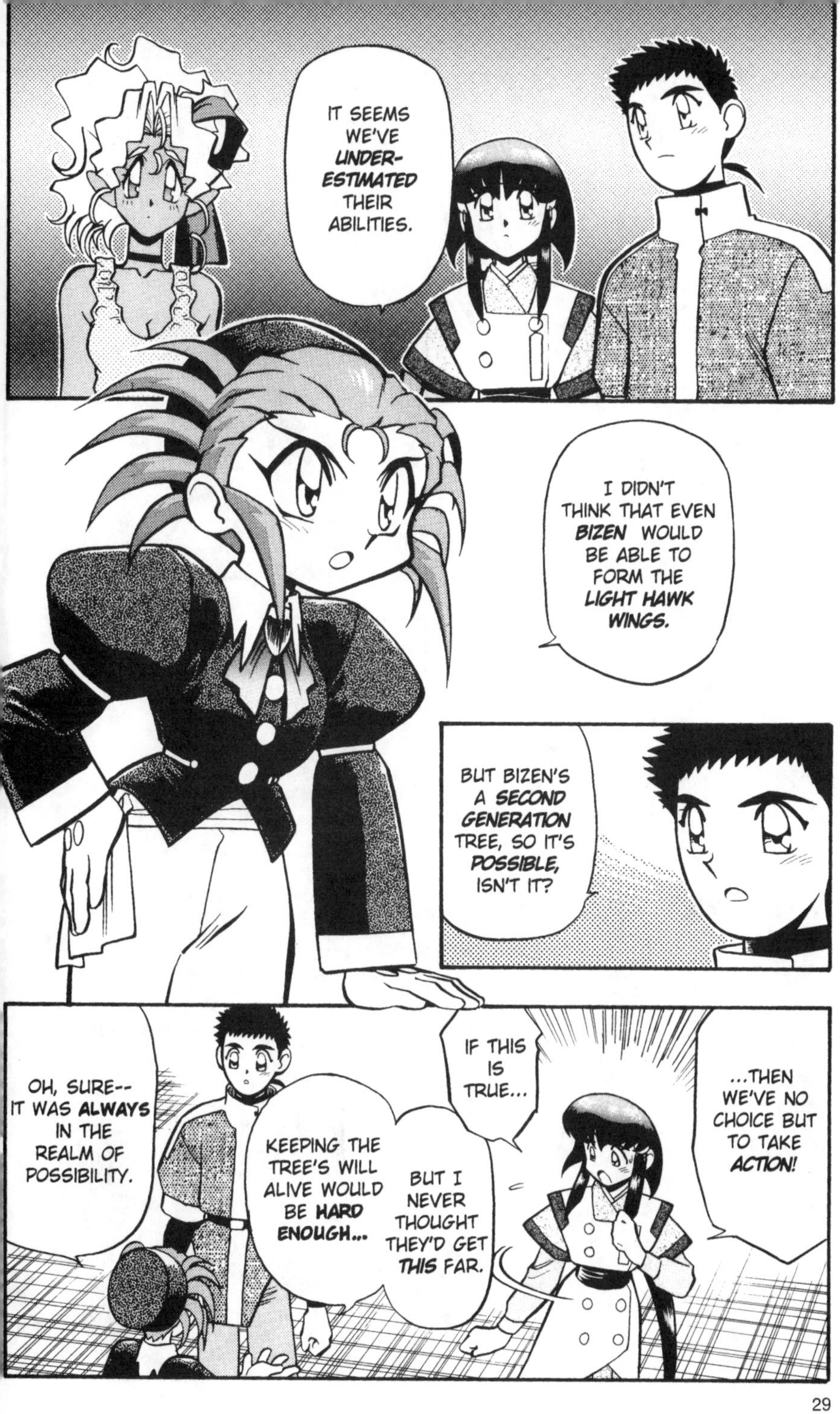
IT SEEMS WE'VE UNDER-ESTIMATED THEIR ABILITIES.
I DIDN'T THINK THAT EVEN BIZEN WOULD BE ABLE TO FORM THE LIGHT HAWK WINGS.
BUT BIZEN'S A SECOND GENERATION TREE, SO IT'S POSSIBLE, ISN'T IT?
OH, SURE-- IT WAS ALWAYS IN THE REALM OF POSSIBILITY.
KEEPING THE TREE'S WILL ALIVE WOULD BE HARD ENOUGH...
BUT I NEVER THOUGHT THEY'D GET THIS FAR.
IF THIS IS TRUE...
...THEN WE'VE NO CHOICE BUT TO TAKE ACTION!

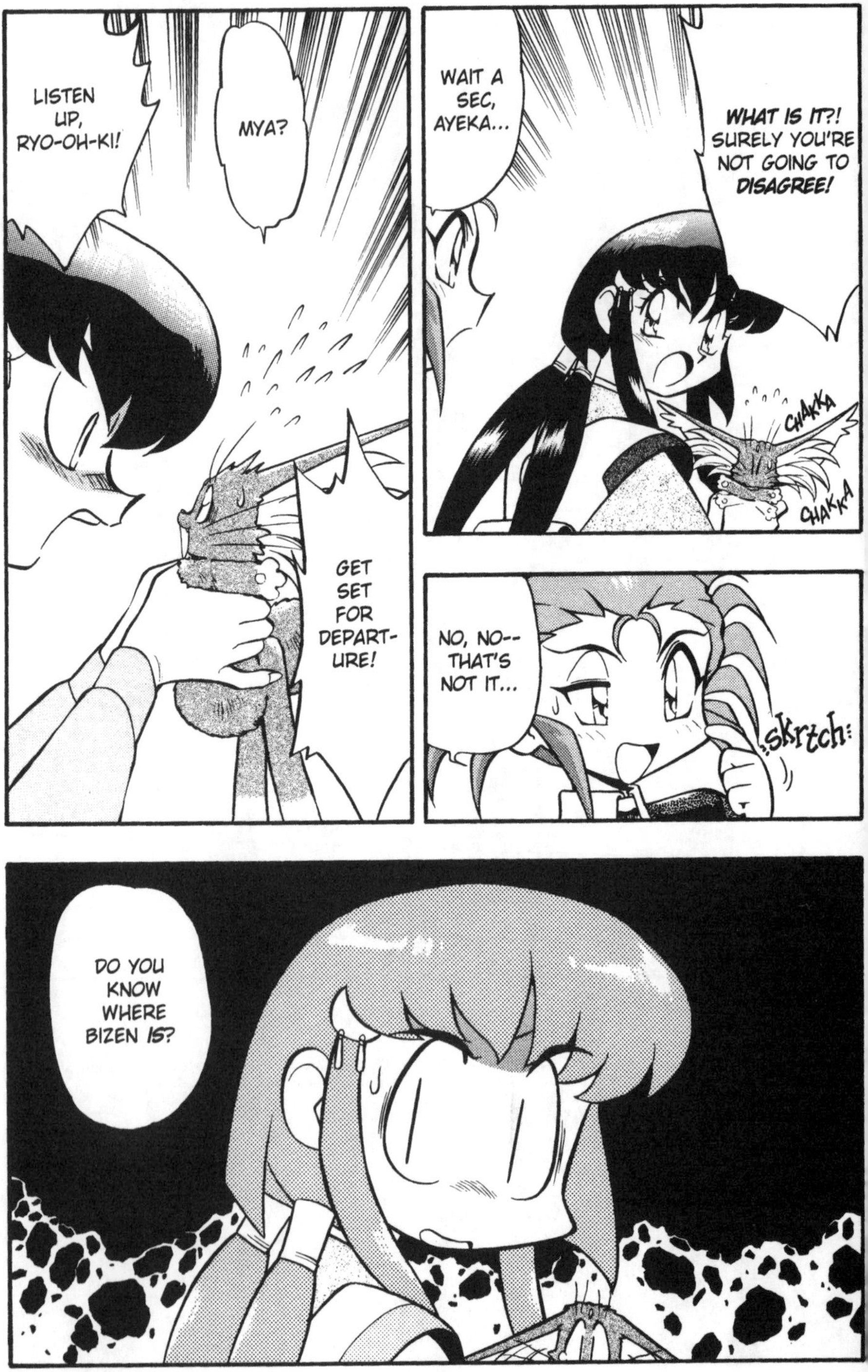
LISTEN UP, RYO-OH-KI!
MYA?
GET SET FOR DEPART-URE!
WAIT A SEC, AYEKA...
WHAT IS IT?! SURELY YOU'RE NOT GOING TO **DISAGREE!**
CHAKKA
CHAKKA
NO, NO--THAT'S NOT IT...
SKRTCH
DO YOU KNOW WHERE BIZEN *IS*?

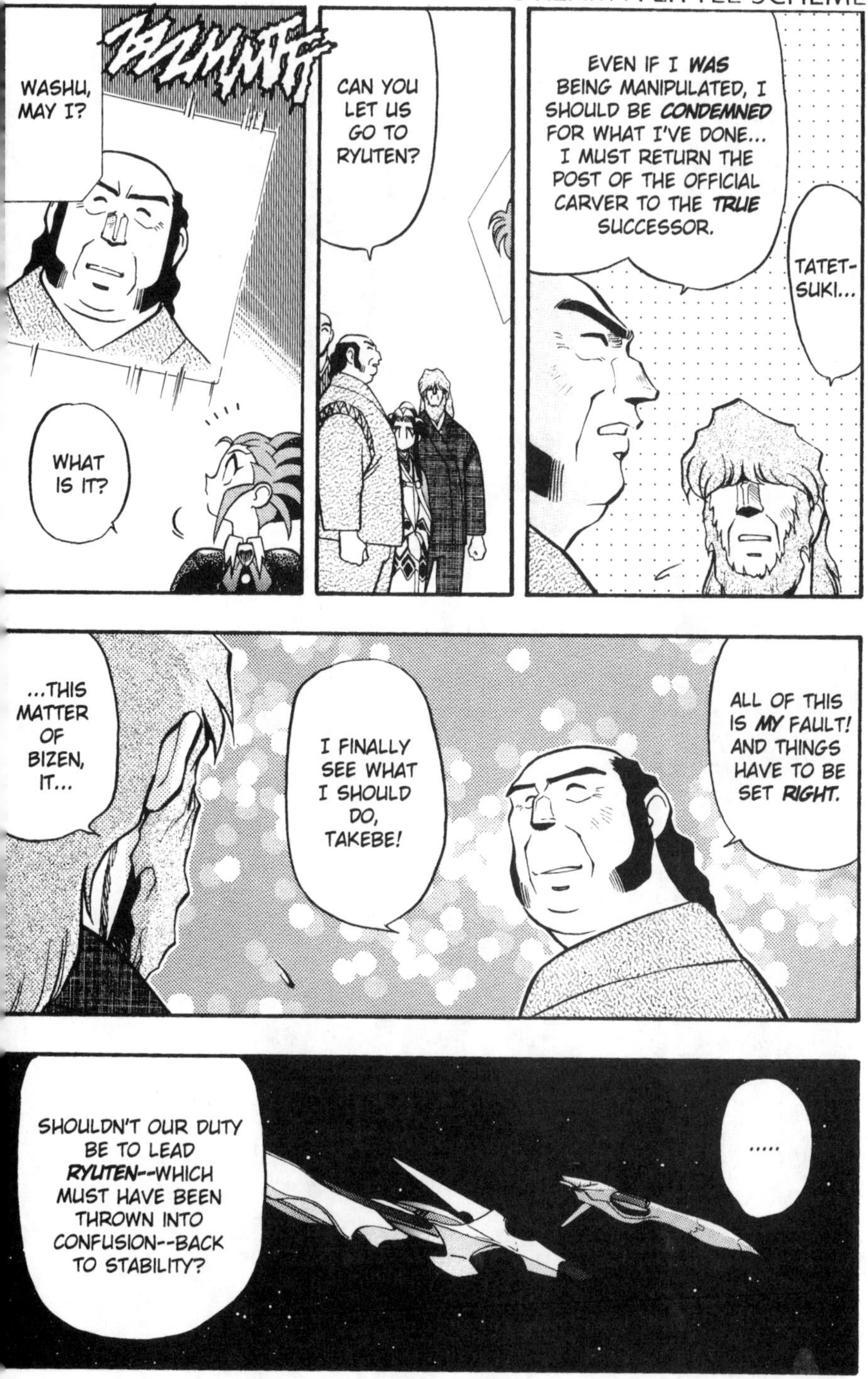
WASHU, MAY I?
WHAT IS IT?
CAN YOU LET US GO TO RYUTEN?
EVEN IF I WAS BEING MANIPULATED, I SHOULD BE CONDEMNED FOR WHAT I'VE DONE... I MUST RETURN THE POST OF THE OFFICIAL CARVER TO THE TRUE SUCCESSOR.
TATET-SUKI...
...THIS MATTER OF BIZEN, IT...
I FINALLY SEE WHAT I SHOULD DO, TAKEBE!
ALL OF THIS IS MY FAULT! AND THINGS HAVE TO BE SET RIGHT.
SHOULDN'T OUR DUTY BE TO LEAD RYUTEN--WHICH MUST HAVE BEEN THROWN INTO CONFUSION--BACK TO STABILITY?
.....

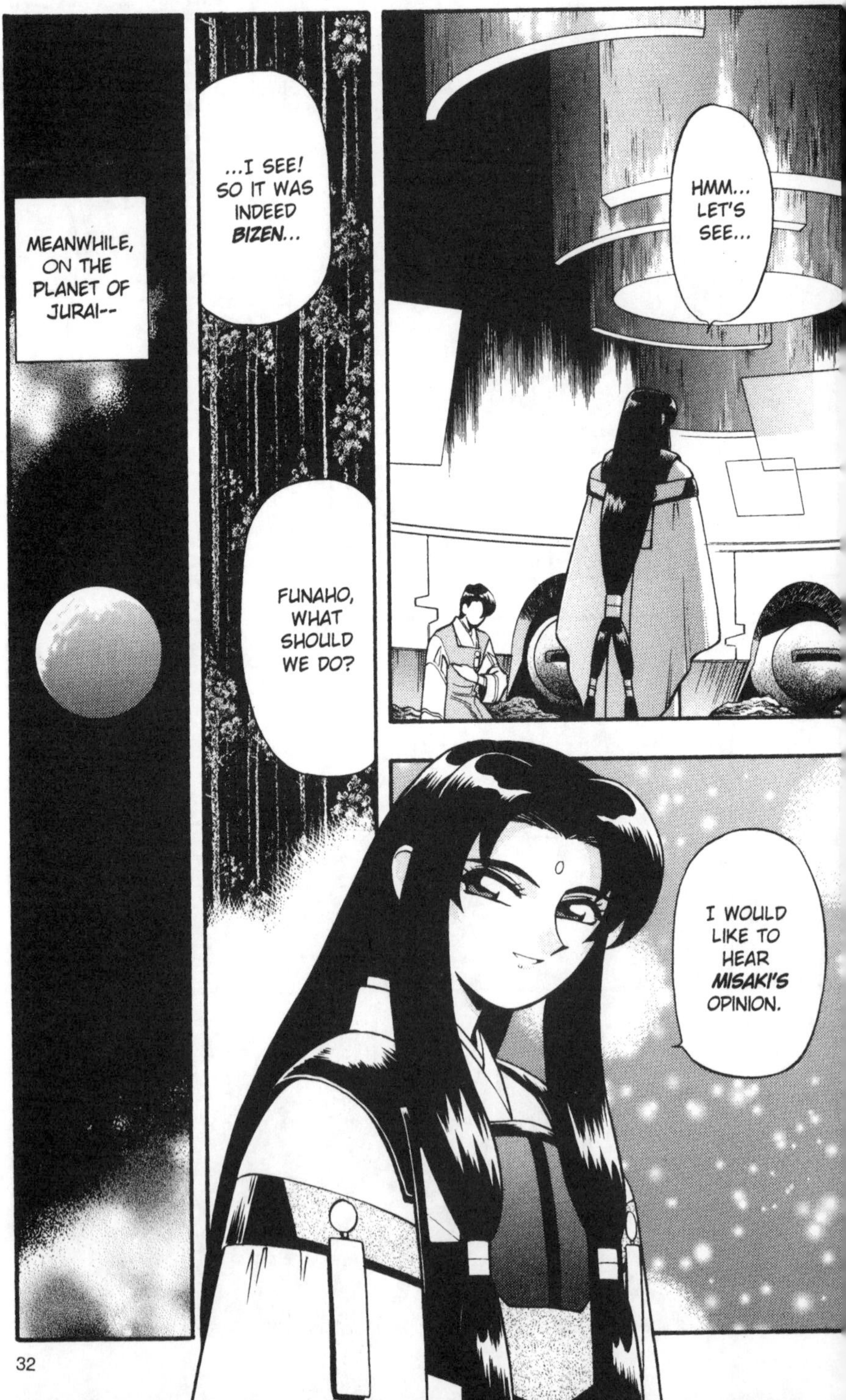
MEANWHILE, ON THE PLANET OF JURAI--
...I SEE! SO IT WAS INDEED **BIZEN**...
FUNAHO, WHAT SHOULD WE DO?
HMM... LET'S SEE...
I WOULD LIKE TO HEAR **MISAKI'S** OPINION.

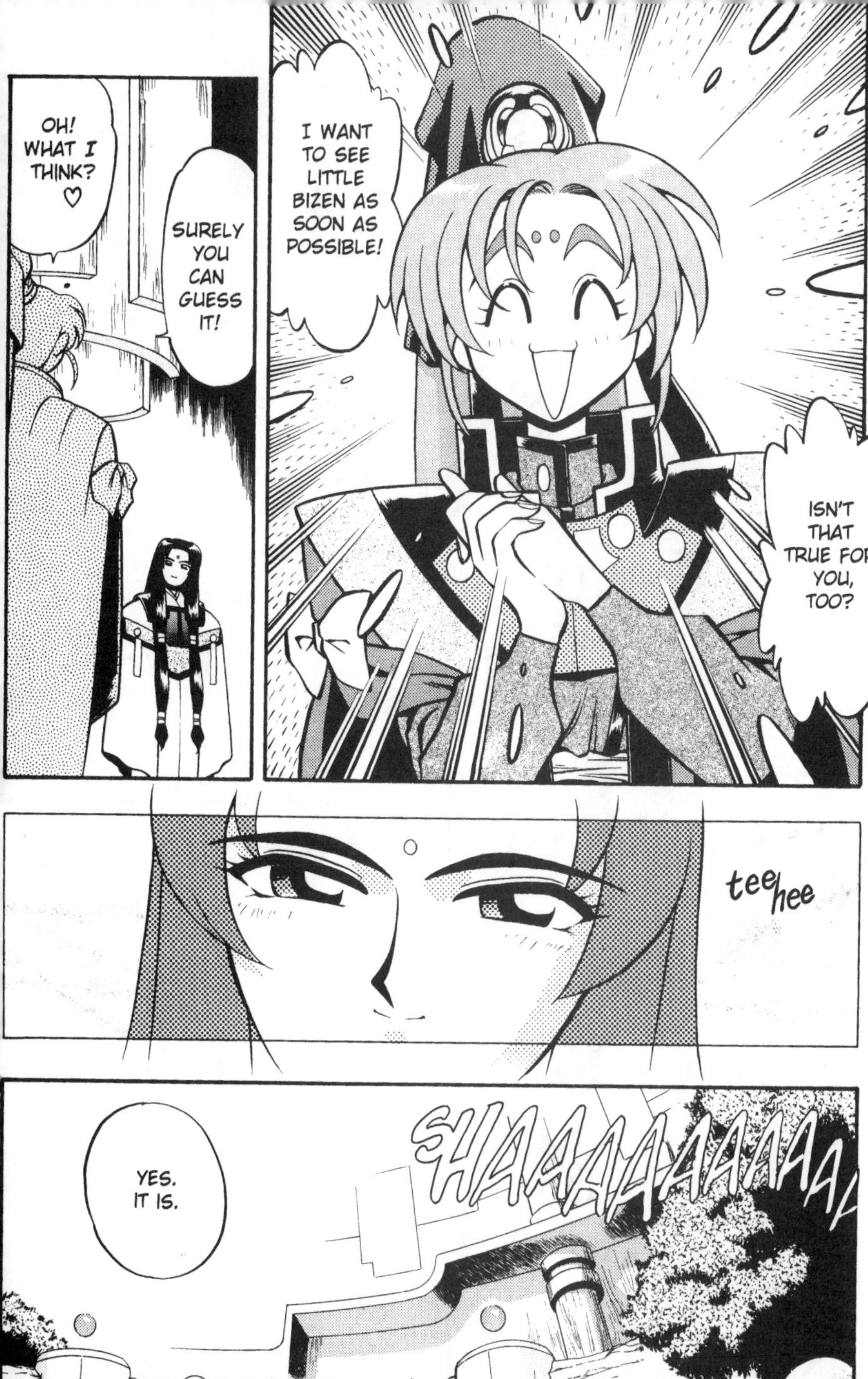
OH! WHAT I THINK? ♡
SURELY YOU CAN GUESS IT!
I WANT TO SEE LITTLE BIZEN AS SOON AS POSSIBLE!
ISN'T THAT TRUE FOR YOU, TOO?
tee hee
YES. IT IS.
SHAAAAAAAAAA

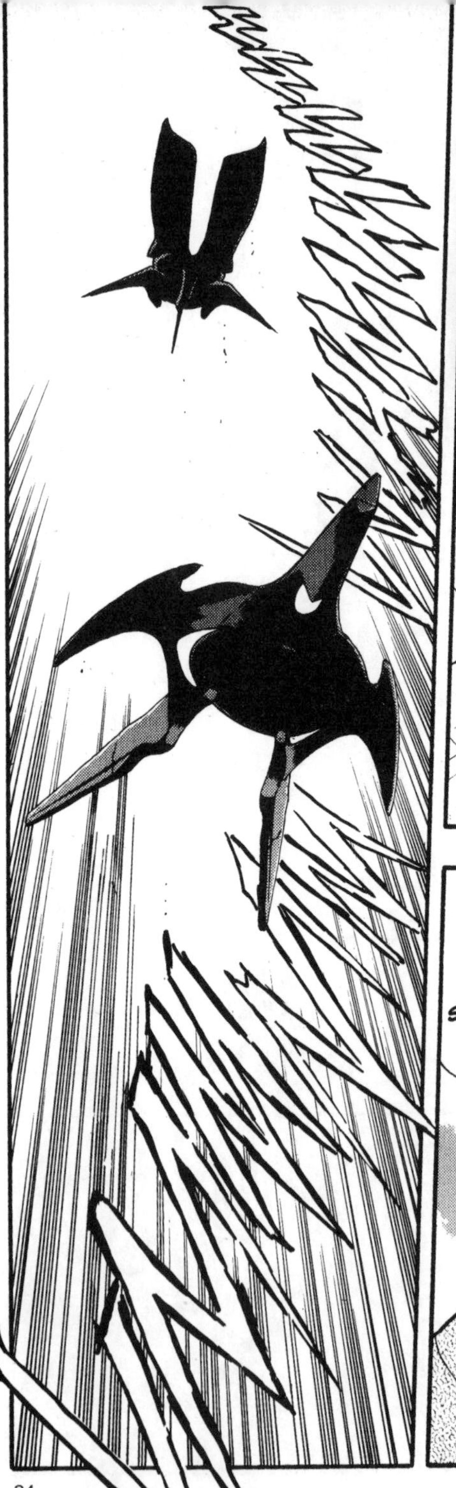

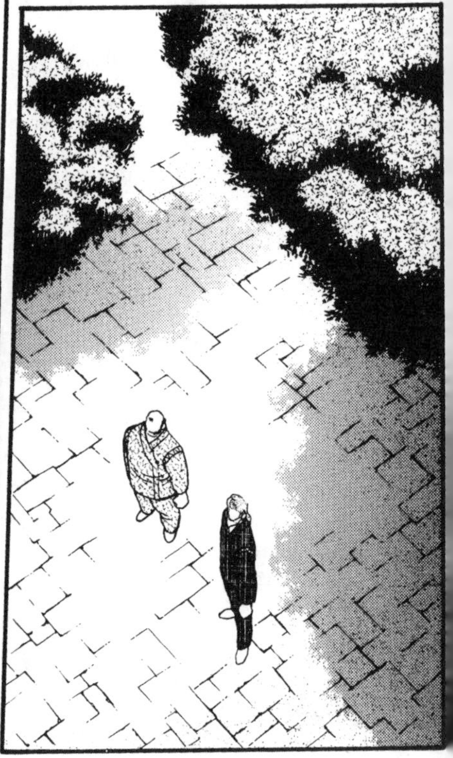

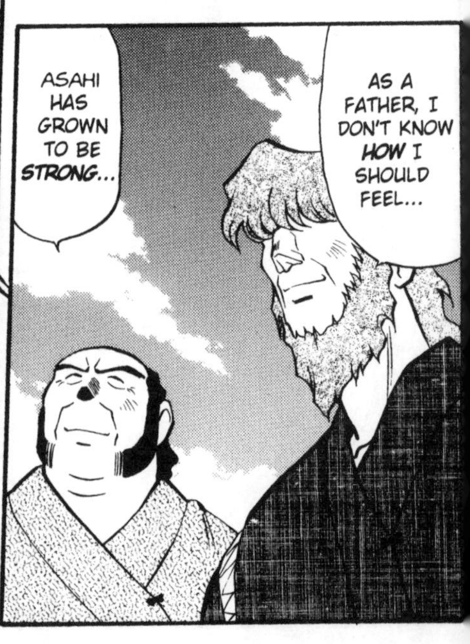

ASAHI HAS GROWN TO BE STRONG...
AS A FATHER, I DON'T KNOW HOW I SHOULD FEEL...

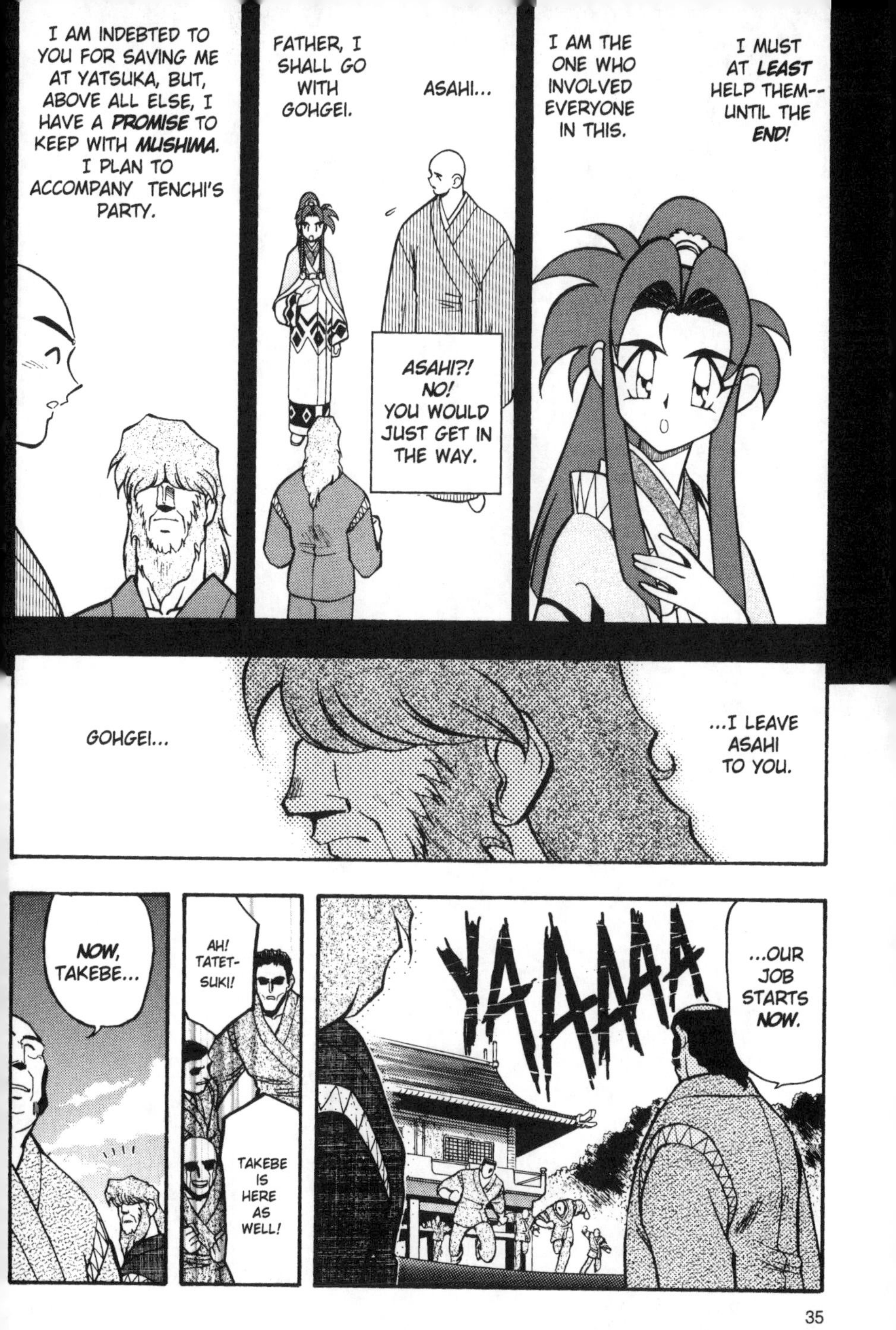
I AM INDEBTED TO YOU FOR SAVING ME AT YATSUKA, BUT, ABOVE ALL ELSE, I HAVE A **PROMISE** TO KEEP WITH **MUSHIMA.** I PLAN TO ACCOMPANY TENCHI'S PARTY.
FATHER, I SHALL GO WITH GOHGEI.
ASAHI...
ASAHI?! NO! YOU WOULD JUST GET IN THE WAY.
I AM THE ONE WHO INVOLVED EVERYONE IN THIS.
I MUST AT **LEAST** HELP THEM--UNTIL THE **END!**
GOHGEI...
...I LEAVE ASAHI TO YOU.
NOW, TAKEBE...
AH! TATET-SUKI!
TAKEBE IS HERE AS WELL!
YAAAAA
...OUR JOB STARTS ***NOW.***

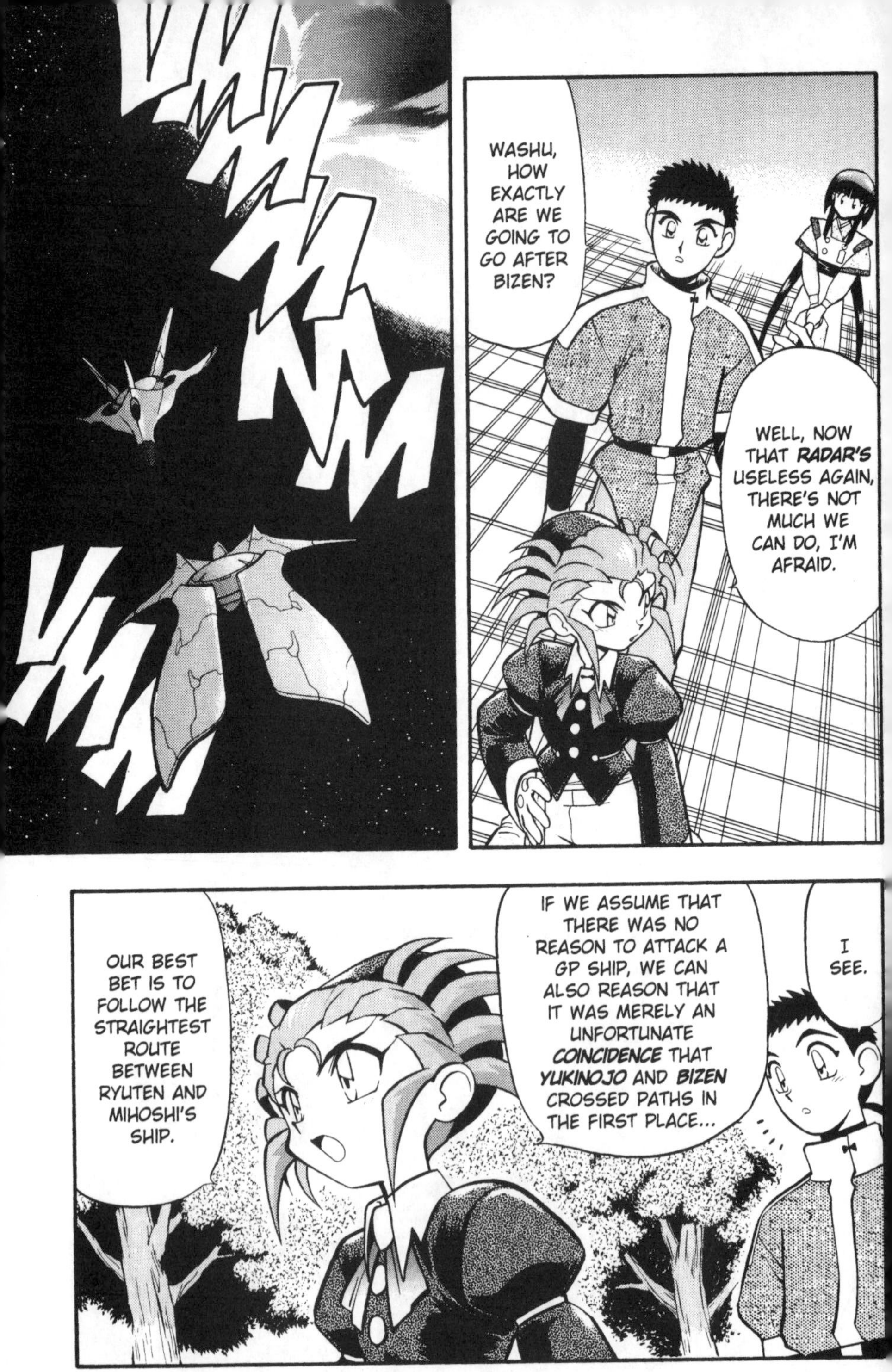
WASHU, HOW EXACTLY ARE WE GOING TO GO AFTER BIZEN?
WELL, NOW THAT **RADAR'S** USELESS AGAIN, THERE'S NOT MUCH WE CAN DO, I'M AFRAID.
OUR BEST BET IS TO FOLLOW THE STRAIGHTEST ROUTE BETWEEN RYUTEN AND MIHOSHI'S SHIP.
IF WE ASSUME THAT THERE WAS NO REASON TO ATTACK A GP SHIP, WE CAN ALSO REASON THAT IT WAS MERELY AN UNFORTUNATE ***COINCIDENCE*** THAT ***YUKINOJO*** AND ***BIZEN*** CROSSED PATHS IN THE FIRST PLACE...
I SEE.

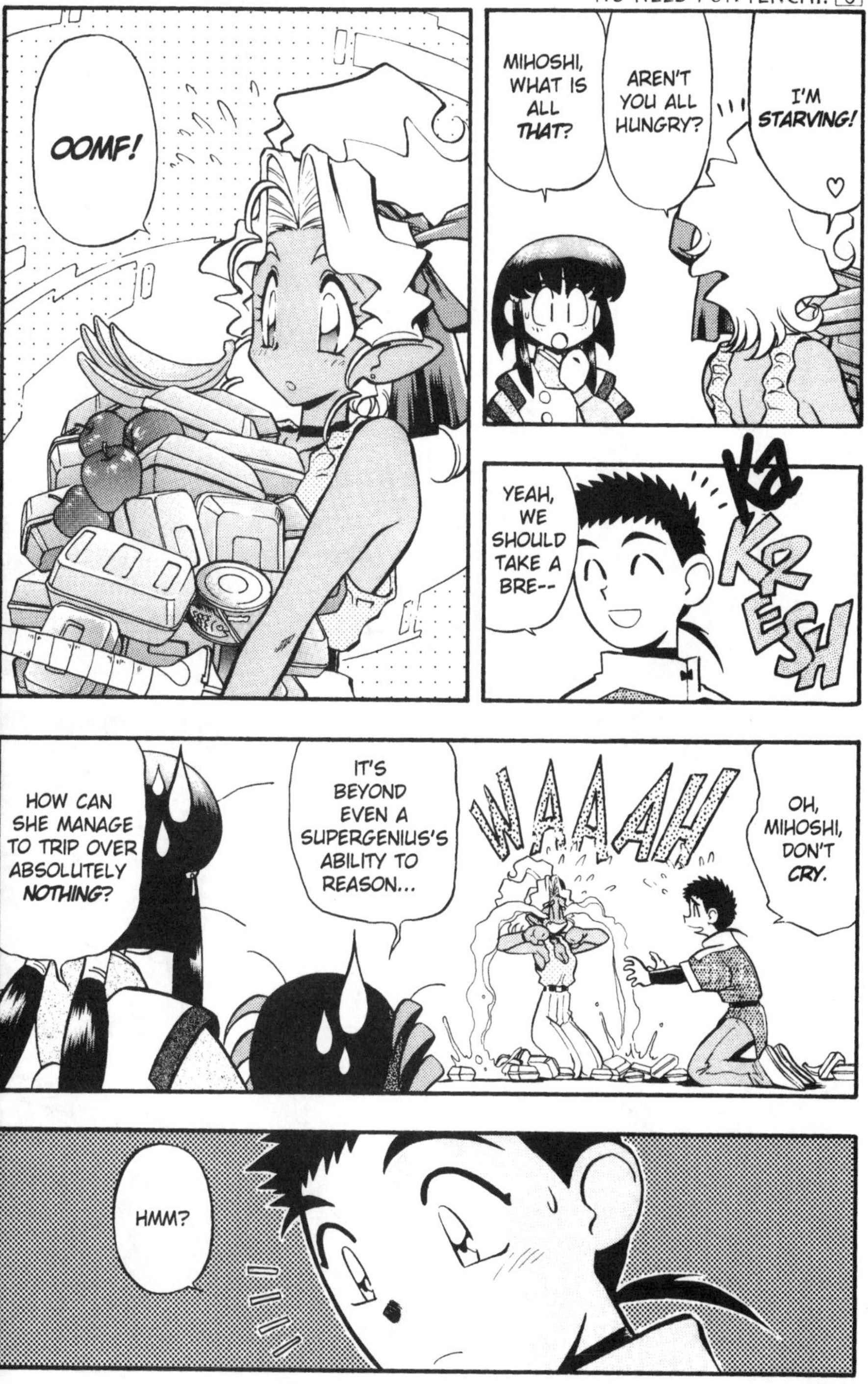
OOMF!
MIHOSHI, WHAT IS ALL THAT?
AREN'T YOU ALL HUNGRY?
I'M STARVING! ♡
YEAH, WE SHOULD TAKE A BRE--
KA KRESH
HOW CAN SHE MANAGE TO TRIP OVER ABSOLUTELY NOTHING?
IT'S BEYOND EVEN A SUPERGENIUS'S ABILITY TO REASON...
WAAAH
OH, MIHOSHI, DON'T CRY.
HMM?

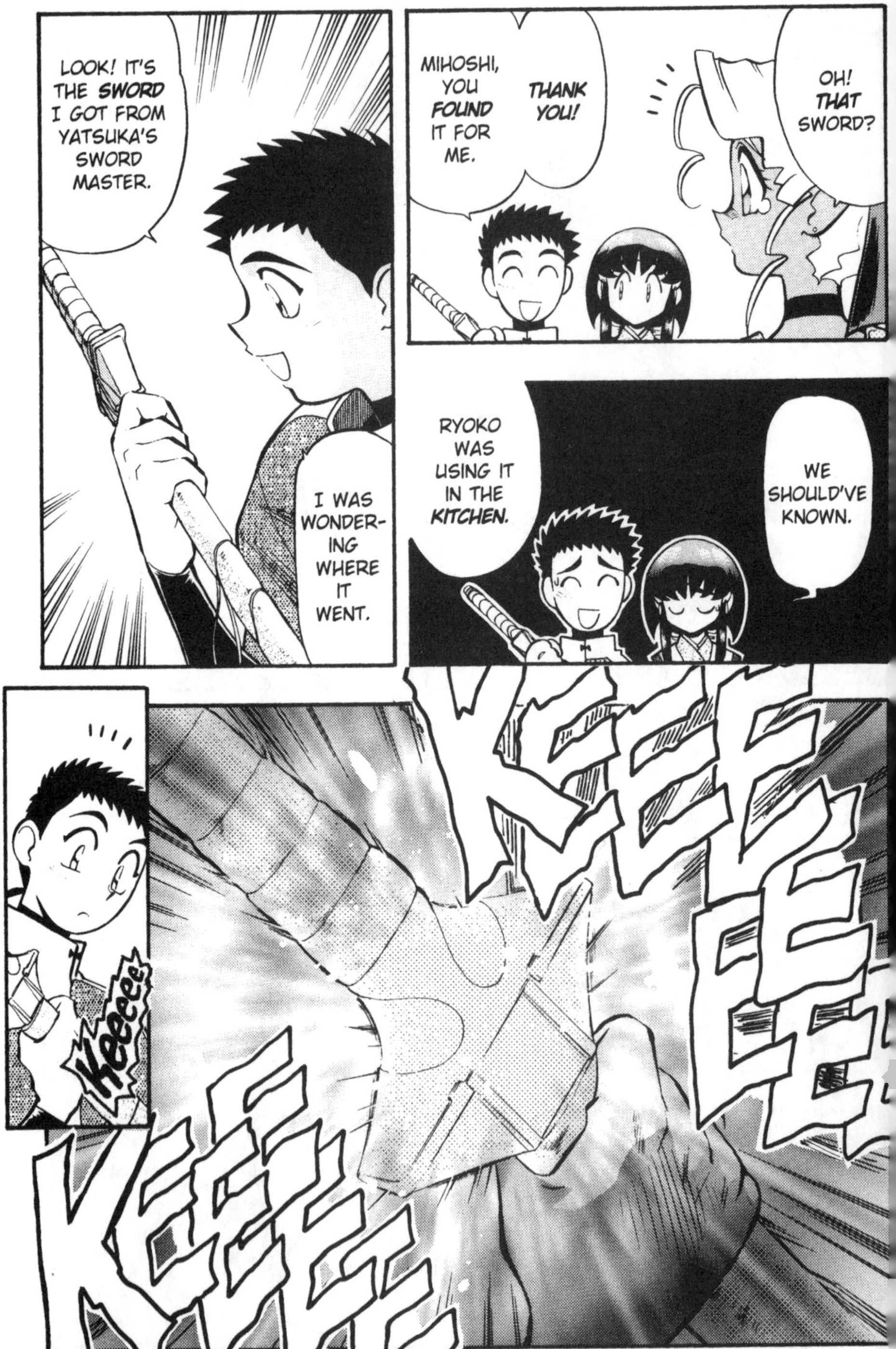
LOOK! IT'S THE SWORD I GOT FROM YATSUKA'S SWORD MASTER.
I WAS WONDERING WHERE IT WENT.
OH! THAT SWORD?
MIHOSHI, YOU FOUND IT FOR ME.
THANK YOU!
RYOKO WAS USING IT IN THE KITCHEN.
WE SHOULD'VE KNOWN.
Keeeee
KEEEEEEE
KEEEEEEE

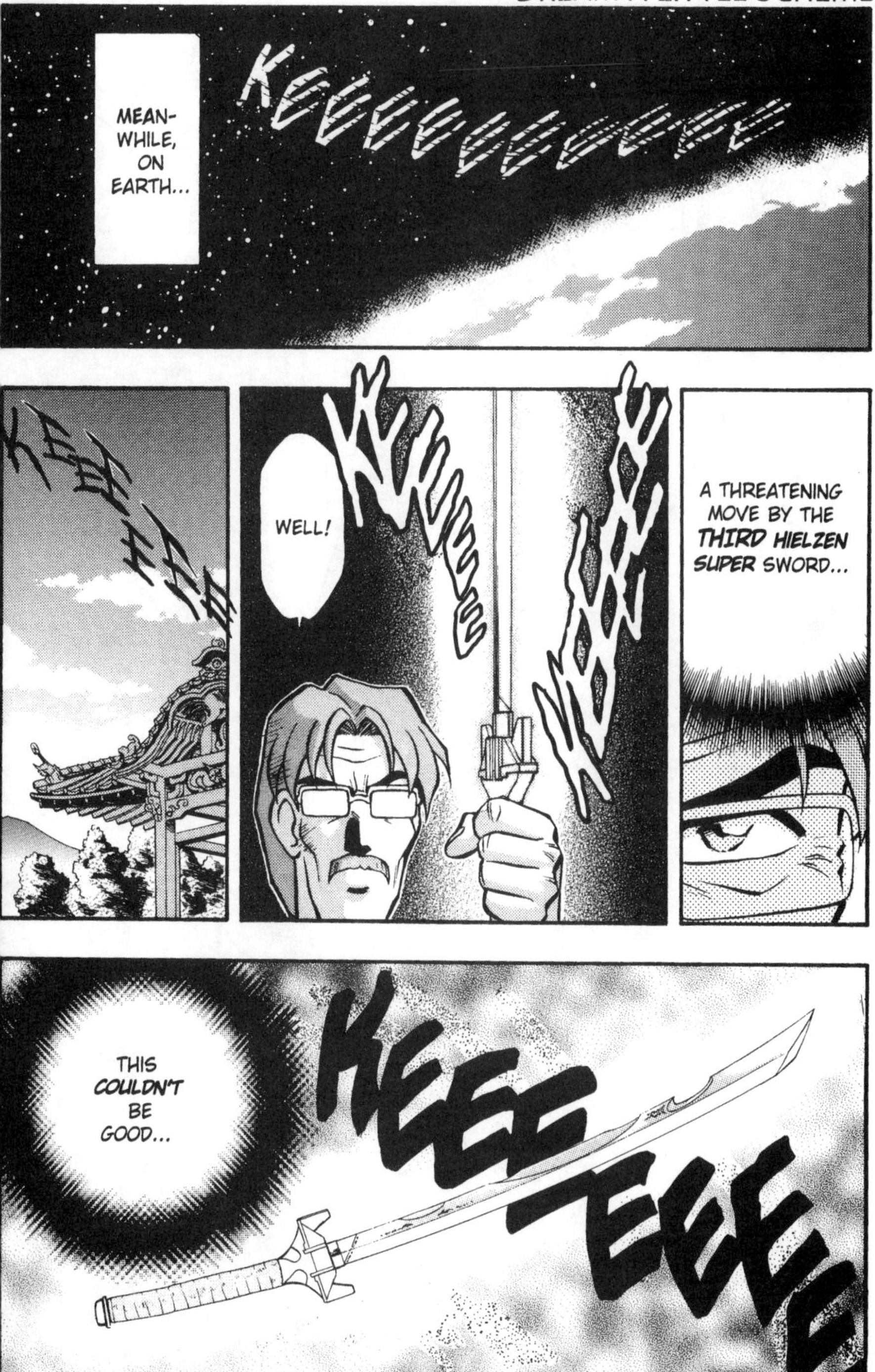
MEAN-WHILE, ON EARTH...
WELL!
A THREATENING MOVE BY THE **THIRD HIELZEN SUPER** SWORD...
THIS **COULDN'T** BE GOOD...

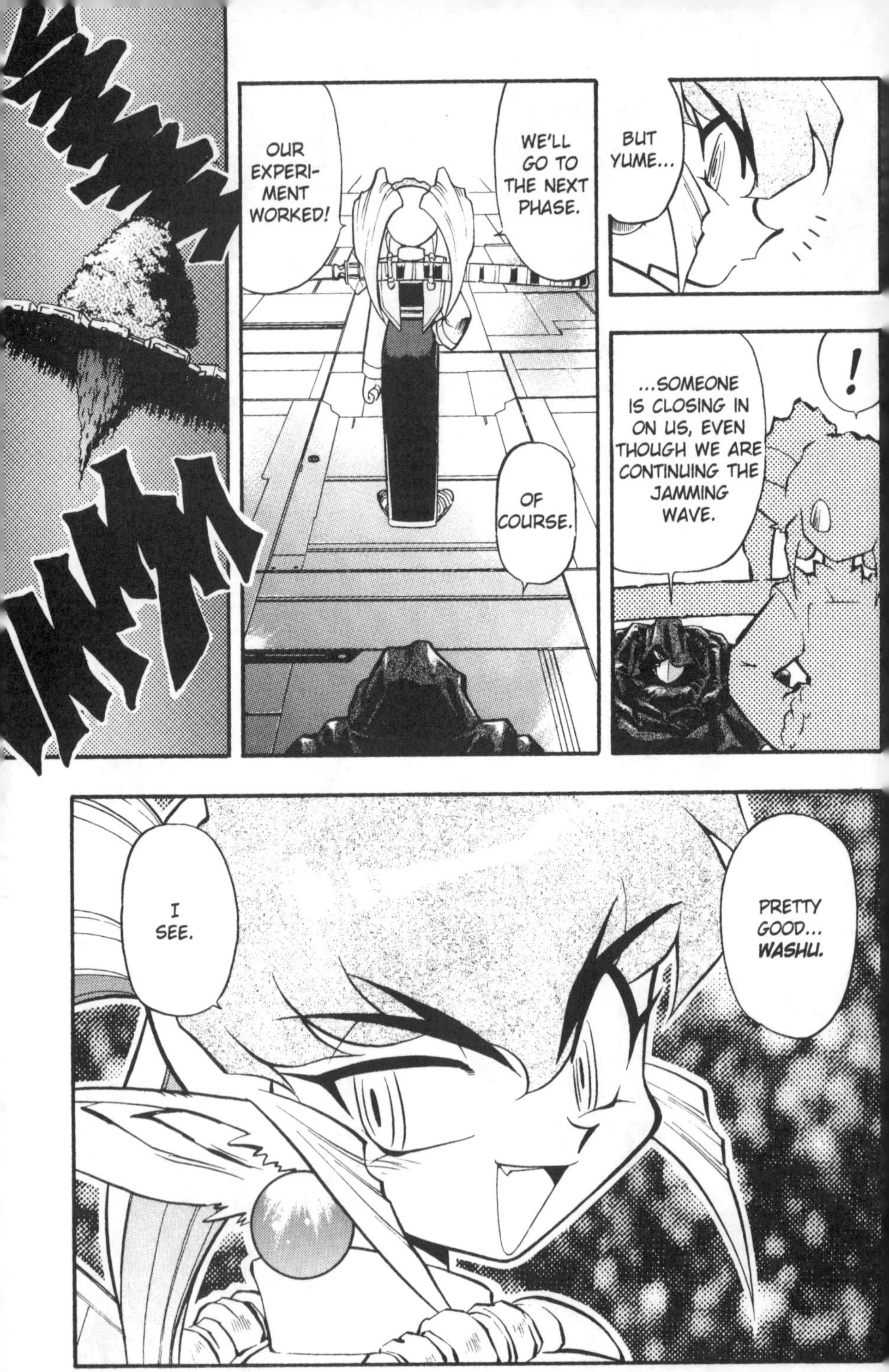
OUR EXPERIMENT WORKED!
WE'LL GO TO THE NEXT PHASE.
OF COURSE.
BUT YUME...
...SOMEONE IS CLOSING IN ON US, EVEN THOUGH WE ARE CONTINUING THE JAMMING WAVE.
!
I SEE.
PRETTY GOOD... **WASHU.**

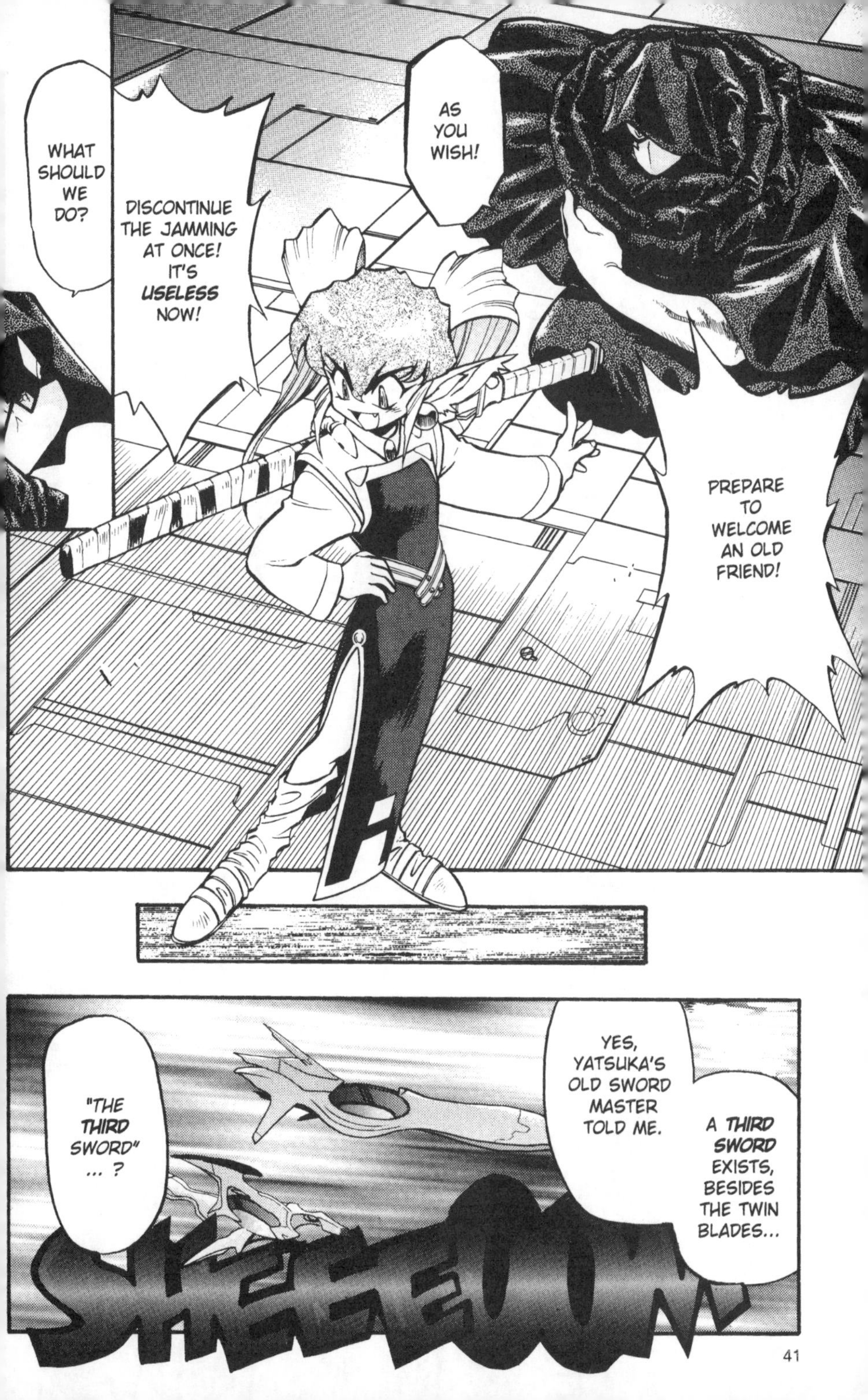
WHAT SHOULD WE DO?
DISCONTINUE THE JAMMING AT ONCE! IT'S **USELESS** NOW!
AS YOU WISH!
PREPARE TO WELCOME AN OLD FRIEND!
"THE **THIRD** SWORD" ... ?
YES, YATSUKA'S OLD SWORD MASTER TOLD ME.
A **THIRD SWORD** EXISTS, BESIDES THE TWIN BLADES...
SHEEEOOM

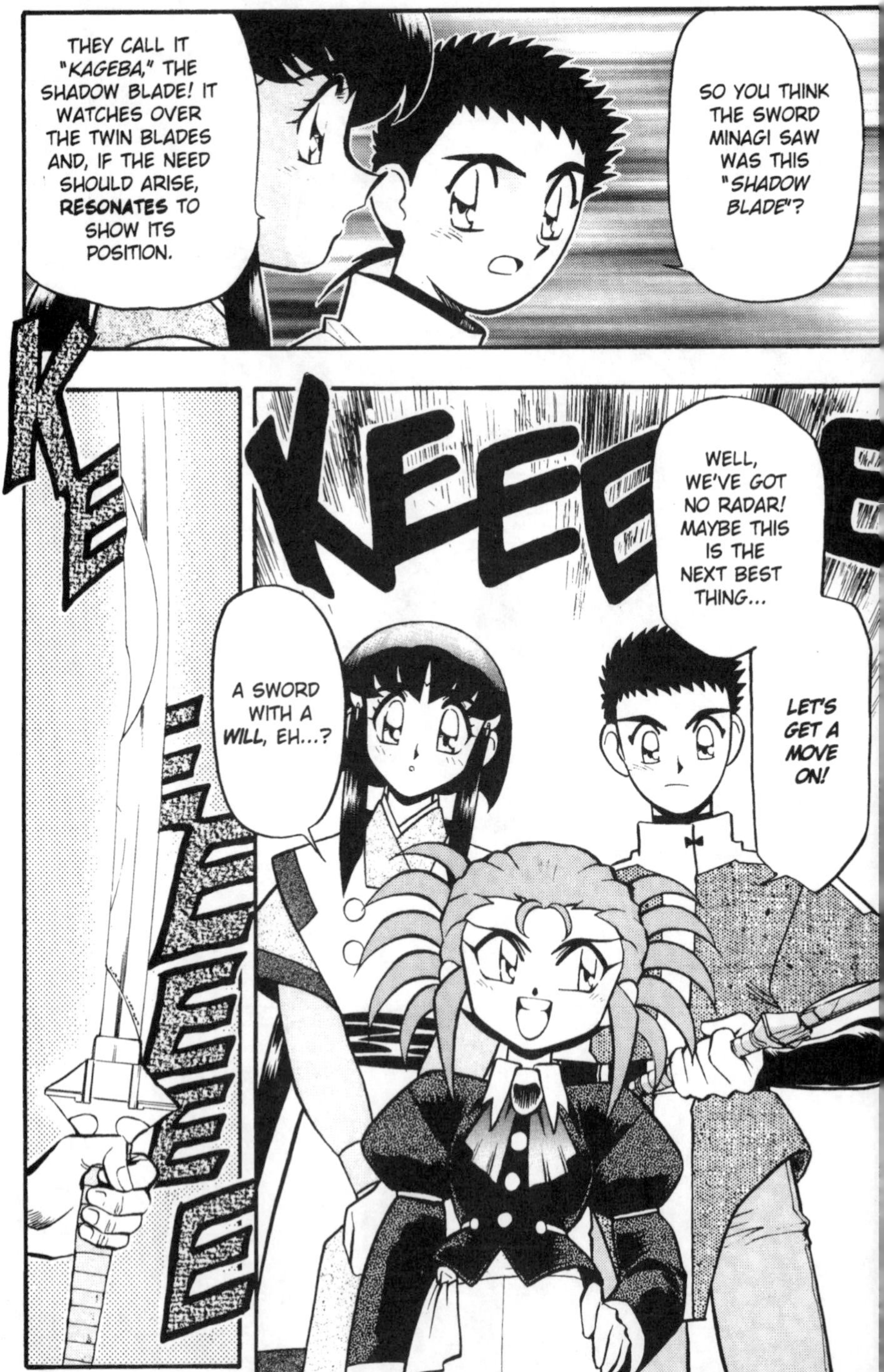
THEY CALL IT "KAGEBA," THE SHADOW BLADE! IT WATCHES OVER THE TWIN BLADES AND, IF THE NEED SHOULD ARISE, RESONATES TO SHOW ITS POSITION.
SO YOU THINK THE SWORD MINAGI SAW WAS THIS "SHADOW BLADE"?
KEEE
WELL, WE'VE GOT NO RADAR! MAYBE THIS IS THE NEXT BEST THING...
A SWORD WITH A WILL, EH...?
LET'S GET A MOVE ON!

Tales of Tenchi #3

A POINTED ENCOUNTER

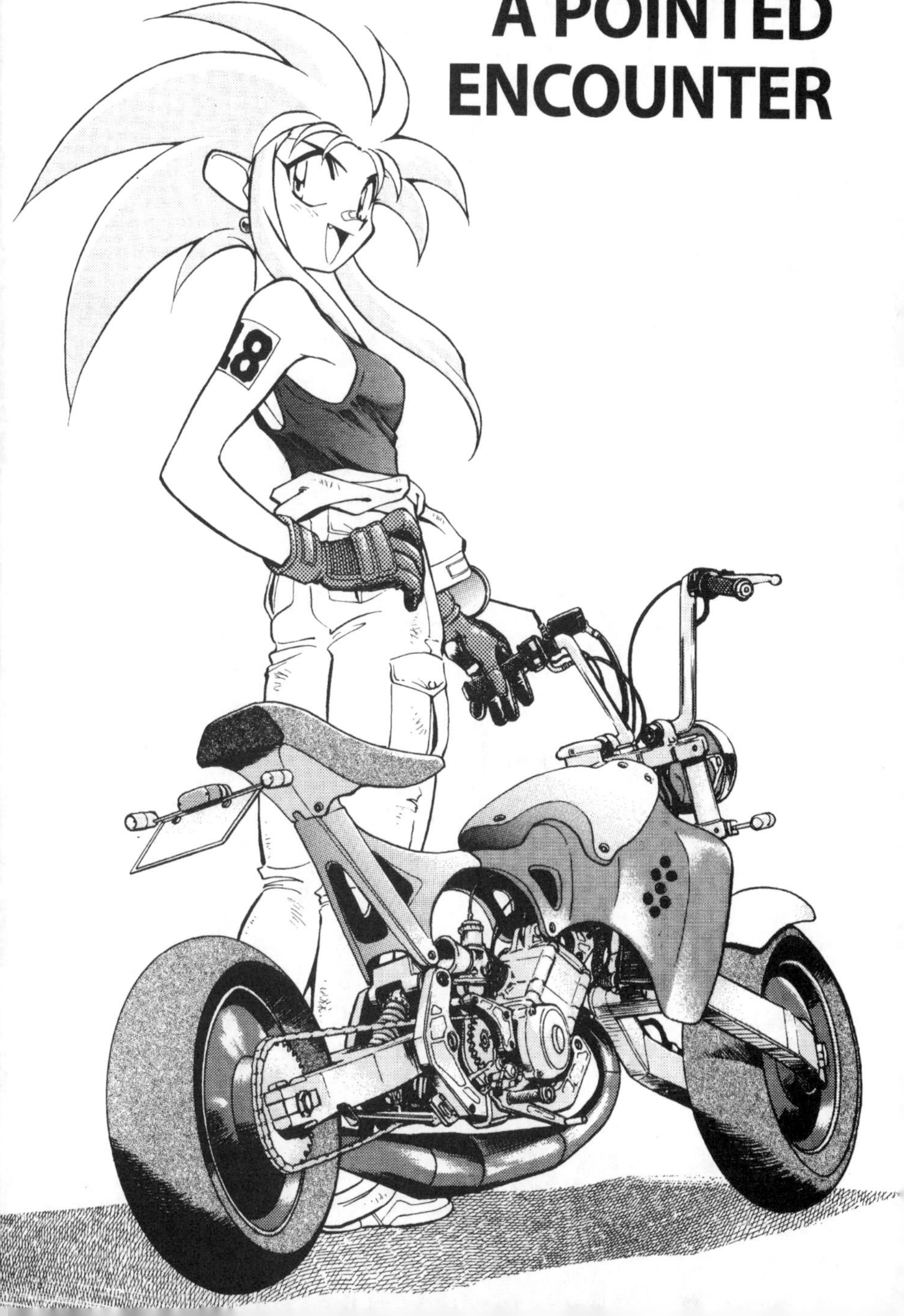
18

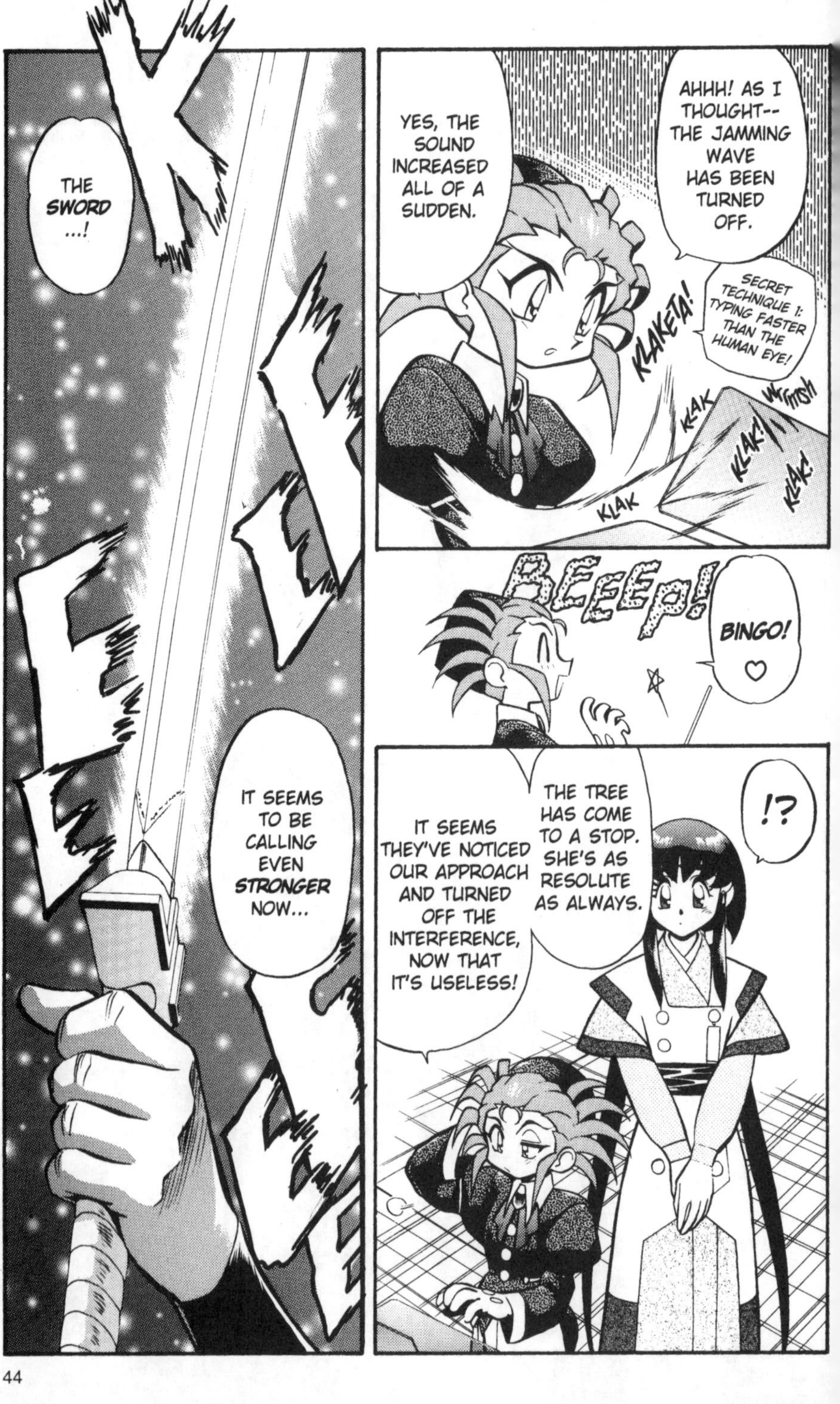
THE SWORD ...!
IT SEEMS TO BE CALLING EVEN STRONGER NOW...
YES, THE SOUND INCREASED ALL OF A SUDDEN.
AHHH! AS I THOUGHT-- THE JAMMING WAVE HAS BEEN TURNED OFF.
KLAKETA!
SECRET TECHNIQUE 1: TYPING FASTER THAN THE HUMAN EYE!
KLAK
KLAK!
KLAK!
KLAK
BEEEP!
BINGO! ♡
IT SEEMS THEY'VE NOTICED OUR APPROACH AND TURNED OFF THE INTERFERENCE, NOW THAT IT'S USELESS!
THE TREE HAS COME TO A STOP. SHE'S AS RESOLUTE AS ALWAYS.
!?

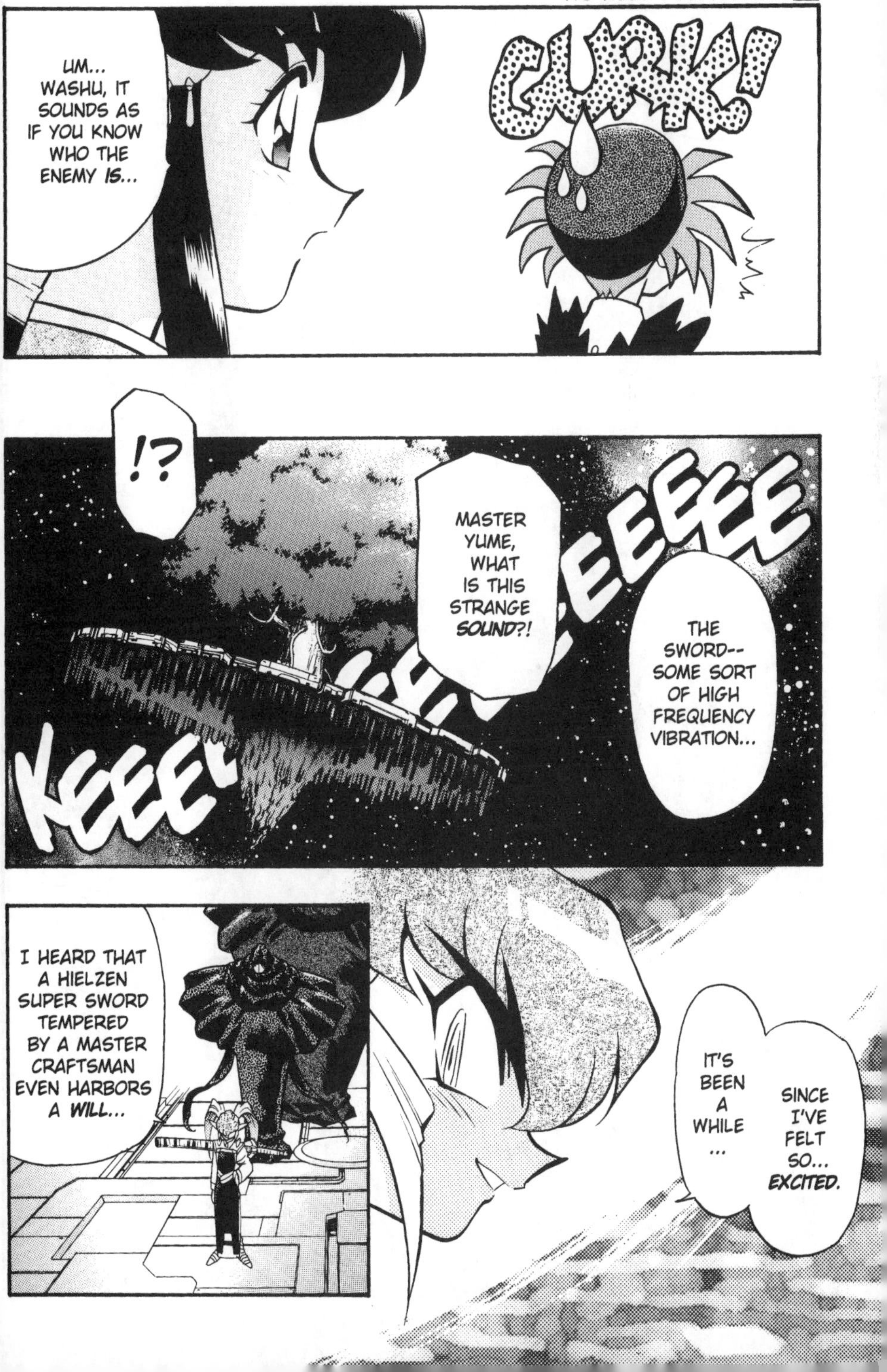
UM... WASHU, IT SOUNDS AS IF YOU KNOW WHO THE ENEMY IS...
GURK!
!?
MASTER YUME, WHAT IS THIS STRANGE SOUND?!
KEEEEEEEEEEEE
THE SWORD-- SOME SORT OF HIGH FREQUENCY VIBRATION...
I HEARD THAT A HIELZEN SUPER SWORD TEMPERED BY A MASTER CRAFTSMAN EVEN HARBORS A WILL...
IT'S BEEN A WHILE ...
SINCE I'VE FELT SO... EXCITED.

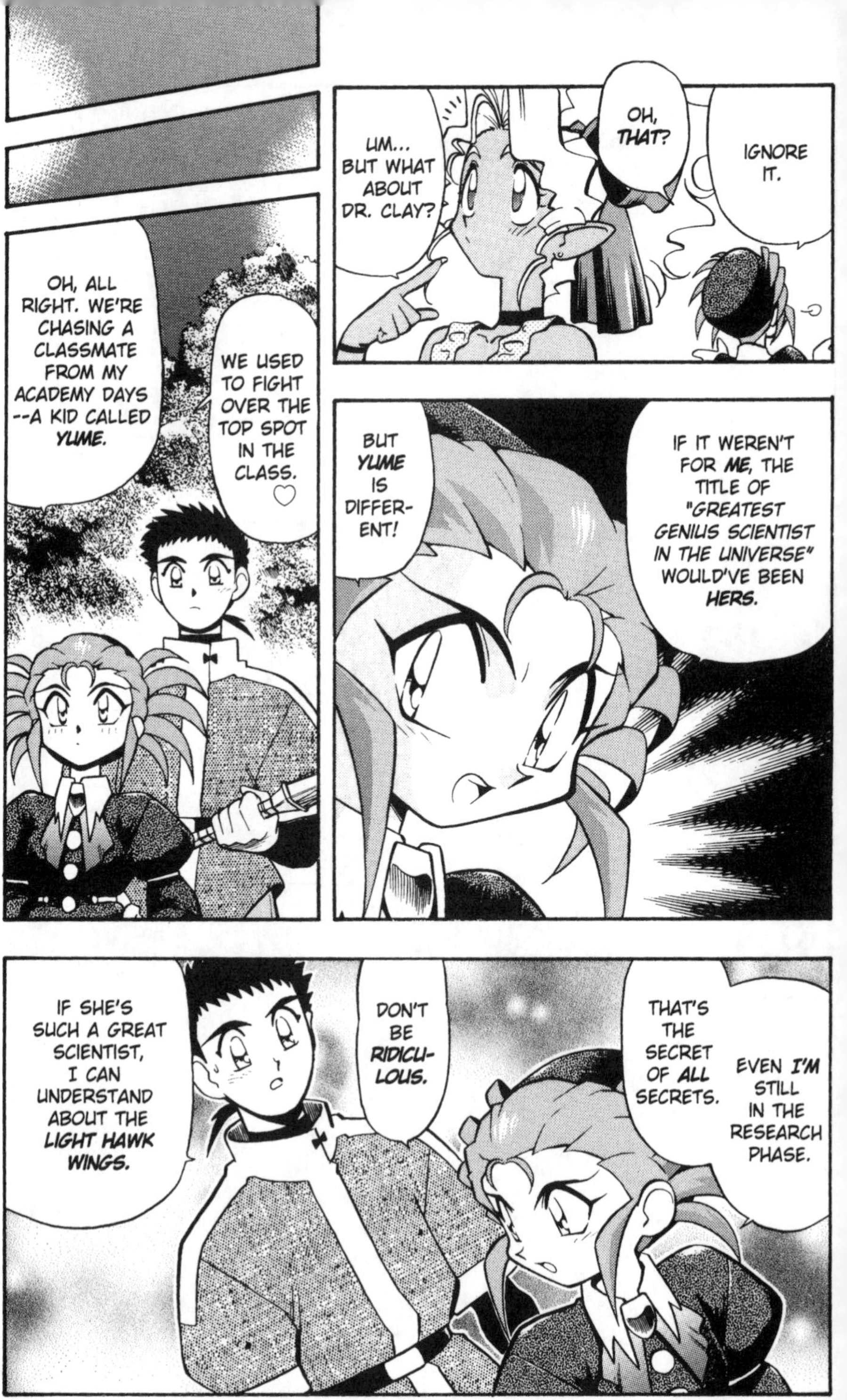
OH, ALL RIGHT. WE'RE CHASING A CLASSMATE FROM MY ACADEMY DAYS --A KID CALLED ***YUME.***
WE USED TO FIGHT OVER THE TOP SPOT IN THE CLASS. ♡
UM... BUT WHAT ABOUT DR. CLAY?
OH, ***THAT?***
IGNORE IT.
BUT ***YUME*** IS DIFFER-ENT!
IF IT WEREN'T FOR ***ME,*** THE TITLE OF ***"GREATEST GENIUS SCIENTIST IN THE UNIVERSE"*** WOULD'VE BEEN ***HERS.***
IF SHE'S SUCH A GREAT SCIENTIST, I CAN UNDERSTAND ABOUT THE ***LIGHT HAWK WINGS.***
DON'T BE ***RIDICU-LOUS.***
THAT'S THE SECRET OF ***ALL*** SECRETS.
EVEN ***I'M*** STILL IN THE RESEARCH PHASE.

! OH

THEN THIS **YUME** MUST BE GREATER THAN WASHU!

WOW! ♡

GREATER THAN WASHU!?

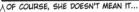
♪ OF COURSE, SHE DOESN'T MEAN IT...

GREATER?! IT'S THOSE FILES!

HUH?

?

WHY ARE YOU ANGRY?

IF **ONLY** I HAD THE SECRET FILES!

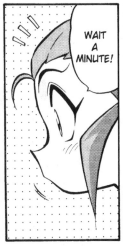

WAIT A MINUTE!

LORRRD TENNNCHIIII? ♡

GULP!

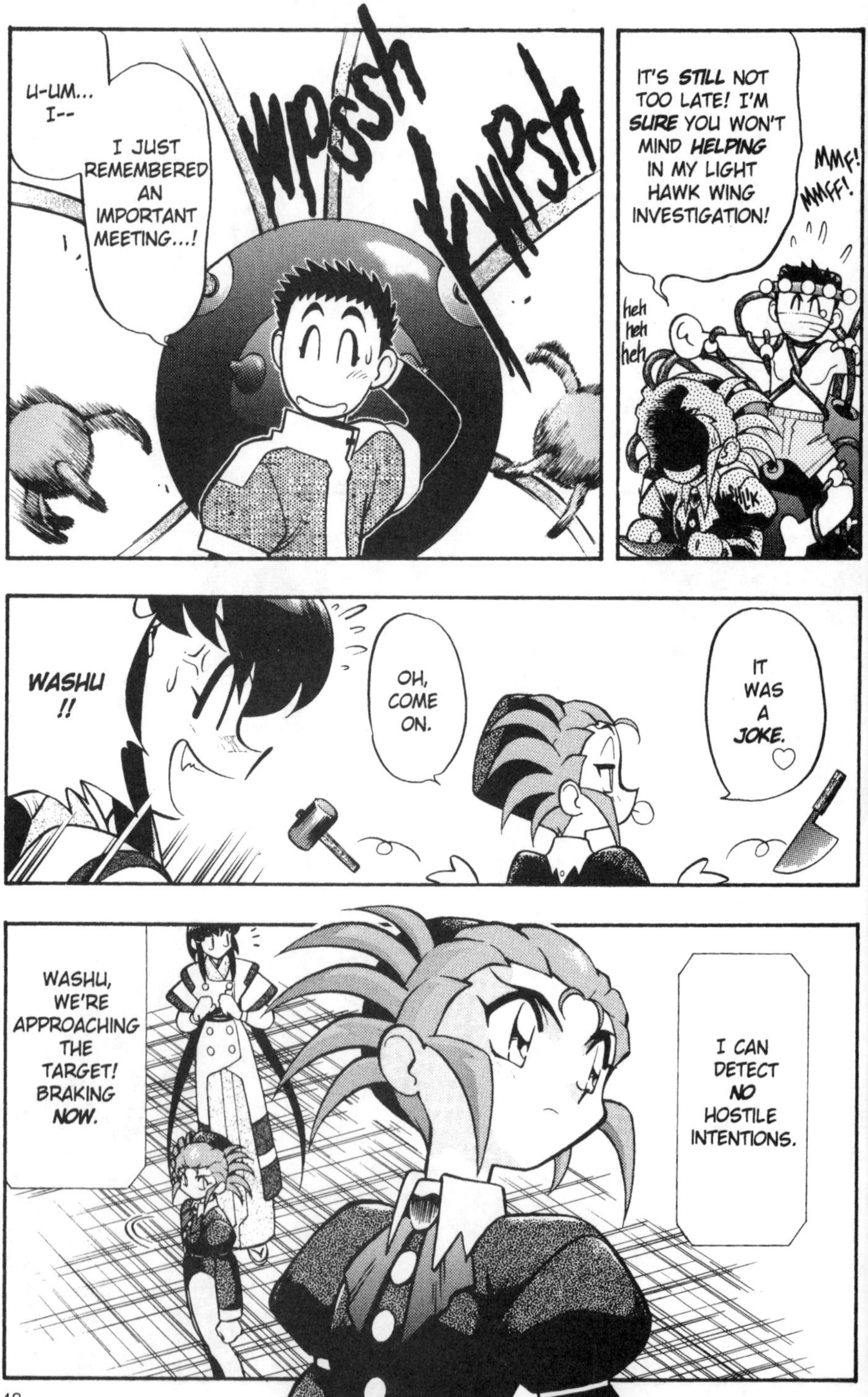
U-UM... I--
I JUST REMEMBERED AN IMPORTANT MEETING...!
WPSSH
KWPSH
IT'S STILL NOT TOO LATE! I'M SURE YOU WON'T MIND HELPING IN MY LIGHT HAWK WING INVESTIGATION!
MMF! MMFF!
heh heh heh
SHLK
WASHU !!
OH, COME ON.
IT WAS A JOKE. ♡
WASHU, WE'RE APPROACHING THE TARGET! BRAKING NOW.
I CAN DETECT NO HOSTILE INTENTIONS.

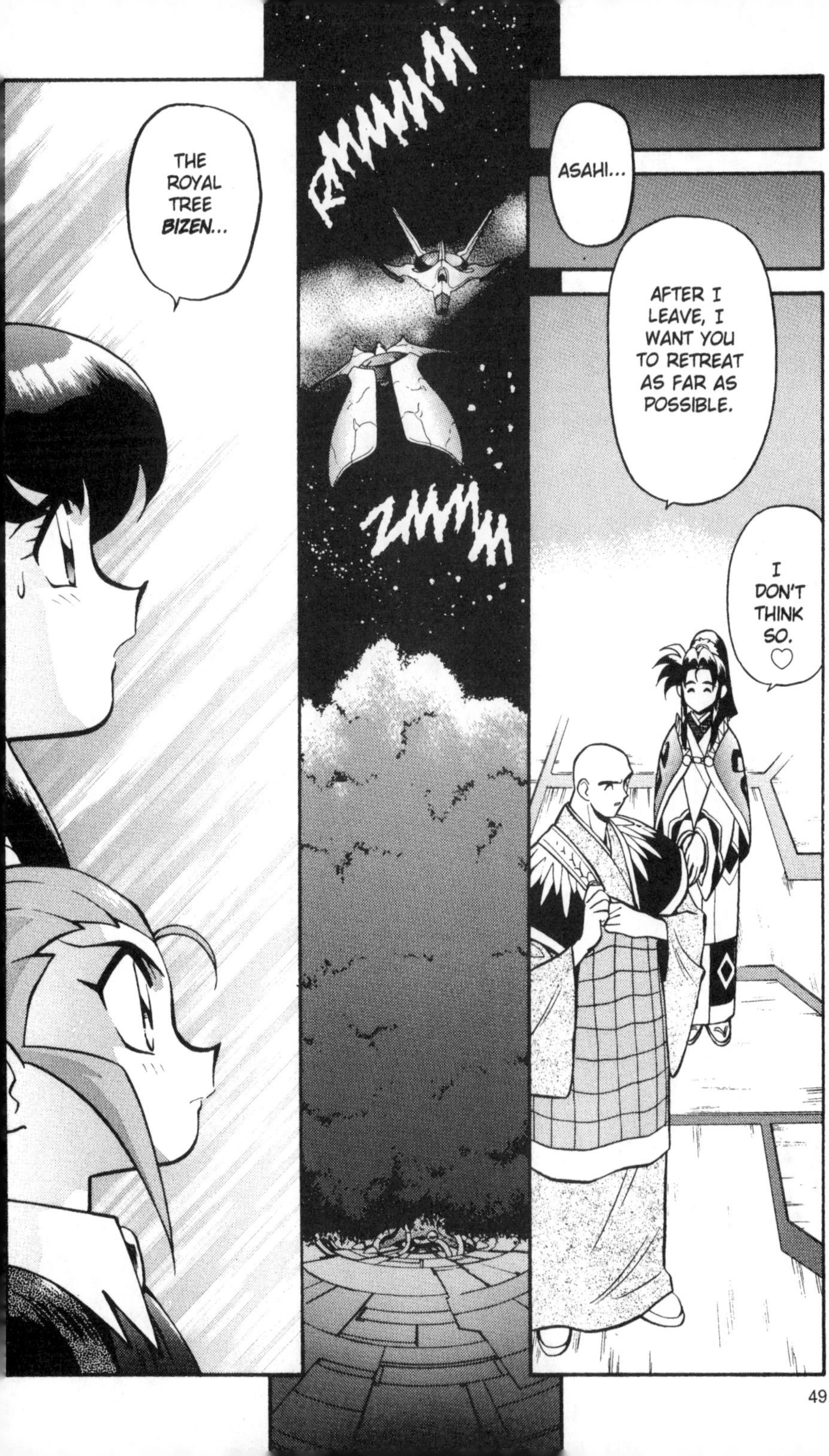
THE ROYAL TREE BIZEN...
RMMMM
ZMMMM
ASAHI...
AFTER I LEAVE, I WANT YOU TO RETREAT AS FAR AS POSSIBLE.
I DON'T THINK SO. ♡

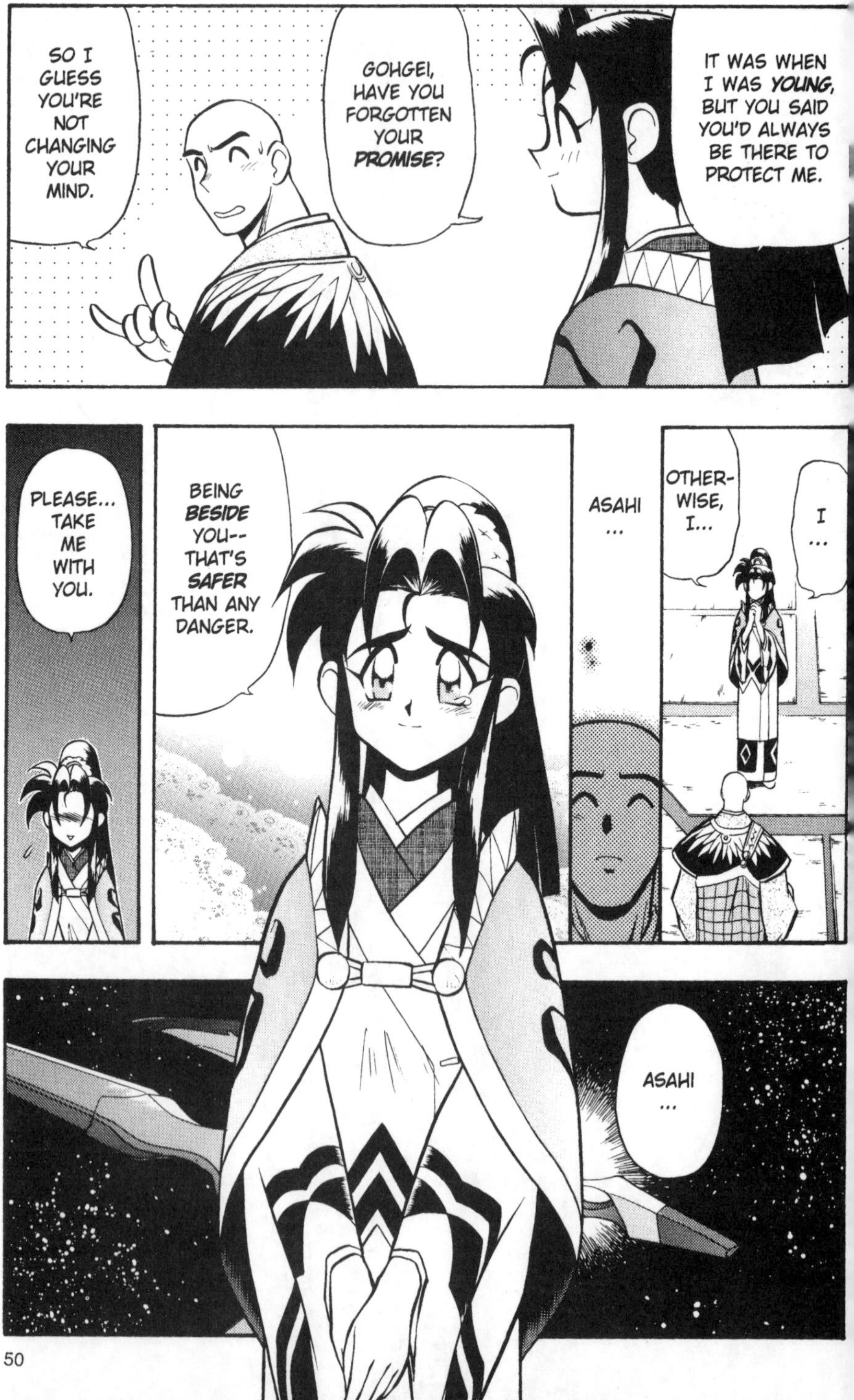
SO I GUESS YOU'RE NOT CHANGING YOUR MIND.
GOHGEI, HAVE YOU FORGOTTEN YOUR PROMISE?
IT WAS WHEN I WAS YOUNG, BUT YOU SAID YOU'D ALWAYS BE THERE TO PROTECT ME.
PLEASE... TAKE ME WITH YOU.
BEING BESIDE YOU--THAT'S SAFER THAN ANY DANGER.
ASAHI ...
OTHER-WISE, I...
I ...
ASAHI ...

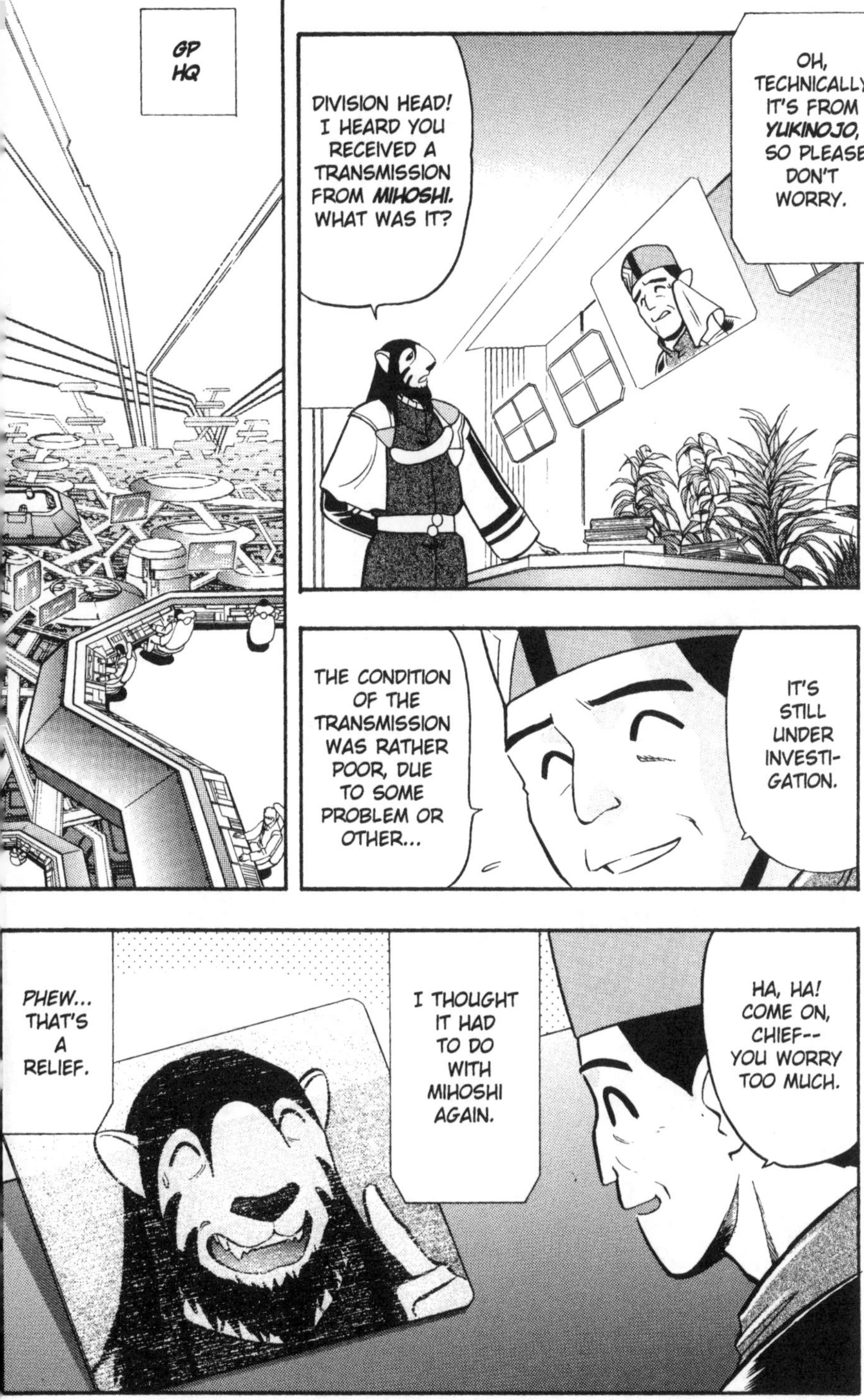
GP HQ
DIVISION HEAD! I HEARD YOU RECEIVED A TRANSMISSION FROM MIHOSHI. WHAT WAS IT?
OH, TECHNICALLY IT'S FROM YUKINOJO, SO PLEASE DON'T WORRY.
THE CONDITION OF THE TRANSMISSION WAS RATHER POOR, DUE TO SOME PROBLEM OR OTHER...
IT'S STILL UNDER INVESTI-GATION.
PHEW... THAT'S A RELIEF.
I THOUGHT IT HAD TO DO WITH MIHOSHI AGAIN.
HA, HA! COME ON, CHIEF-- YOU WORRY TOO MUCH.

GOOD
DAY.

heh!

WELL,
THAT
BOUGHT
US
SOME
TIME.

THIS **DOES**
HAVE TO DO
WITH A
ROYAL TREE,
AFTER ALL...

THE JURAI
ROYAL FAMILY
WOULDN'T WANT
TO BE BEATEN
TO IT BY GP...

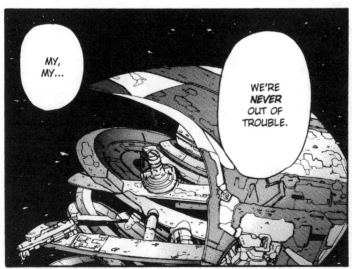

MY,
MY...

WE'RE
NEVER
OUT OF
TROUBLE.

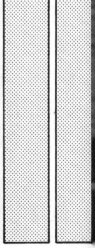

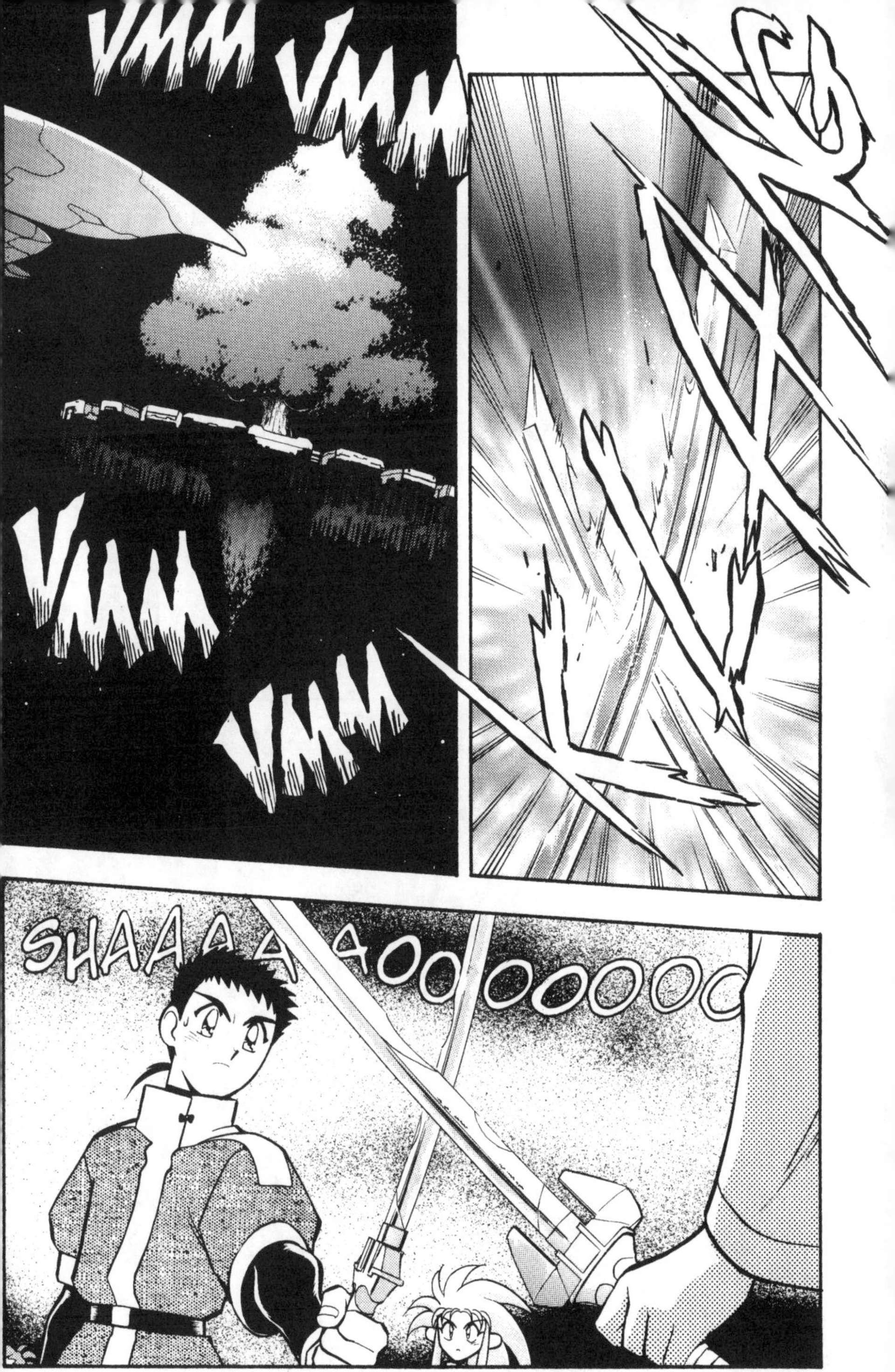
VMM VMM
VMM
VMM
SHAAAAAOOOOOOOOC

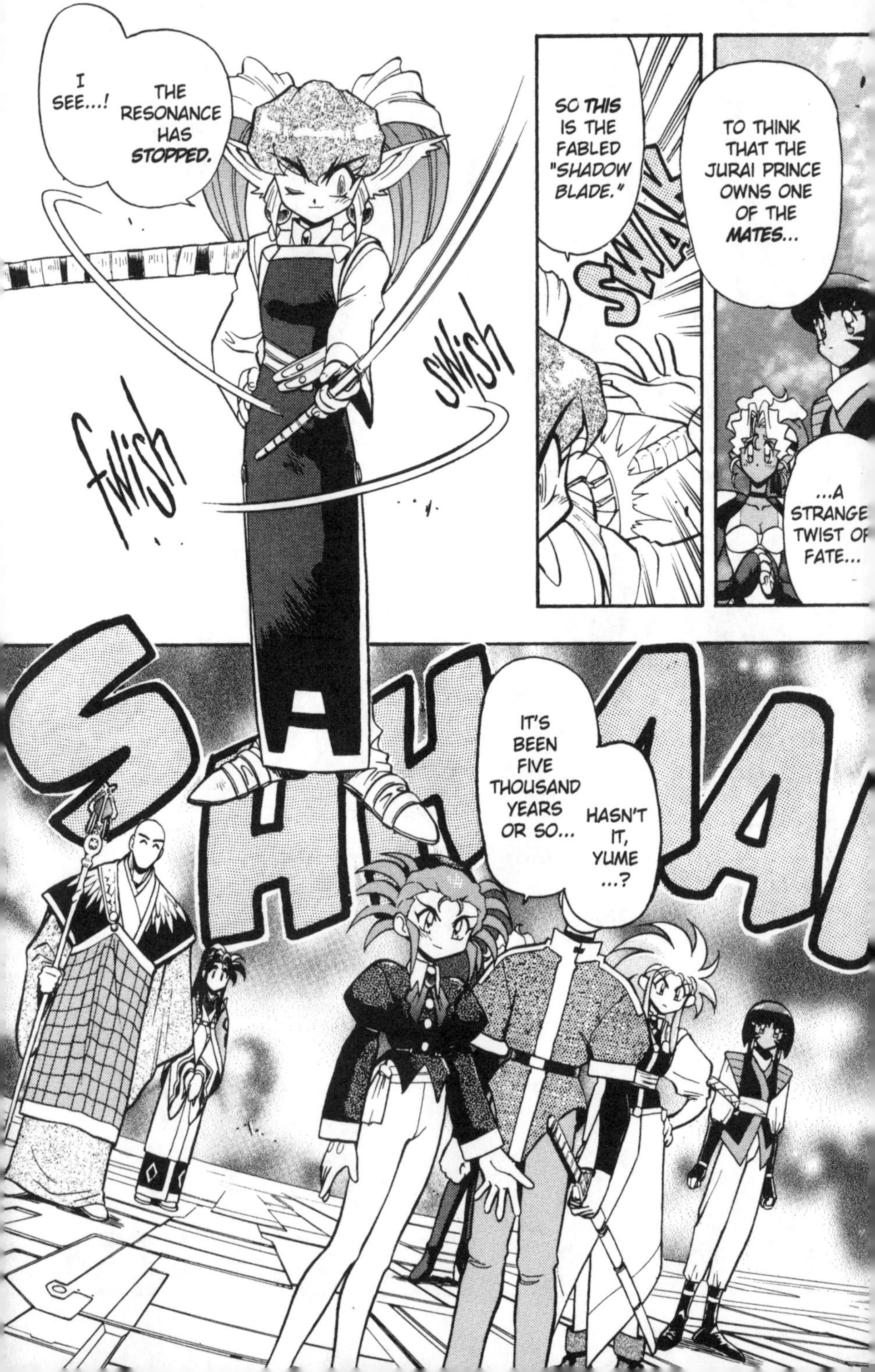

I SEE...!
THE RESONANCE HAS STOPPED.
fwish
swish
SO THIS IS THE FABLED "SHADOW BLADE."
SWAK
TO THINK THAT THE JURAI PRINCE OWNS ONE OF THE MATES...
...A STRANGE TWIST OF FATE...
SHAA
IT'S BEEN FIVE THOUSAND YEARS OR SO...
HASN'T IT, YUME ...?

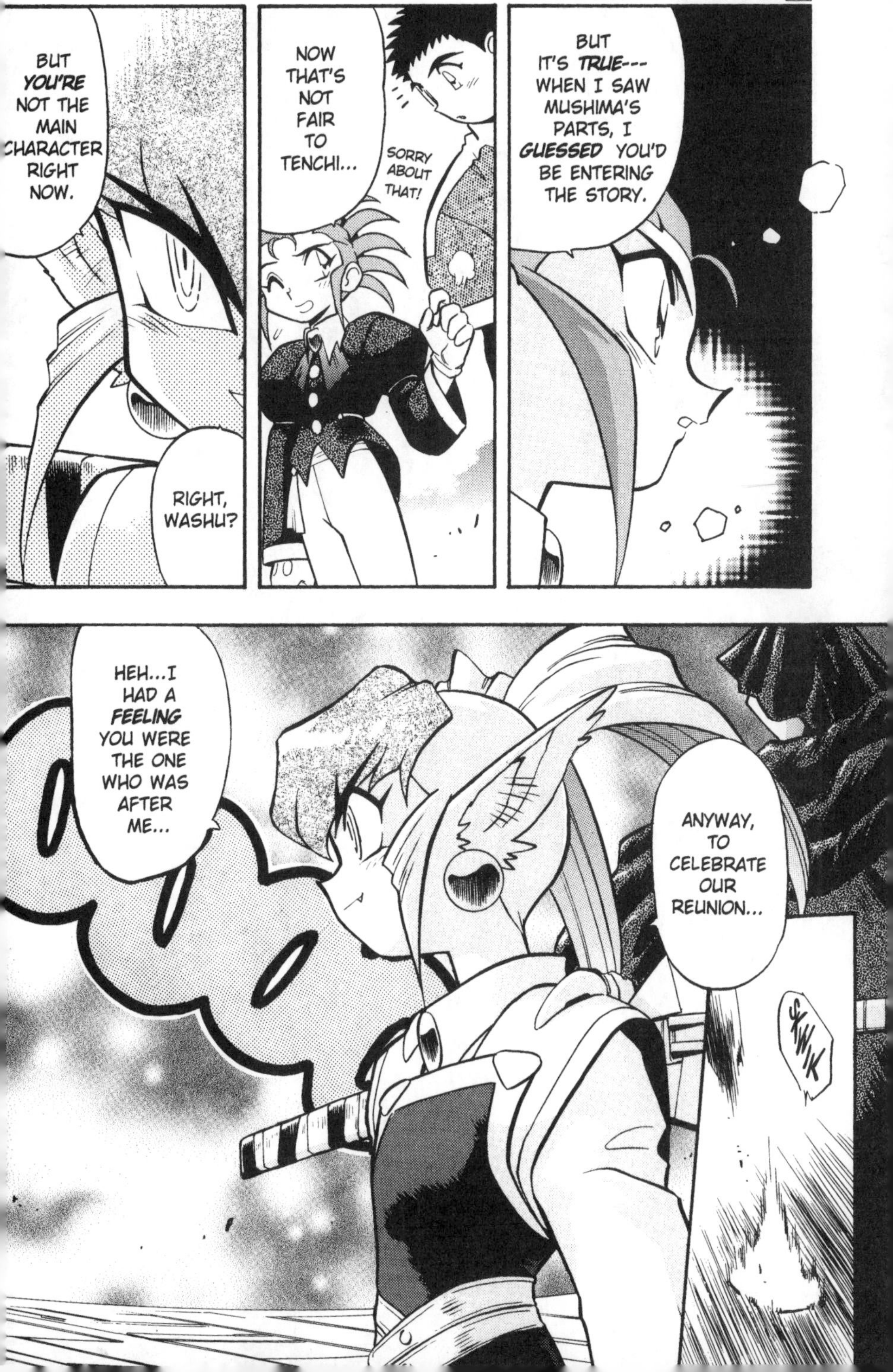
BUT YOU'RE NOT THE MAIN CHARACTER RIGHT NOW.
RIGHT, WASHU?
NOW THAT'S NOT FAIR TO TENCHI...
SORRY ABOUT THAT!
BUT IT'S TRUE--- WHEN I SAW MUSHIMA'S PARTS, I GUESSED YOU'D BE ENTERING THE STORY.
HEH...I HAD A FEELING YOU WERE THE ONE WHO WAS AFTER ME...
ANYWAY, TO CELEBRATE OUR REUNION...
SKWIK

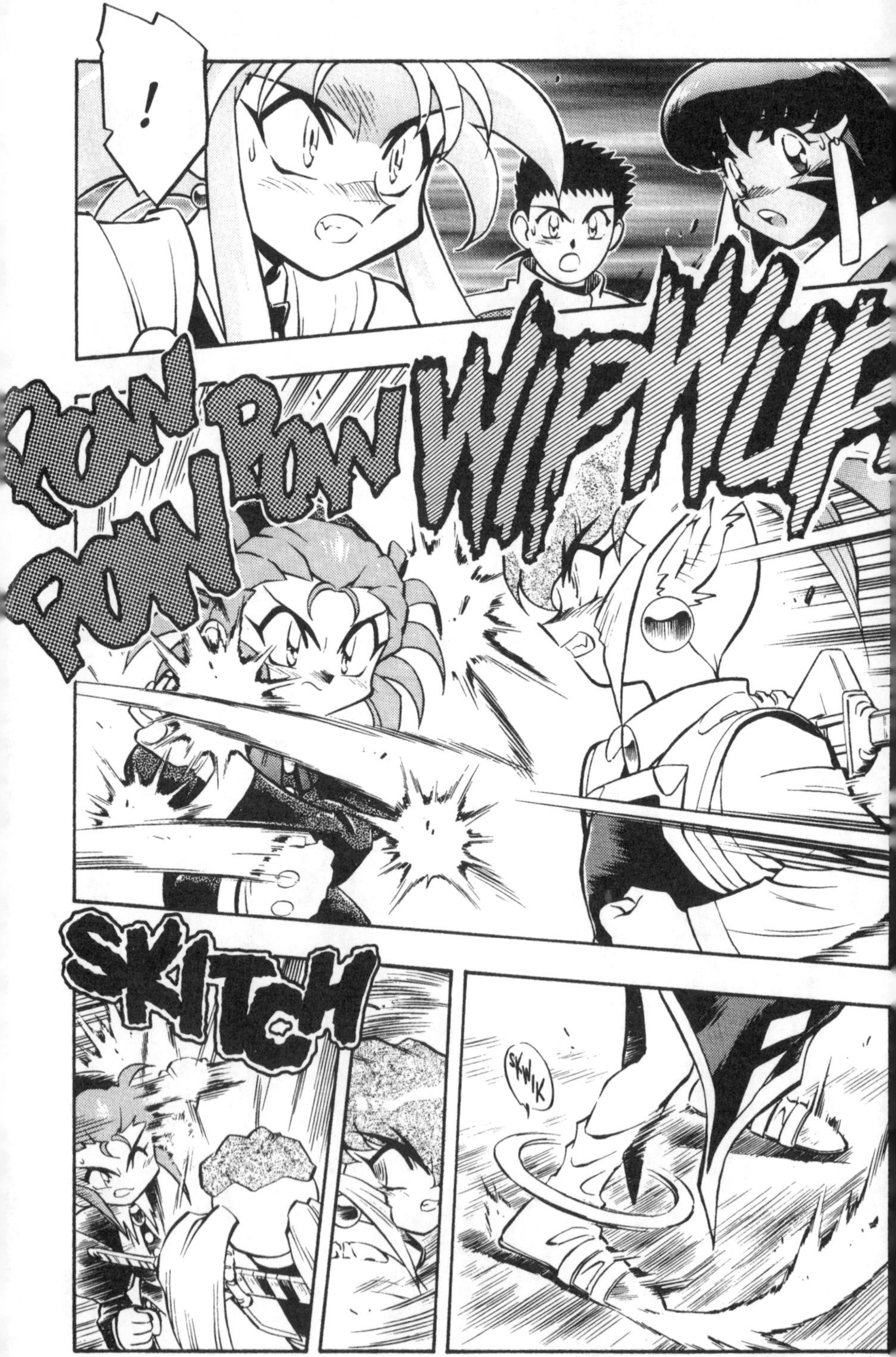
!
POW POW
POW POW
WIPWIP
SKITCH
SKWIK

♡ SHIFTING WEIGHT AT SUPER SPEED--TEE HEE

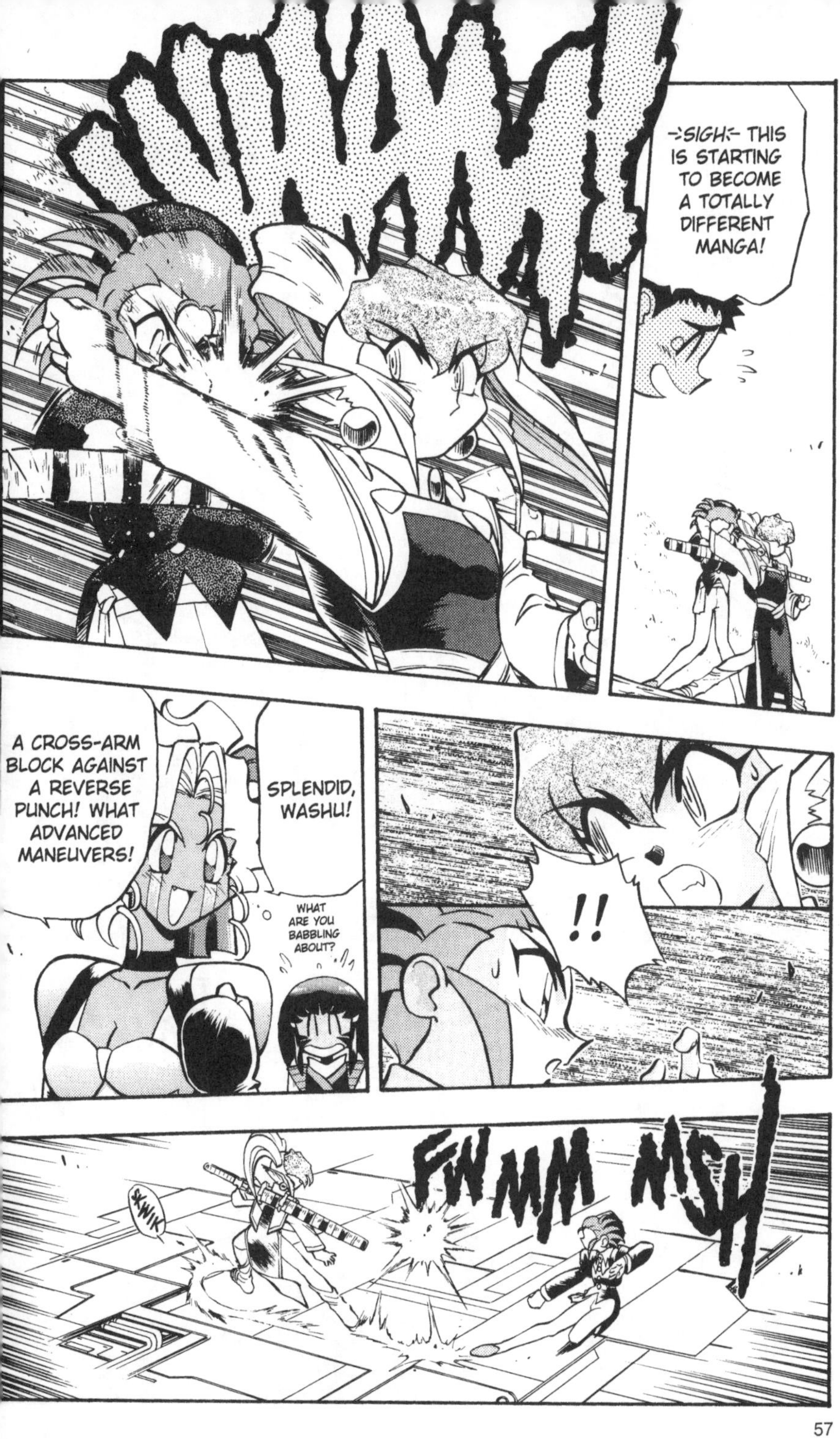
-SIGH- THIS IS STARTING TO BECOME A TOTALLY DIFFERENT MANGA!
A CROSS-ARM BLOCK AGAINST A REVERSE PUNCH! WHAT ADVANCED MANEUVERS!
SPLENDID, WASHU!
WHAT ARE YOU BABBLING ABOUT?
!!
SKWIK
FWMM MSH

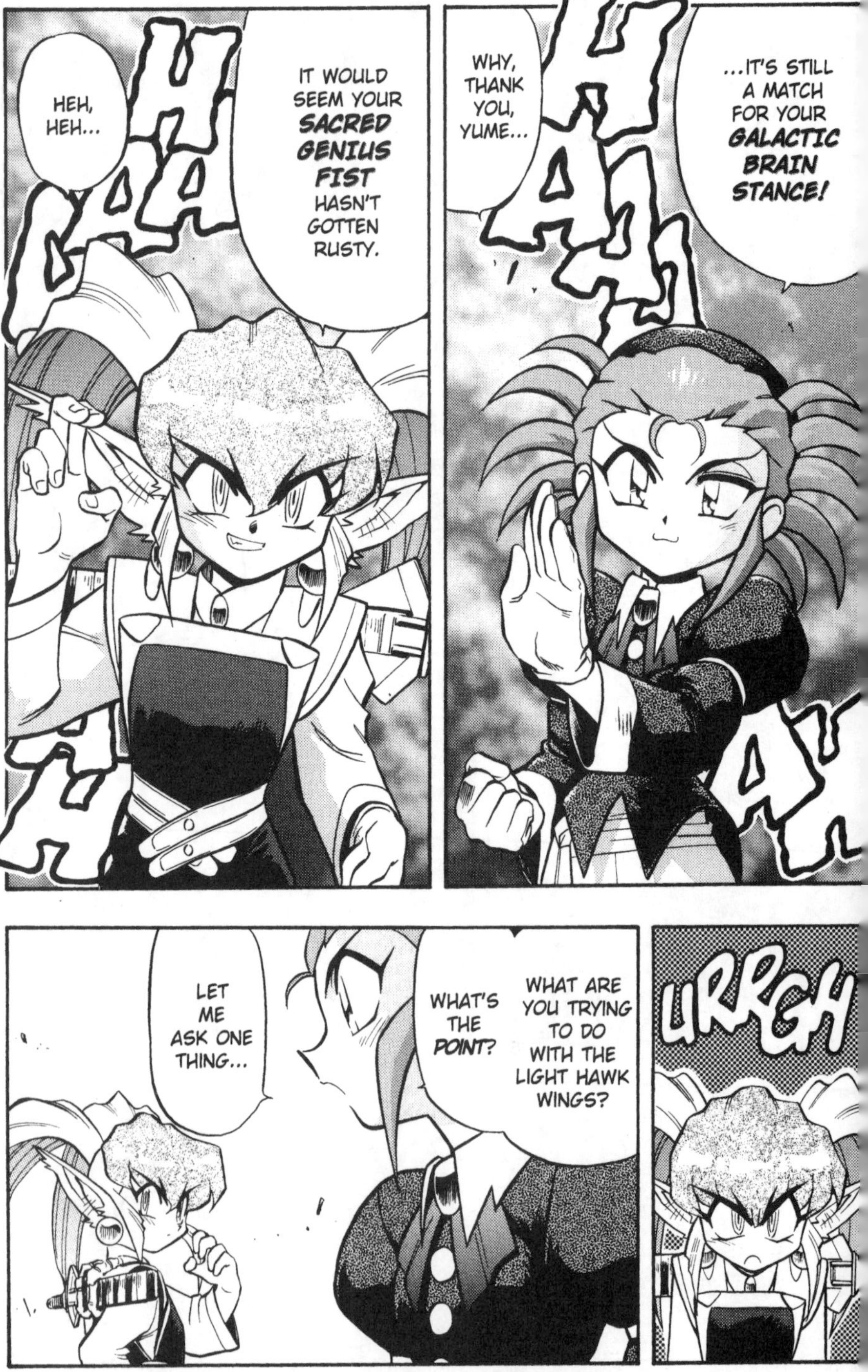
HEH, HEH...
IT WOULD SEEM YOUR **SACRED GENIUS FIST** HASN'T GOTTEN RUSTY.
WHY, THANK YOU, YUME...
...IT'S STILL A MATCH FOR YOUR ***GALACTIC BRAIN STANCE!***
LET ME ASK ONE THING...
WHAT'S THE *POINT?*
WHAT ARE YOU TRYING TO DO WITH THE LIGHT HAWK WINGS?
URRGH

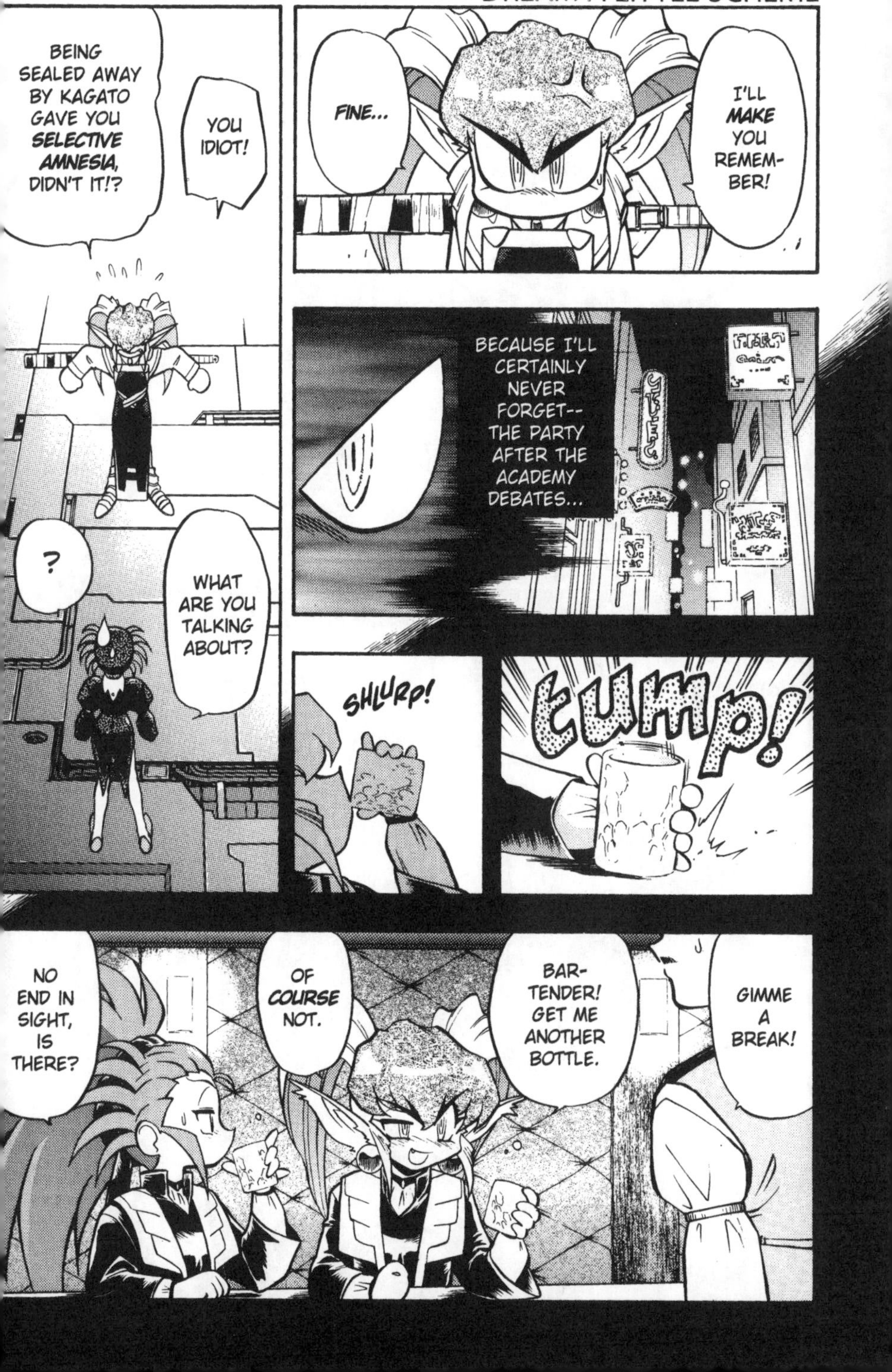
BEING SEALED AWAY BY KAGATO GAVE YOU SELECTIVE AMNESIA, DIDN'T IT!?
YOU IDIOT!
?
WHAT ARE YOU TALKING ABOUT?
FINE...
I'LL MAKE YOU REMEMBER!
BECAUSE I'LL CERTAINLY NEVER FORGET-- THE PARTY AFTER THE ACADEMY DEBATES...
SHLURP!
tump!
NO END IN SIGHT, IS THERE?
OF COURSE NOT.
BARTENDER! GET ME ANOTHER BOTTLE.
GIMME A BREAK!

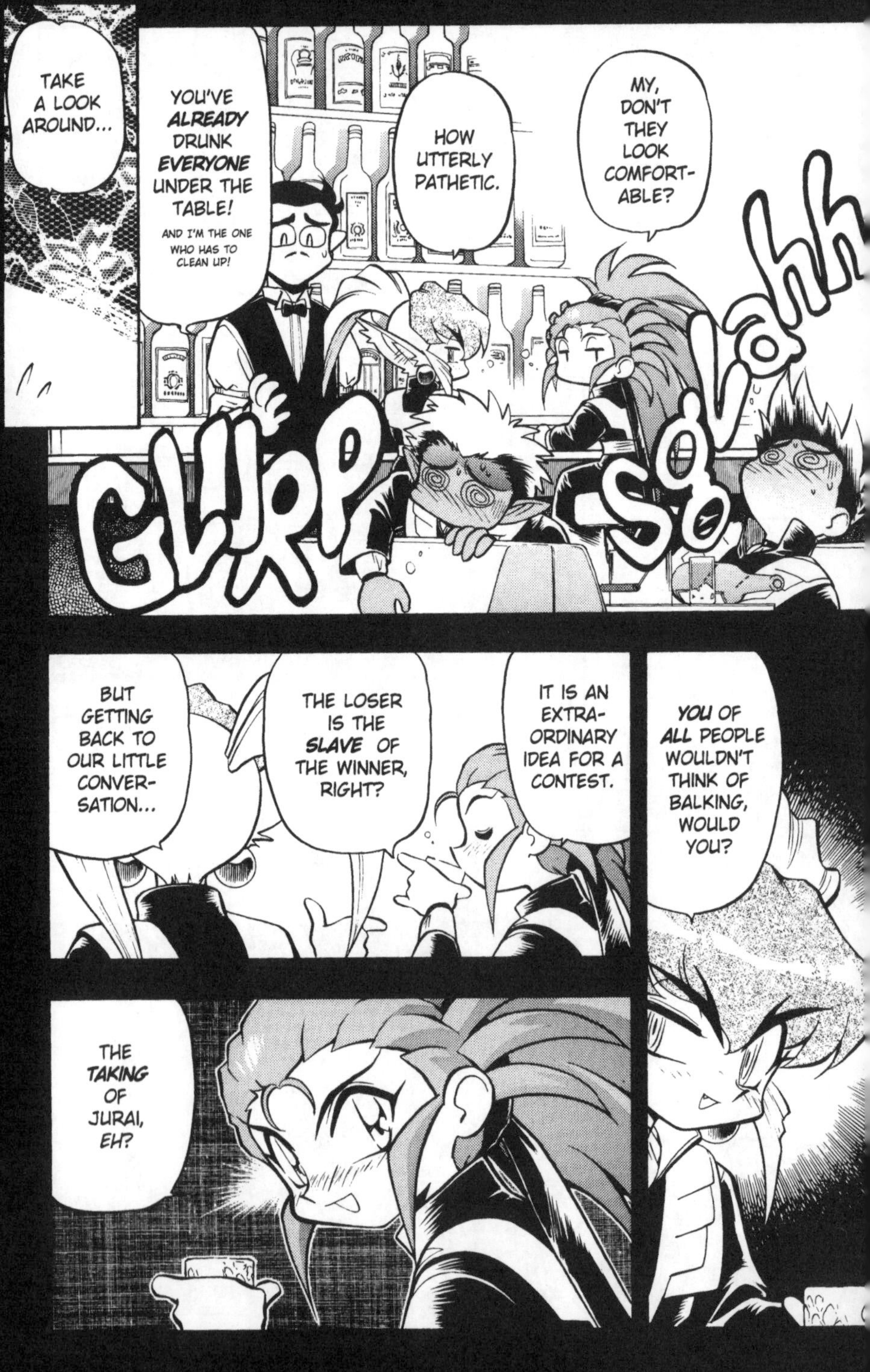
TAKE A LOOK AROUND...
YOU'VE *ALREADY* DRUNK *EVERYONE* UNDER THE TABLE!
AND I'M THE ONE WHO HAS TO CLEAN UP!
HOW UTTERLY PATHETIC.
MY, DON'T THEY LOOK COMFORTABLE?
GLUPP
SGOLAHH
BUT GETTING BACK TO OUR LITTLE CONVERSATION...
THE LOSER IS THE *SLAVE* OF THE WINNER, RIGHT?
IT IS AN EXTRAORDINARY IDEA FOR A CONTEST.
YOU OF *ALL* PEOPLE WOULDN'T THINK OF BALKING, WOULD YOU?
THE *TAKING* OF JURAI, EH?

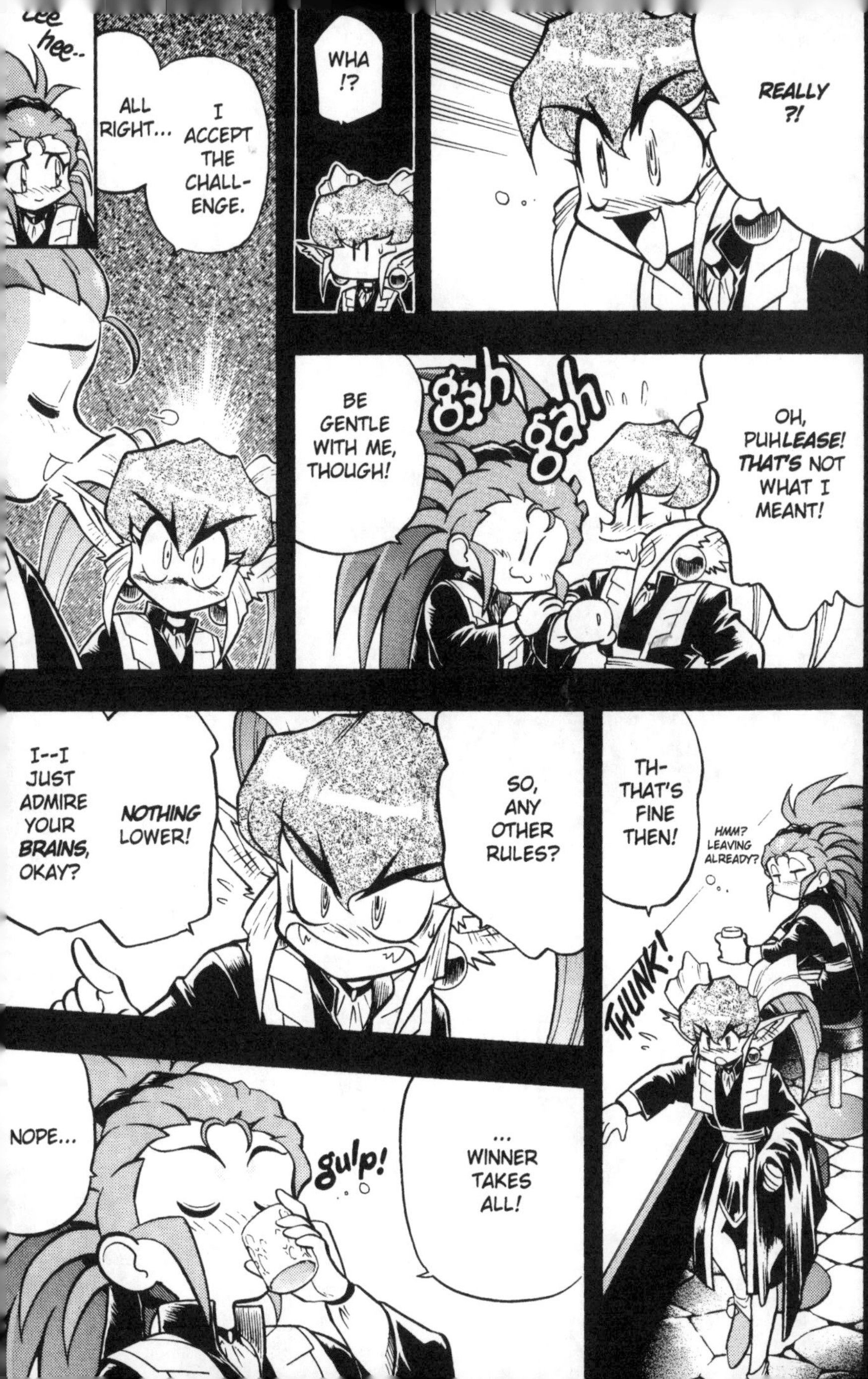
tee hee..
ALL RIGHT...
I ACCEPT THE CHALL-ENGE.
WHA !?
REALLY ?!
BE GENTLE WITH ME, THOUGH!
gah gah
OH, PUHLEASE! THAT'S NOT WHAT I MEANT!
I--I JUST ADMIRE YOUR BRAINS, OKAY?
NOTHING LOWER!
SO, ANY OTHER RULES?
TH-THAT'S FINE THEN!
HMM? LEAVING ALREADY?
THUNK!
NOPE...
gulp!
... WINNER TAKES ALL!

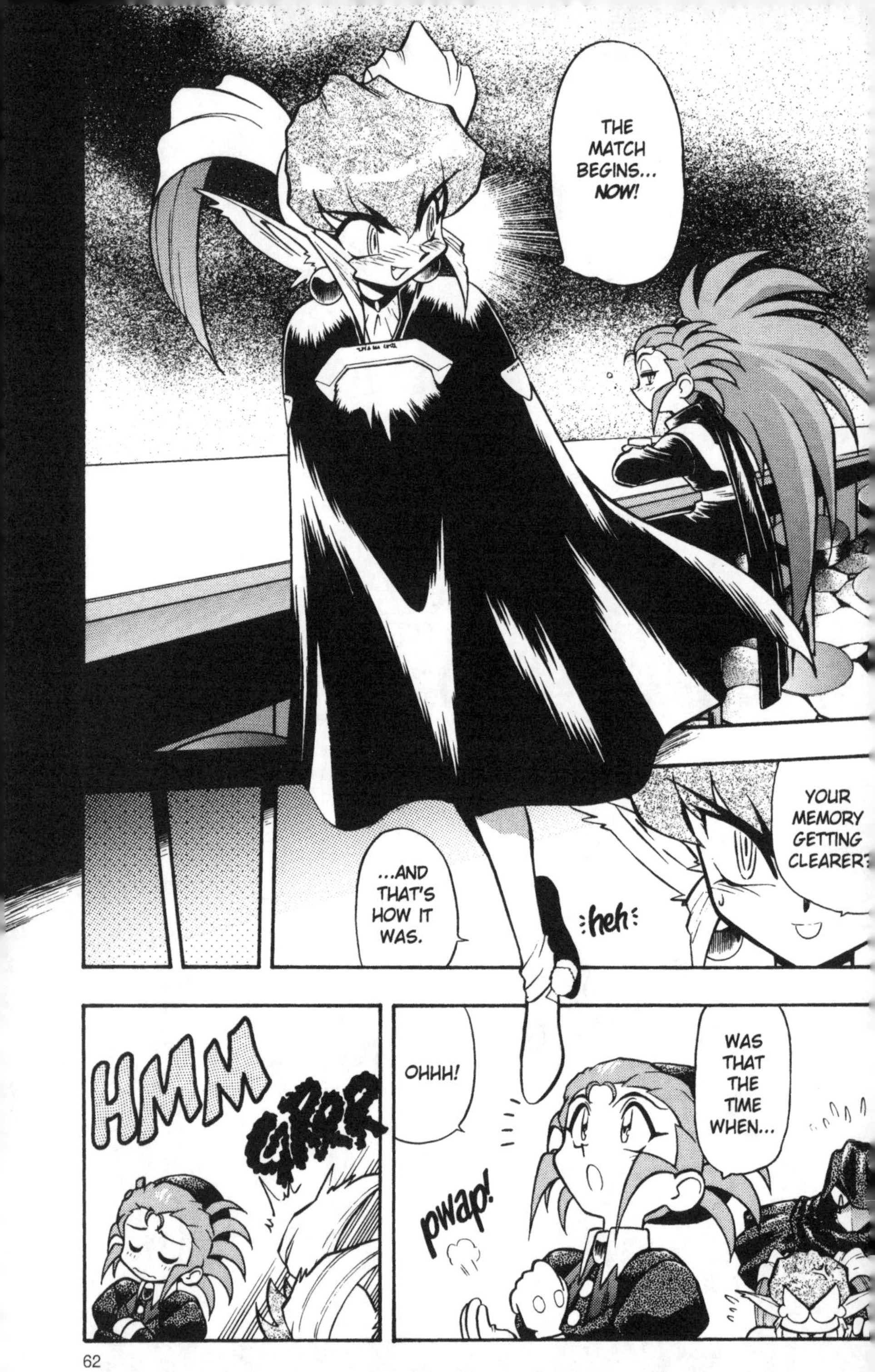
THE MATCH BEGINS... NOW!
...AND THAT'S HOW IT WAS.
heh
YOUR MEMORY GETTING CLEARER?
HMM
GRRR
OHHH!
pwap!
WAS THAT THE TIME WHEN...

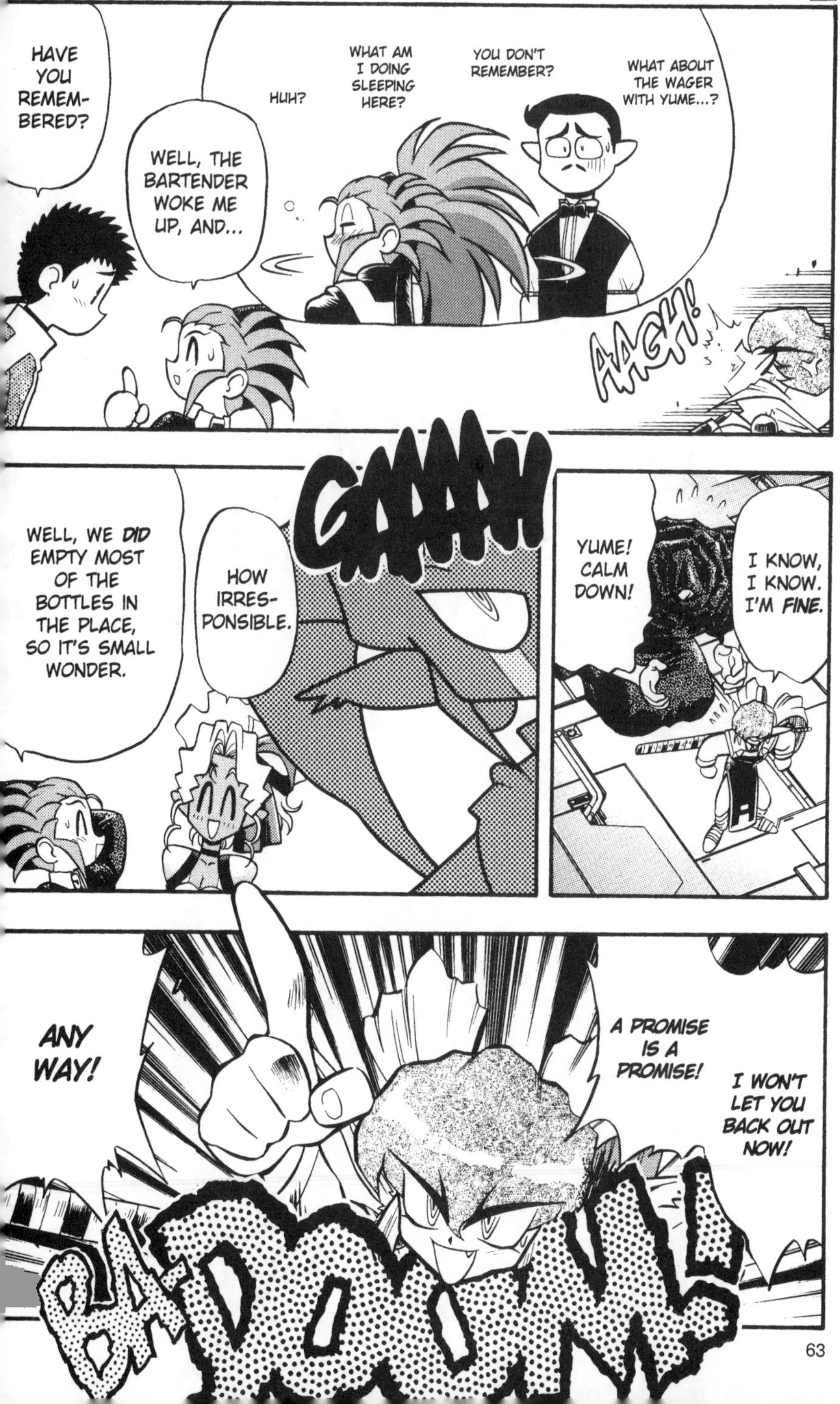
HAVE YOU REMEMBERED?
WELL, THE BARTENDER WOKE ME UP, AND...
HUH?
WHAT AM I DOING SLEEPING HERE?
YOU DON'T REMEMBER?
WHAT ABOUT THE WAGER WITH YUME...?
AAGH!
WELL, WE *DID* EMPTY MOST OF THE BOTTLES IN THE PLACE, SO IT'S SMALL WONDER.
HOW IRRESPONSIBLE.
GAAAH
YUME! CALM DOWN!
I KNOW, I KNOW. I'M *FINE*.
ANY WAY!
A PROMISE IS A PROMISE!
I WON'T LET YOU BACK OUT NOW!
BADOOM!

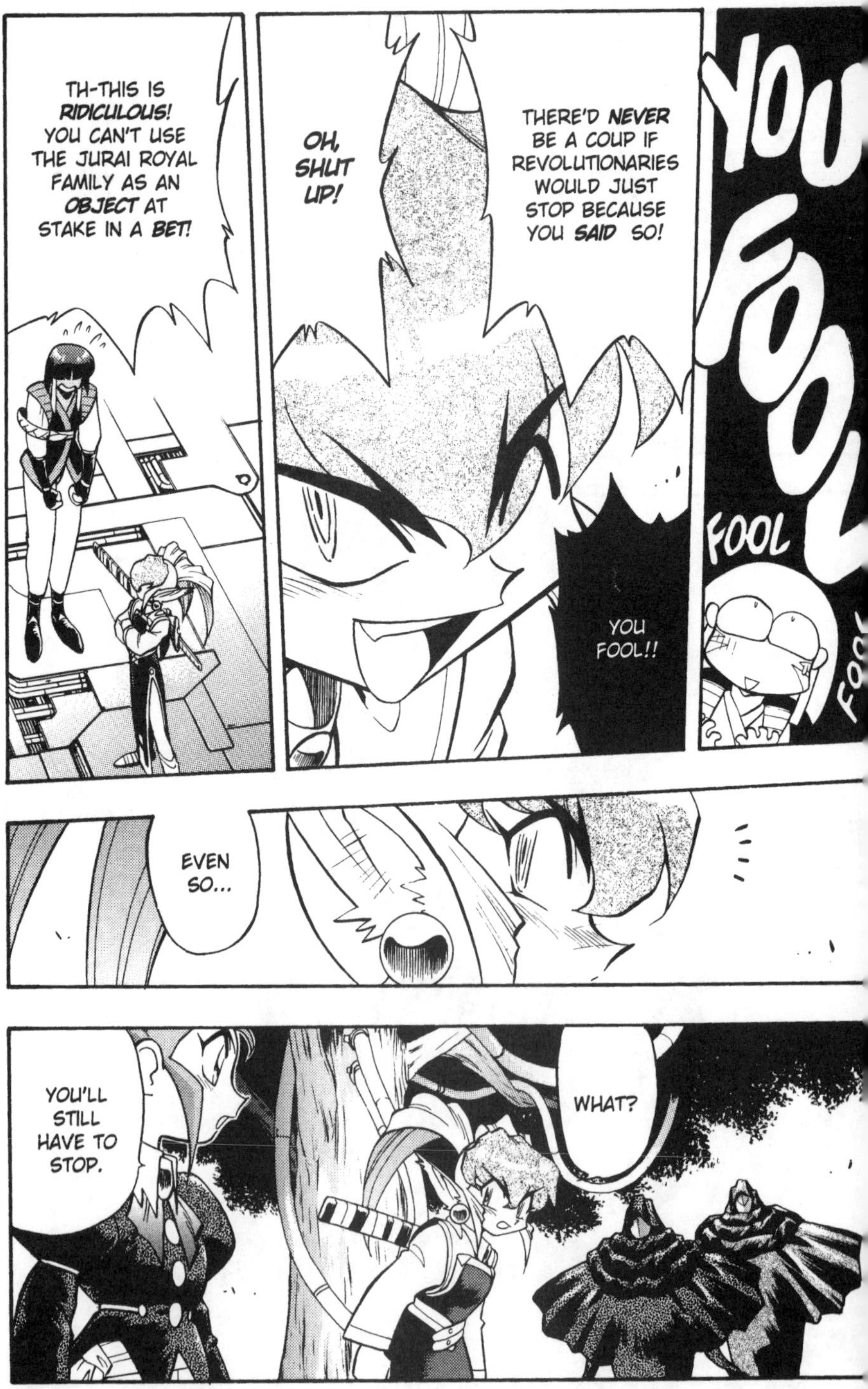
TH-THIS IS RIDICULOUS! YOU CAN'T USE THE JURAI ROYAL FAMILY AS AN OBJECT AT STAKE IN A BET!
OH, SHUT UP!
THERE'D NEVER BE A COUP IF REVOLUTIONARIES WOULD JUST STOP BECAUSE YOU SAID SO!
YOU FOOL!!
YOU FOOL
FOOL
FOO
EVEN SO...
YOU'LL STILL HAVE TO STOP.
WHAT?

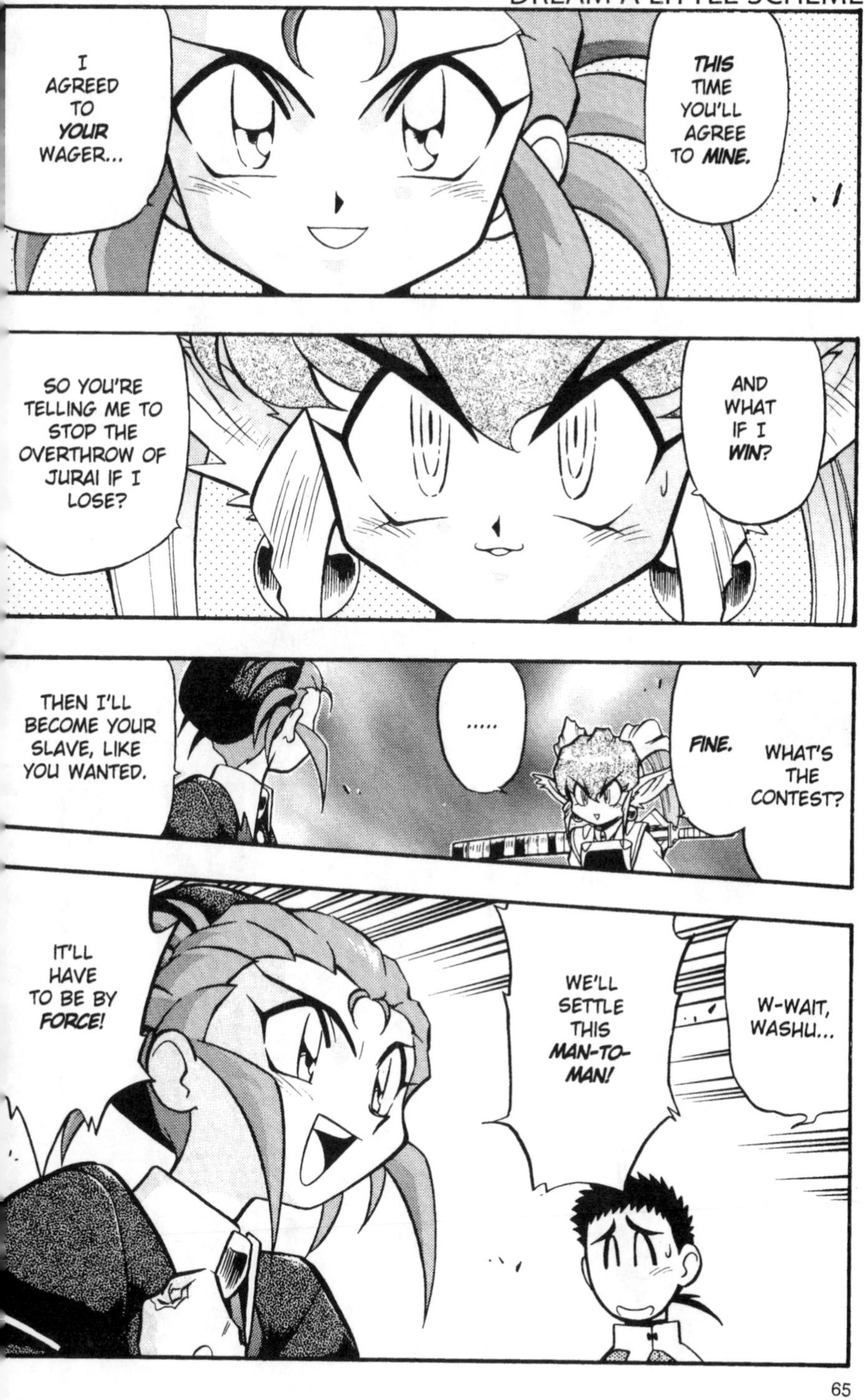
I AGREED TO *YOUR* WAGER...
THIS TIME YOU'LL AGREE TO *MINE.*
SO YOU'RE TELLING ME TO STOP THE OVERTHROW OF JURAI IF I LOSE?
AND WHAT IF I *WIN?*
THEN I'LL BECOME YOUR SLAVE, LIKE YOU WANTED.
.....
FINE.
WHAT'S THE CONTEST?
IT'LL HAVE TO BE BY *FORCE!*
WE'LL SETTLE THIS *MAN-TO-MAN!*
W-WAIT, WASHU...

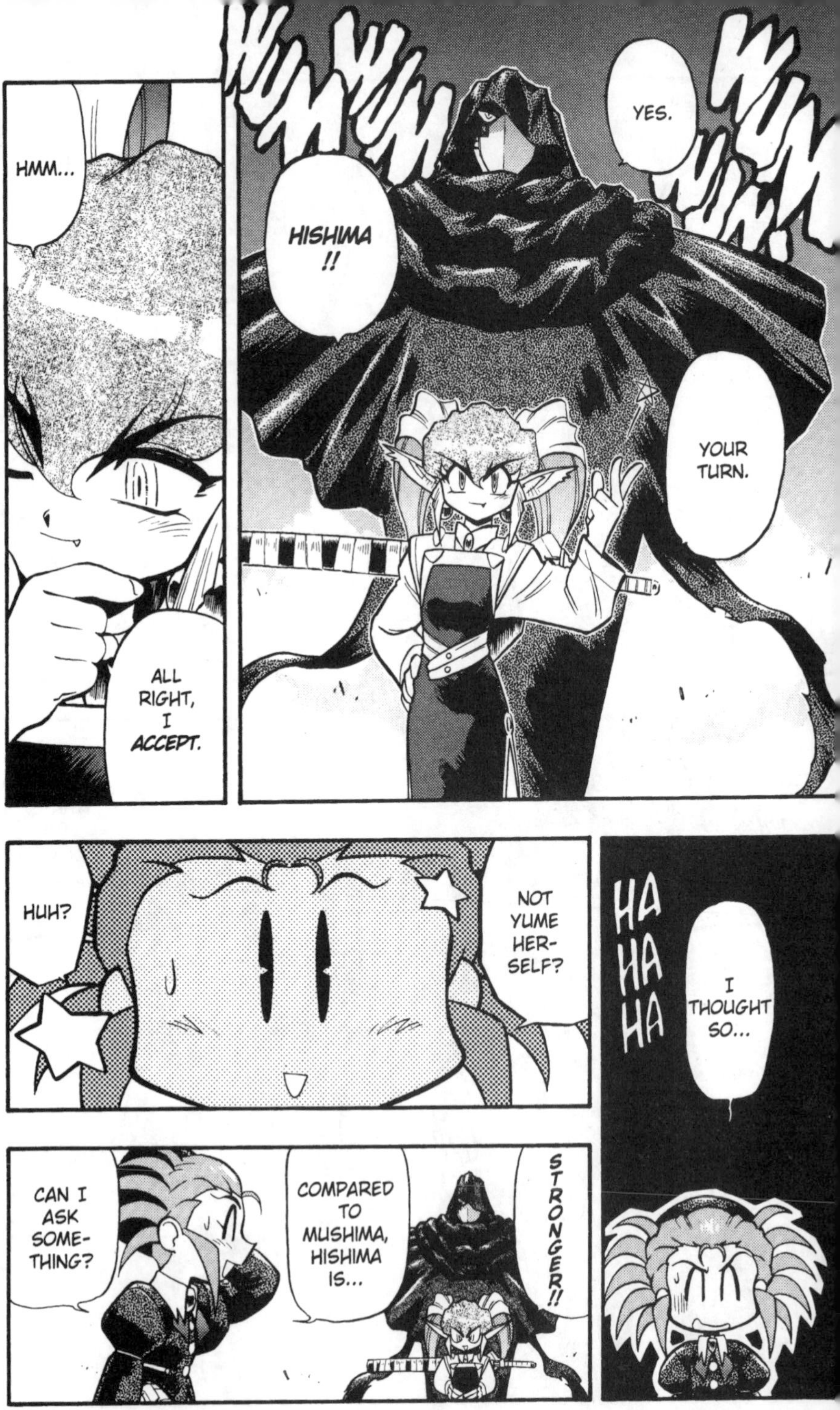
HMM...
ALL RIGHT, I ACCEPT.
HISHIMA !!
YES.
YOUR TURN.
HUH?
NOT YUME HER-SELF?
CAN I ASK SOME-THING?
COMPARED TO MUSHIMA, HISHIMA IS...
STRONGER!!
HA HA HA
I THOUGHT SO...

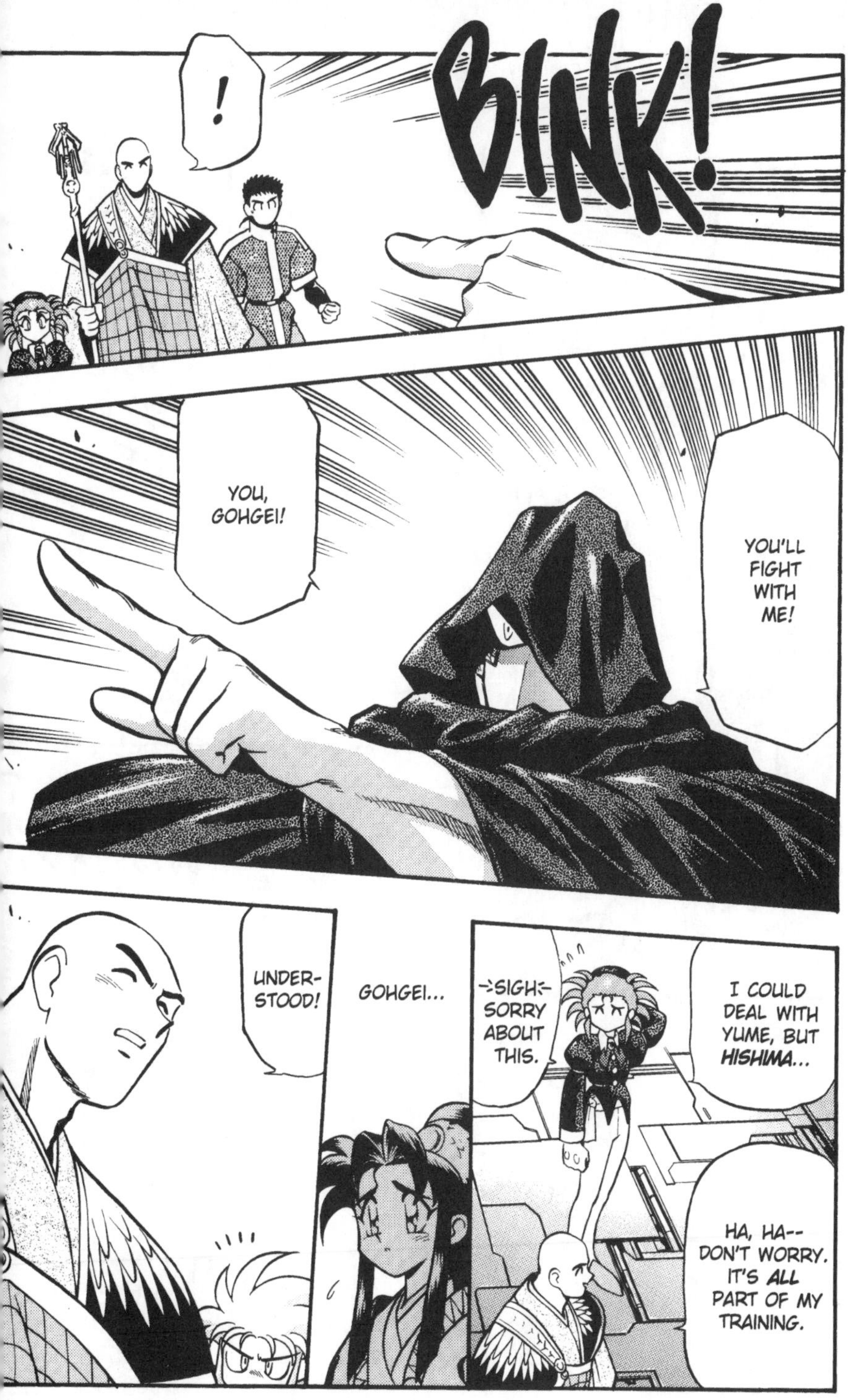
BINK!
!
YOU, GOHGEI!
YOU'LL FIGHT WITH ME!
I COULD DEAL WITH YUME, BUT HISHIMA...
HA, HA-- DON'T WORRY. IT'S ALL PART OF MY TRAINING.
-SIGH- SORRY ABOUT THIS.
GOHGEI...
UNDER-STOOD!

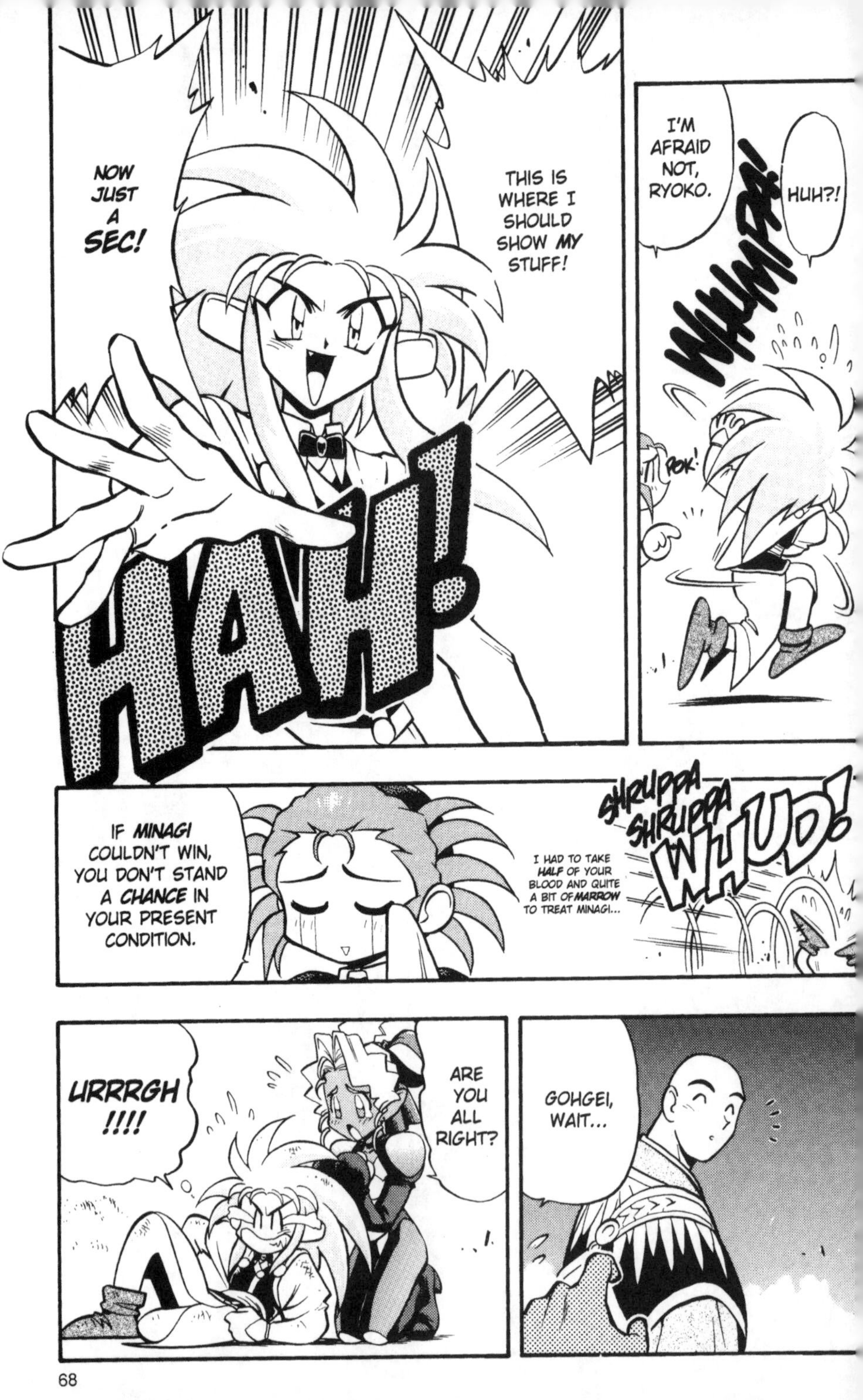
NOW JUST A SEC!
THIS IS WHERE I SHOULD SHOW MY STUFF!
HAH!
I'M AFRAID NOT, RYOKO.
HUH?!
WHUMPA!
POK!
IF MINAGI COULDN'T WIN, YOU DON'T STAND A CHANCE IN YOUR PRESENT CONDITION.
I HAD TO TAKE HALF OF YOUR BLOOD AND QUITE A BIT OF MARROW TO TREAT MINAGI...
SHRUPPA SHRUPPA WHUD!
URRRGH !!!!
ARE YOU ALL RIGHT?
GOHGEI, WAIT...

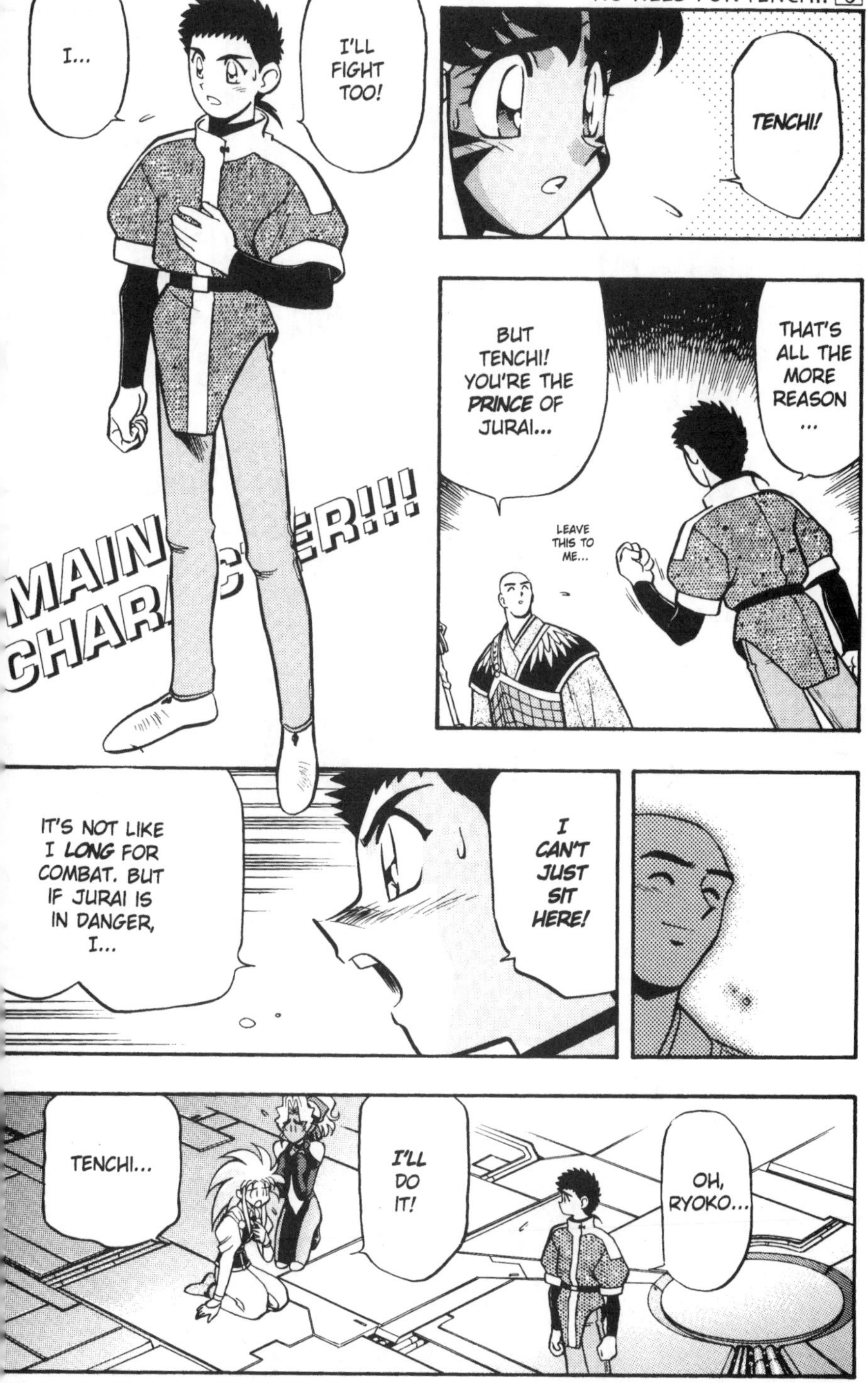
I...
I'LL FIGHT TOO!
MAIN CHARA C ER!!!
TENCHI!
BUT TENCHI! YOU'RE THE PRINCE OF JURAI...
THAT'S ALL THE MORE REASON...
LEAVE THIS TO ME...
IT'S NOT LIKE I LONG FOR COMBAT. BUT IF JURAI IS IN DANGER, I...
I CAN'T JUST SIT HERE!
TENCHI...
I'LL DO IT!
OH, RYOKO...

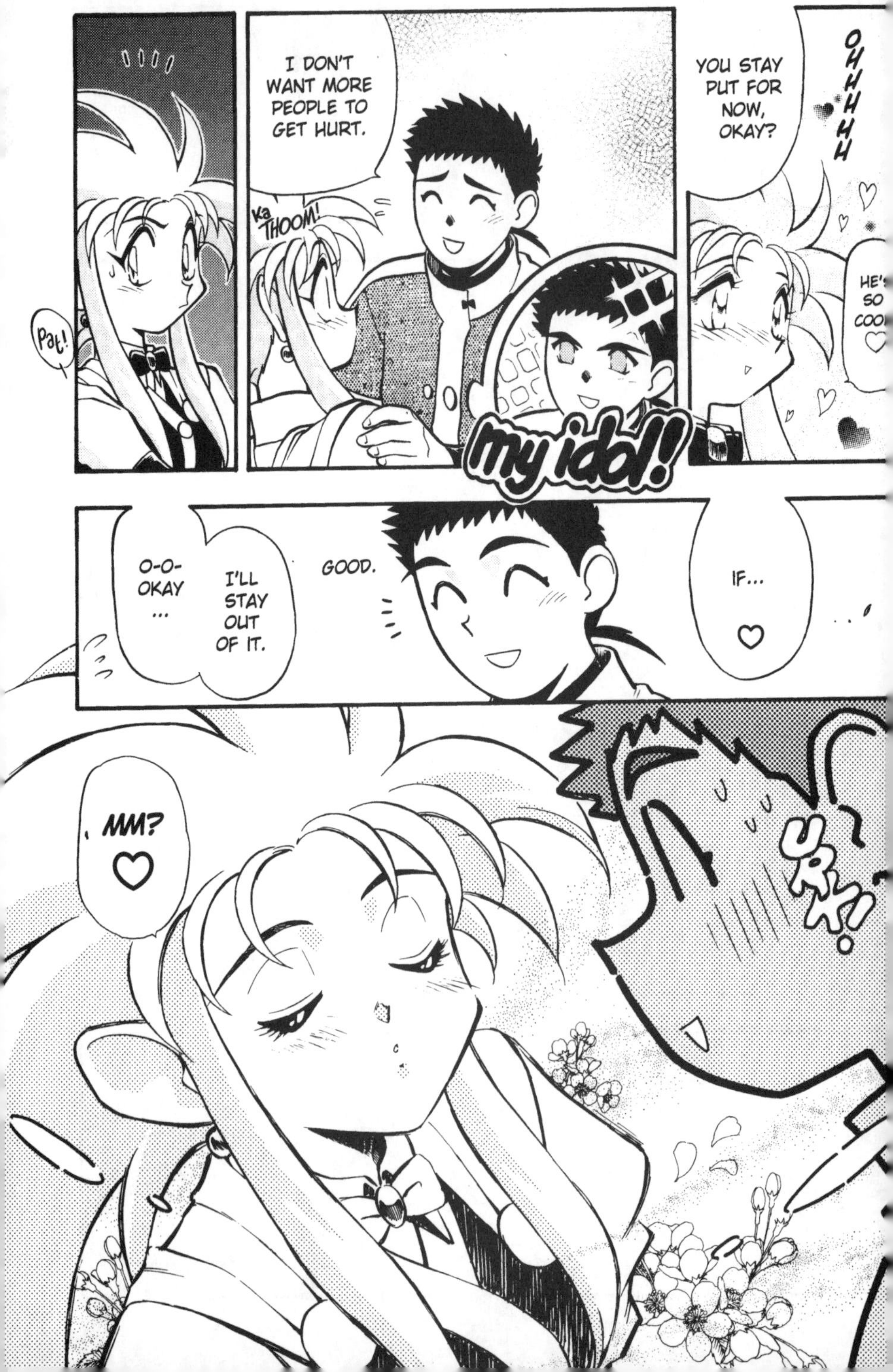

Pat!
I DON'T WANT MORE PEOPLE TO GET HURT.
Ka THOOM!
YOU STAY PUT FOR NOW, OKAY?
OHHHHHH
HE'S SO COO ♡
my idol!
O-O-OKAY ...
I'LL STAY OUT OF IT.
GOOD.
IF... ♡
MM? ♡
URK!

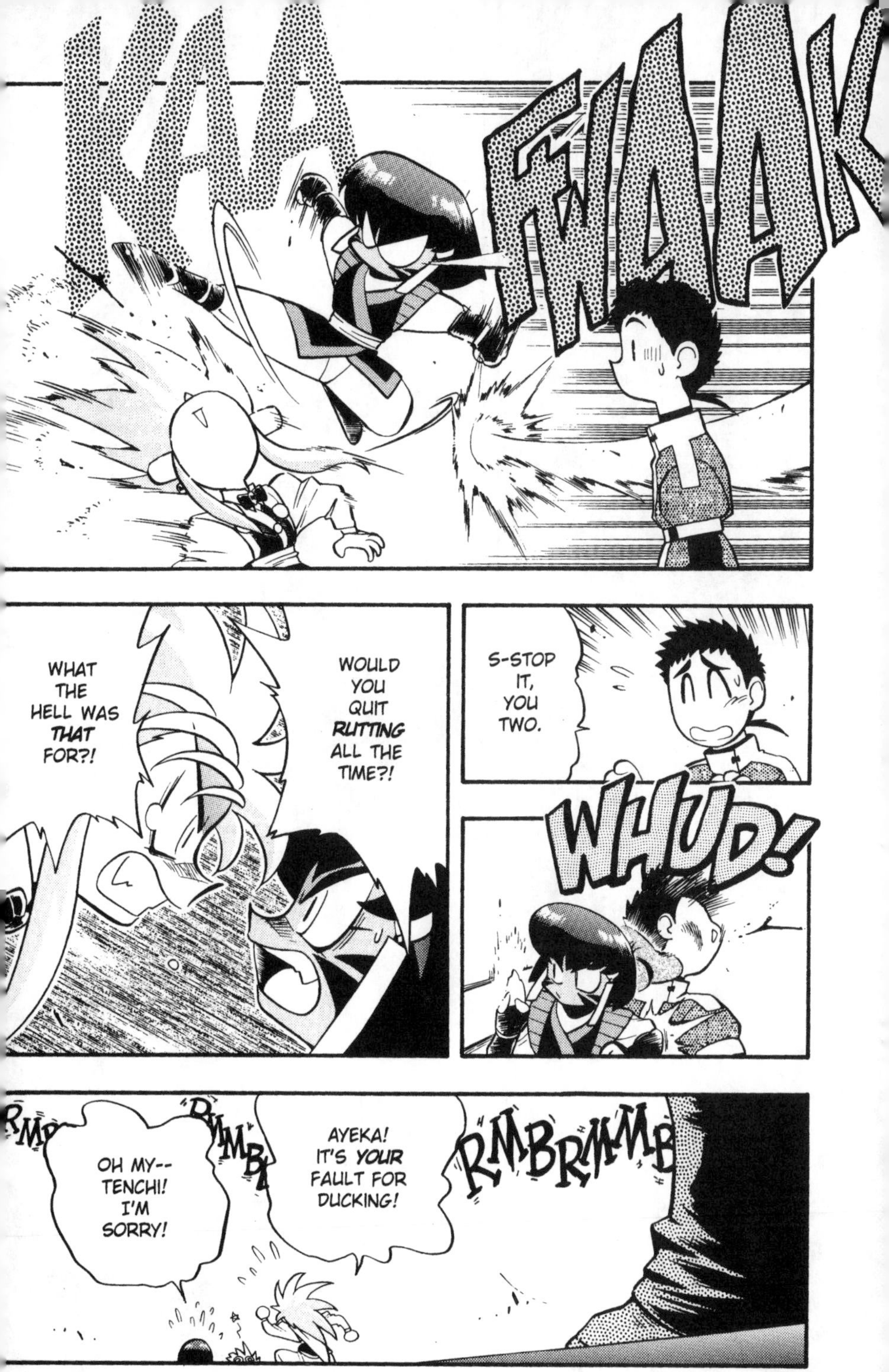
KAA
FWAAK
WHAT THE HELL WAS THAT FOR?!
WOULD YOU QUIT RUTTING ALL THE TIME?!
S-STOP IT, YOU TWO.
WHUD!
RMP
OH MY-- TENCHI! I'M SORRY!
RMMB
AYEKA! IT'S YOUR FAULT FOR DUCKING!
RMBRMMB

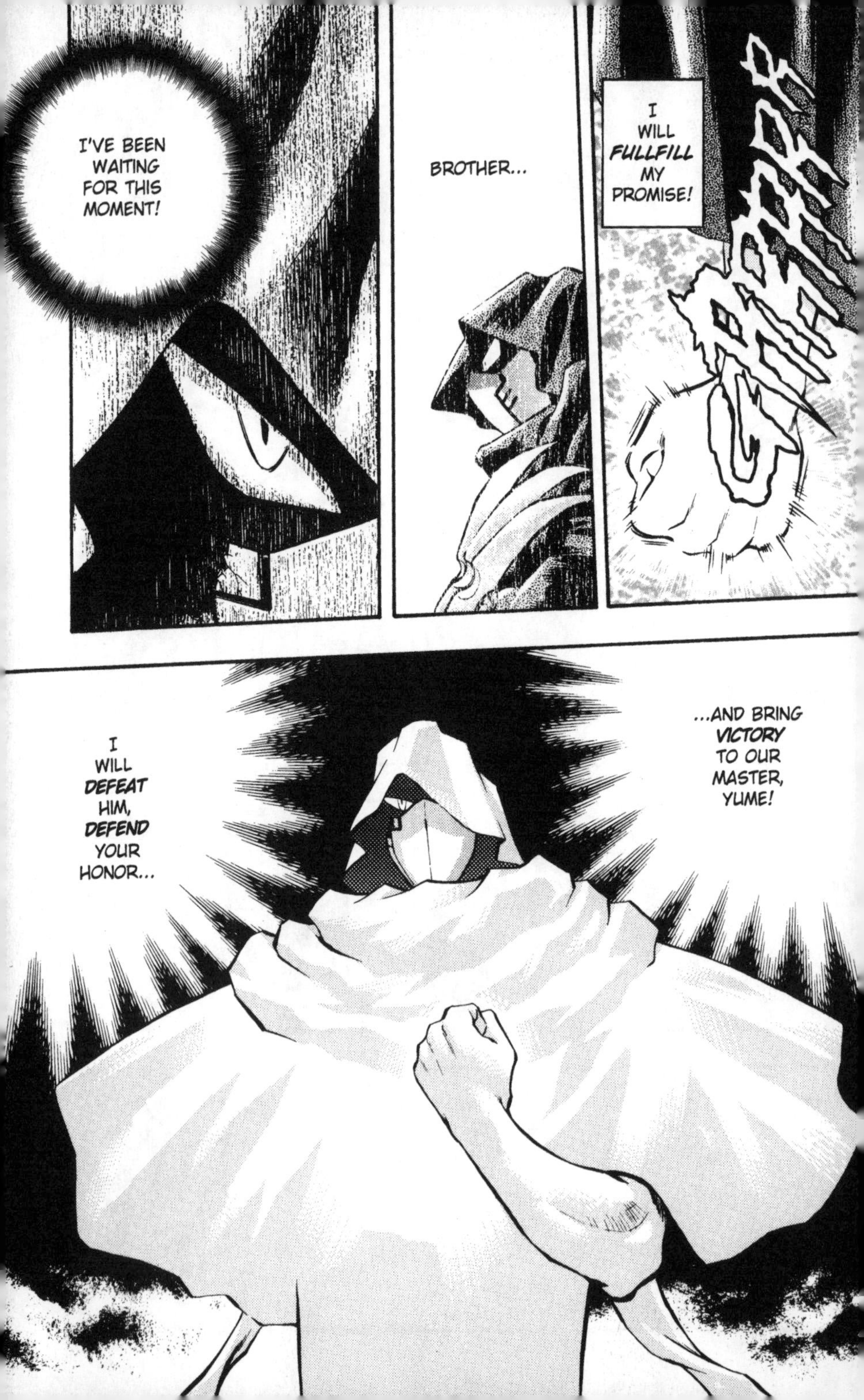
I'VE BEEN WAITING FOR THIS MOMENT!
BROTHER...
I WILL **FULLFILL** MY PROMISE!
I WILL **DEFEAT** HIM, **DEFEND** YOUR HONOR...
...AND BRING **VICTORY** TO OUR MASTER, YUME!

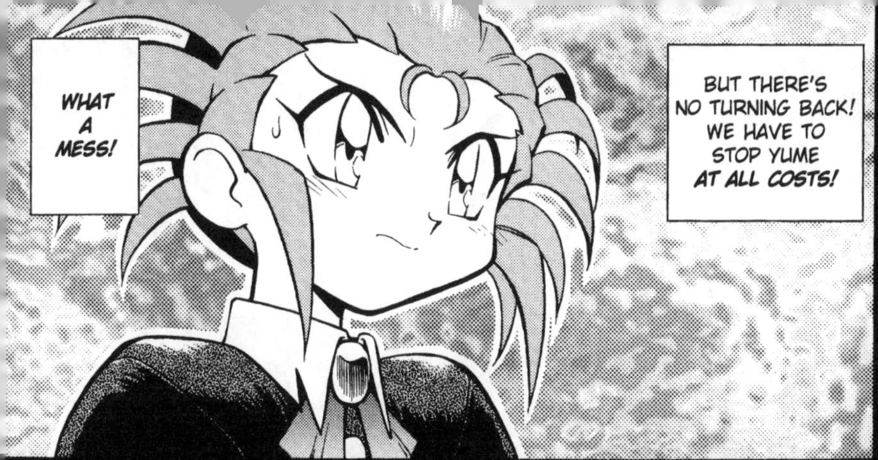
WHAT A MESS!
BUT THERE'S NO TURNING BACK! WE HAVE TO STOP YUME AT ALL COSTS!

Tales of Tenchi #4

FIRST STRIKE

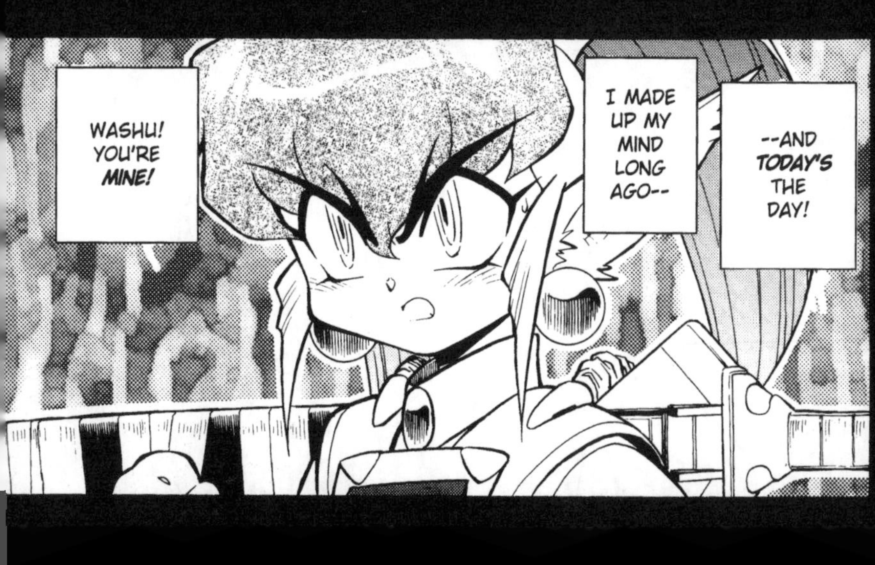
WASHU! YOU'RE MINE!
I MADE UP MY MIND LONG AGO--
--AND TODAY'S THE DAY!

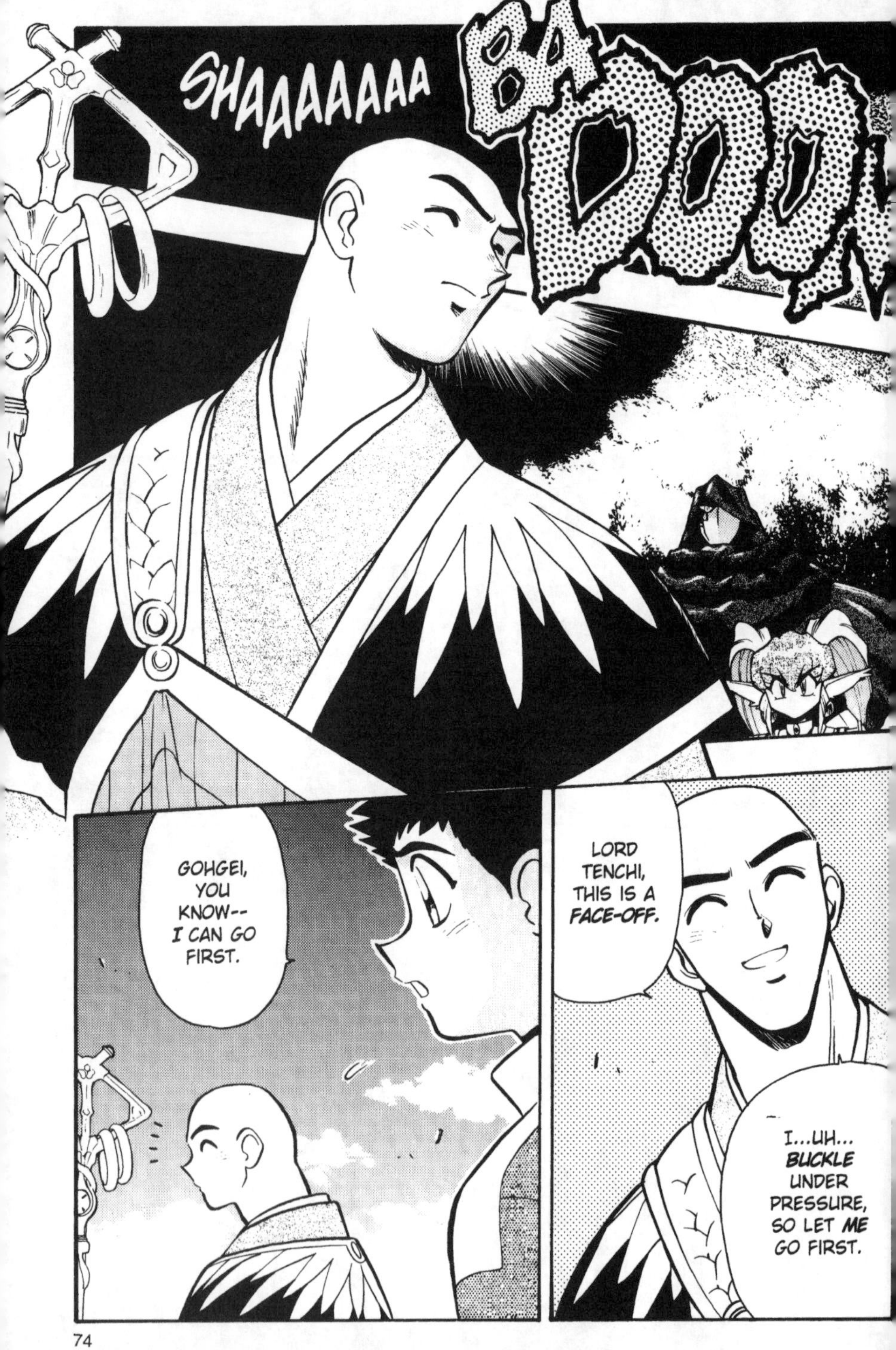
SHAAAAAAAA
BA DOOM
GOHGEI, YOU KNOW-- I CAN GO FIRST.
LORD TENCHI, THIS IS A FACE-OFF.
I...UH... BUCKLE UNDER PRESSURE, SO LET ME GO FIRST.

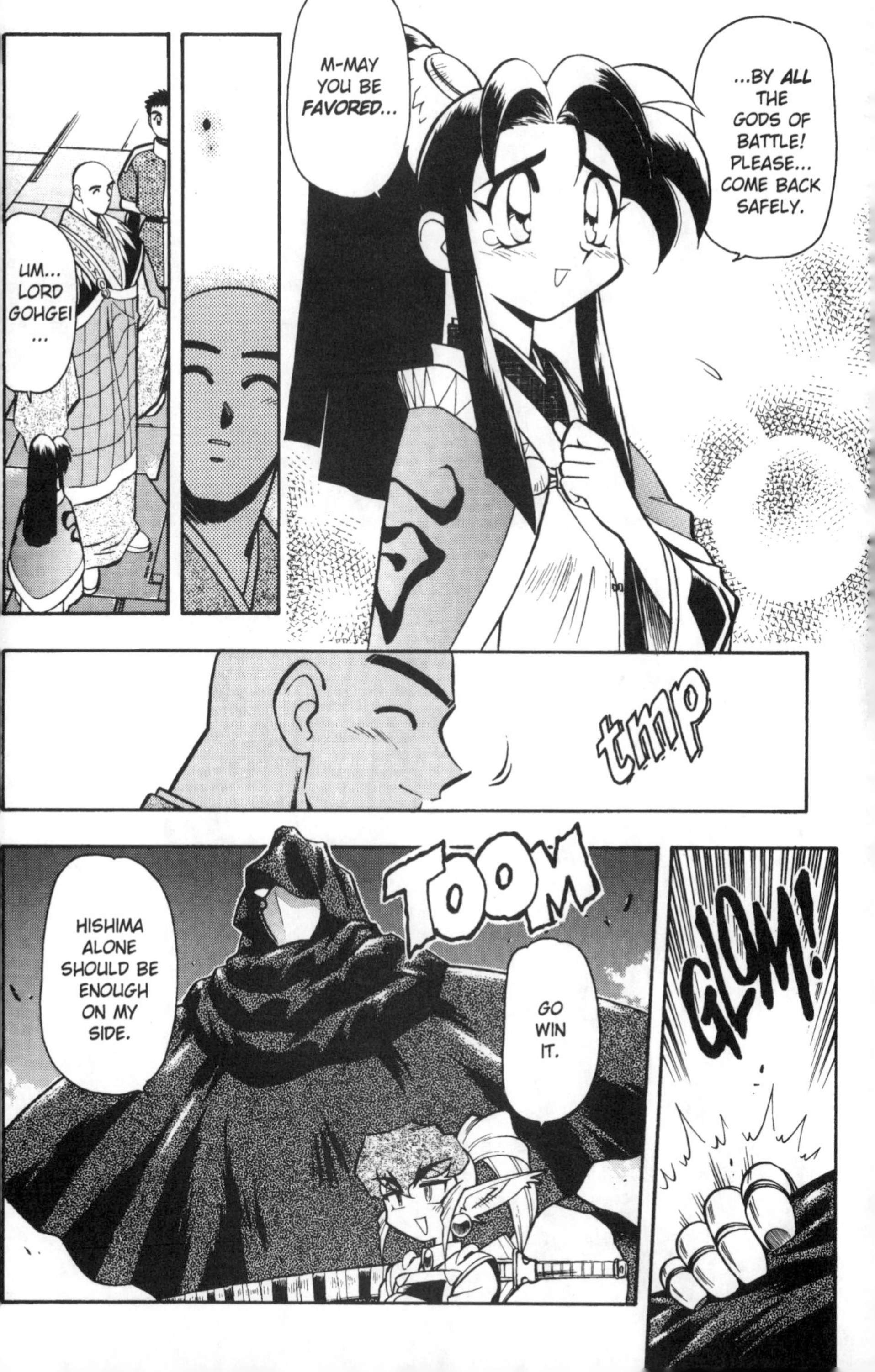
UM... LORD GOHGEI ...
M-MAY YOU BE FAVORED...
...BY ALL THE GODS OF BATTLE! PLEASE... COME BACK SAFELY.
tmp
TOOM
HISHIMA ALONE SHOULD BE ENOUGH ON MY SIDE.
GO WIN IT.
GLOM!

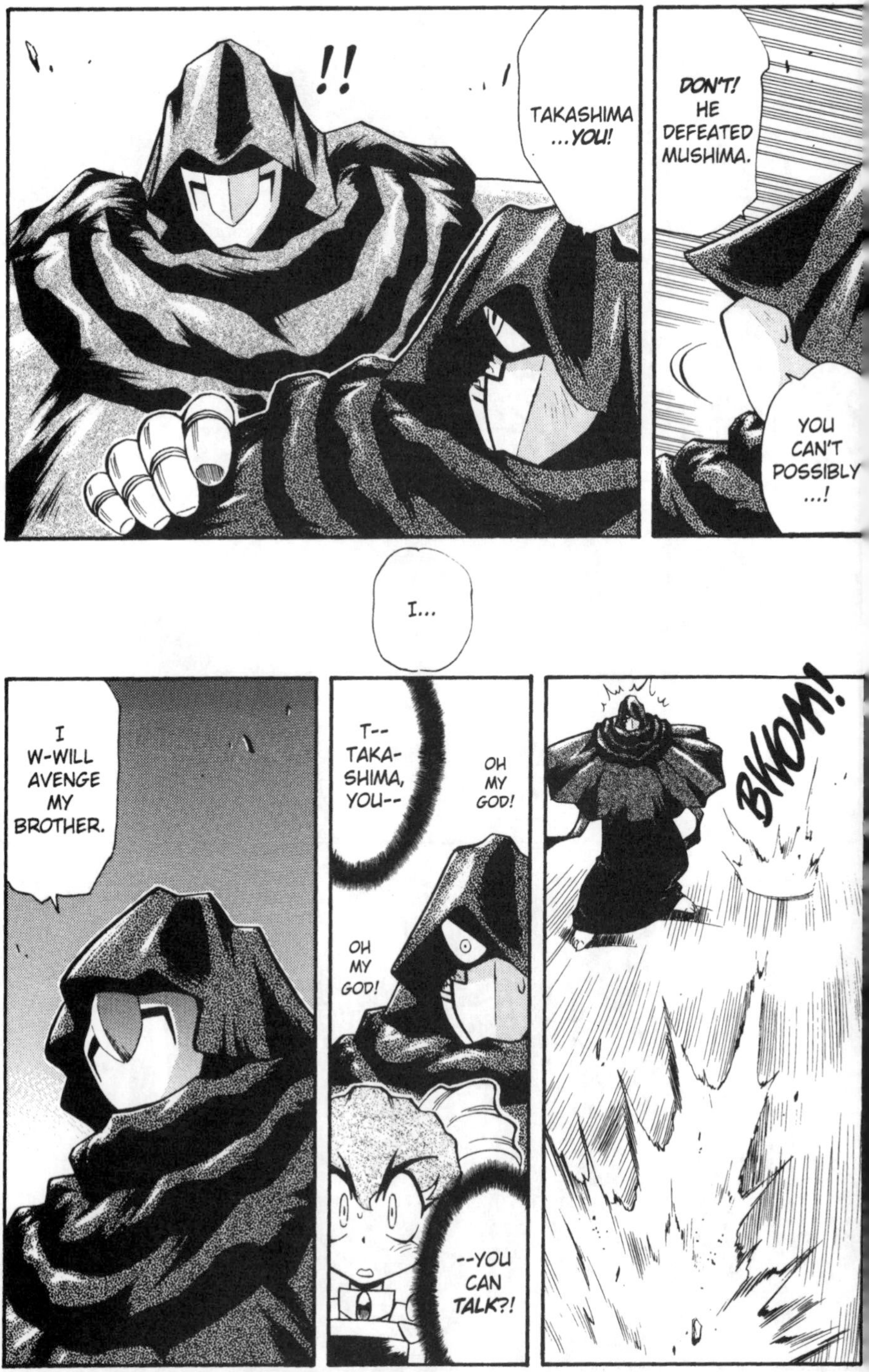
!!
TAKASHIMA ...YOU!
DON'T! HE DEFEATED MUSHIMA.
YOU CAN'T POSSIBLY ...!
I...
I W-WILL AVENGE MY BROTHER.
T-- TAKA-SHIMA, YOU--
OH MY GOD!
OH MY GOD!
--YOU CAN TALK?!
BWOM!

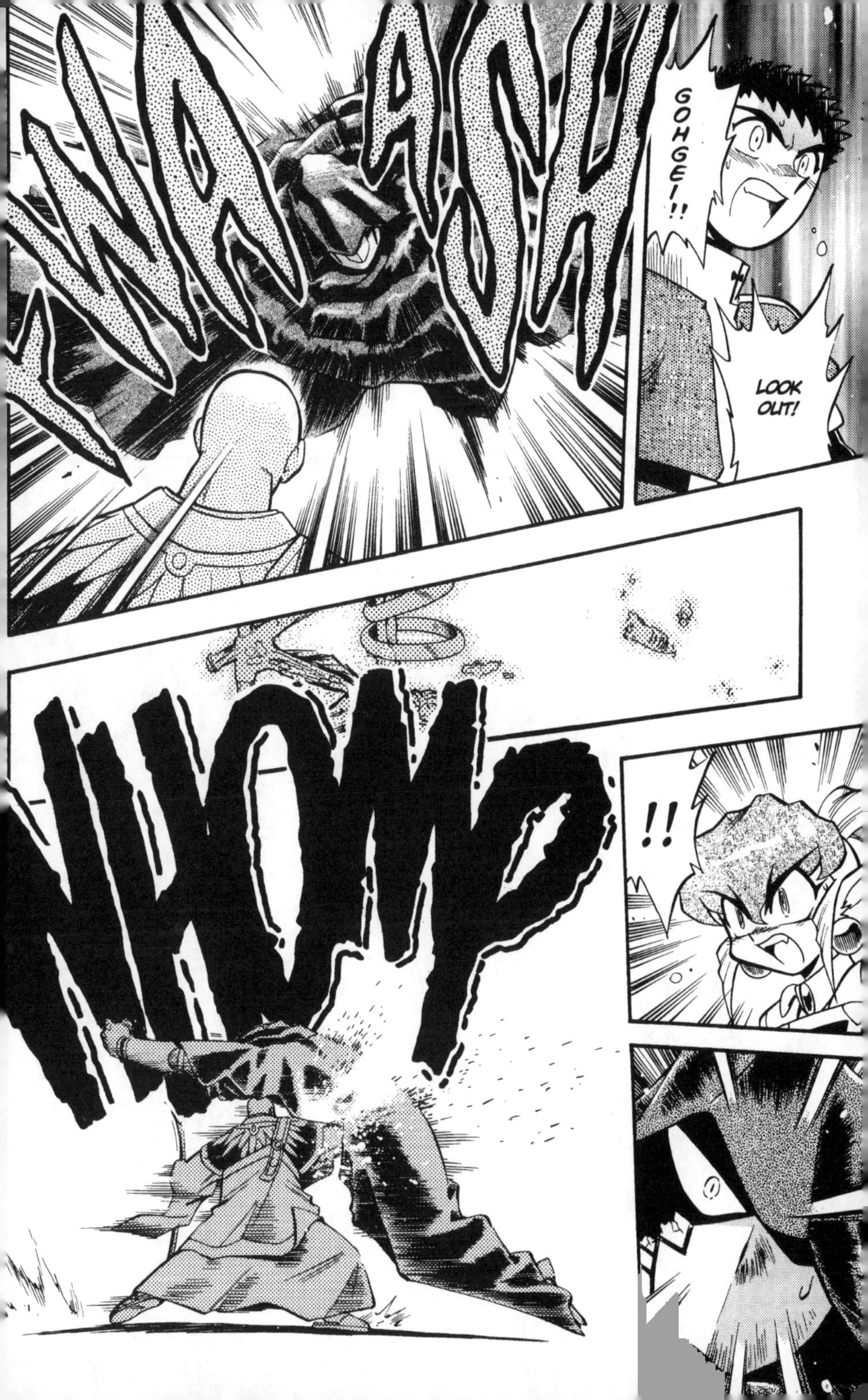
WAAGH
GOHGEI!!
LOOK OUT!
WHOMP
!!

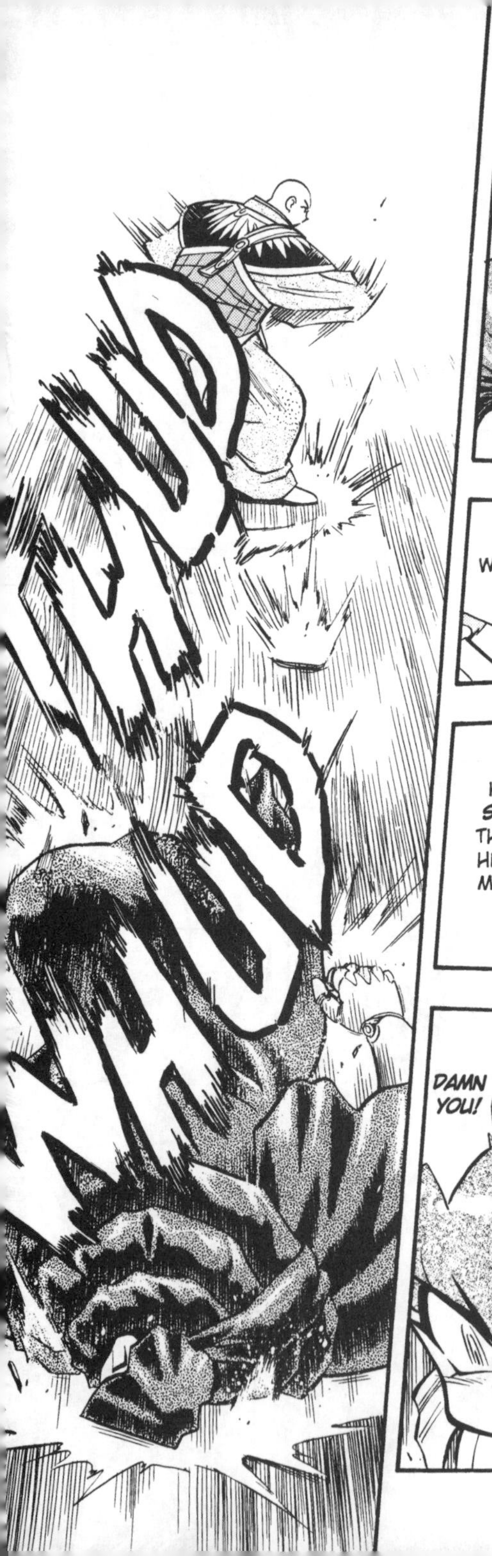

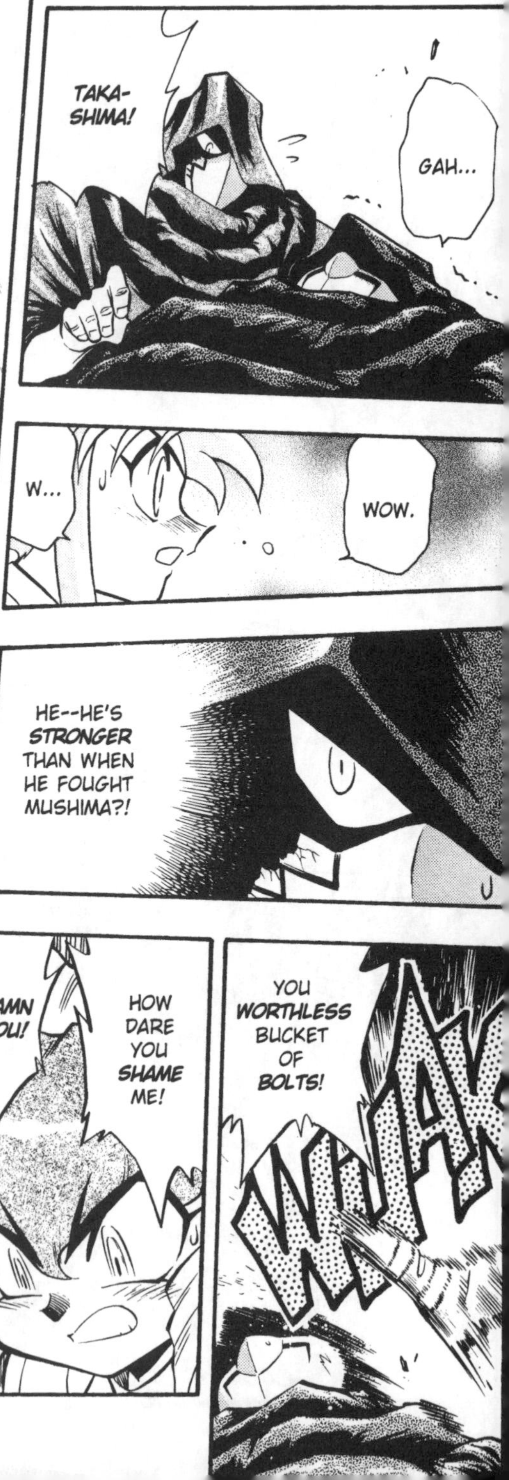
TAKA-SHIMA!
GAH...
W...
WOW.
HE--HE'S STRONGER THAN WHEN HE FOUGHT MUSHIMA?!
DAMN YOU!
HOW DARE YOU SHAME ME!
YOU WORTHLESS BUCKET OF BOLTS!

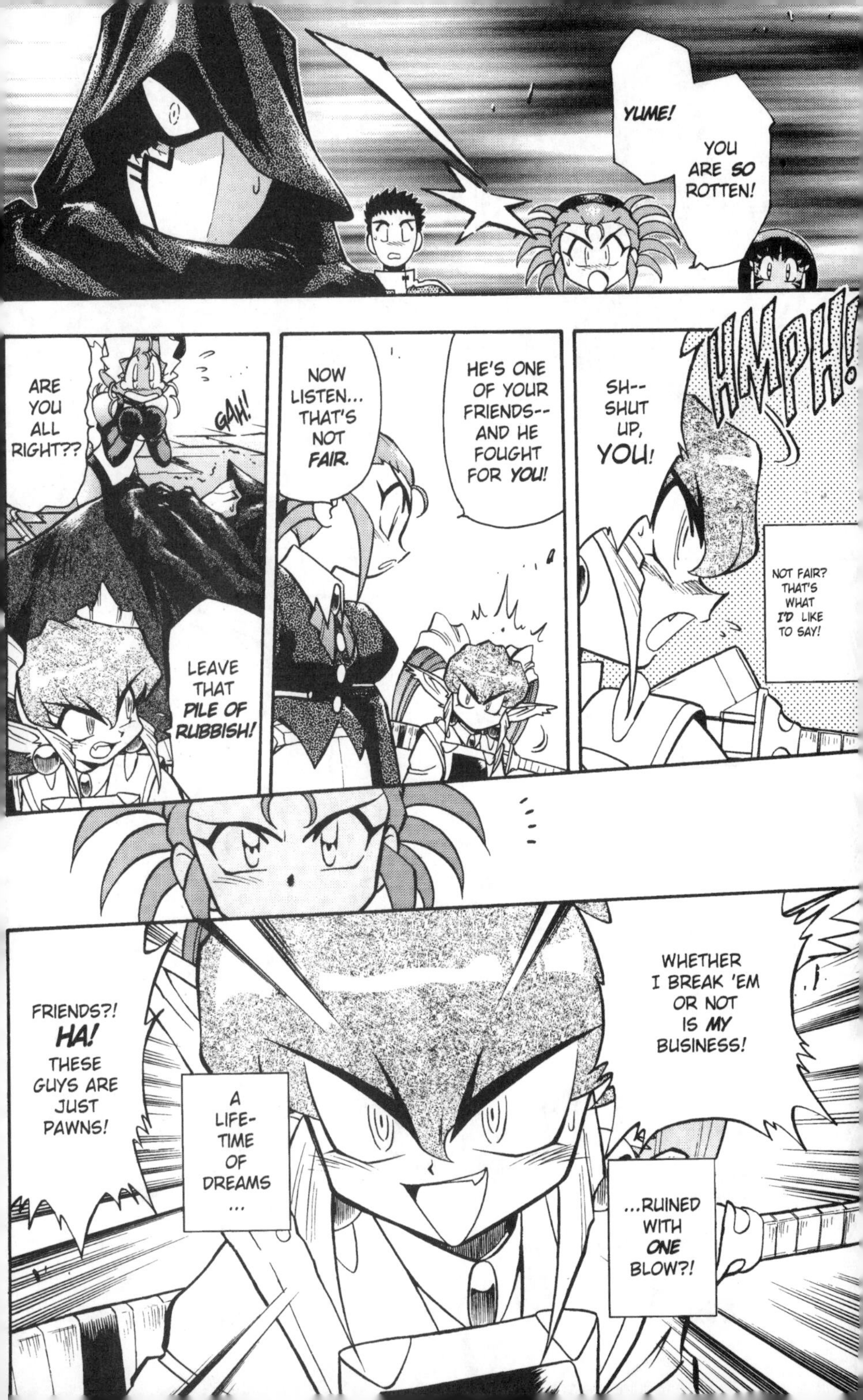
YUME!
YOU ARE SO ROTTEN!
ARE YOU ALL RIGHT??
GAH!
LEAVE THAT PILE OF RUBBISH!
NOW LISTEN... THAT'S NOT FAIR.
HE'S ONE OF YOUR FRIENDS--AND HE FOUGHT FOR YOU!
SH--SHUT UP, YOU!
THMPH!
NOT FAIR? THAT'S WHAT I'D LIKE TO SAY!
FRIENDS?! HA! THESE GUYS ARE JUST PAWNS!
A LIFE-TIME OF DREAMS...
WHETHER I BREAK 'EM OR NOT IS MY BUSINESS!
...RUINED WITH ONE BLOW?!

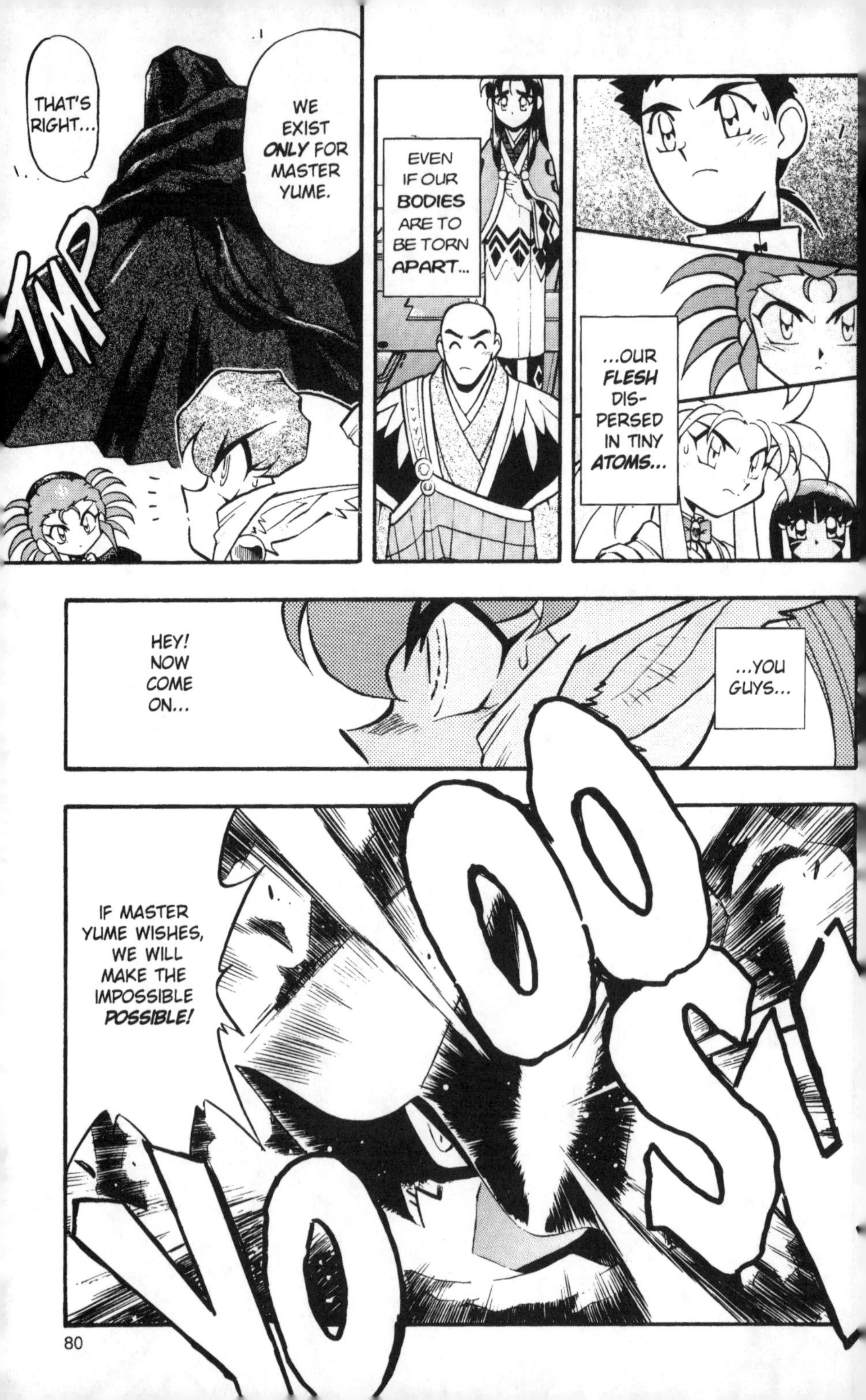
THAT'S RIGHT...
WE EXIST ONLY FOR MASTER YUME.
TMP
EVEN IF OUR BODIES ARE TO BE TORN APART...
...OUR FLESH DIS-PERSED IN TINY ATOMS...
HEY! NOW COME ON...
...YOU GUYS...
IF MASTER YUME WISHES, WE WILL MAKE THE IMPOSSIBLE POSSIBLE!
VOOOS

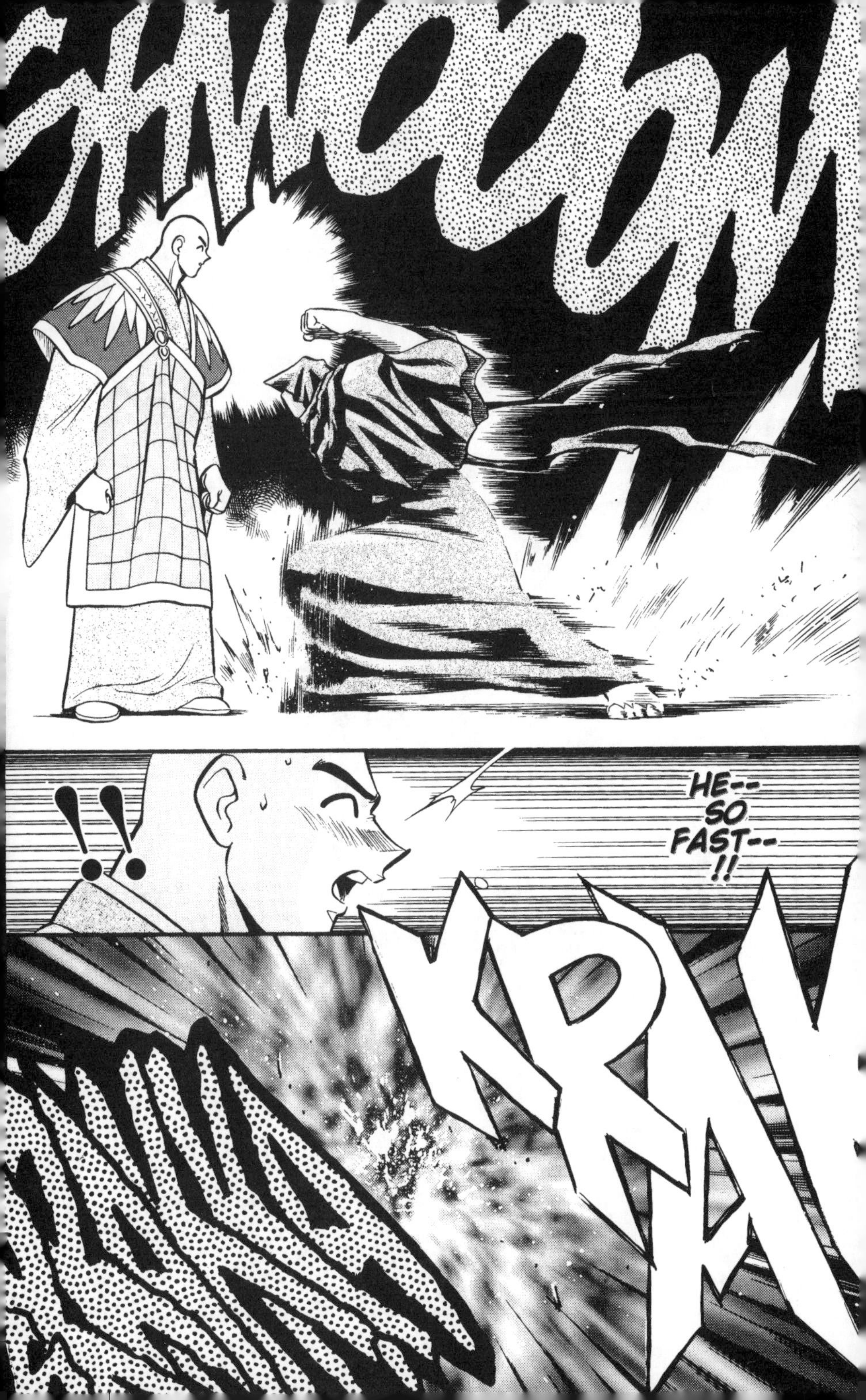
!!
HE-- SO FAST-- !!

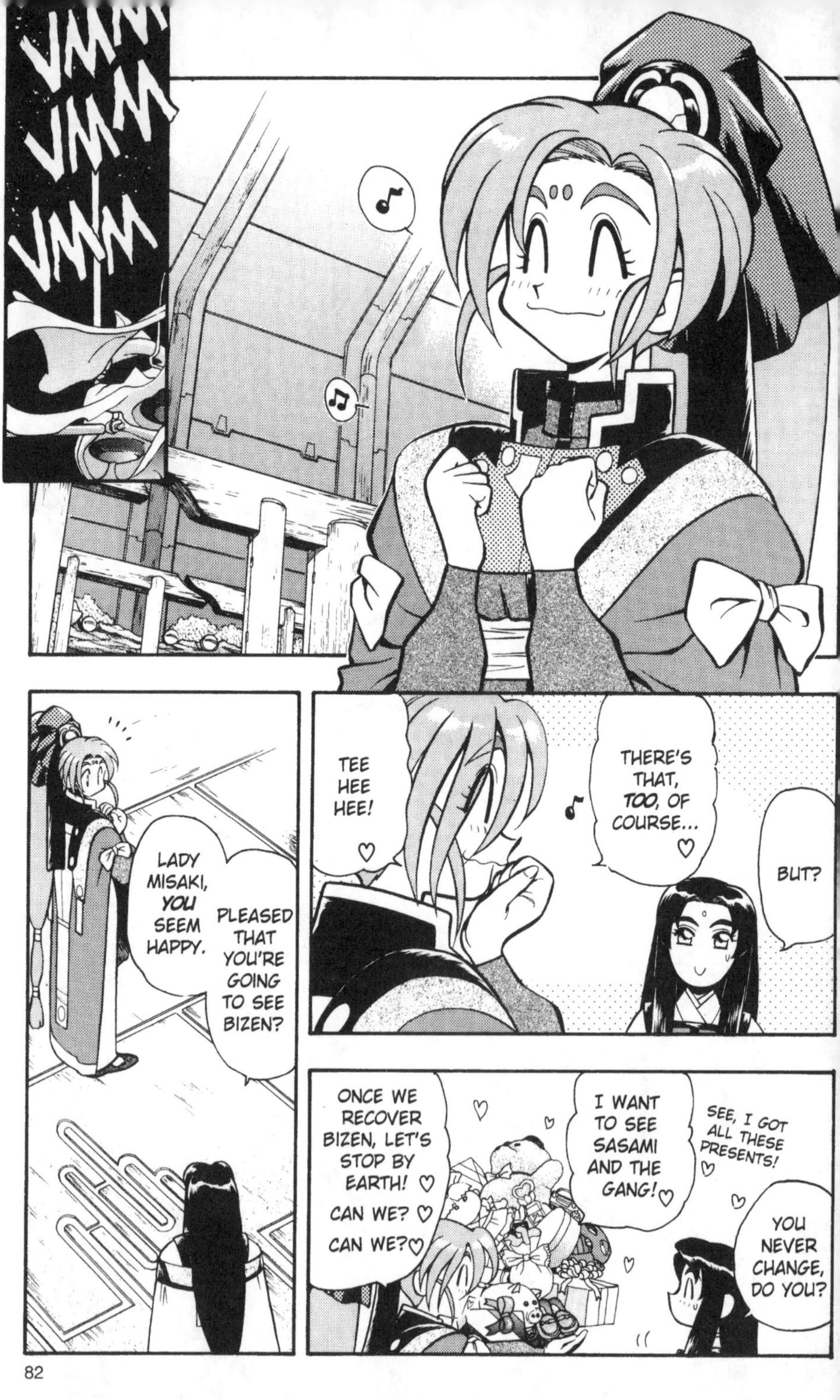
VMM
VMM
VMM
LADY MISAKI, *YOU* SEEM HAPPY.
PLEASED THAT YOU'RE GOING TO SEE BIZEN?
TEE HEE HEE! ♡
THERE'S THAT, *TOO*, OF COURSE... ♡
BUT?
ONCE WE RECOVER BIZEN, LET'S STOP BY EARTH! ♡
CAN WE? ♡
CAN WE? ♡
I WANT TO SEE SASAMI AND THE GANG! ♡
SEE, I GOT ALL THESE PRESENTS! ♡
YOU NEVER CHANGE, DO YOU?

WHY DO I FEEL SO UNEASY?

IT'S AS IF...

AS LONG AS WE'RE LEADING JURAI'S FLEET, THE GREATEST FLEET IN THE UNIVERSE, I SHOULDN'T FEEL EVEN A DROP OF ANXIETY...

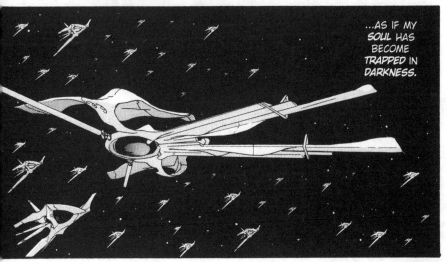

...AS IF MY *SOUL* HAS BECOME *TRAPPED* IN *DARKNESS.*

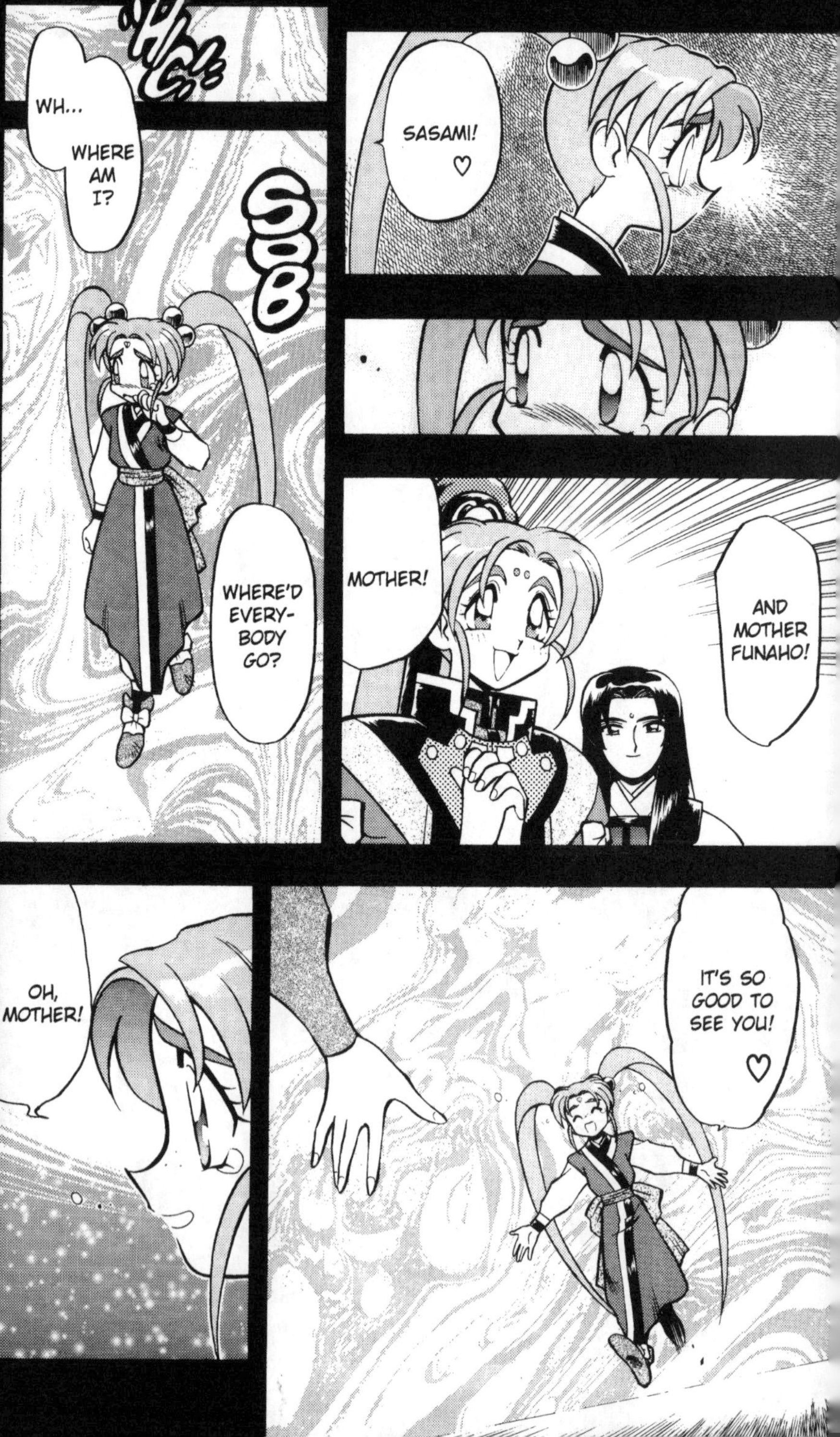
HIC
WH... WHERE AM I?
SOB
WHERE'D EVERY-BODY GO?
SASAMI! ♡
MOTHER!
AND MOTHER FUNAHO!
OH, MOTHER!
IT'S SO GOOD TO SEE YOU! ♡

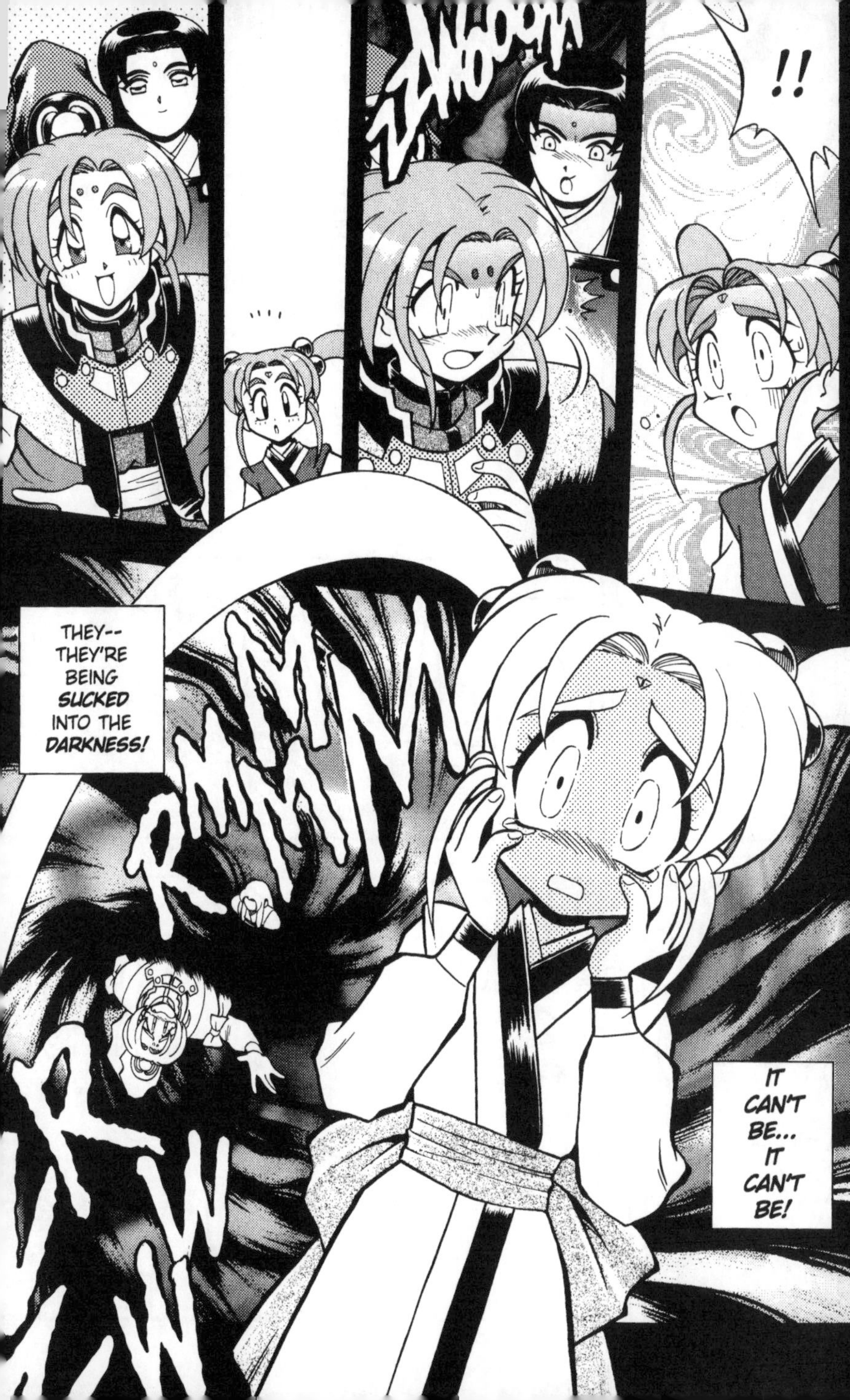
ZZANOOOM
!!
THEY-- THEY'RE BEING SUCKED INTO THE DARKNESS!
IT CAN'T BE... IT CAN'T BE!

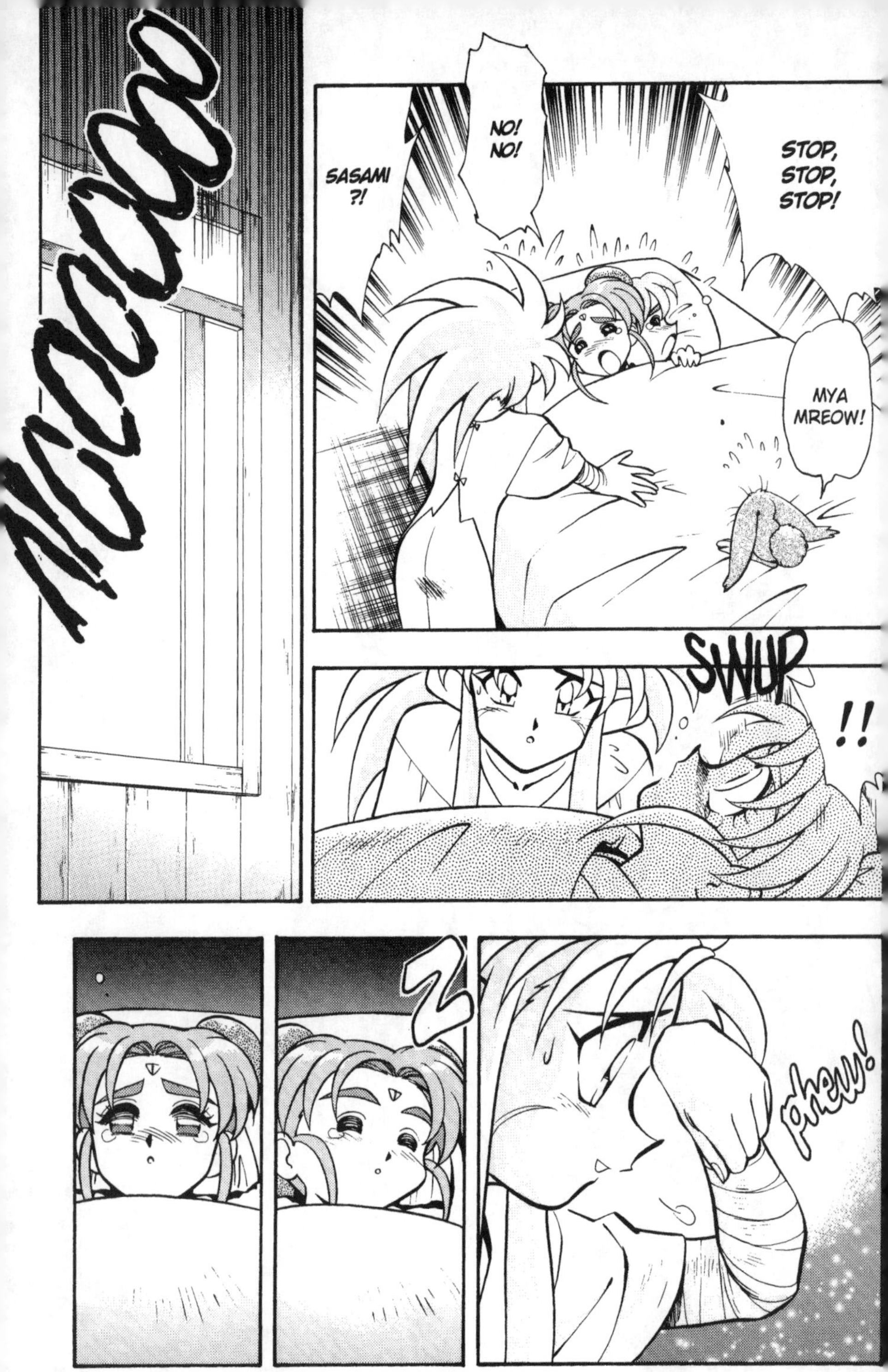
NOOOOOO
SASAMI ?!
NO! NO!
STOP, STOP, STOP!
MYA MREOW!
SWUP
!!
Z
phew!

MREOWW?

AWWW... YOU MUST BE WORRIED ABOUT SASAMI TOO.

SLP SLP

YOU HAVEN'T EVEN *TOUCHED* YOUR FAVORITE CARROTS...

MREOOOOW !!!

IT'S OKAY, RYO-OH-KI! REALLY! ♡

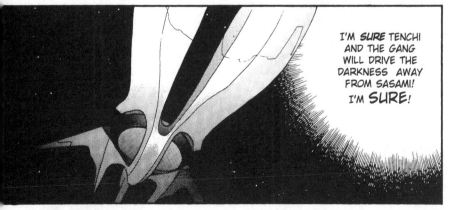

I'M *SURE* TENCHI AND THE GANG WILL DRIVE THE DARKNESS AWAY FROM SASAMI! I'M **SURE**!

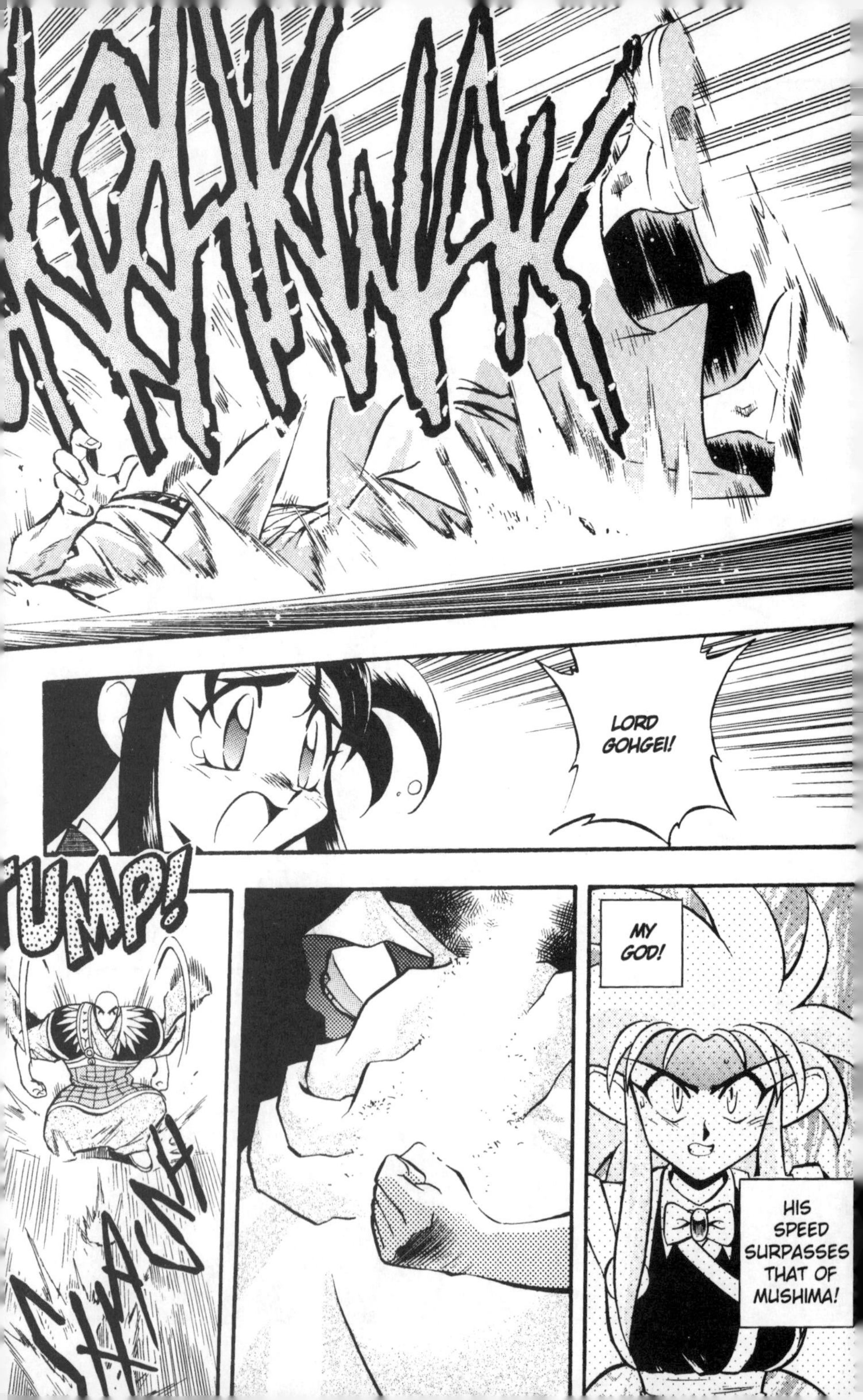
LORD GOHGEI!
TUMP!
MY GOD!
HIS SPEED SURPASSES THAT OF MUSHIMA!

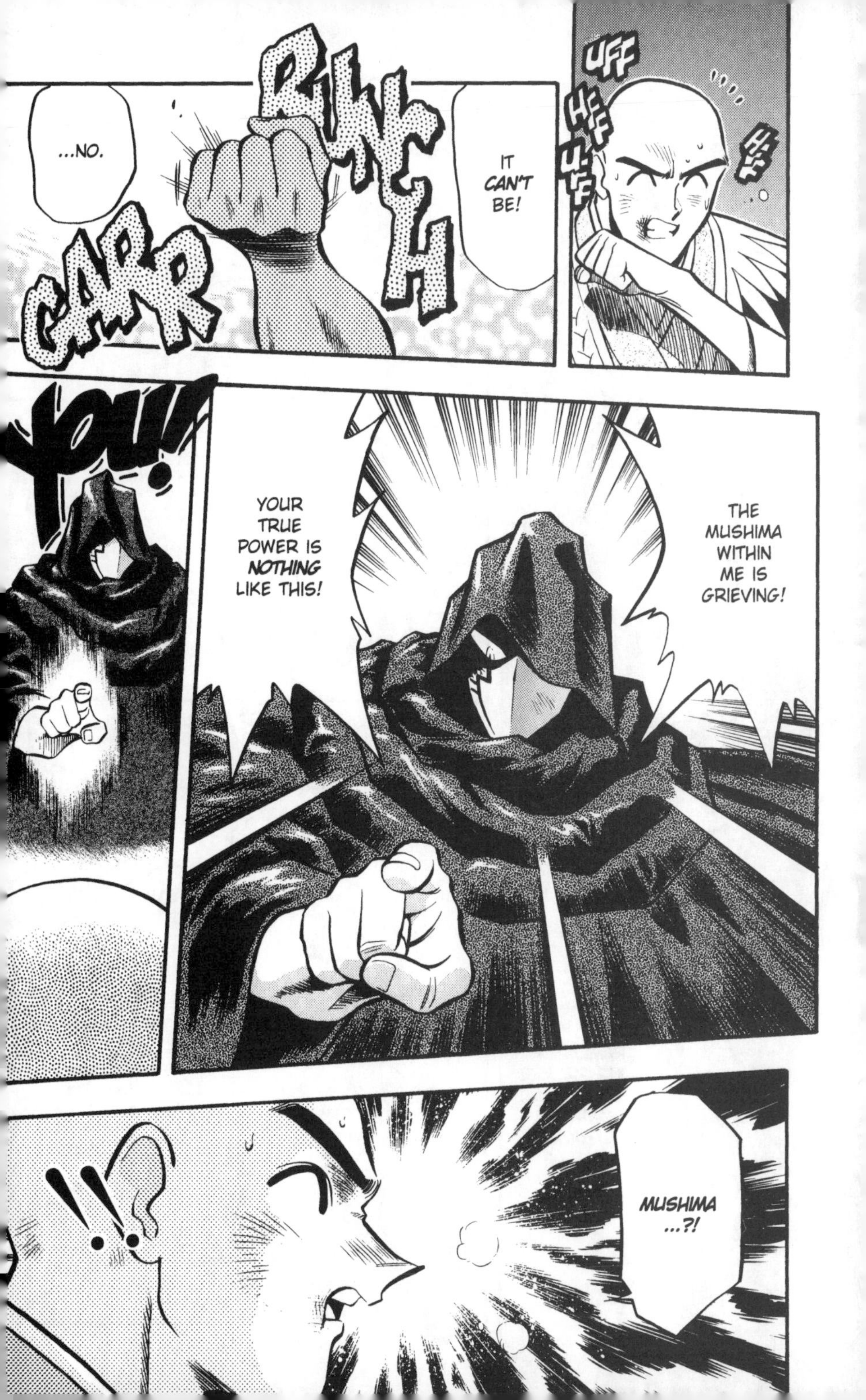

...NO.
CARR
RUNCH
IT CAN'T BE!
UFF
HUFF
UFF
HUFF
YOU!!
YOUR TRUE POWER IS NOTHING LIKE THIS!
THE MUSHIMA WITHIN ME IS GRIEVING!
!!
MUSHIMA ...?!

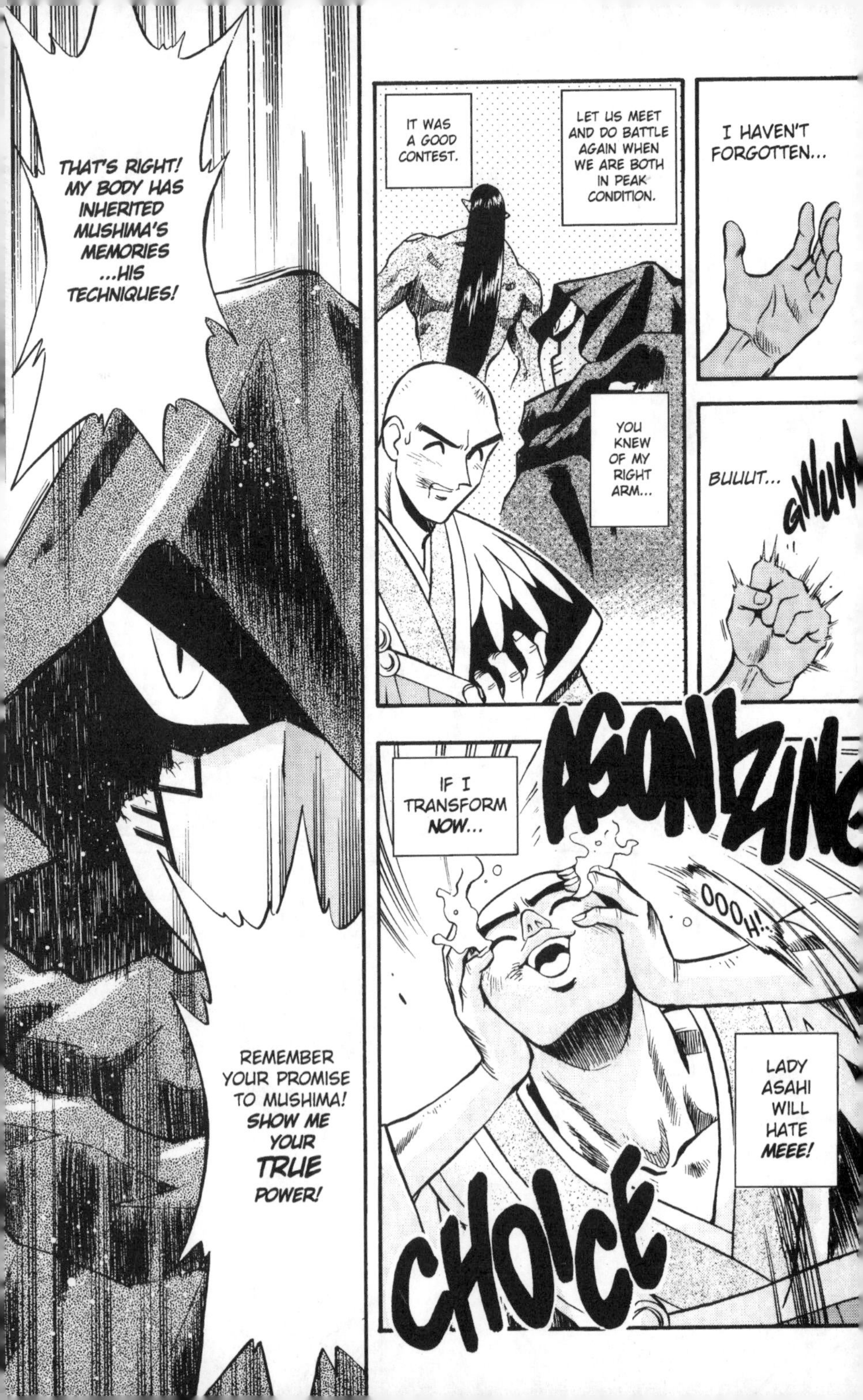
THAT'S RIGHT! MY BODY HAS INHERITED MUSHIMA'S MEMORIES ...HIS TECHNIQUES!
REMEMBER YOUR PROMISE TO MUSHIMA! SHOW ME YOUR TRUE POWER!
IT WAS A GOOD CONTEST.
LET US MEET AND DO BATTLE AGAIN WHEN WE ARE BOTH IN PEAK CONDITION.
YOU KNEW OF MY RIGHT ARM...
I HAVEN'T FORGOTTEN...
BUUUT...
GWUM
IF I TRANSFORM NOW...
AGONIZING
OOOH!!
LADY ASAHI WILL HATE MEEE!
CHOICE

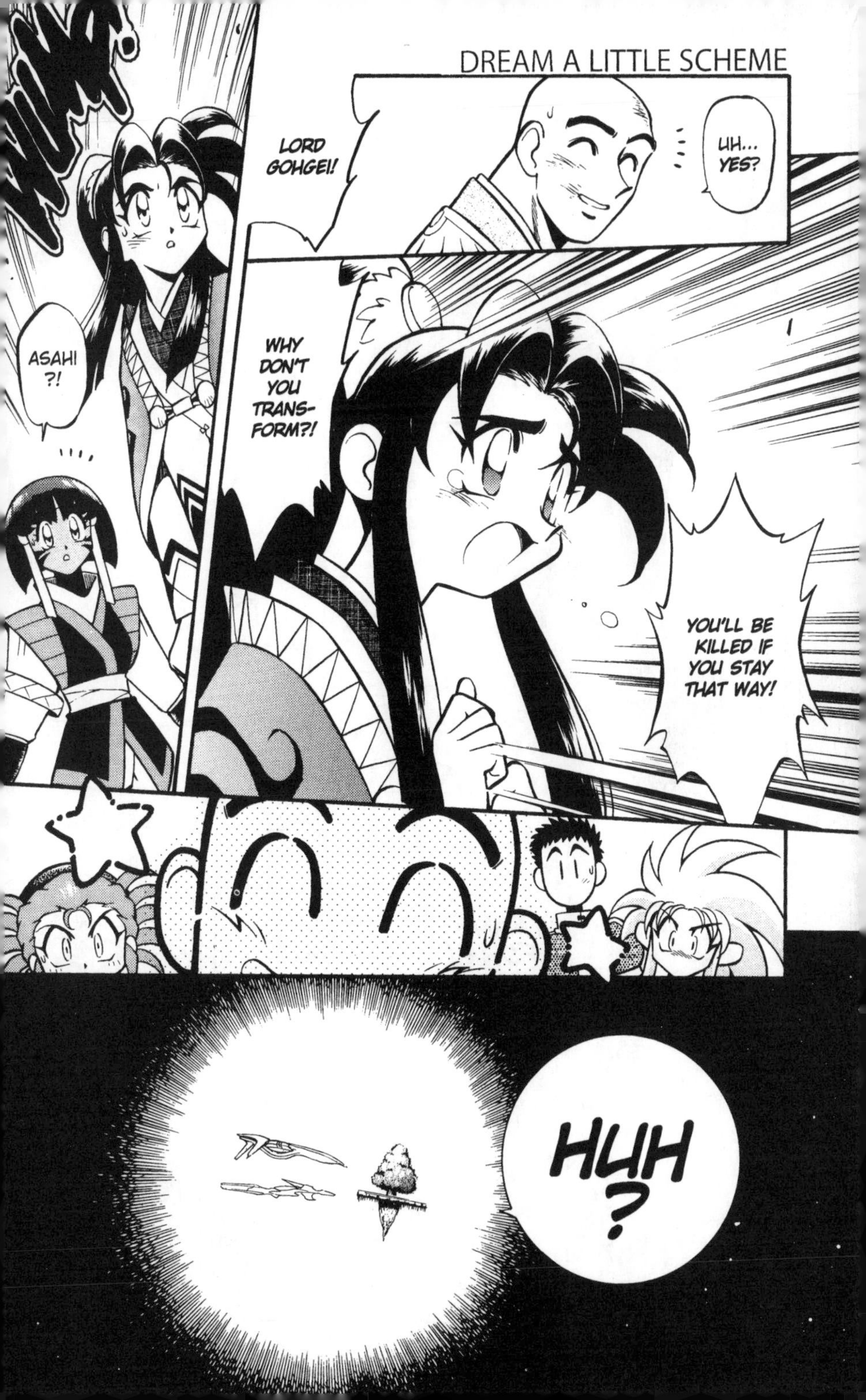
ASAHI ?!
LORD GOHGEI!
UH... YES?
WHY DON'T YOU TRANSFORM?!
YOU'LL BE KILLED IF YOU STAY THAT WAY!
HUH ?

RIGHT?

SO, UM...

YOU **KNEW** ABOUT HIS TRANSFORMATION?

SO, GOHGEI?! YOU GOT AN EXPLANATION?

GRRRR!

WELL, IF I WERE TO **INFER...**

OH, DON'T TELL ME **YOU** DIDN'T KNOW!

ah ha, ha!

LORD GOHGEI IS A GAGUTIAN! EVERYONE KNOWS THEY BECOME STRONGER WHEN THEY TRANSFORM.

LITTLE ASAHI IS BEING ATTACKED BY A RYUTEN BROWN BEAR.

GRRR!

OH NO!

EEP!

TRANS-FORM!

THE CHAMPION OF JUSTICE SAVES THE GIRL.

HE IS GONE WITH THE WIND, LEAVING NO NAME.

UM...

HAHA! I'M NOT **GOHGEI** OR ANYTHING-- I'M JUST A CHAMPION OF JUSTICE PASSING THROUGH.

BYE!

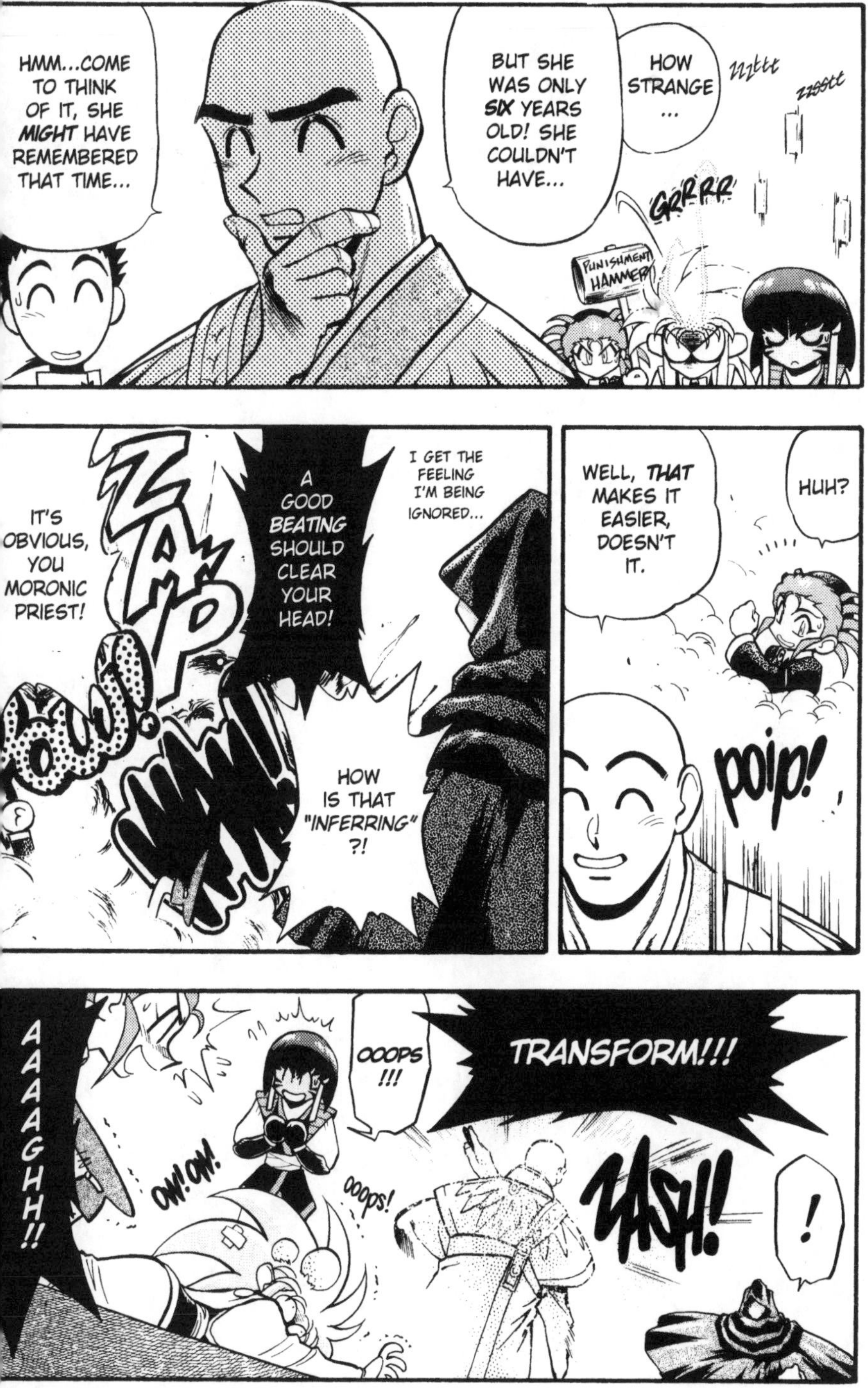
HMM...COME TO THINK OF IT, SHE MIGHT HAVE REMEMBERED THAT TIME...
BUT SHE WAS ONLY SIX YEARS OLD! SHE COULDN'T HAVE...
HOW STRANGE ...
zzzttt
zzzsst
GRRRR
PUNISHMENT HAMMER
IT'S OBVIOUS, YOU MORONIC PRIEST!
A GOOD BEATING SHOULD CLEAR YOUR HEAD!
I GET THE FEELING I'M BEING IGNORED...
HOW IS THAT "INFERRING" ?!
WELL, THAT MAKES IT EASIER, DOESN'T IT.
HUH?
poip!
AAAAAGHH!!
OOOPS !!!
OW! OW!
ooops!
TRANSFORM!!!
ZASH!
!

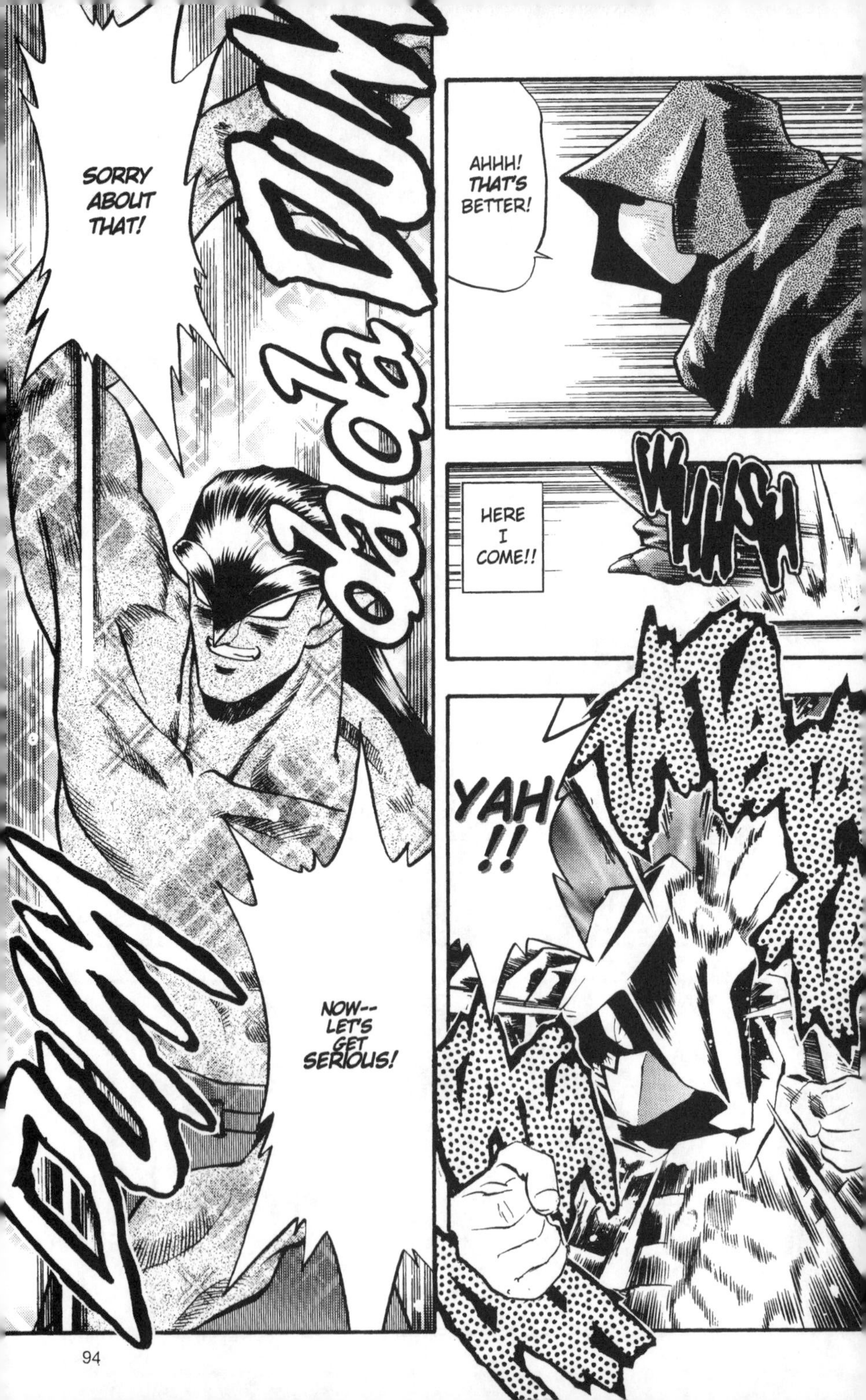
SORRY ABOUT THAT!
NOW-- LET'S GET SERIOUS!
AHHH! THAT'S BETTER!
HERE I COME!!
WHUSH
YAH !!

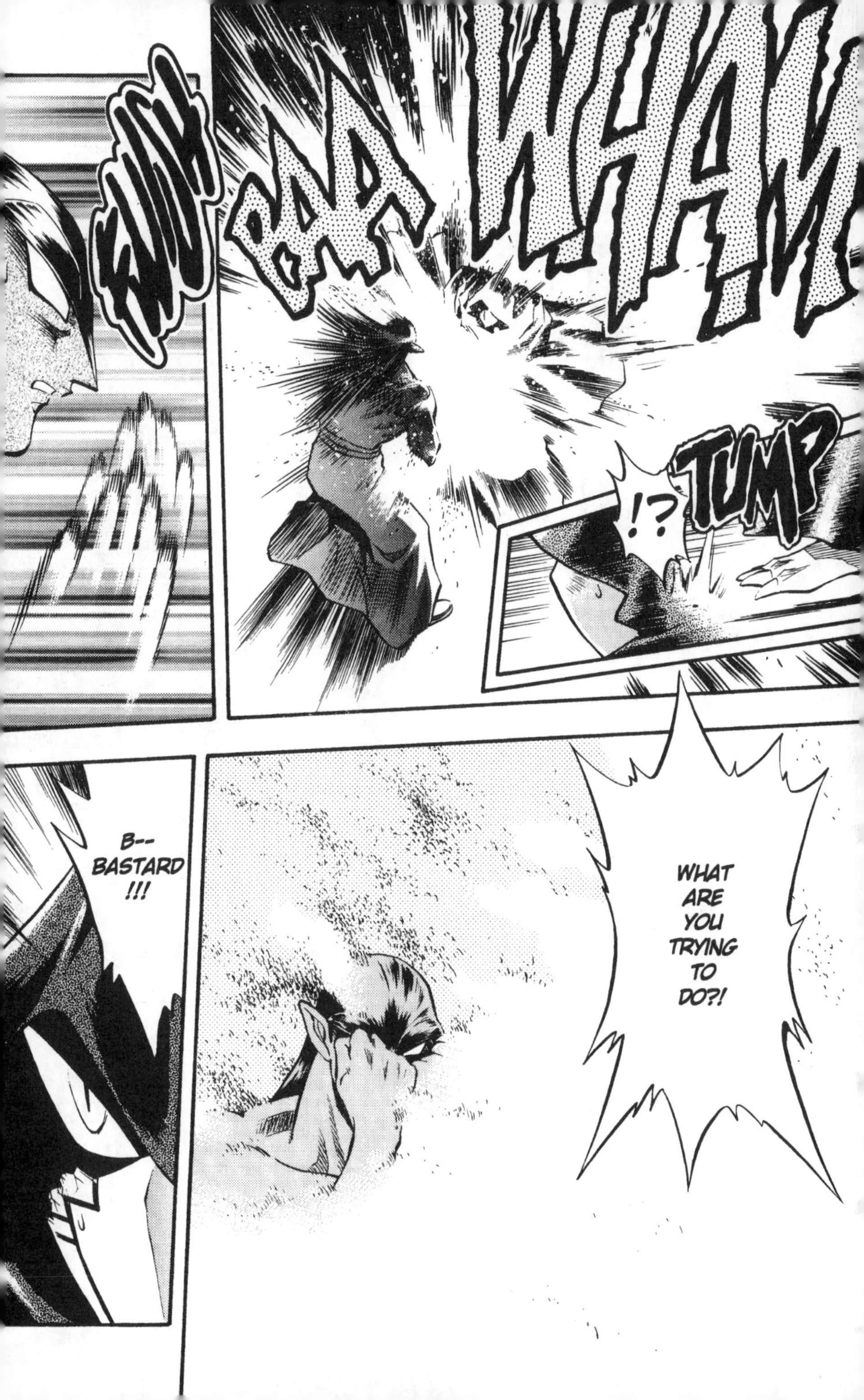
WHAM
!?
TUMP
B-- BASTARD !!!
WHAT ARE YOU TRYING TO DO?!

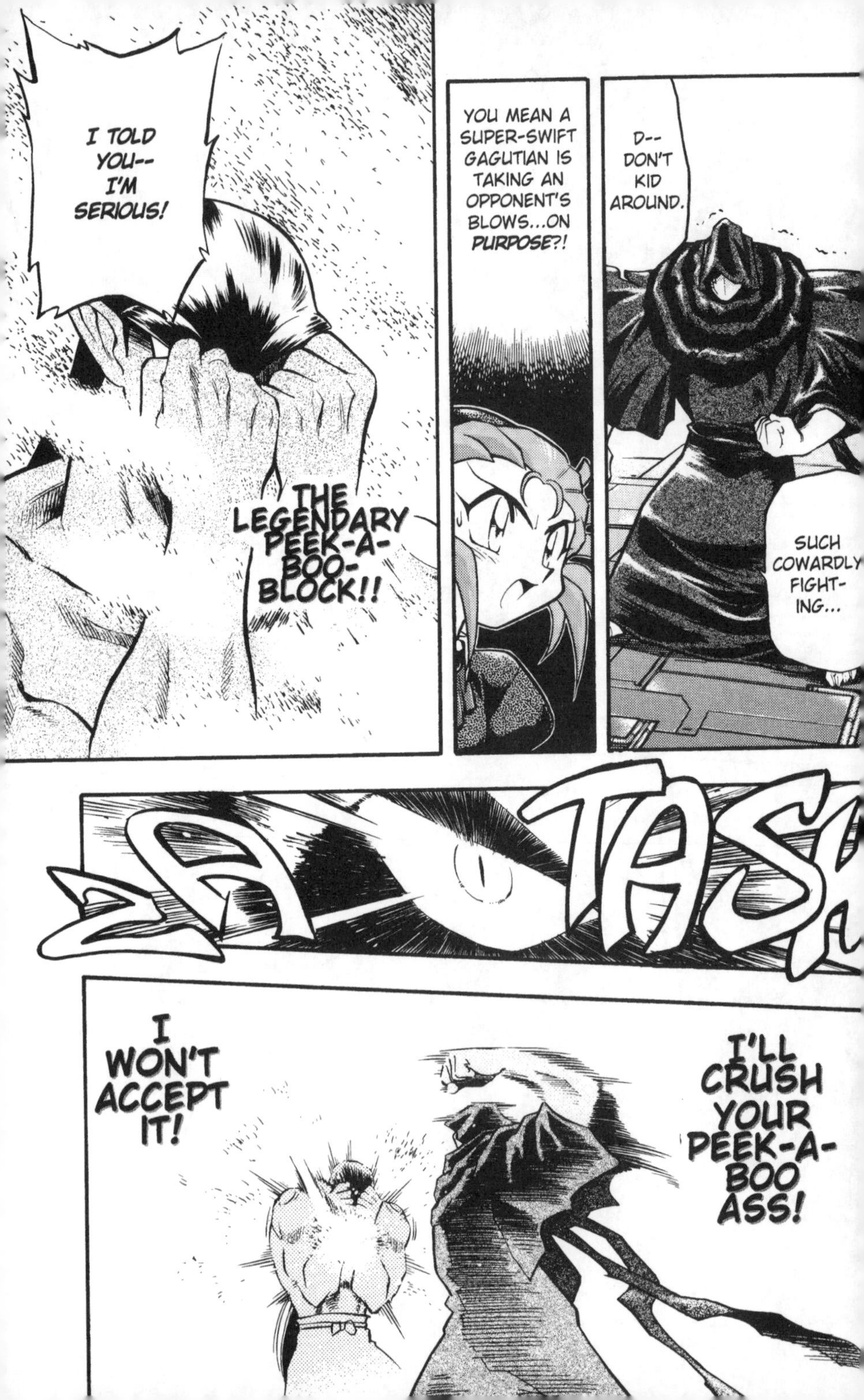
I TOLD YOU-- I'M SERIOUS!
THE LEGENDARY PEEK-A-BOO-BLOCK!!
YOU MEAN A SUPER-SWIFT GAGUTIAN IS TAKING AN OPPONENT'S BLOWS...ON PURPOSE?!
D-- DON'T KID AROUND.
SUCH COWARDLY FIGHTING...
TAS
I WON'T ACCEPT IT!
I'LL CRUSH YOUR PEEK-A-BOO ASS!

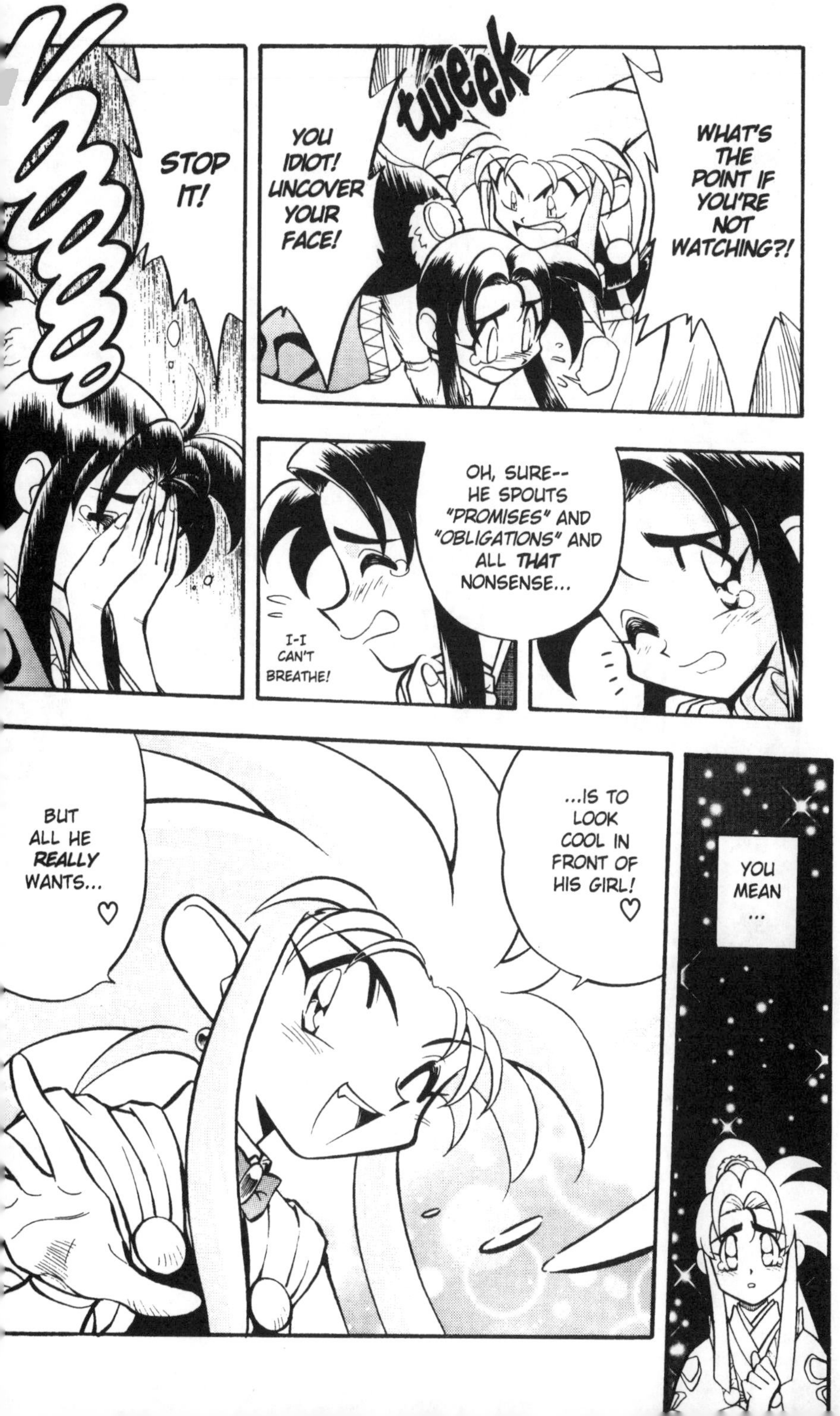
STOP IT!
YOU IDIOT! UNCOVER YOUR FACE!
tweek
WHAT'S THE POINT IF YOU'RE NOT WATCHING?!
I-I CAN'T BREATHE!
OH, SURE-- HE SPOUTS "PROMISES" AND "OBLIGATIONS" AND ALL THAT NONSENSE...
BUT ALL HE REALLY WANTS... ♡
...IS TO LOOK COOL IN FRONT OF HIS GIRL! ♡
YOU MEAN ...

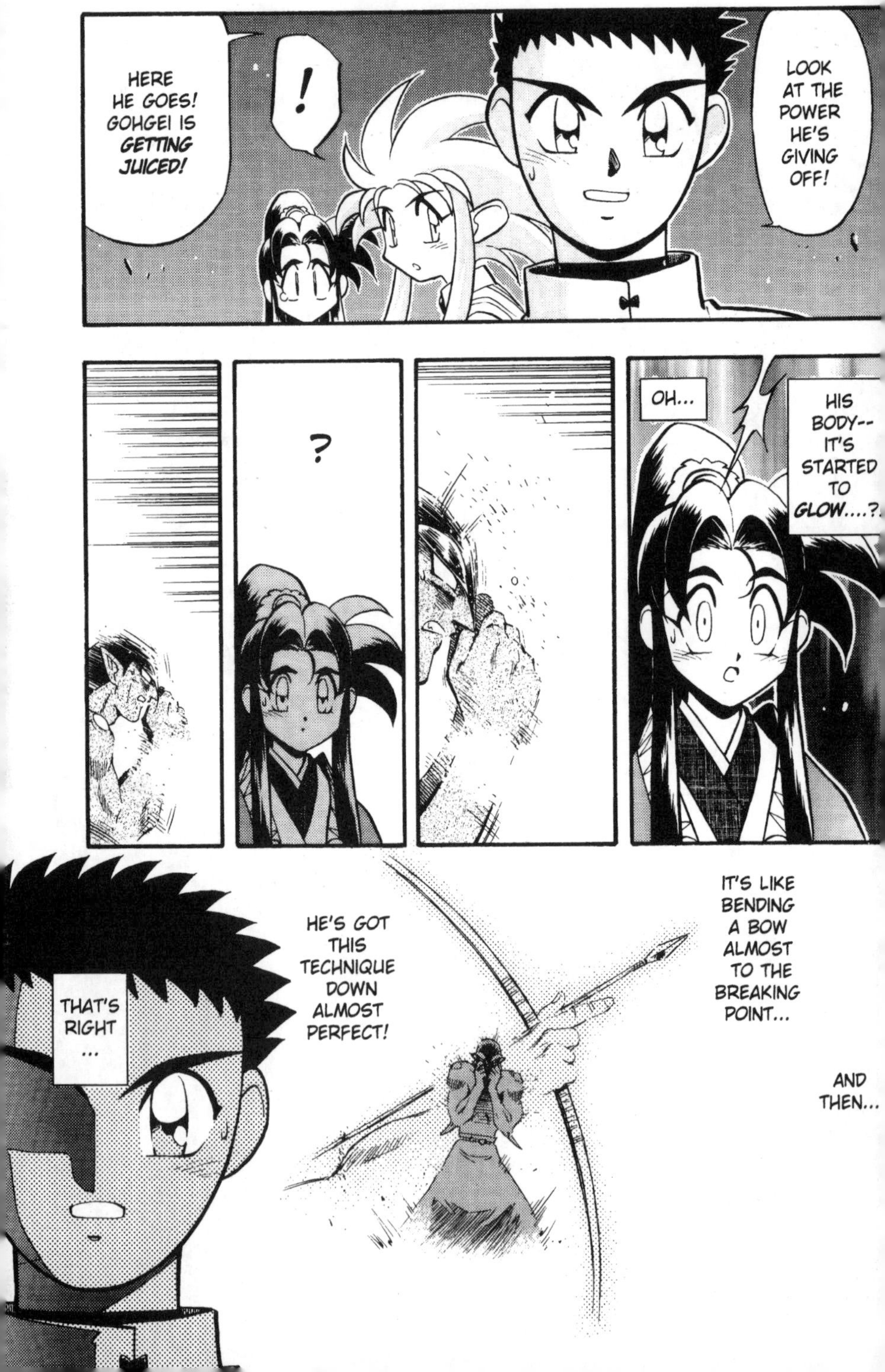
HERE HE GOES! GOHGEI IS GETTING JUICED!
!
LOOK AT THE POWER HE'S GIVING OFF!
?
OH...
HIS BODY-- IT'S STARTED TO GLOW....?
THAT'S RIGHT ...
HE'S GOT THIS TECHNIQUE DOWN ALMOST PERFECT!
IT'S LIKE BENDING A BOW ALMOST TO THE BREAKING POINT...
AND THEN...

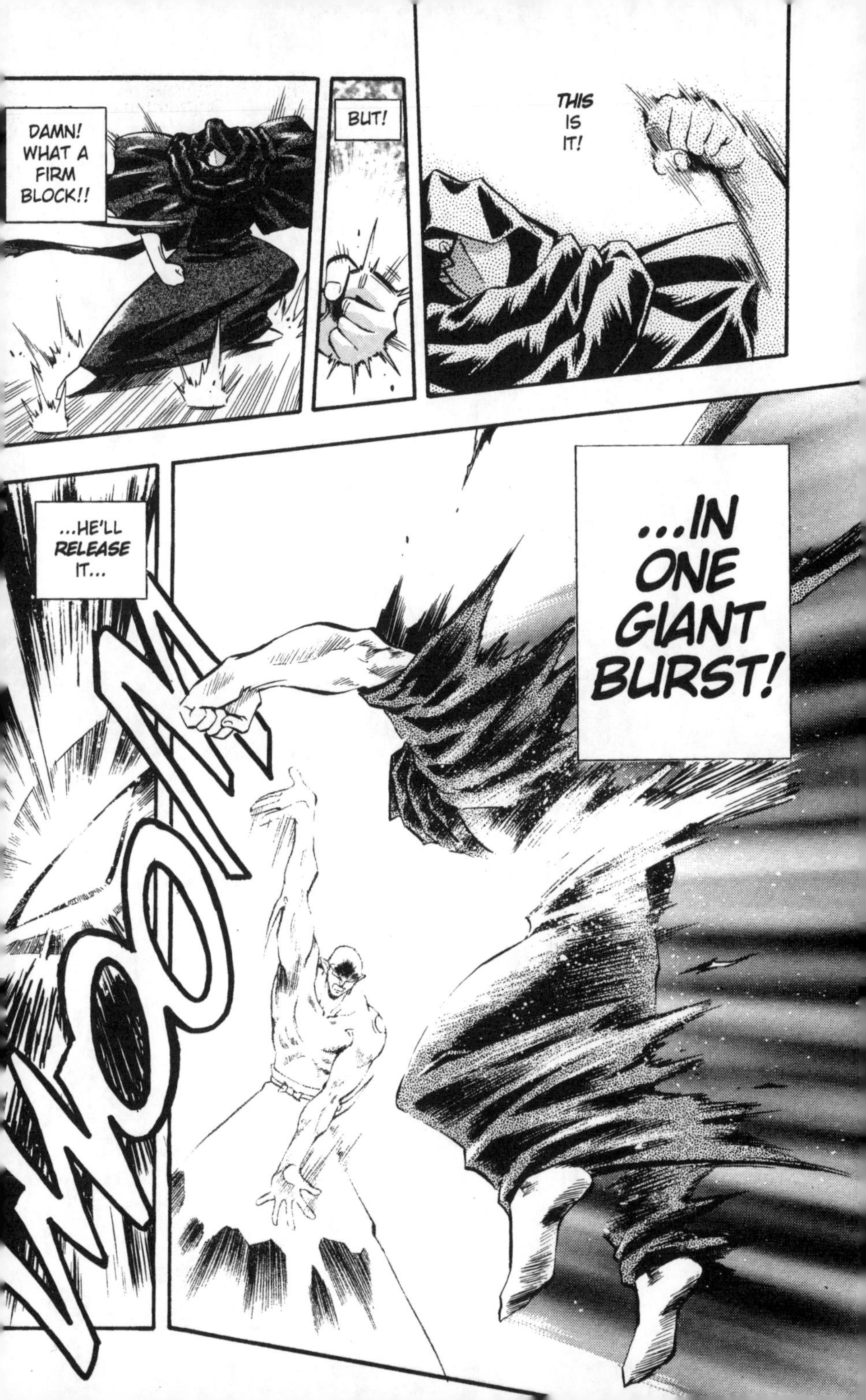
DAMN! WHAT A FIRM BLOCK!!
BUT!
THIS IS IT!
...HE'LL RELEASE IT...
...IN ONE GIANT BURST!
WHOOSH

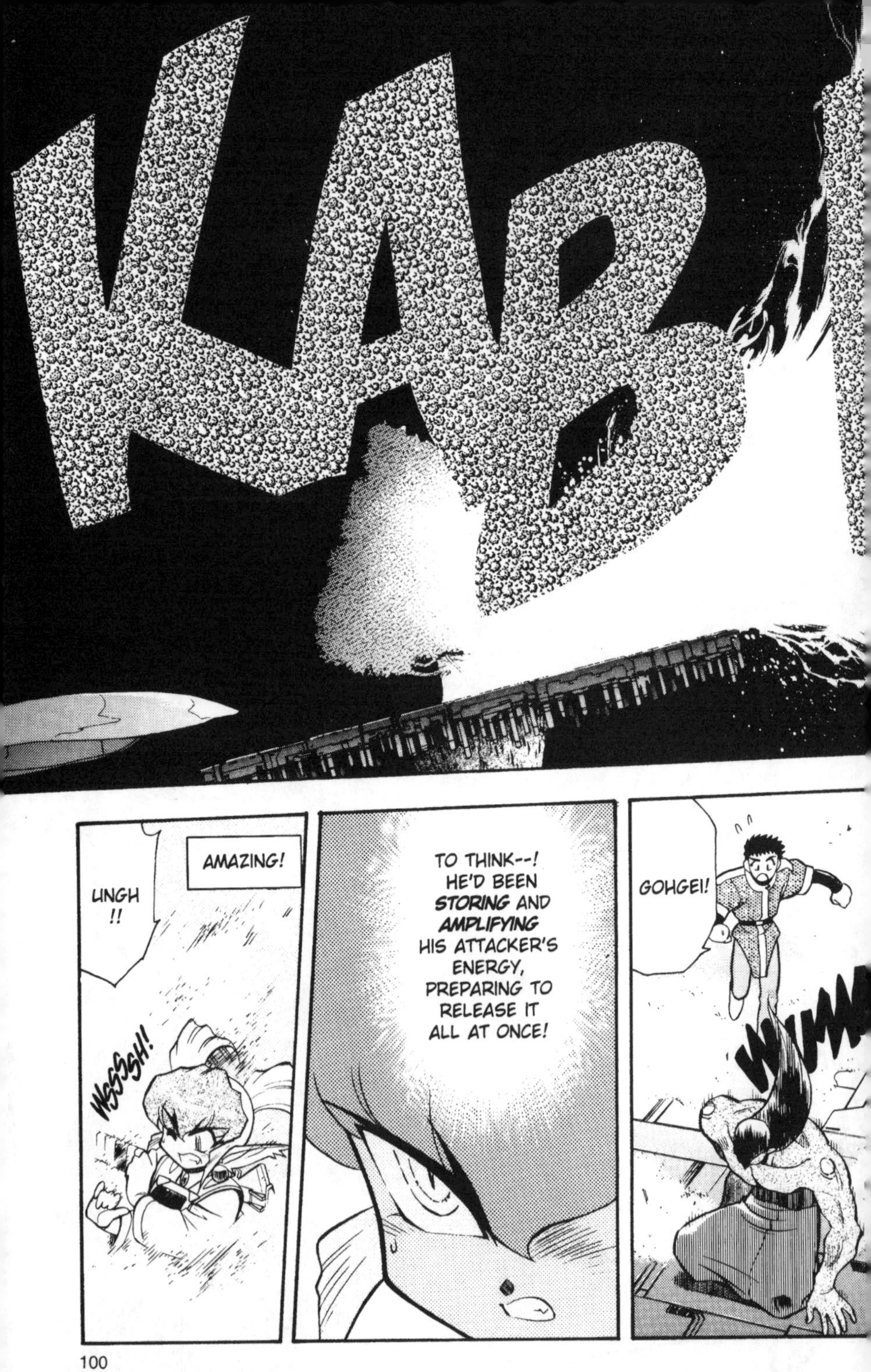
KLAB
UNGH !!
AMAZING!
WSSSH!
TO THINK--! HE'D BEEN STORING AND AMPLIFYING HIS ATTACKER'S ENERGY, PREPARING TO RELEASE IT ALL AT ONCE!
GOHGEI!

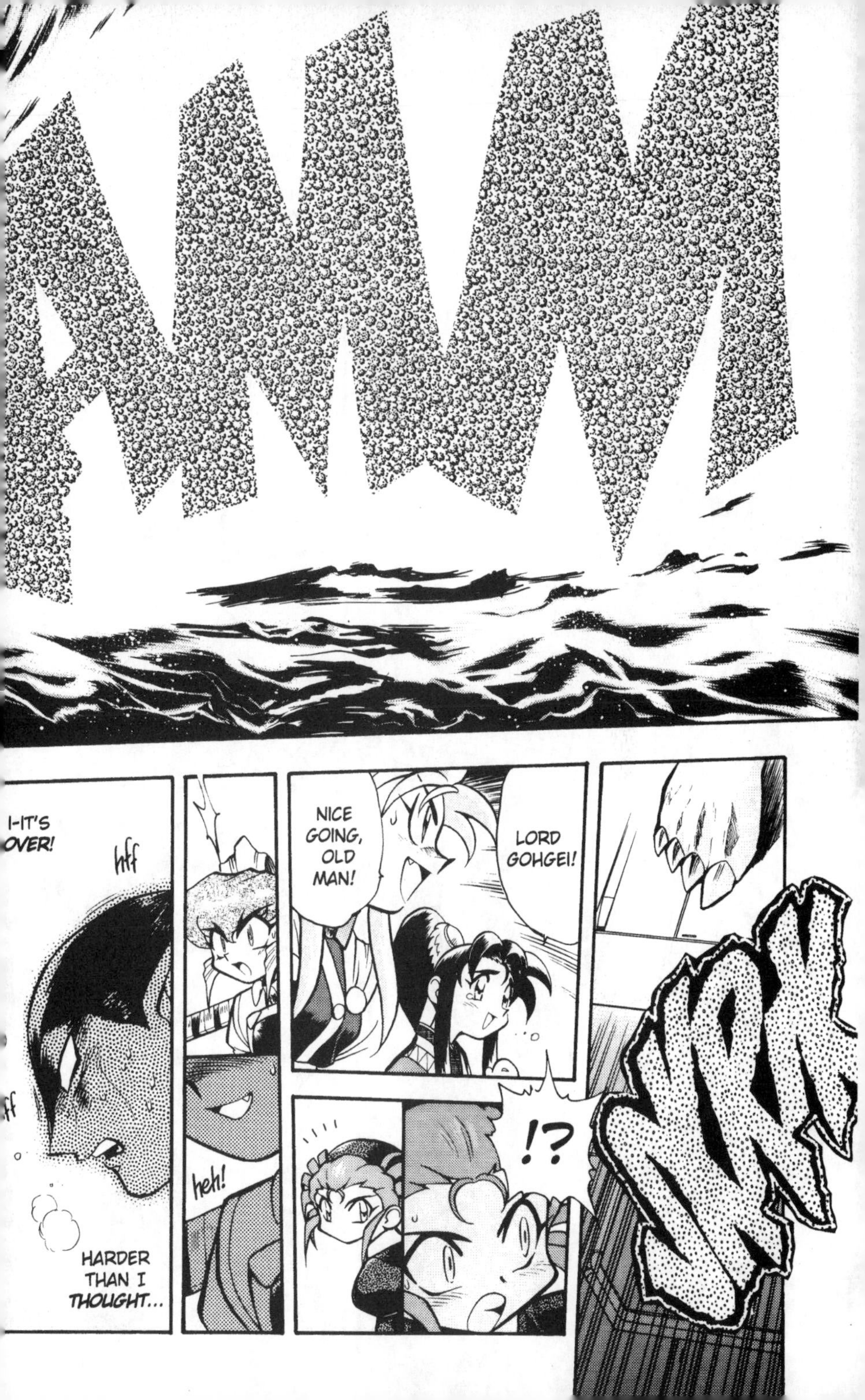
I-IT'S OVER!
hff
hff
HARDER THAN I THOUGHT...
NICE GOING, OLD MAN!
LORD GOHGEI!
heh!
!?

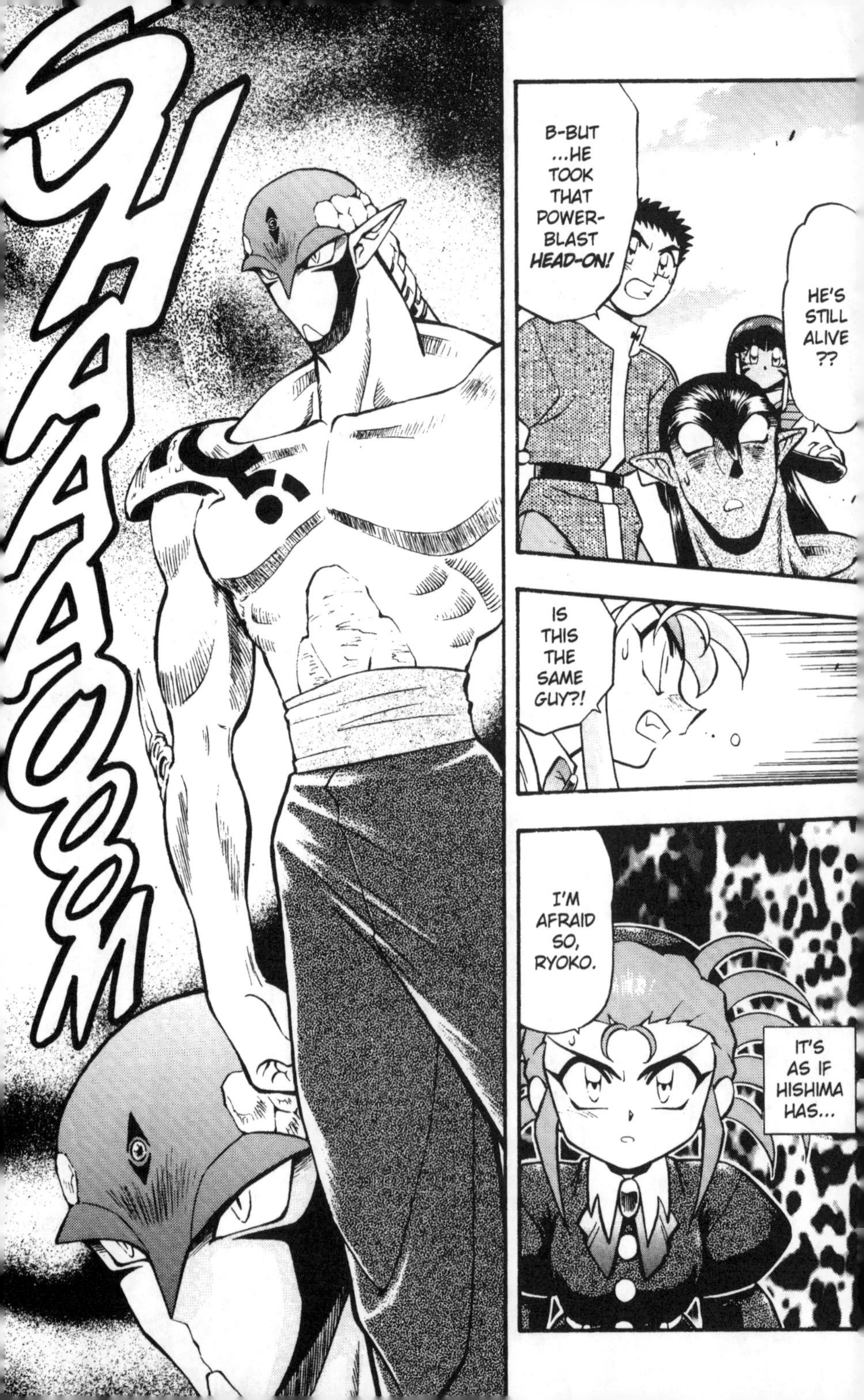
SHAAAOOOM
B-BUT ...HE TOOK THAT POWER-BLAST *HEAD-ON!*
HE'S STILL ALIVE ??
IS THIS THE SAME GUY?!
I'M AFRAID SO, RYOKO.
IT'S AS IF HISHIMA HAS...

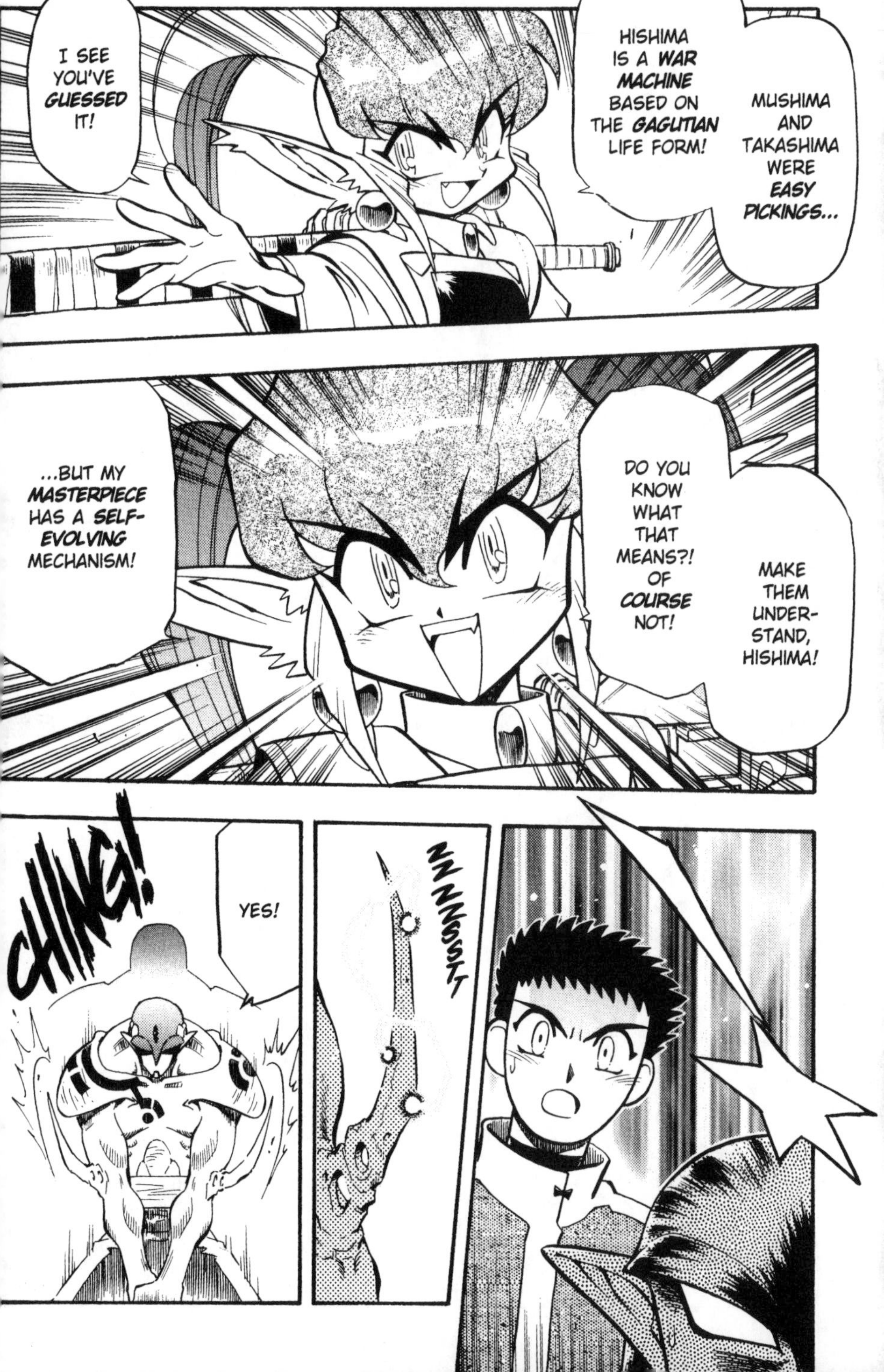
I SEE YOU'VE GUESSED IT!
HISHIMA IS A WAR MACHINE BASED ON THE GAGUTIAN LIFE FORM!
MUSHIMA AND TAKASHIMA WERE EASY PICKINGS...
...BUT MY MASTERPIECE HAS A SELF-EVOLVING MECHANISM!
DO YOU KNOW WHAT THAT MEANS?! OF COURSE NOT!
MAKE THEM UNDER-STAND, HISHIMA!
CHING!
YES!
NNNNSSKT

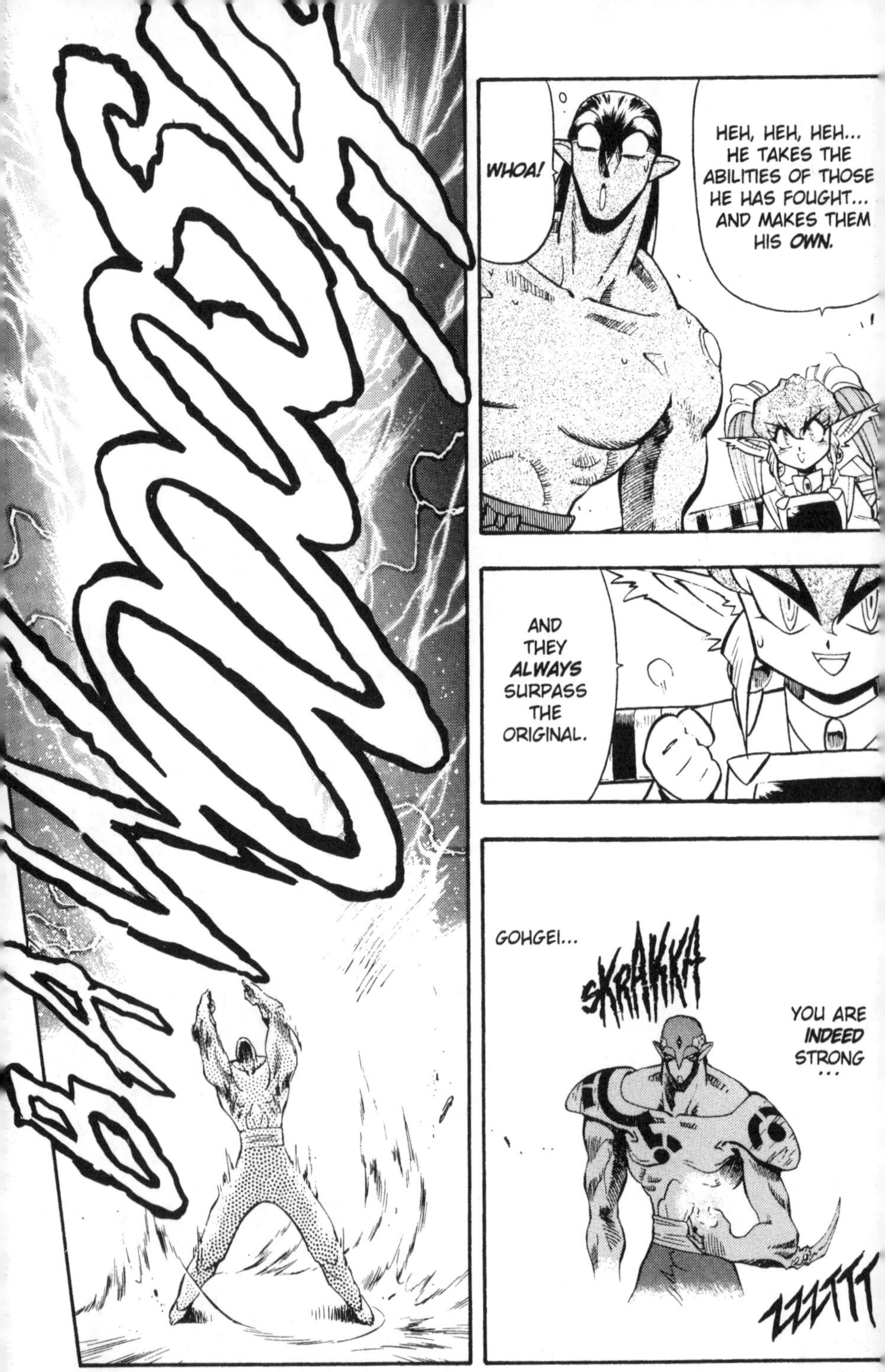
WHOA!
HEH, HEH, HEH... HE TAKES THE ABILITIES OF THOSE HE HAS FOUGHT... ...AND MAKES THEM HIS *OWN.*
AND THEY *ALWAYS* SURPASS THE ORIGINAL.
GOHGEI...
SKRAKKA
YOU ARE *INDEED* STRONG ...
ZZZTTT

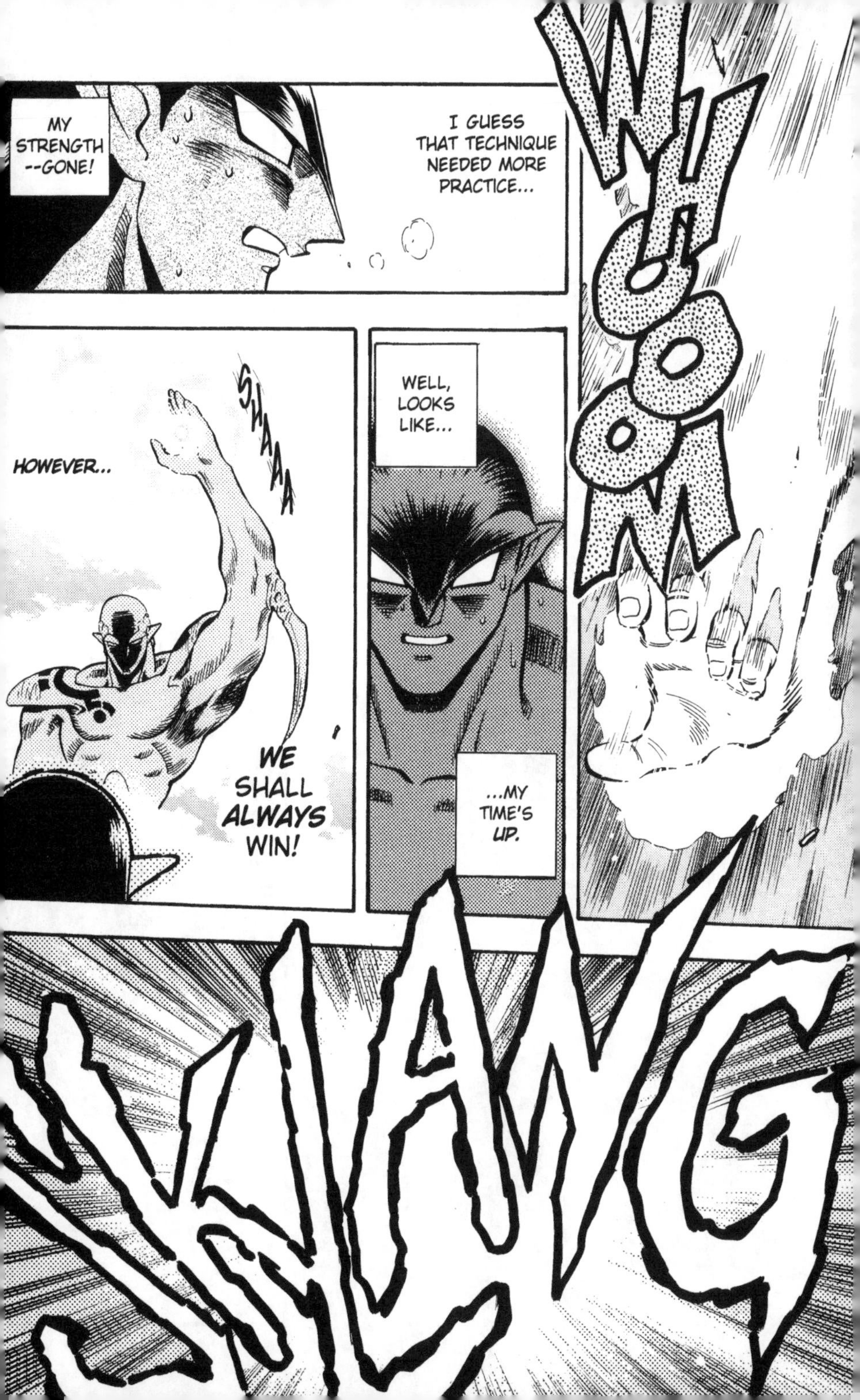
MY STRENGTH --GONE!
I GUESS THAT TECHNIQUE NEEDED MORE PRACTICE...
HOWEVER...
SHAAAA
WE SHALL ALWAYS WIN!
WELL, LOOKS LIKE...
...MY TIME'S UP.
WHOOOOM
KLANG

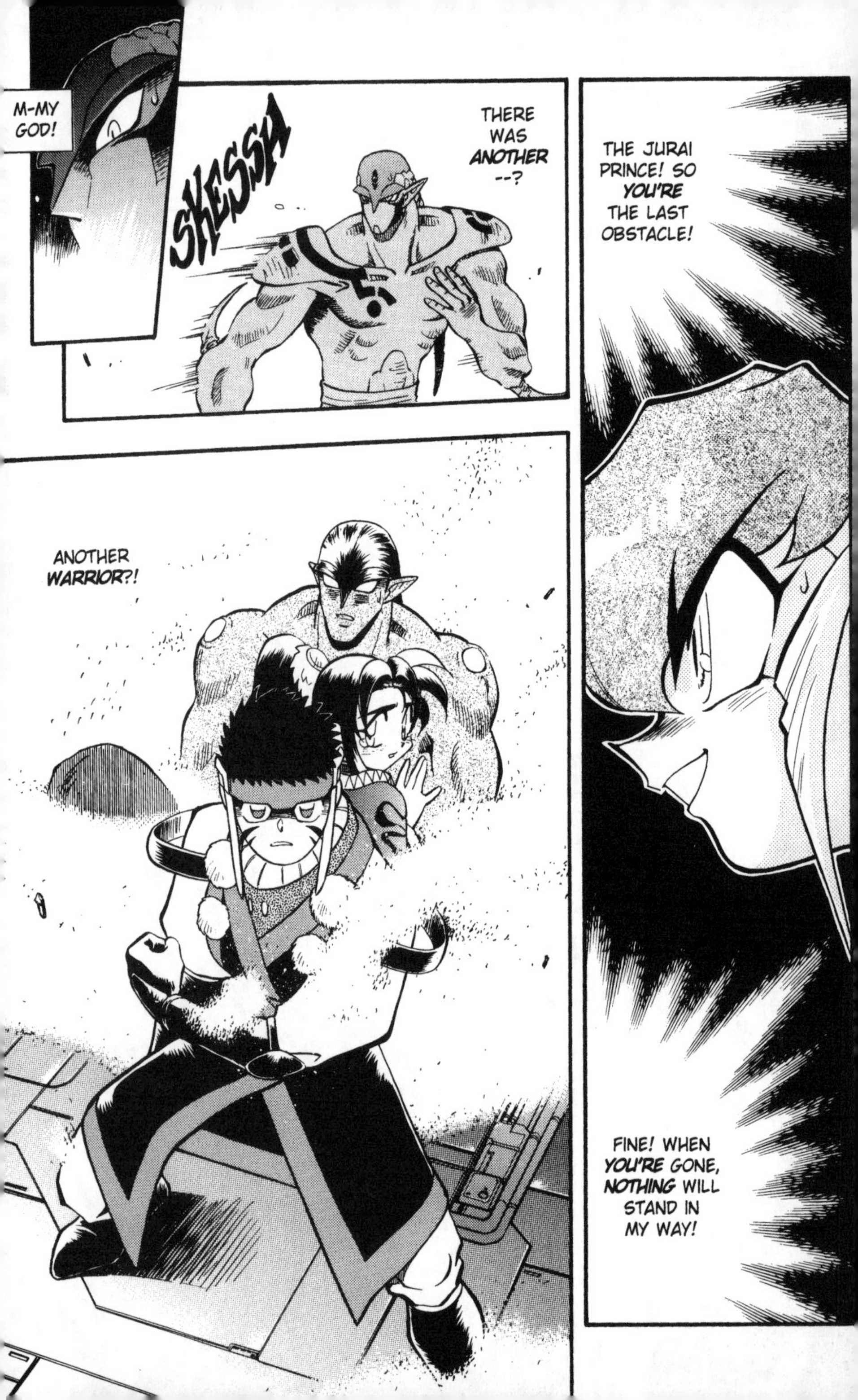
M-MY GOD!
SKESSH
THERE WAS ANOTHER --?
ANOTHER WARRIOR?!
THE JURAI PRINCE! SO YOU'RE THE LAST OBSTACLE!
FINE! WHEN YOU'RE GONE, NOTHING WILL STAND IN MY WAY!

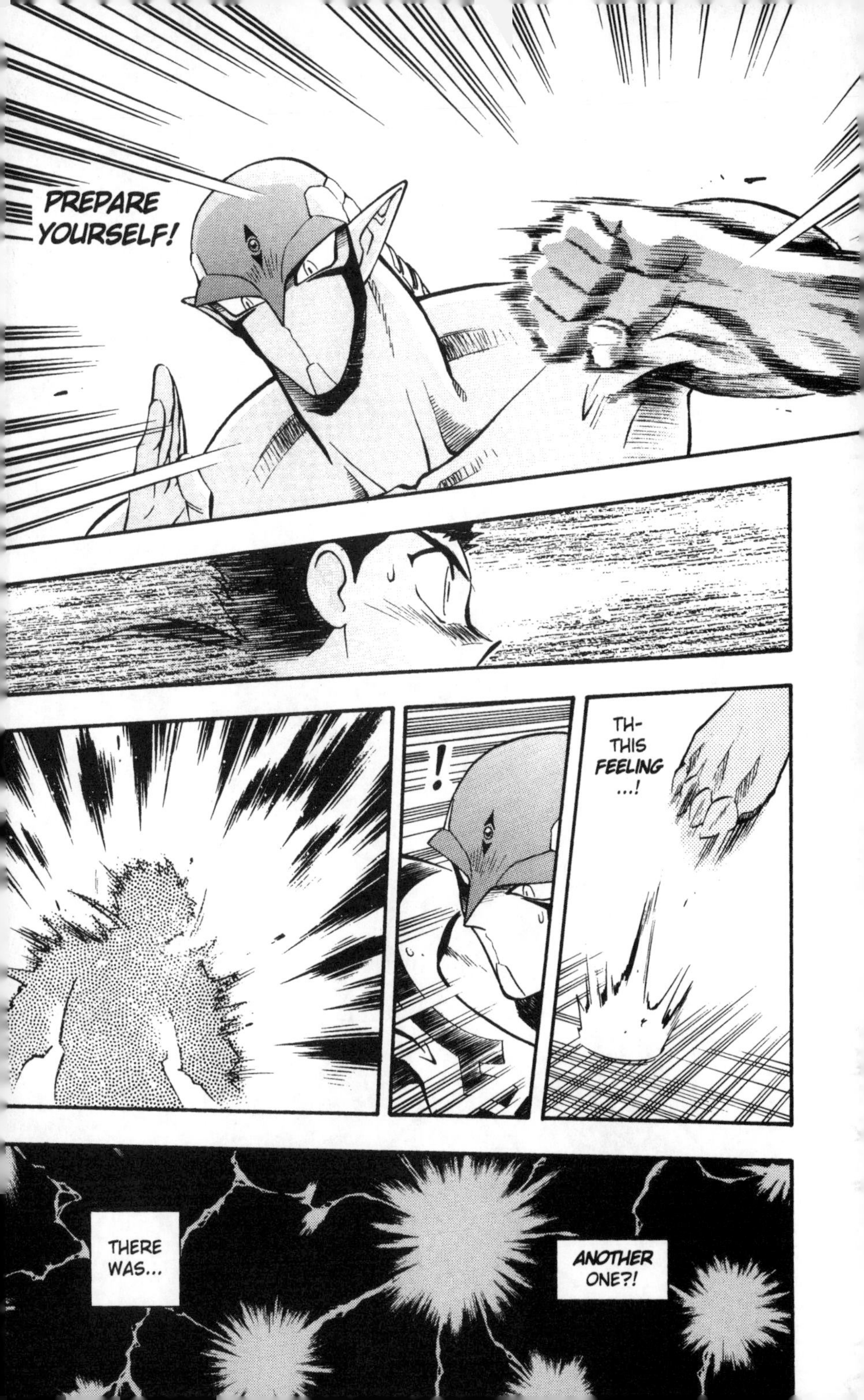
PREPARE YOURSELF!
TH- THIS FEELING ...!
!
THERE WAS...
ANOTHER ONE?!

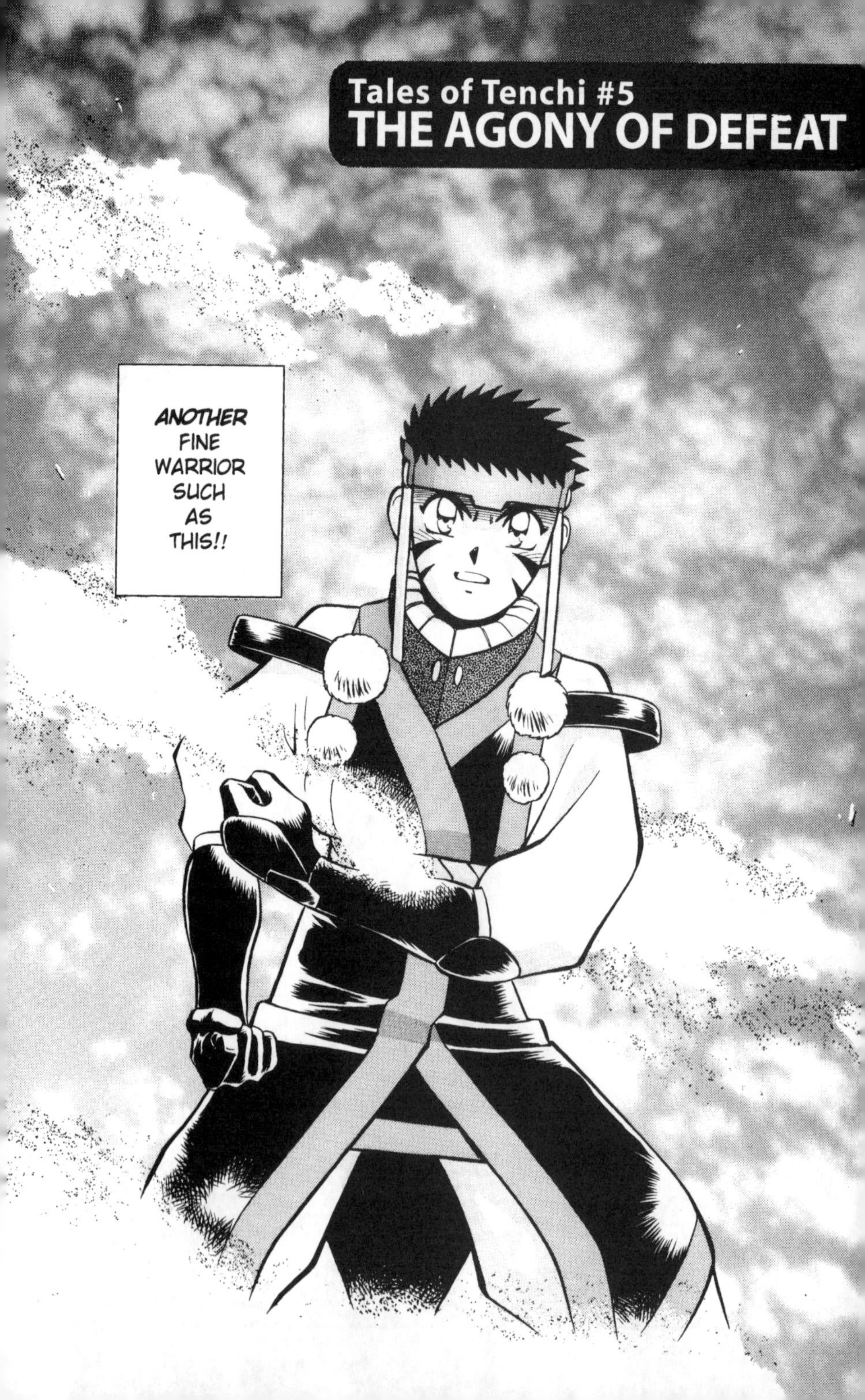
Tales of Tenchi #5
THE AGONY OF DEFEAT
ANOTHER FINE WARRIOR SUCH AS THIS!!

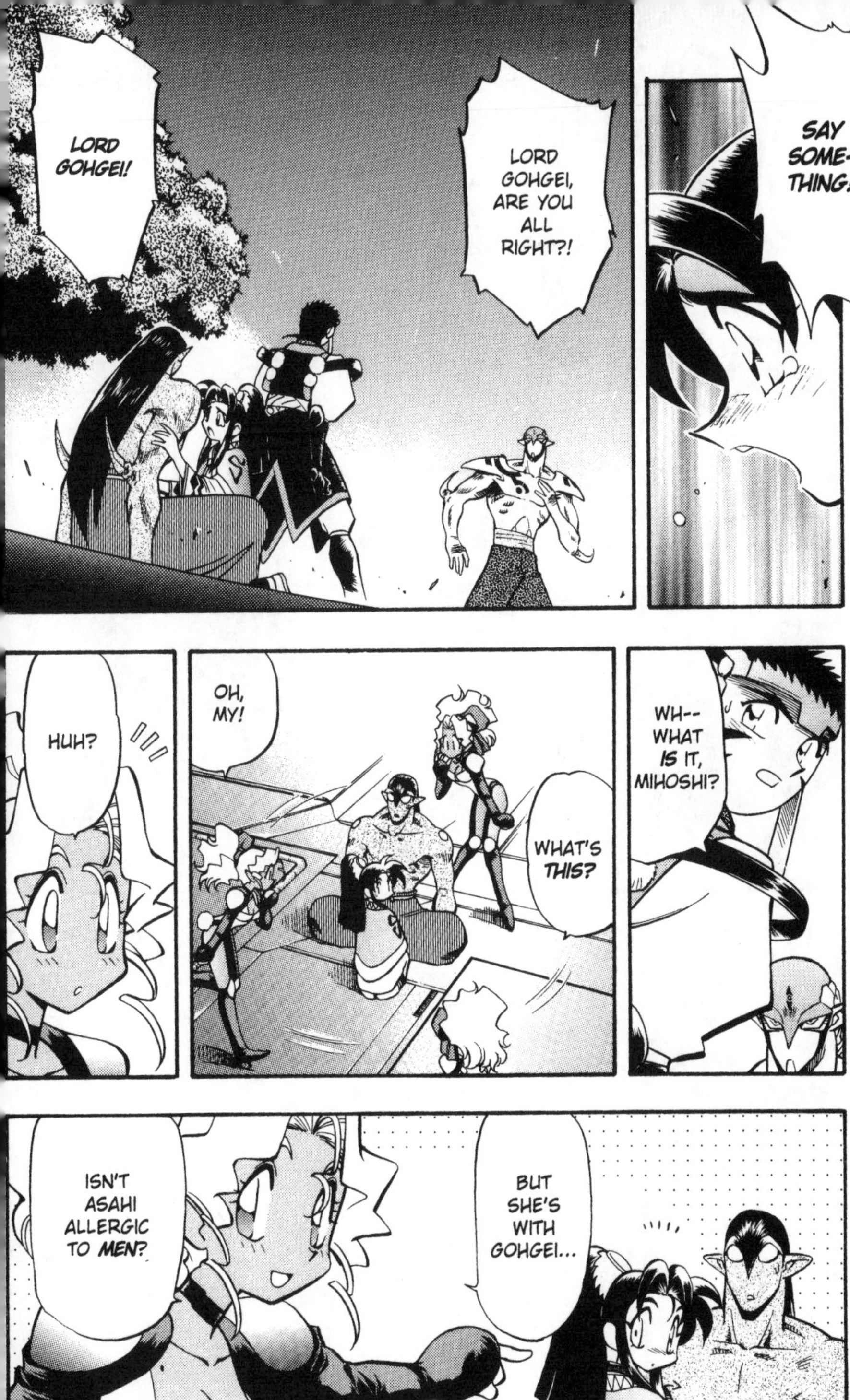
LORD GOHGEI!
LORD GOHGEI, ARE YOU ALL RIGHT?!
SAY SOME-THING!
HUH?
OH, MY!
WHAT'S THIS?
WH--WHAT IS IT, MIHOSHI?
ISN'T ASAHI ALLERGIC TO MEN?
BUT SHE'S WITH GOHGEI...

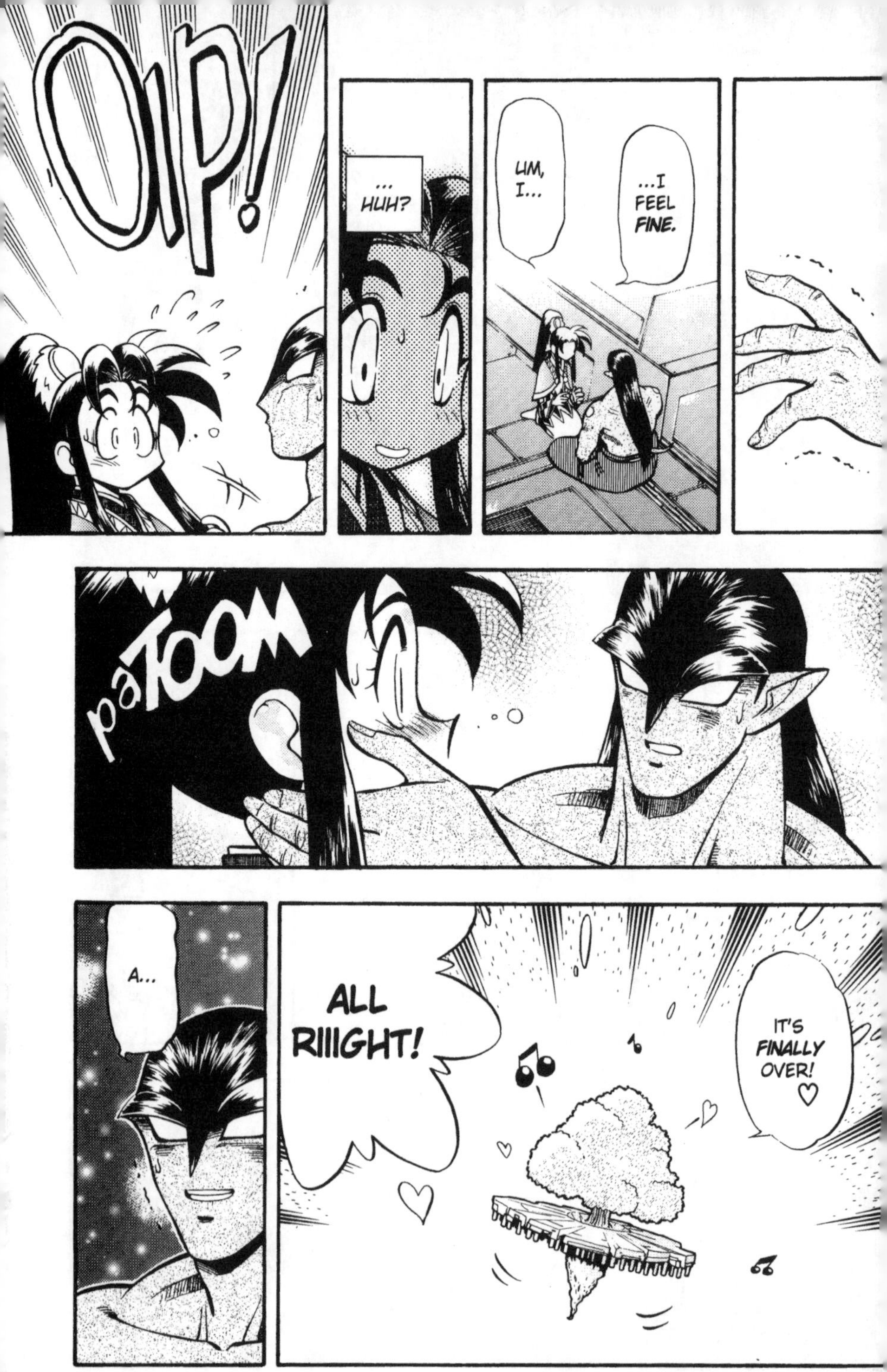
OIP!
... HUH?
UM, I...
...I FEEL FINE.
paTOOM
A...
ALL RIIIGHT!
IT'S FINALLY OVER! ♡

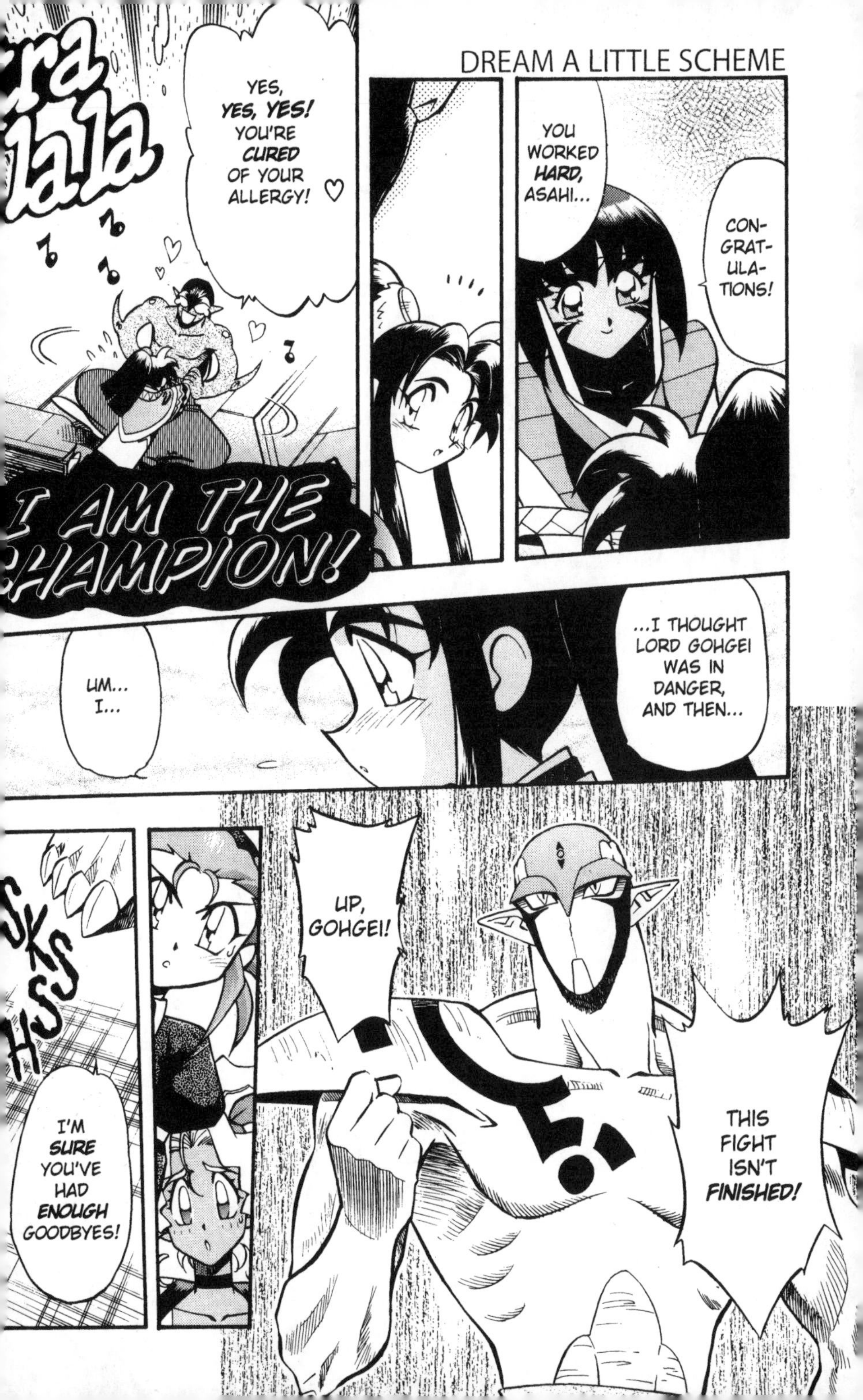
YES, YES, YES! YOU'RE CURED OF YOUR ALLERGY! ♡
I AM THE CHAMPION!
YOU WORKED HARD, ASAHI...
CON-GRAT-ULA-TIONS!
UM... I...
...I THOUGHT LORD GOHGEI WAS IN DANGER, AND THEN...
I'M SURE YOU'VE HAD ENOUGH GOODBYES!
UP, GOHGEI!
THIS FIGHT ISN'T FINISHED!

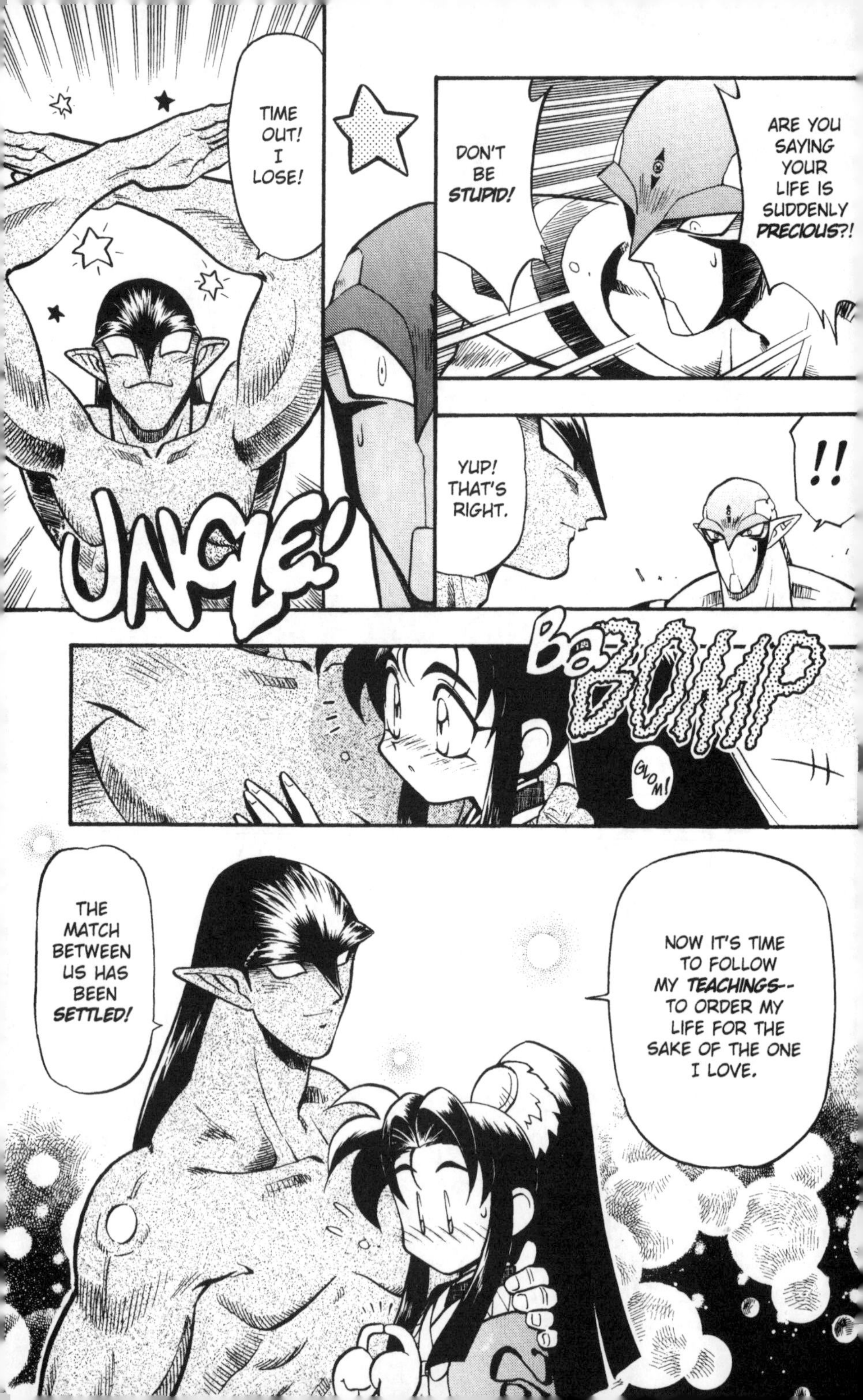
TIME OUT! I LOSE!
UNCLE!
DON'T BE STUPID!
ARE YOU SAYING YOUR LIFE IS SUDDENLY PRECIOUS?!
YUP! THAT'S RIGHT.
!!
BA-BOMP
GYOM!
THE MATCH BETWEEN US HAS BEEN SETTLED!
NOW IT'S TIME TO FOLLOW MY TEACHINGS-- TO ORDER MY LIFE FOR THE SAKE OF THE ONE I LOVE.

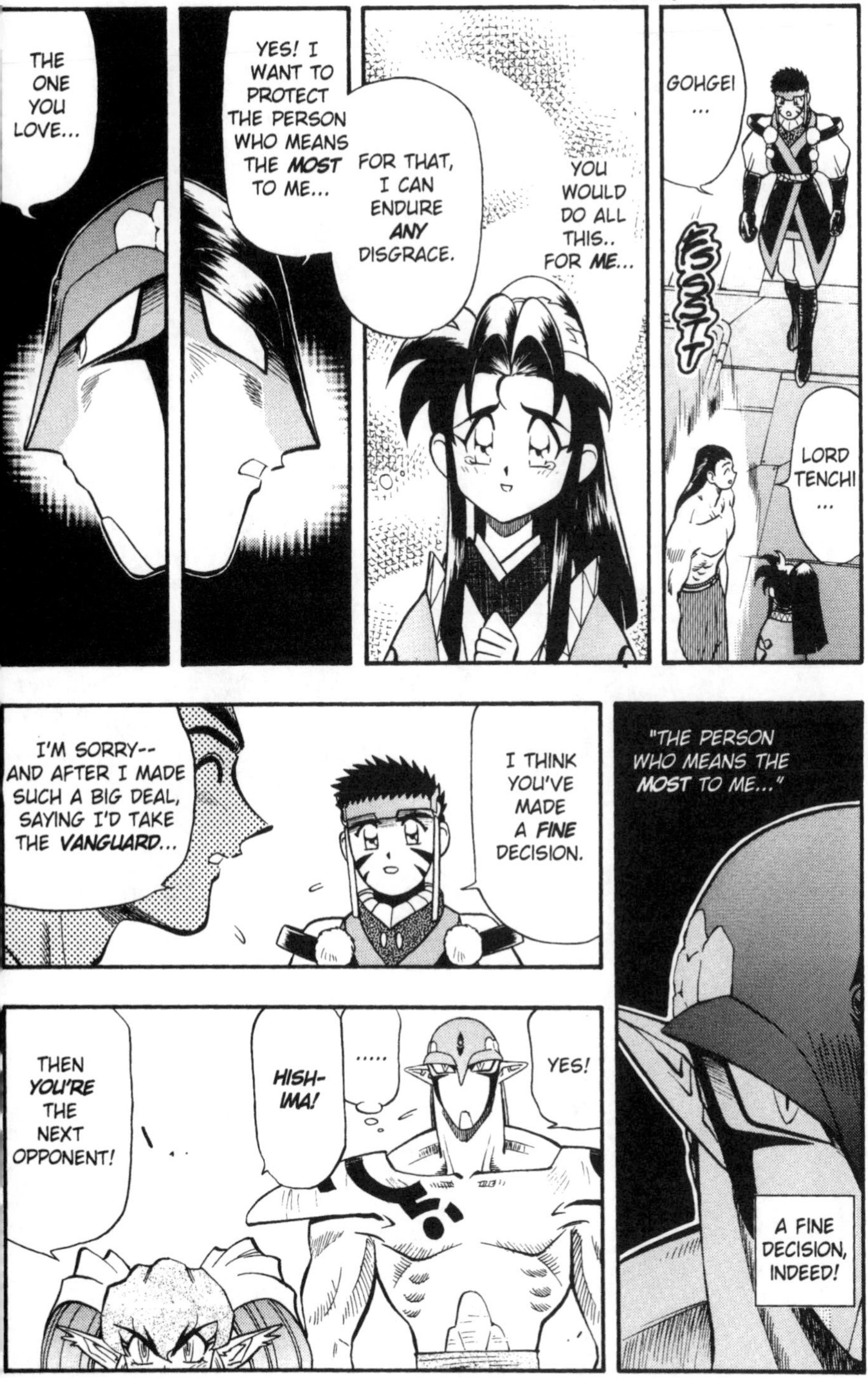
THE ONE YOU LOVE...
YES! I WANT TO PROTECT THE PERSON WHO MEANS THE **MOST** TO ME...
FOR THAT, I CAN ENDURE **ANY** DISGRACE.
YOU WOULD DO ALL THIS.. FOR **ME**...
GOHGEI ...
KSSSTT
LORD TENCHI ...
I'M SORRY-- AND AFTER I MADE SUCH A BIG DEAL, SAYING I'D TAKE THE **VANGUARD**...
I THINK YOU'VE MADE A **FINE** DECISION.
THEN **YOU'RE** THE NEXT OPPONENT!
HISH-IMA!
.....
YES!
"THE PERSON WHO MEANS THE **MOST** TO ME..."
A FINE DECISION, INDEED!

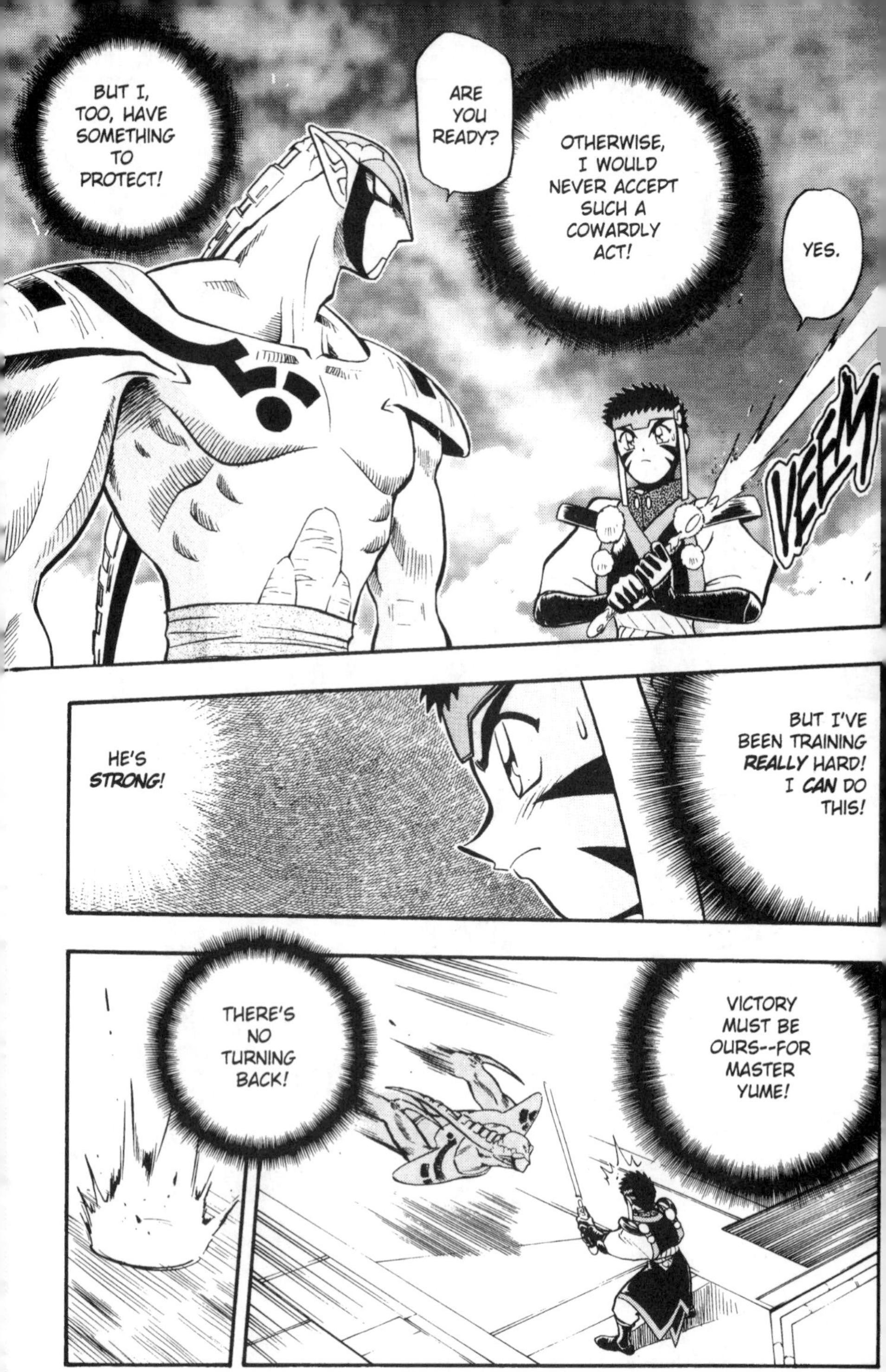
BUT I, TOO, HAVE SOMETHING TO PROTECT!
ARE YOU READY?
OTHERWISE, I WOULD NEVER ACCEPT SUCH A COWARDLY ACT!
YES.
VEEM
HE'S STRONG!
BUT I'VE BEEN TRAINING REALLY HARD! I CAN DO THIS!
THERE'S NO TURNING BACK!
VICTORY MUST BE OURS--FOR MASTER YUME!

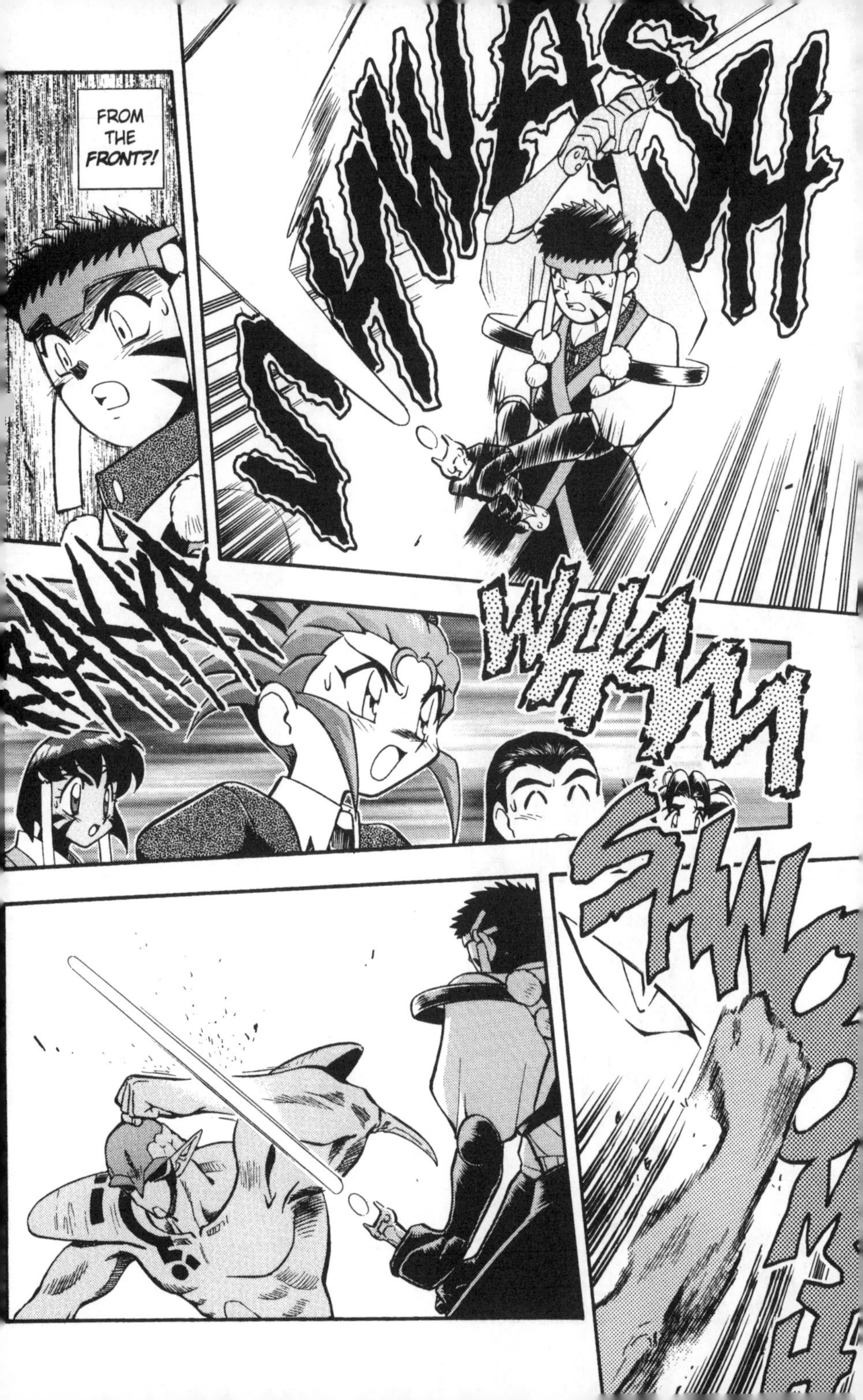
FROM THE FRONT?!
WHASH
WHAM

HE...

TH--TH LIGHTEST IMPACT...

...HAS THE POWER OF MY OWN SWORD...?!

HE CAN COPY THE ABILITIES OF HIS OPPONENT SO QUICKLY?!

HE DODGED IT?!

DAMN!

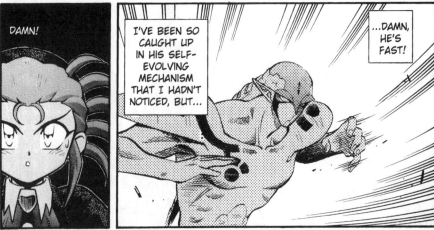

I'VE BEEN SO CAUGHT UP IN HIS SELF-EVOLVING MECHANISM THAT I HADN'T NOTICED, BUT...

...DAMN, HE'S FAST!

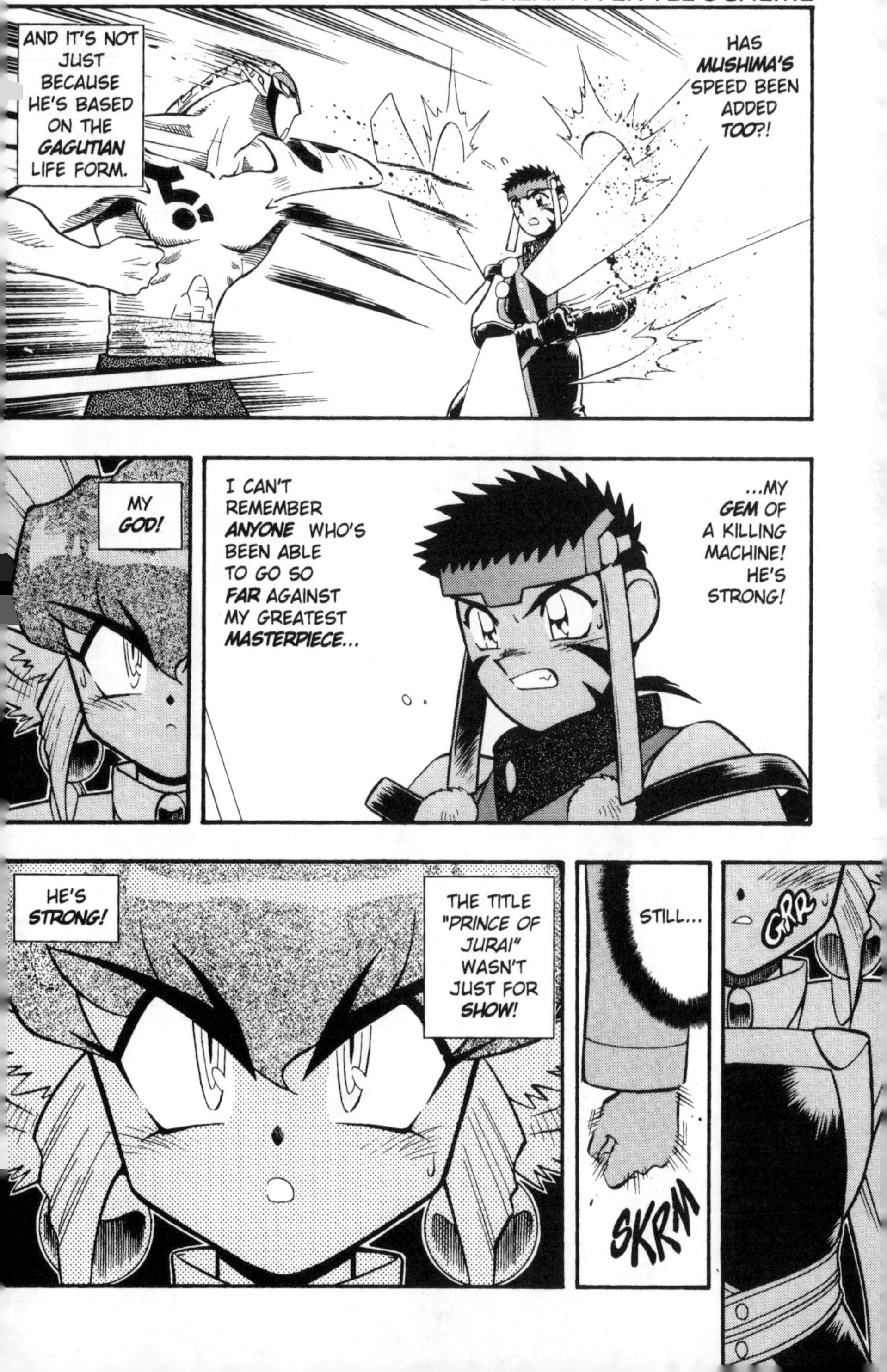
AND IT'S NOT JUST BECAUSE HE'S BASED ON THE GAGUTIAN LIFE FORM.
HAS MUSHIMA'S SPEED BEEN ADDED TOO?!
MY GOD!
I CAN'T REMEMBER ANYONE WHO'S BEEN ABLE TO GO SO FAR AGAINST MY GREATEST MASTERPIECE...
...MY GEM OF A KILLING MACHINE! HE'S STRONG!
HE'S STRONG!
THE TITLE "PRINCE OF JURAI" WASN'T JUST FOR SHOW!
STILL...
SKRM
GRR

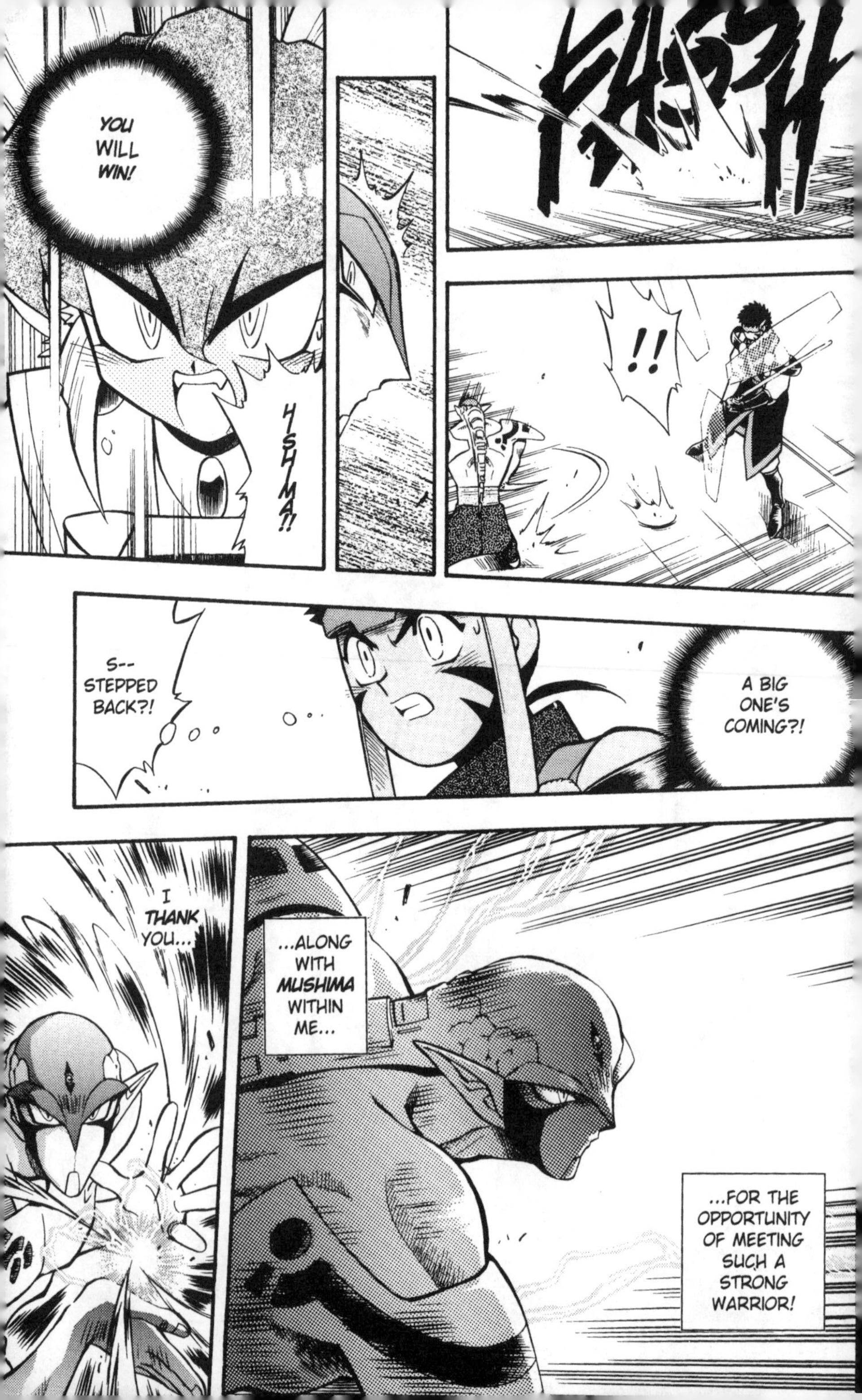
YOU WILL WIN!
MUSHIMA!!
FASSH
!!
S-- STEPPED BACK?!
A BIG ONE'S COMING?!
I THANK YOU...
...ALONG WITH MUSHIMA WITHIN ME...
...FOR THE OPPORTUNITY OF MEETING SUCH A STRONG WARRIOR!

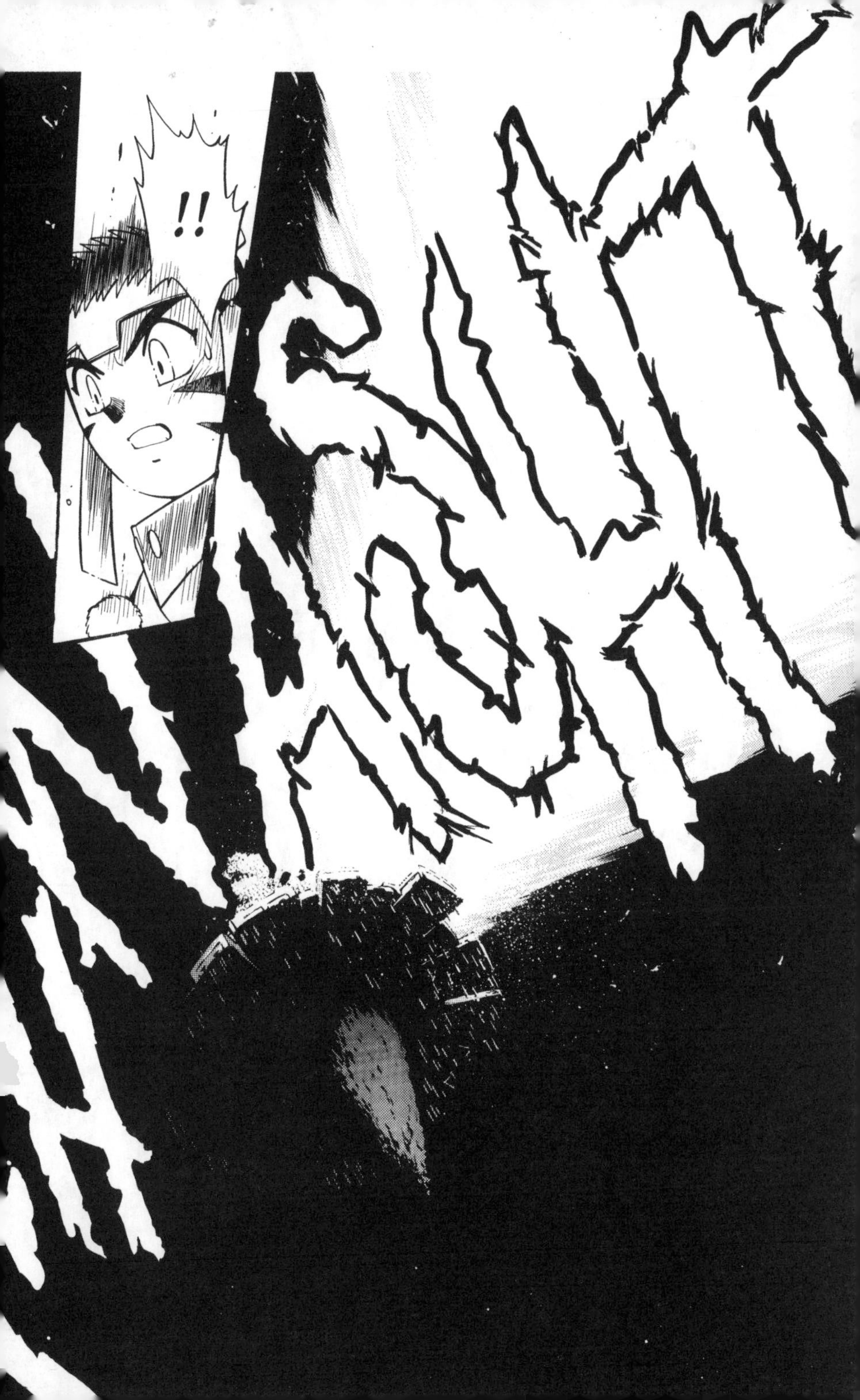
!!

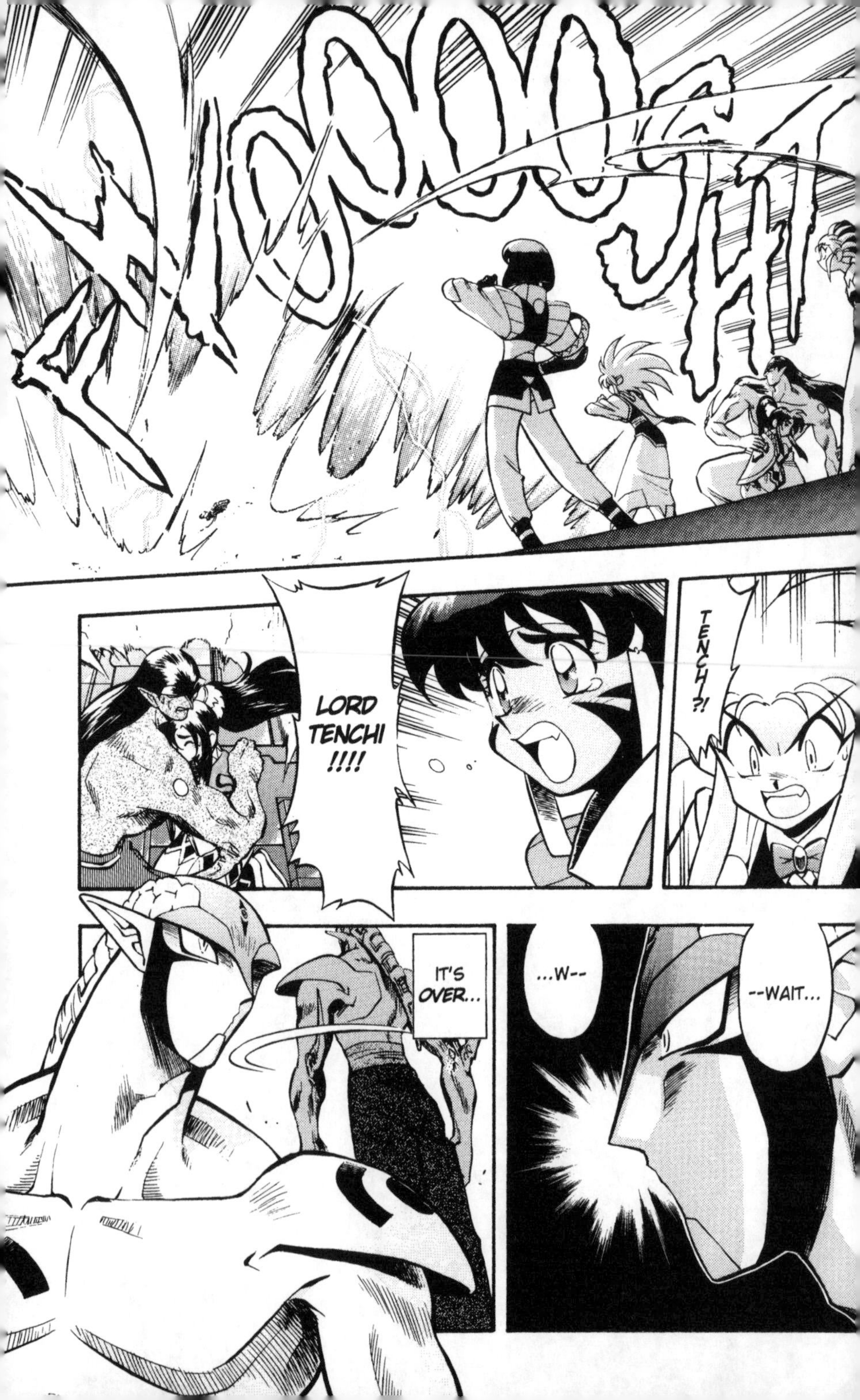

FWOOOOOSH
LORD TENCHI !!!!
TENCHI?!
IT'S OVER...
...W--
--WAIT...

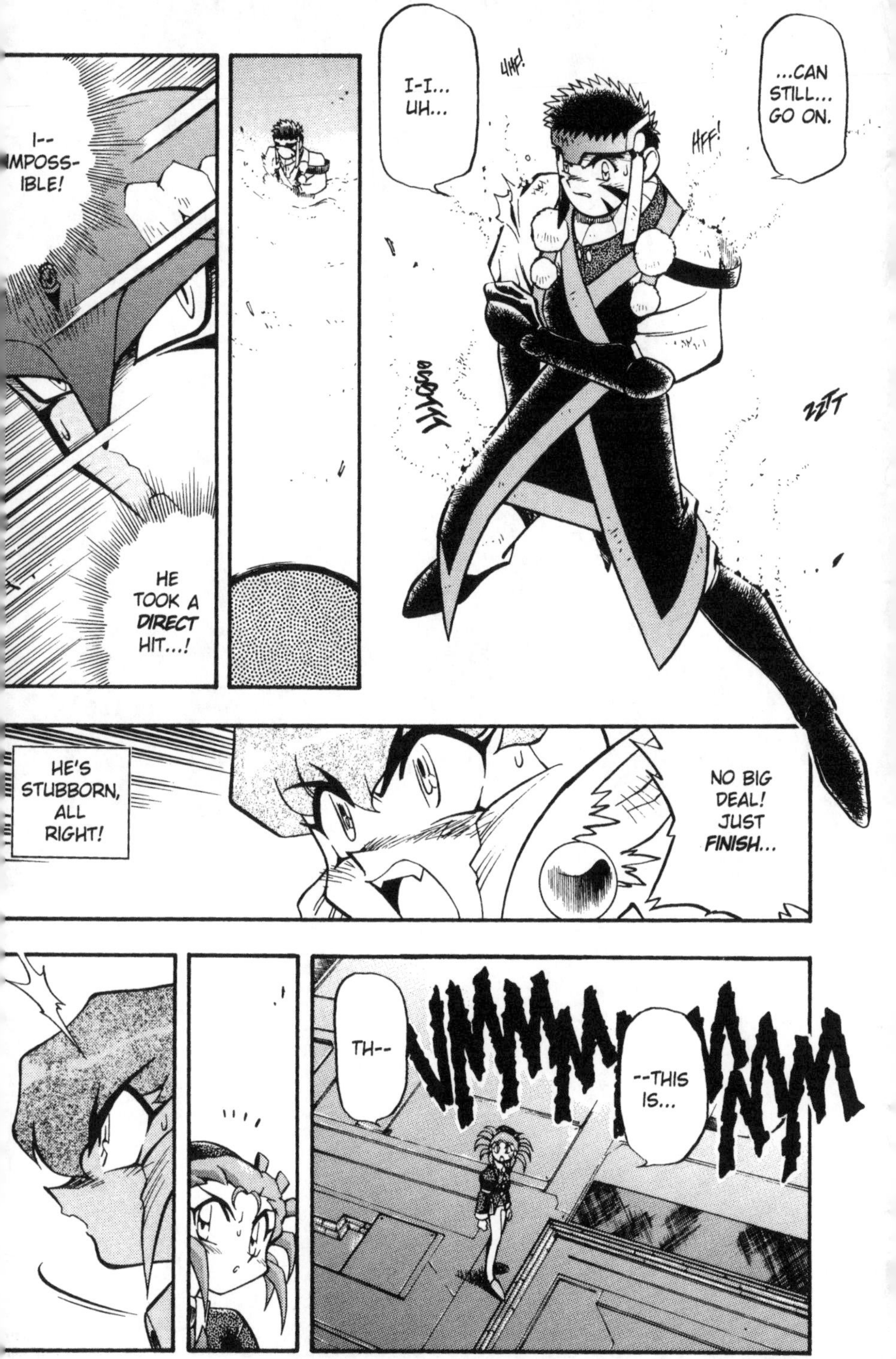

I-- IMPOSSIBLE!
HE TOOK A DIRECT HIT...!
I-I... UH...
UHF!
HFF!
...CAN STILL... GO ON.
ZZTT
HE'S STUBBORN, ALL RIGHT!
NO BIG DEAL! JUST FINISH...
TH--
--THIS IS...

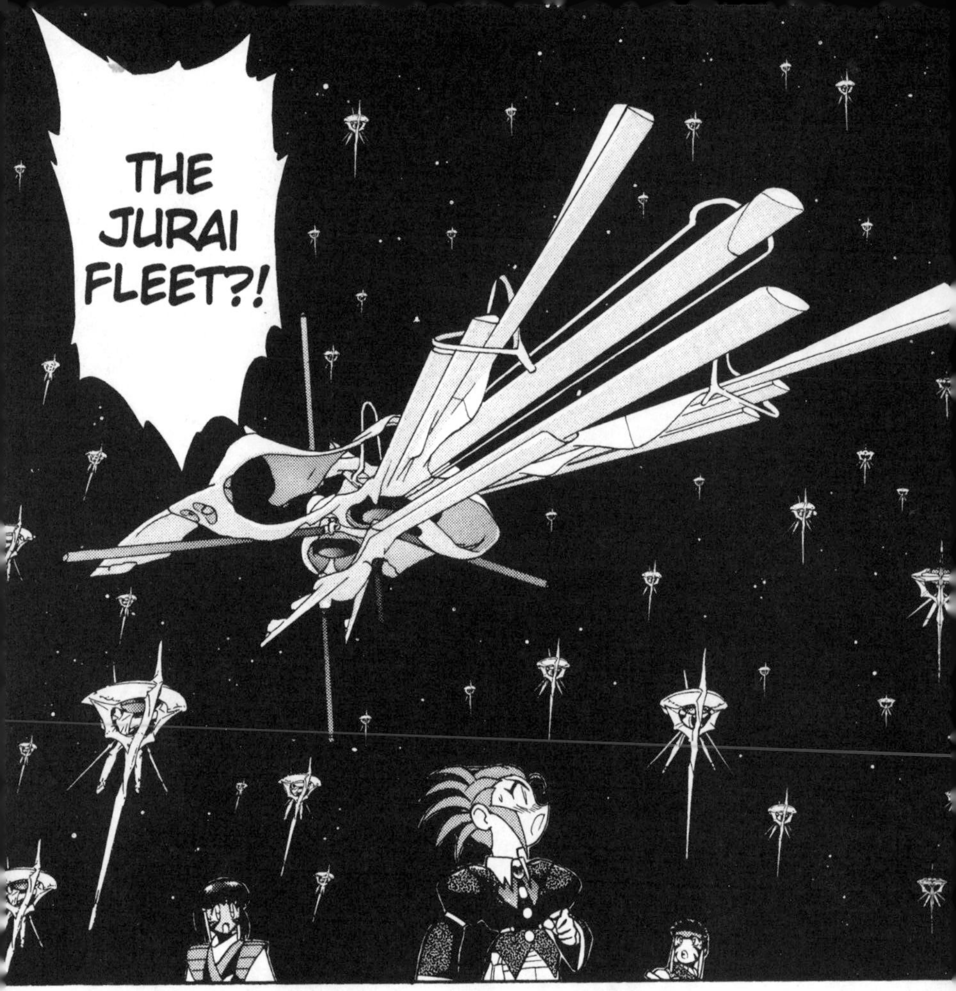
THE JURAI FLEET?!
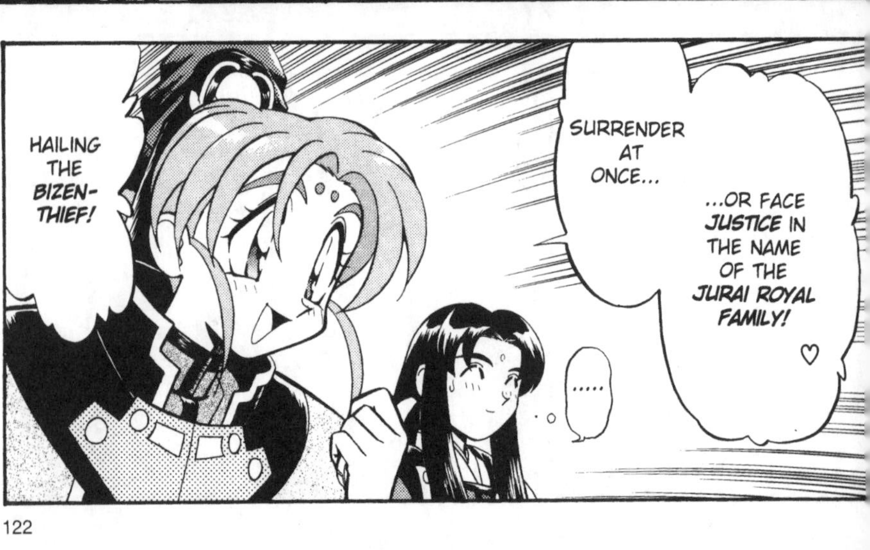
HAILING THE BIZEN-THIEF!
SURRENDER AT ONCE...
...OR FACE JUSTICE IN THE NAME OF THE JURAI ROYAL FAMILY! ♡
.....

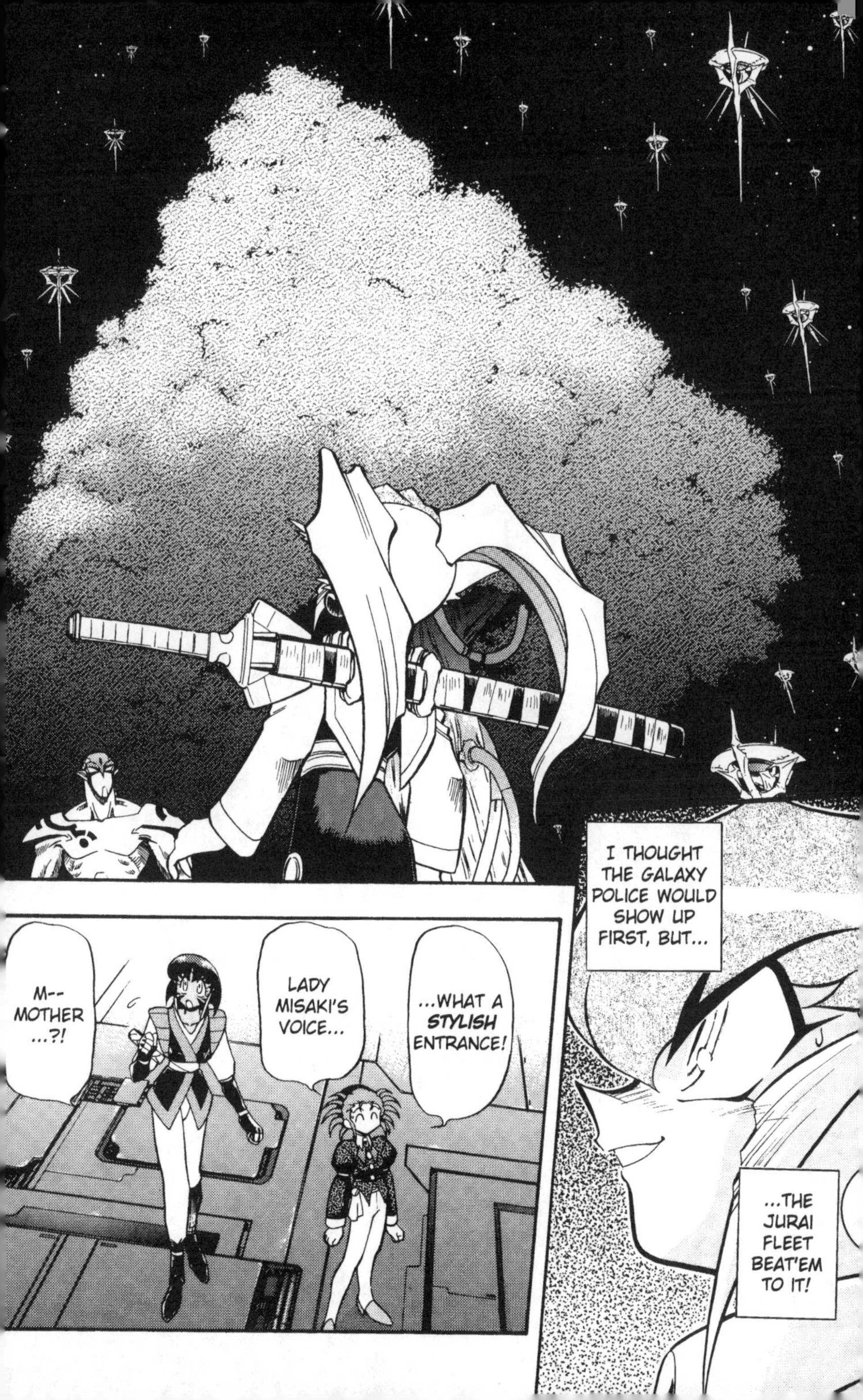
M-- MOTHER ...?!
LADY MISAKI'S VOICE...
...WHAT A **STYLISH** ENTRANCE!
I THOUGHT THE GALAXY POLICE WOULD SHOW UP FIRST, BUT...
...THE JURAI FLEET BEAT'EM TO IT!

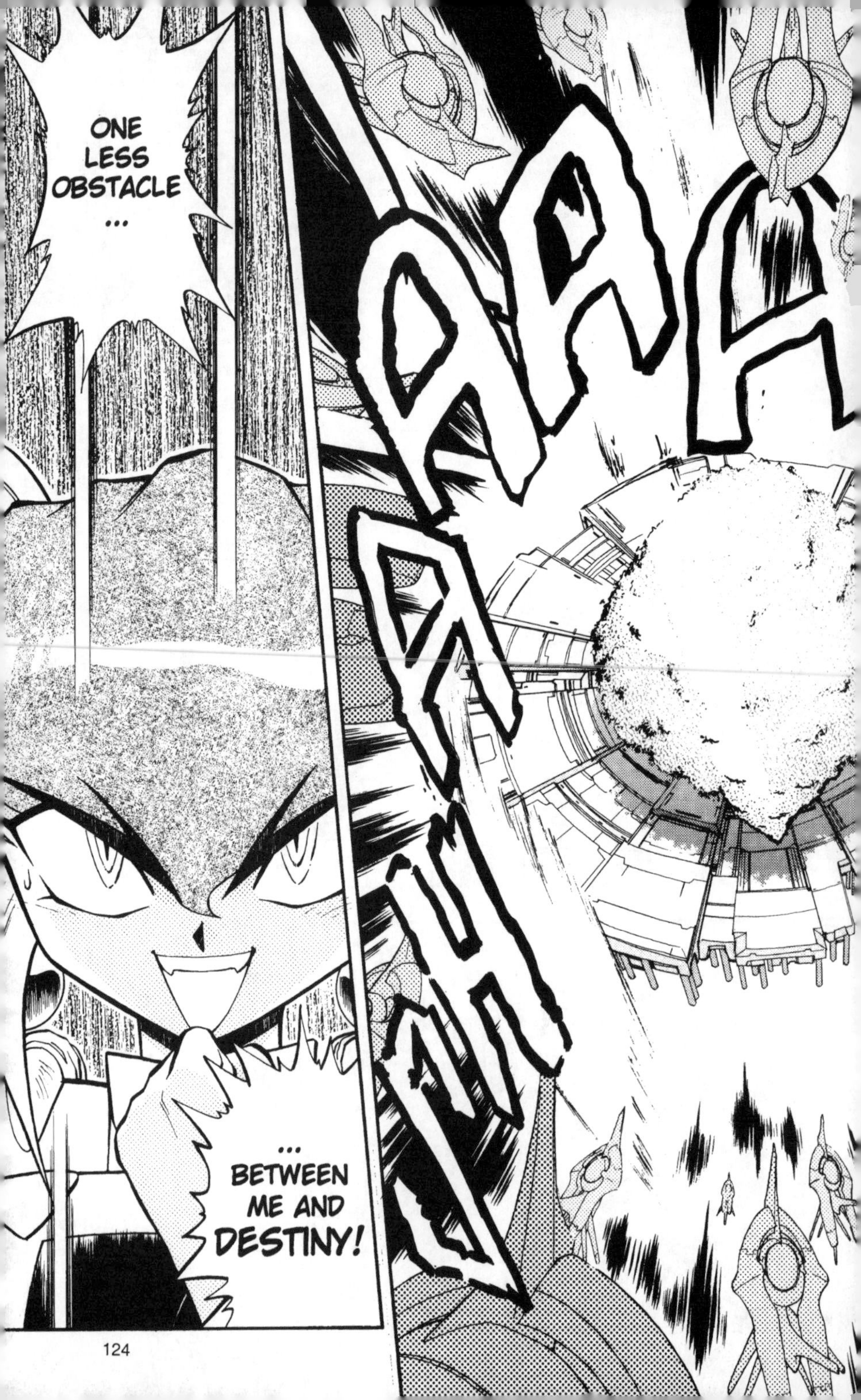
ONE LESS OBSTACLE ...
... BETWEEN ME AND DESTINY!

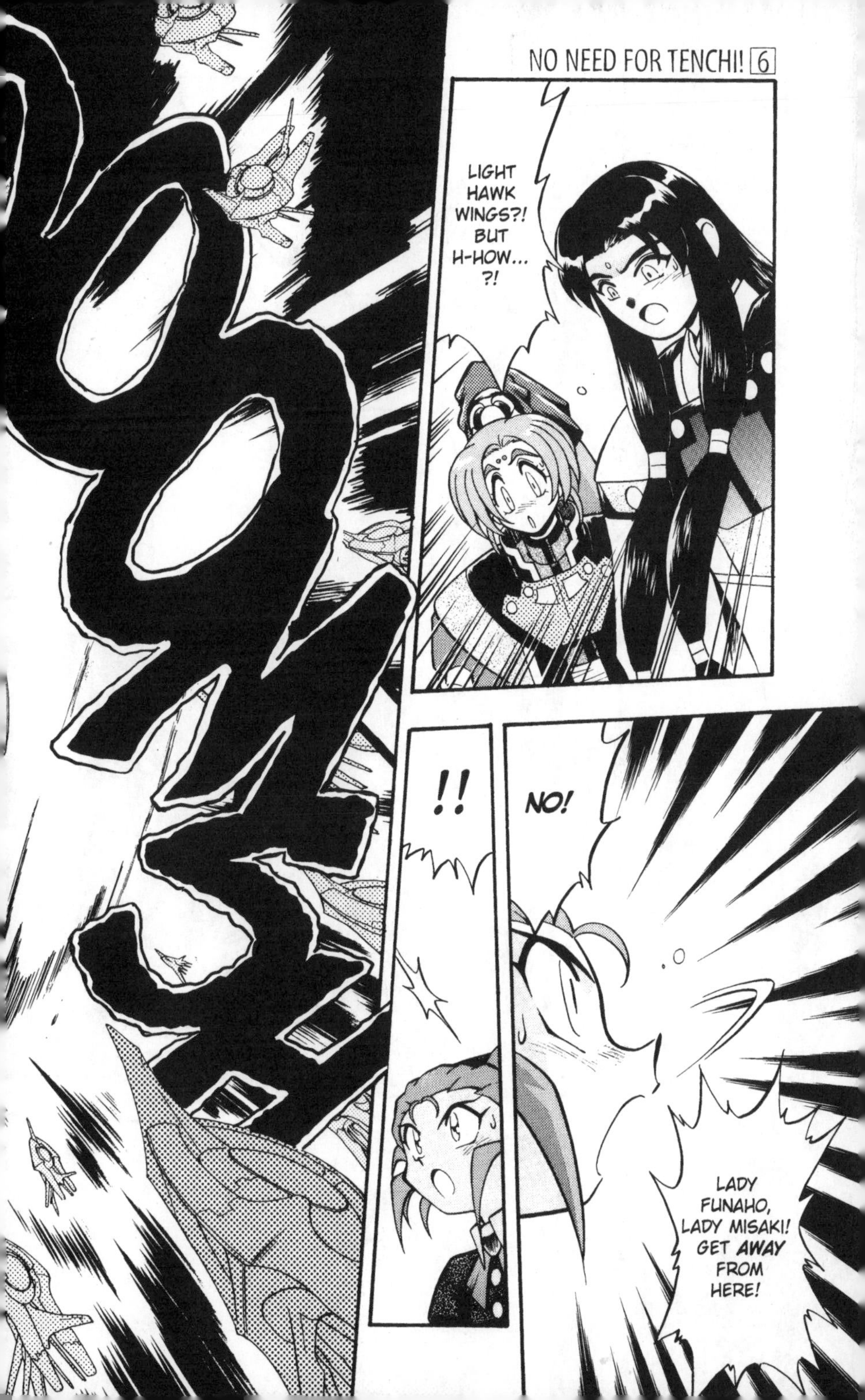
LIGHT HAWK WINGS?! BUT H-HOW... ?!
!!
NO!
LADY FUNAHO, LADY MISAKI! GET AWAY FROM HERE!

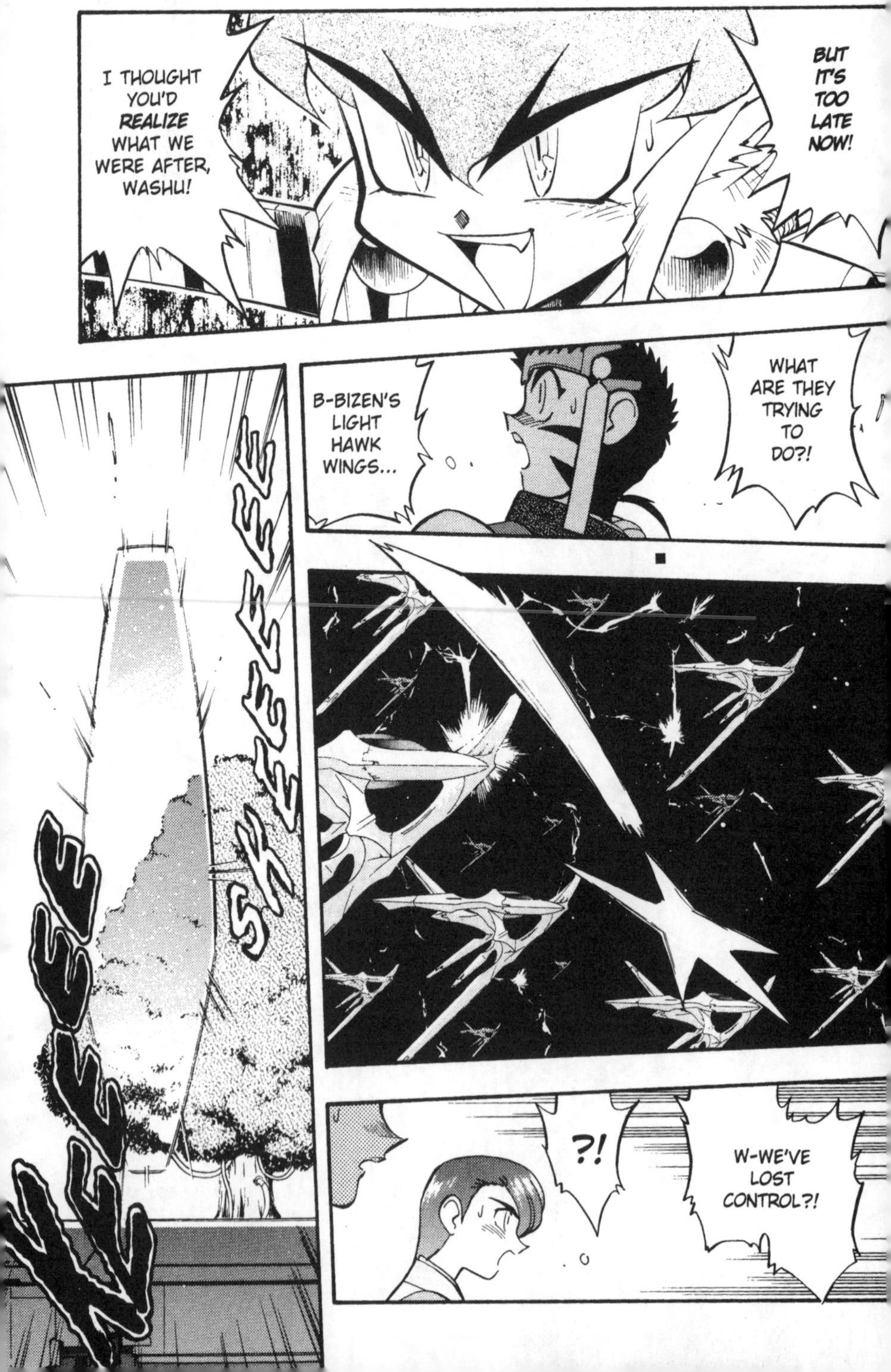
I THOUGHT YOU'D REALIZE WHAT WE WERE AFTER, WASHU!
BUT IT'S TOO LATE NOW!
SKREEEE
B-BIZEN'S LIGHT HAWK WINGS...
WHAT ARE THEY TRYING TO DO?!
?!
W-WE'VE LOST CONTROL?!

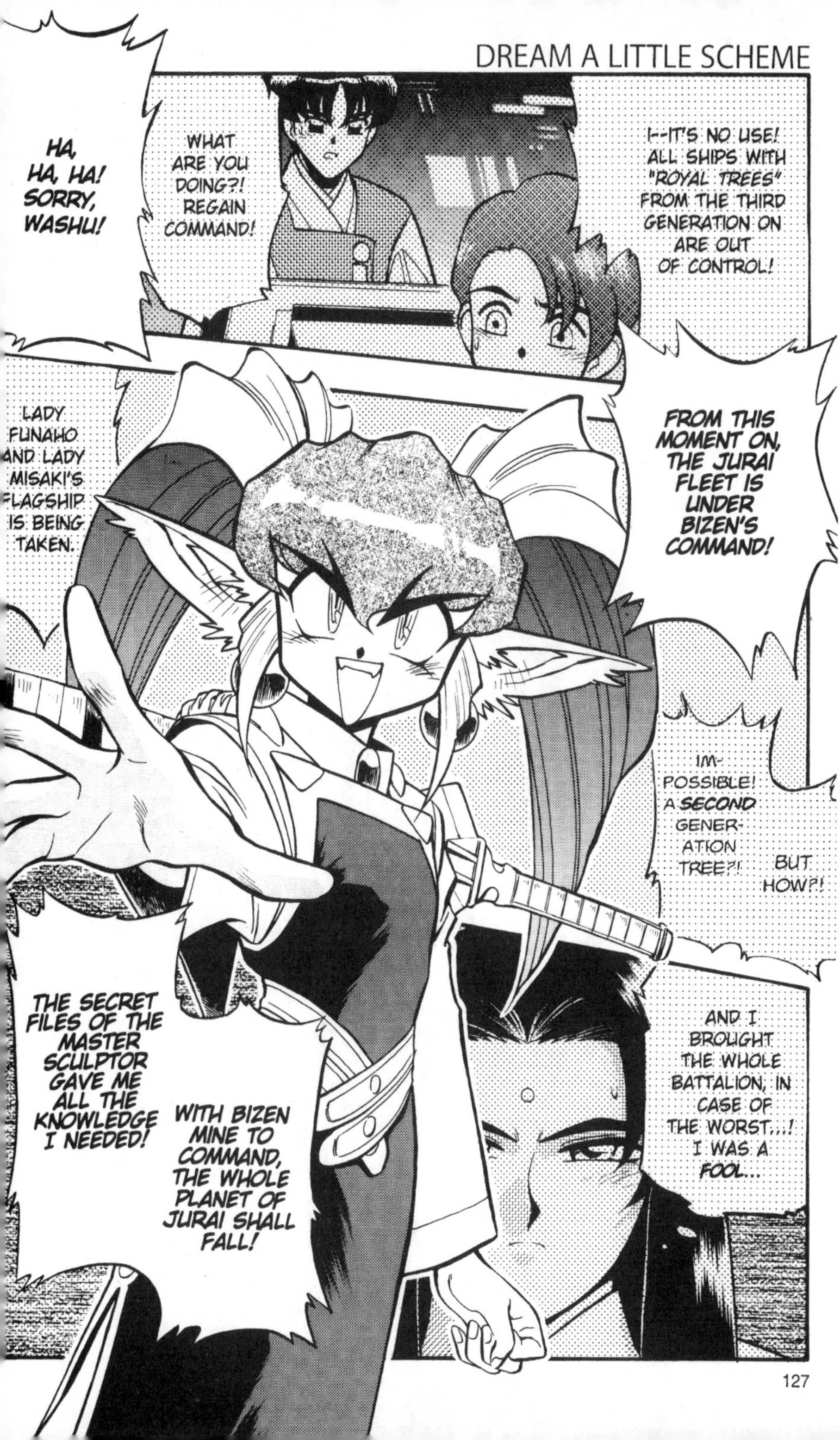
HA, HA, HA! SORRY, WASHU!
WHAT ARE YOU DOING?! REGAIN COMMAND!
I--IT'S NO USE! ALL SHIPS WITH "ROYAL TREES" FROM THE THIRD GENERATION ON ARE OUT OF CONTROL!
LADY FUNAHO AND LADY MISAKI'S FLAGSHIP IS BEING TAKEN.
FROM THIS MOMENT ON, THE JURAI FLEET IS UNDER BIZEN'S COMMAND!
IM-POSSIBLE! A SECOND GENER-ATION TREE?!
BUT HOW?!
THE SECRET FILES OF THE MASTER SCULPTOR GAVE ME ALL THE KNOWLEDGE I NEEDED!
WITH BIZEN MINE TO COMMAND, THE WHOLE PLANET OF JURAI SHALL FALL!
AND I BROUGHT THE WHOLE BATTALION, IN CASE OF THE WORST...! I WAS A FOOL...

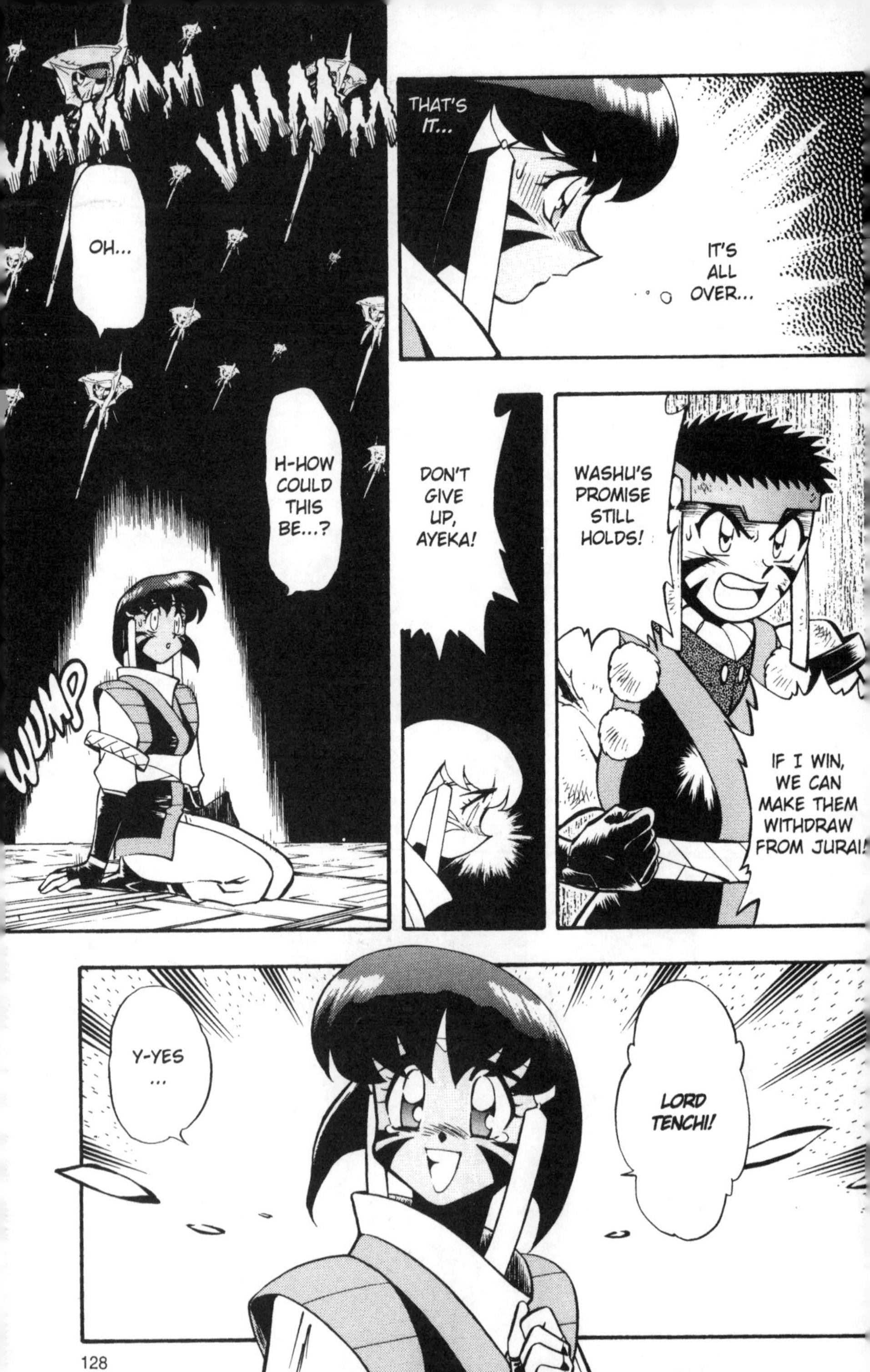
VMMMM VMMMM
OH...
H-HOW COULD THIS BE...?
WUMP
THAT'S IT...
IT'S ALL OVER...
DON'T GIVE UP, AYEKA!
WASHU'S PROMISE STILL HOLDS!
IF I WIN, WE CAN MAKE THEM WITHDRAW FROM JURAI!
Y-YES ...
LORD TENCHI!

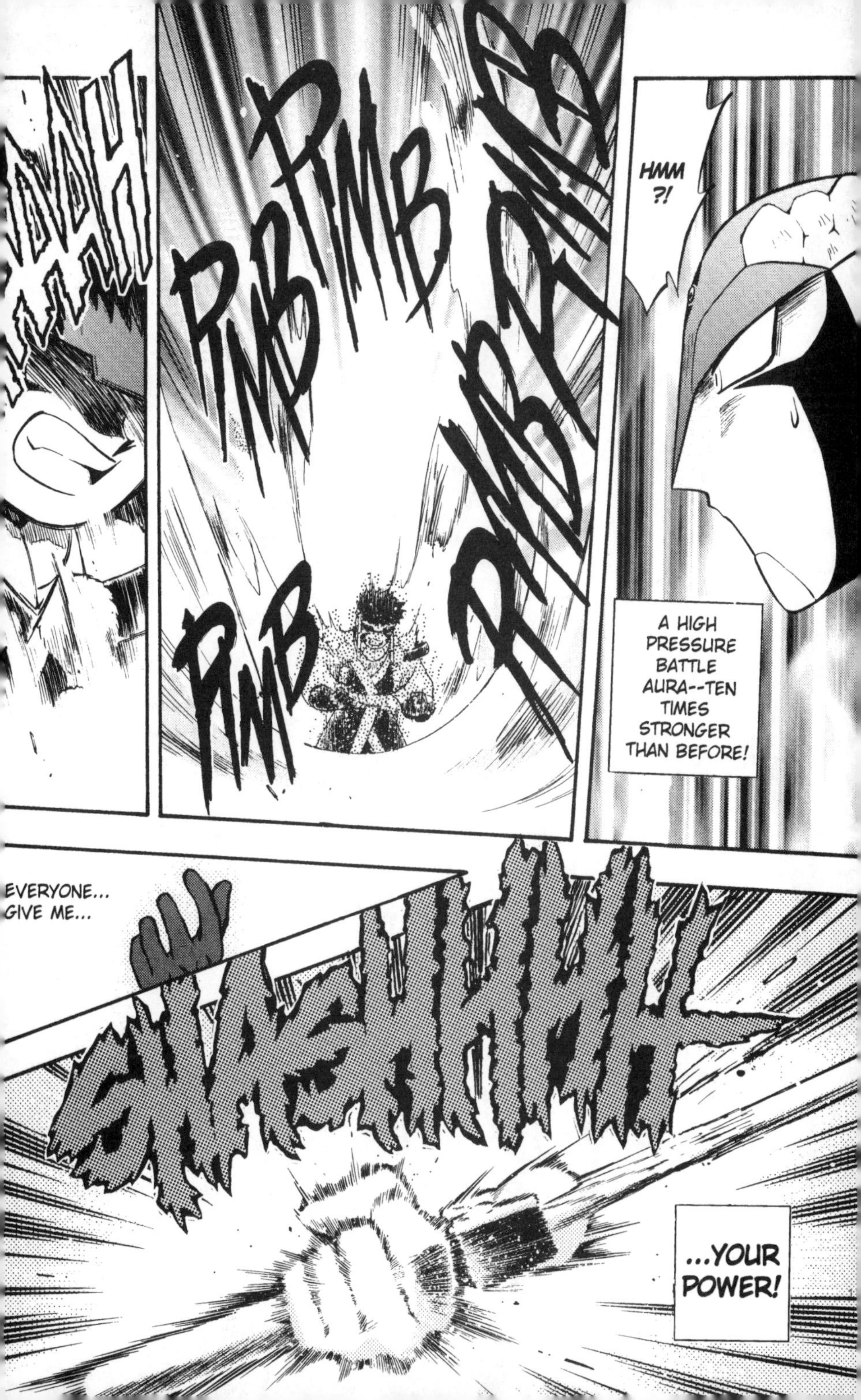
HMM ?!
A HIGH PRESSURE BATTLE AURA--TEN TIMES STRONGER THAN BEFORE!
EVERYONE... GIVE ME...
...YOUR POWER!

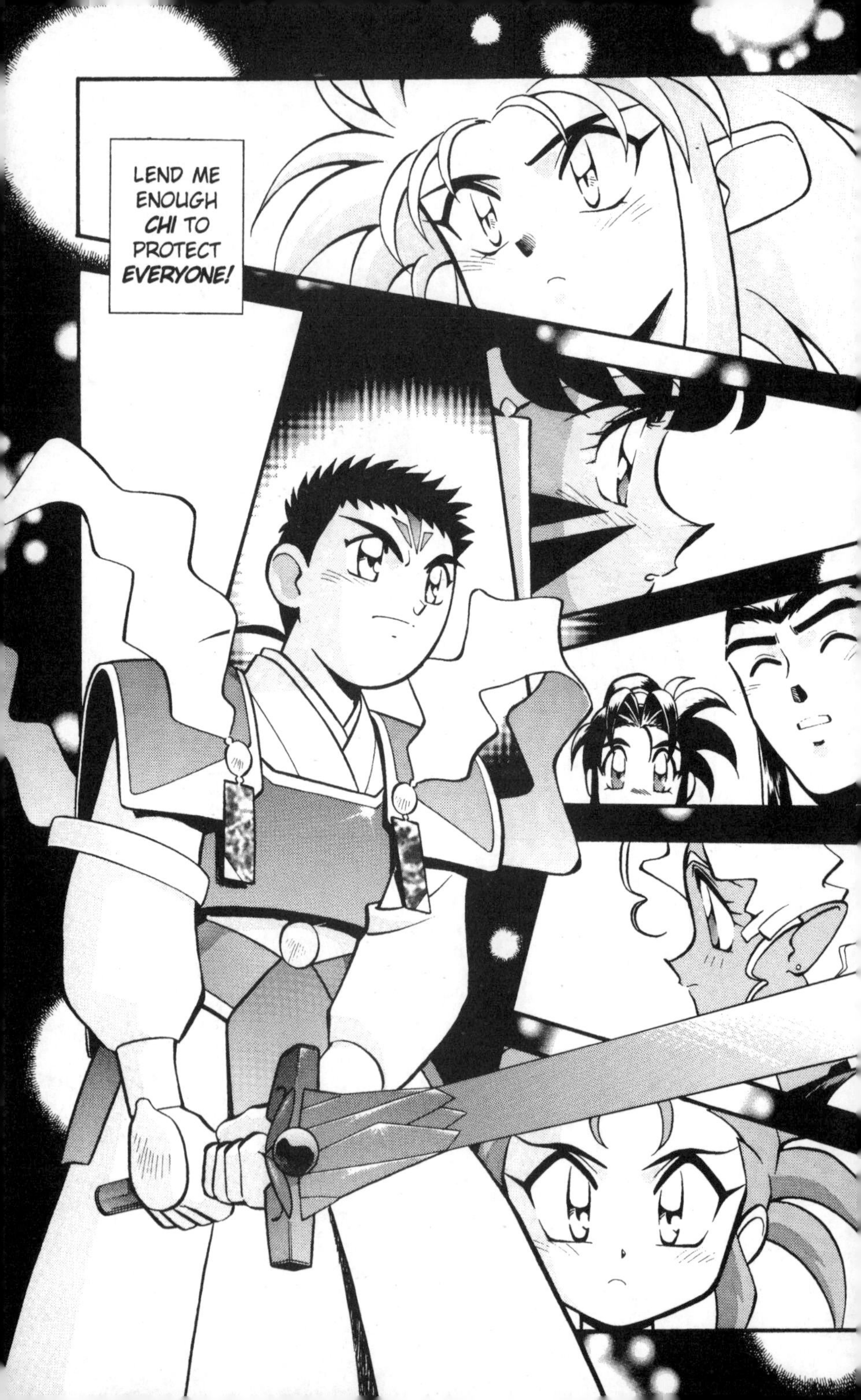
LEND ME ENOUGH CHI TO PROTECT EVERYONE!

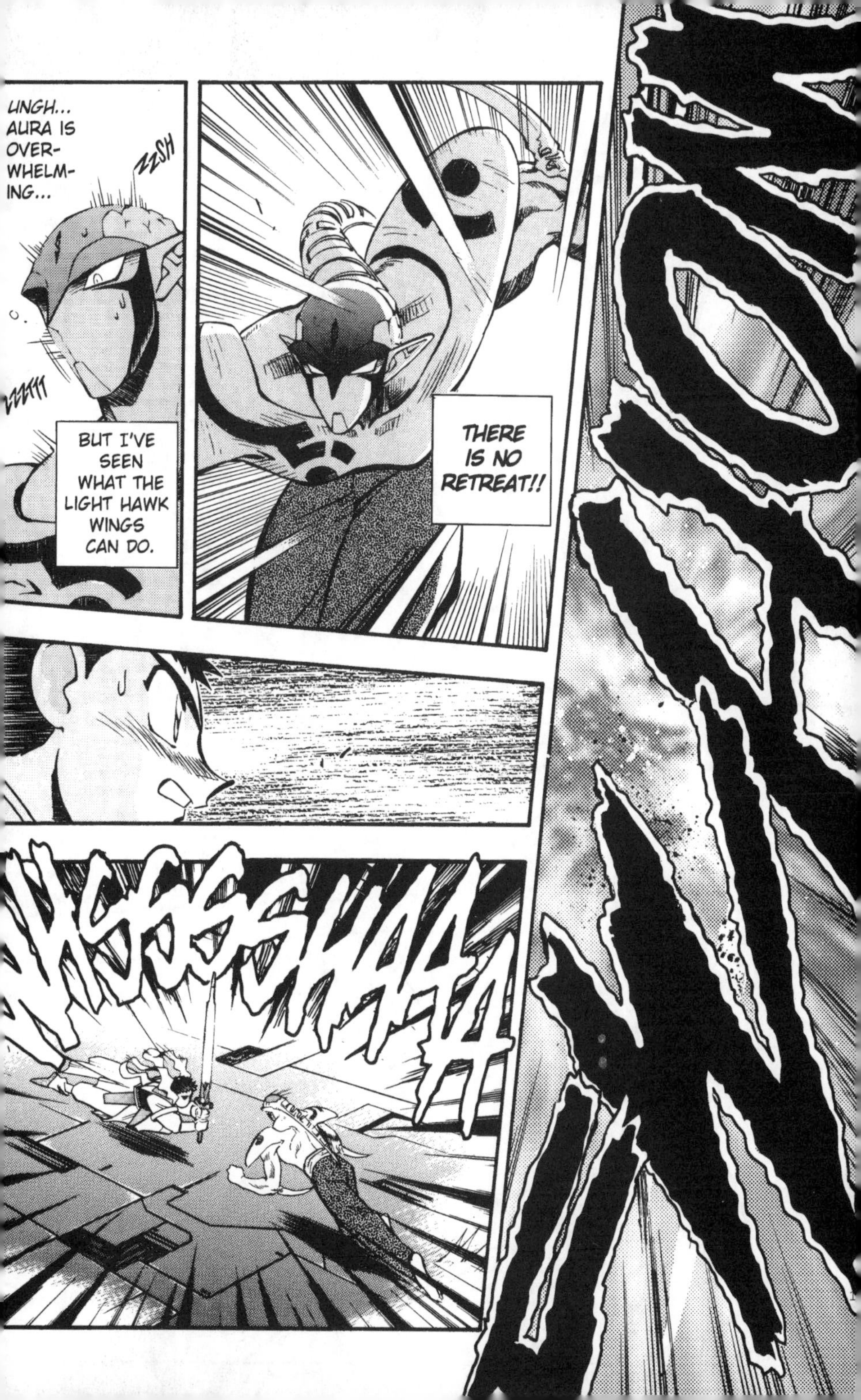
UNGH... AURA IS OVER-WHELM-ING...
ZZSH
BUT I'VE SEEN WHAT THE LIGHT HAWK WINGS CAN DO.
THERE IS NO RETREAT!!

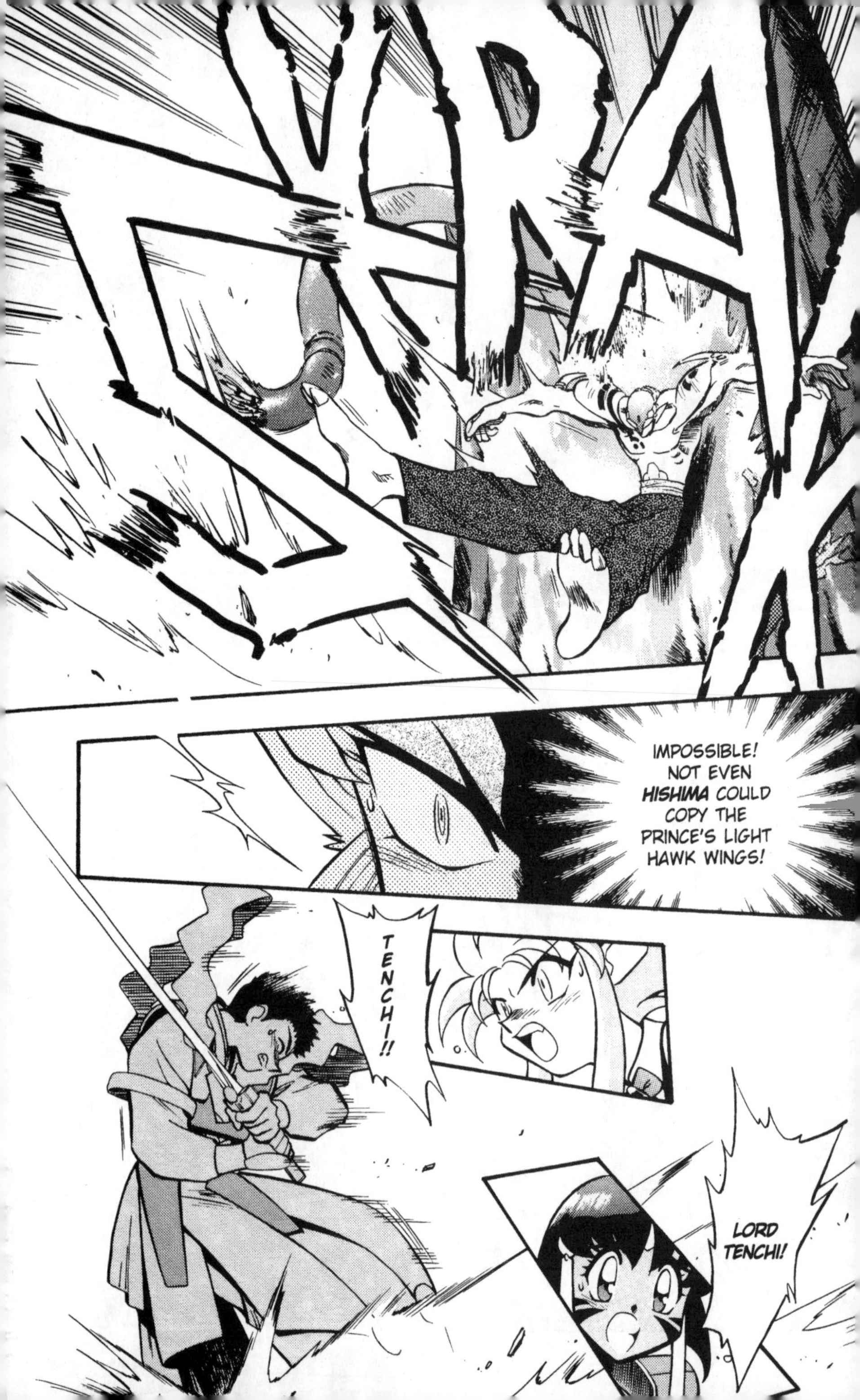
IMPOSSIBLE! NOT EVEN HISHIMA COULD COPY THE PRINCE'S LIGHT HAWK WINGS!
TENCHI!!
LORD TENCHI!

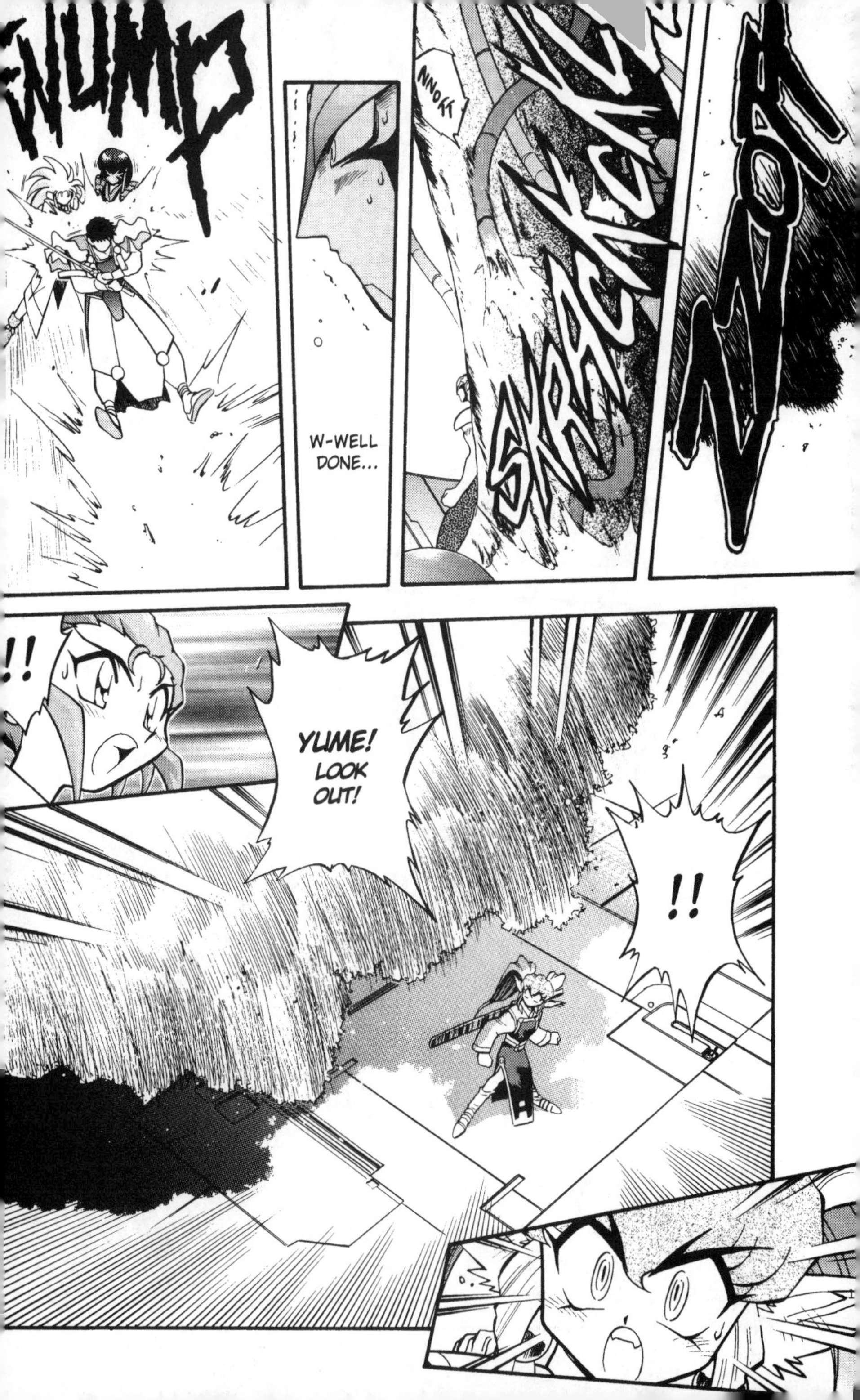
NNOFF
W-WELL DONE...
!!
YUME! LOOK OUT!
!!

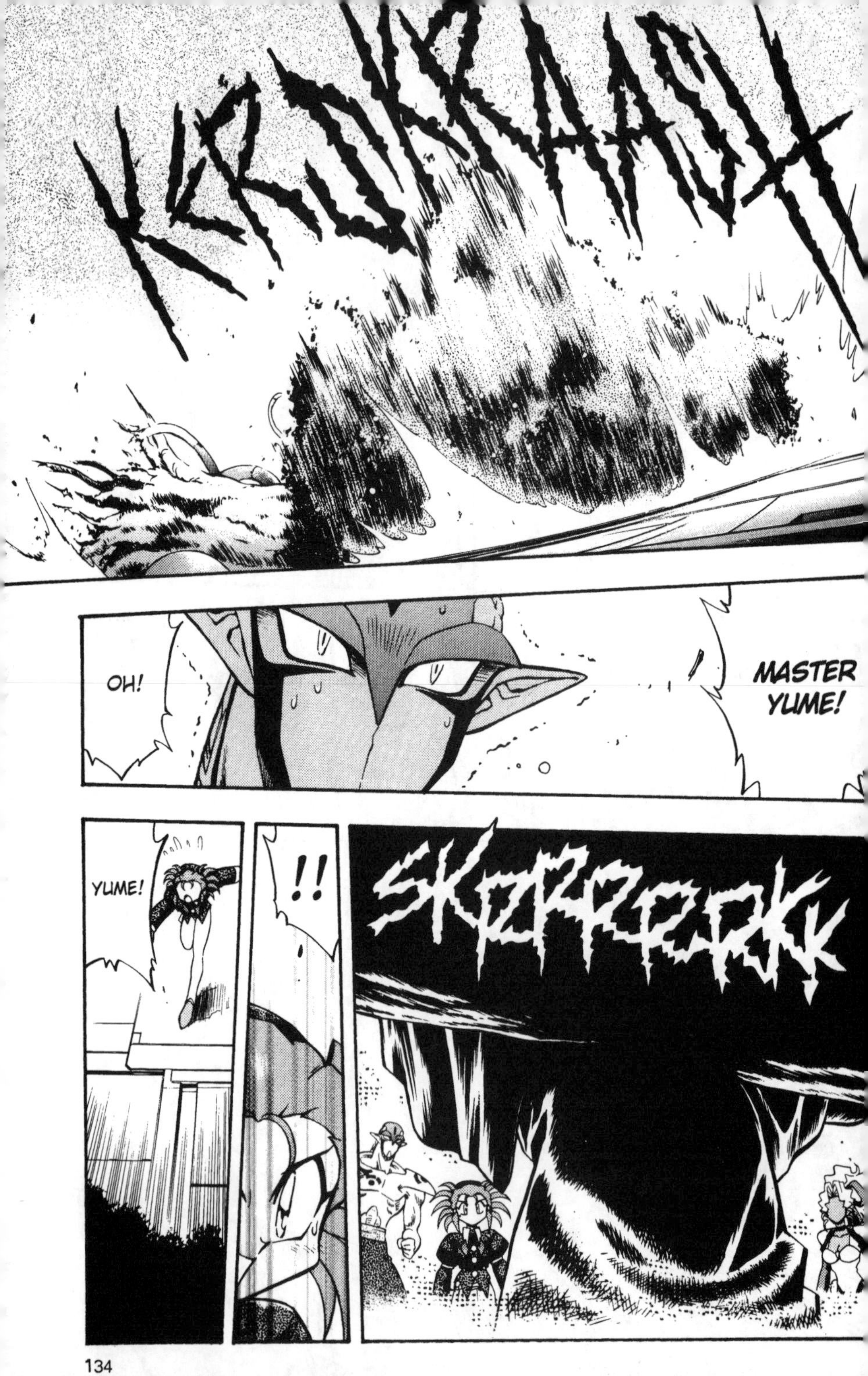
KRDKRAASH
OH!
MASTER YUME!
YUME!
!!
SKRRRRKK

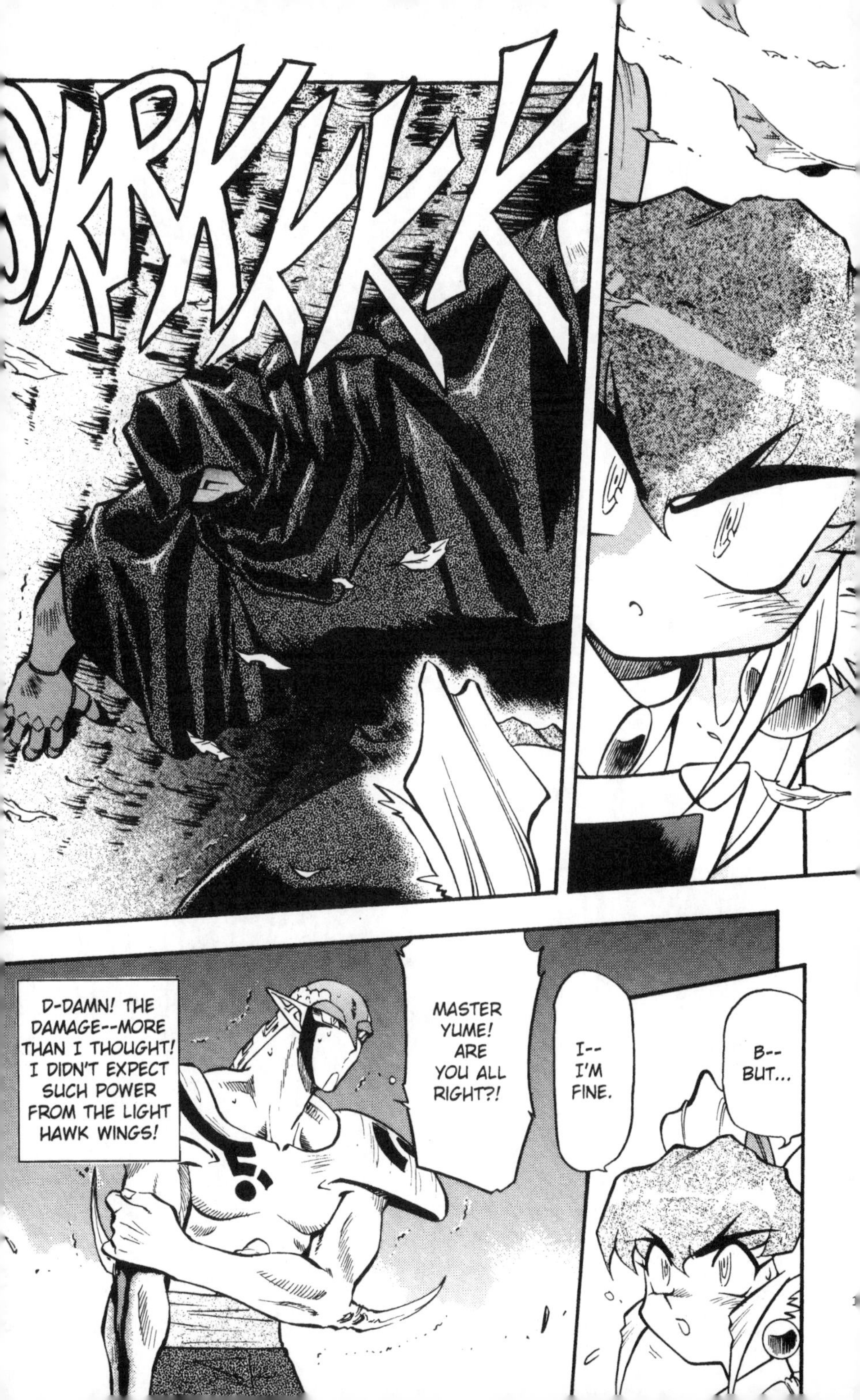
SKRKKKK
D-DAMN! THE DAMAGE--MORE THAN I THOUGHT! I DIDN'T EXPECT SUCH POWER FROM THE LIGHT HAWK WINGS!
MASTER YUME! ARE YOU ALL RIGHT?!
I-- I'M FINE.
B-- BUT...

TAKA-
SHIMA...

SKKK

BECAUSE
OF MY
KICK...

MASTER
YUME,
HURRY!

B--
BUT...

WHMSK

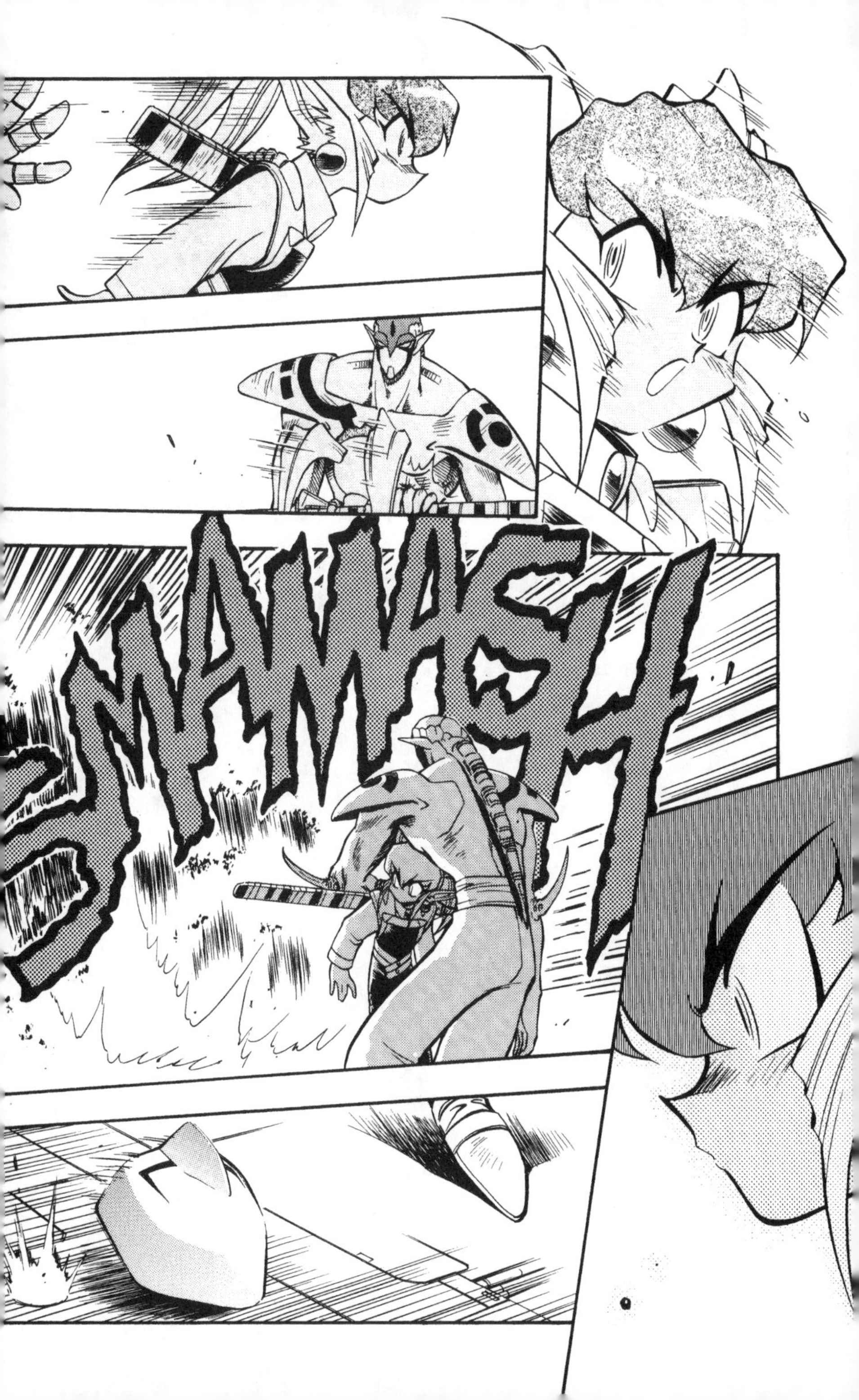
SMAAASH

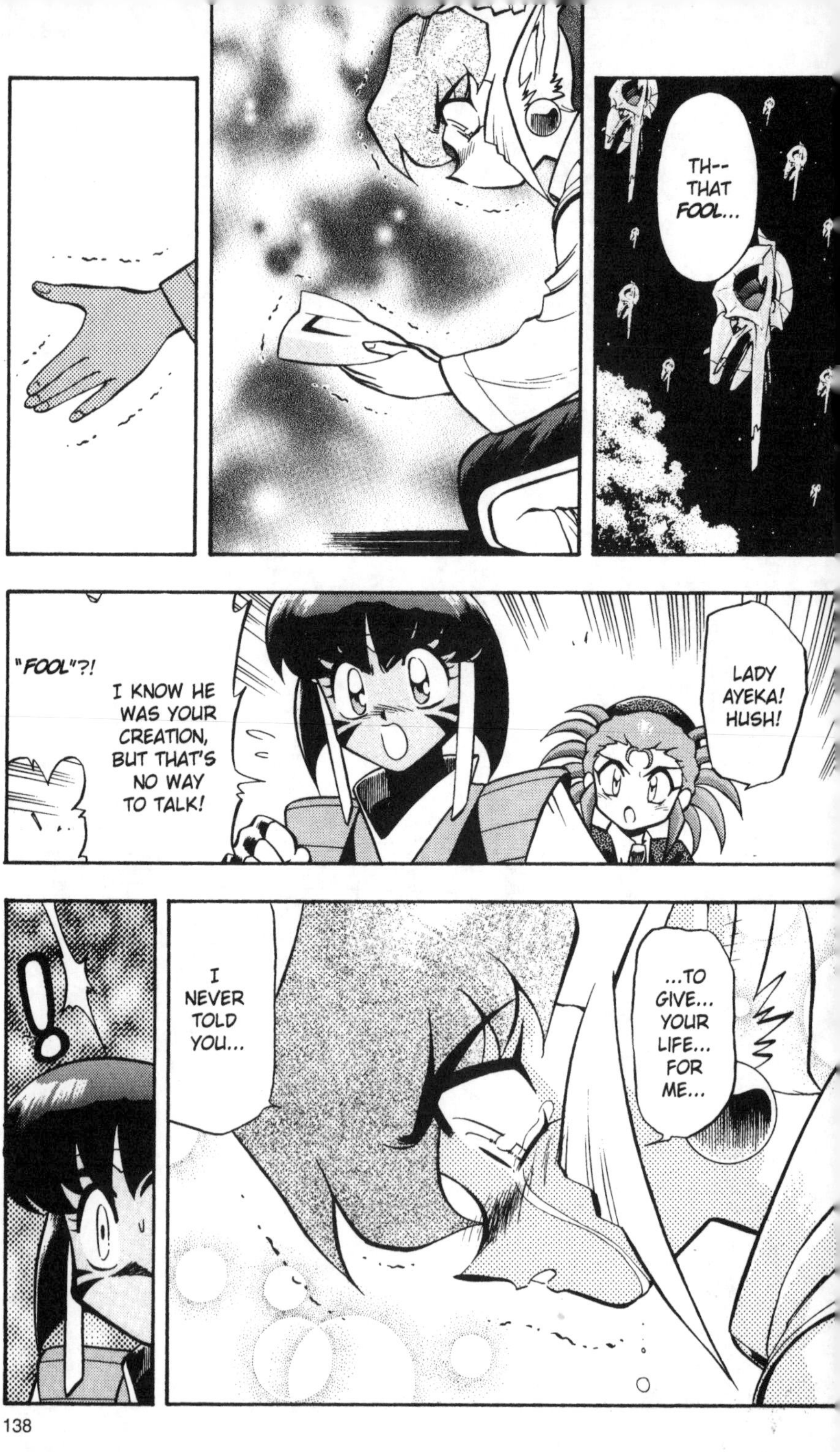
TH-- THAT FOOL...
"FOOL"?!
I KNOW HE WAS YOUR CREATION, BUT THAT'S NO WAY TO TALK!
LADY AYEKA! HUSH!
!
I NEVER TOLD YOU...
...TO GIVE... YOUR LIFE... FOR ME...

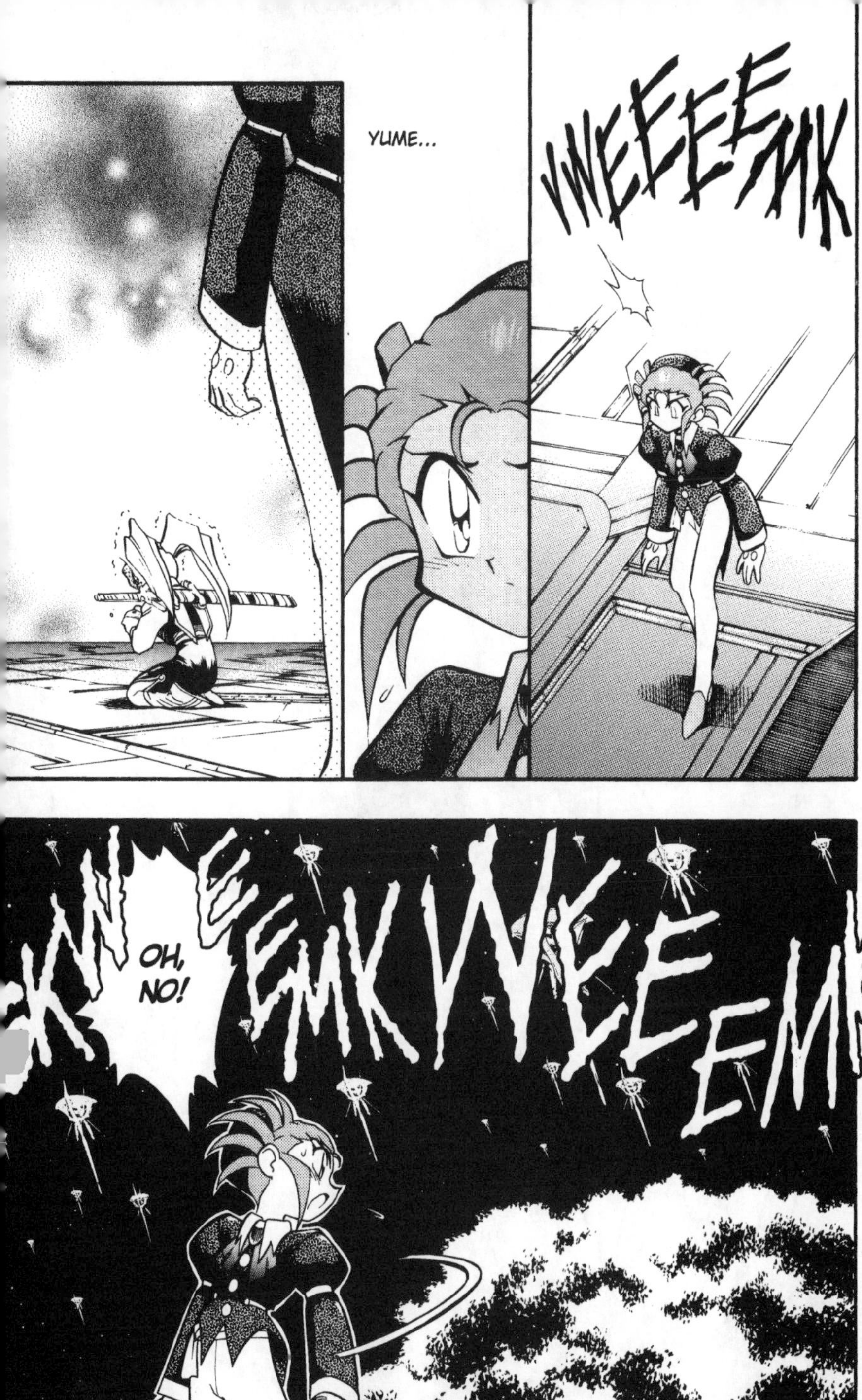
YUME...
OH, NO!

ALL RIGHT, WASHU! **NOW** WHAT'S GOING ON?

IF WE DON'T DO SOMETHING **FAST**, THE **ROYAL TREES** UNDER BIZEN'S COMMAND WILL SET OFF A **CHAIN REACTION** OF EXPLOSIVE CONTRACTIONS!

THE SHOCK-- IT'S CAUSED **BIZEN** TO COMPLETELY LOSE CONTROL!

I'M AFRAID THAT THE WORST CASE SCENARIO, IN SUCH A SITUATION, IS THE **UTTER DESTRUCTION** OF OUR **GALAXY**!

ales of Tenchi #6

PEACE AT LAST

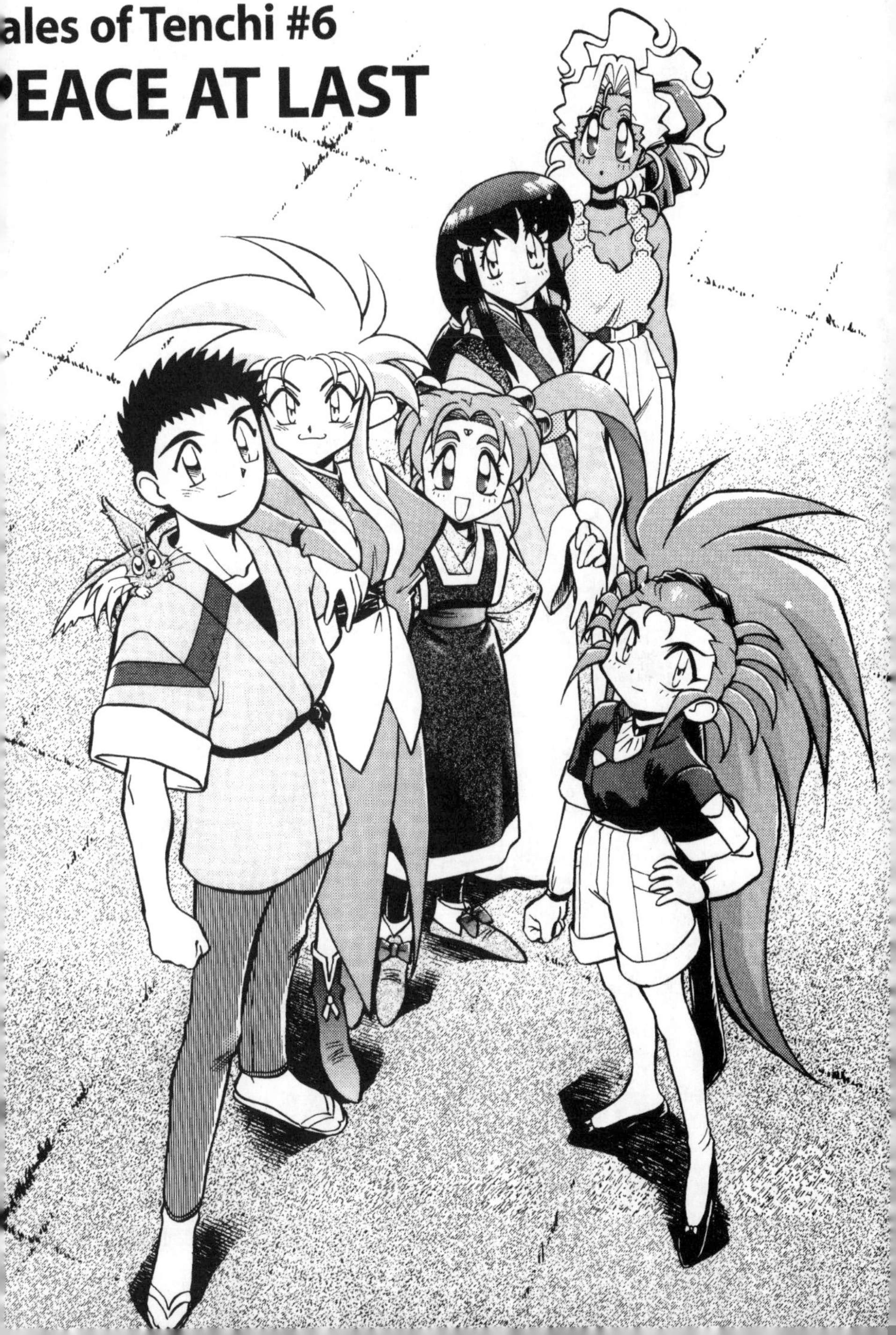

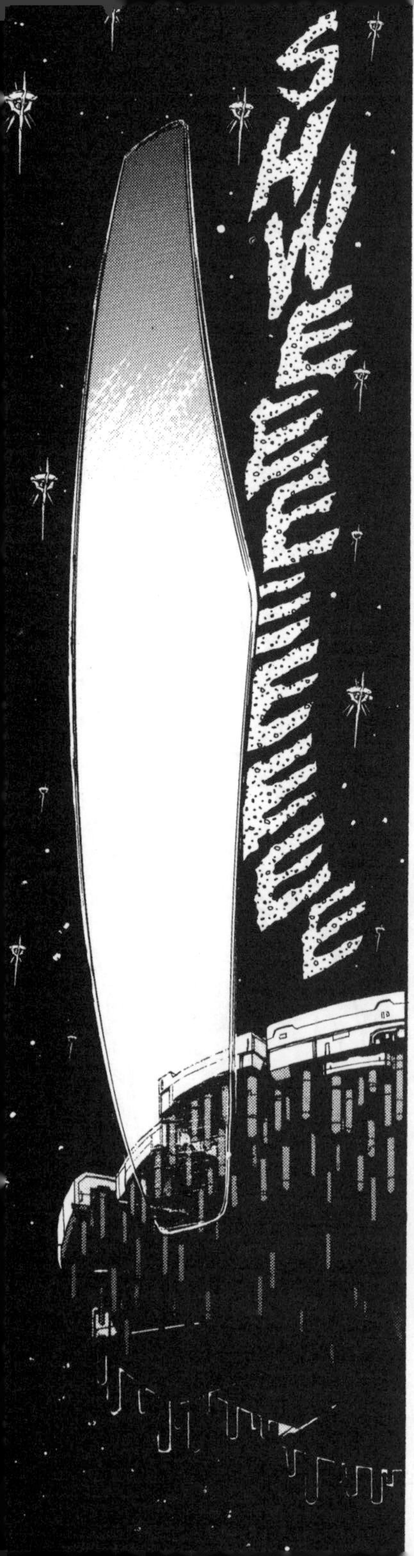
SHWEEEEEEEEEW

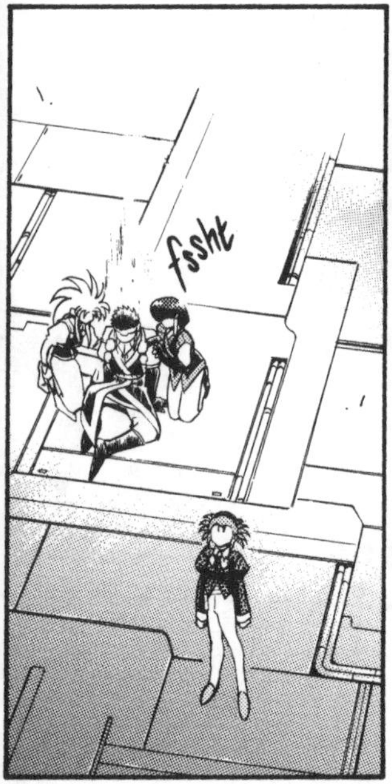
fssht

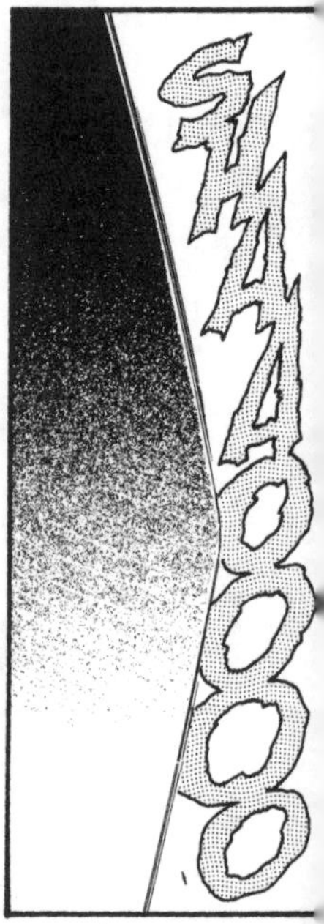
SHAAOOOO

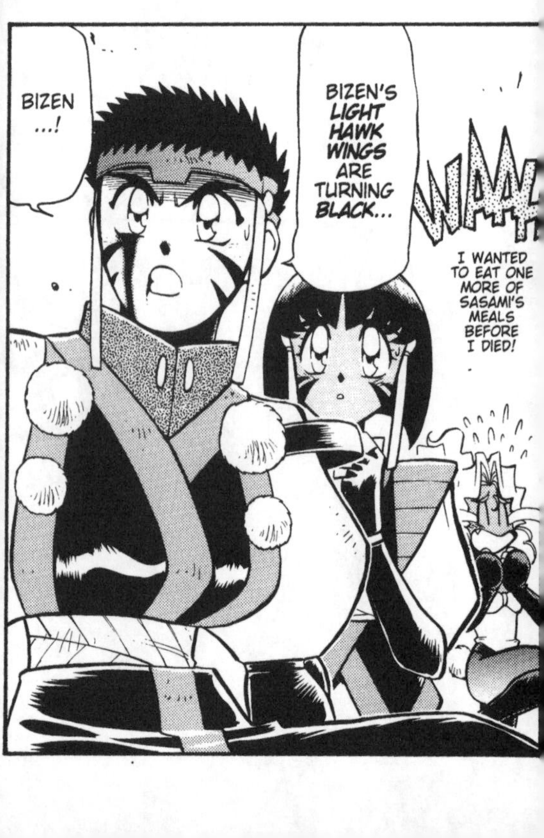
BIZEN ...!
BIZEN'S LIGHT HAWK WINGS ARE TURNING BLACK...
WAAAH
I WANTED TO EAT ONE MORE OF SASAMI'S MEALS BEFORE I DIED!

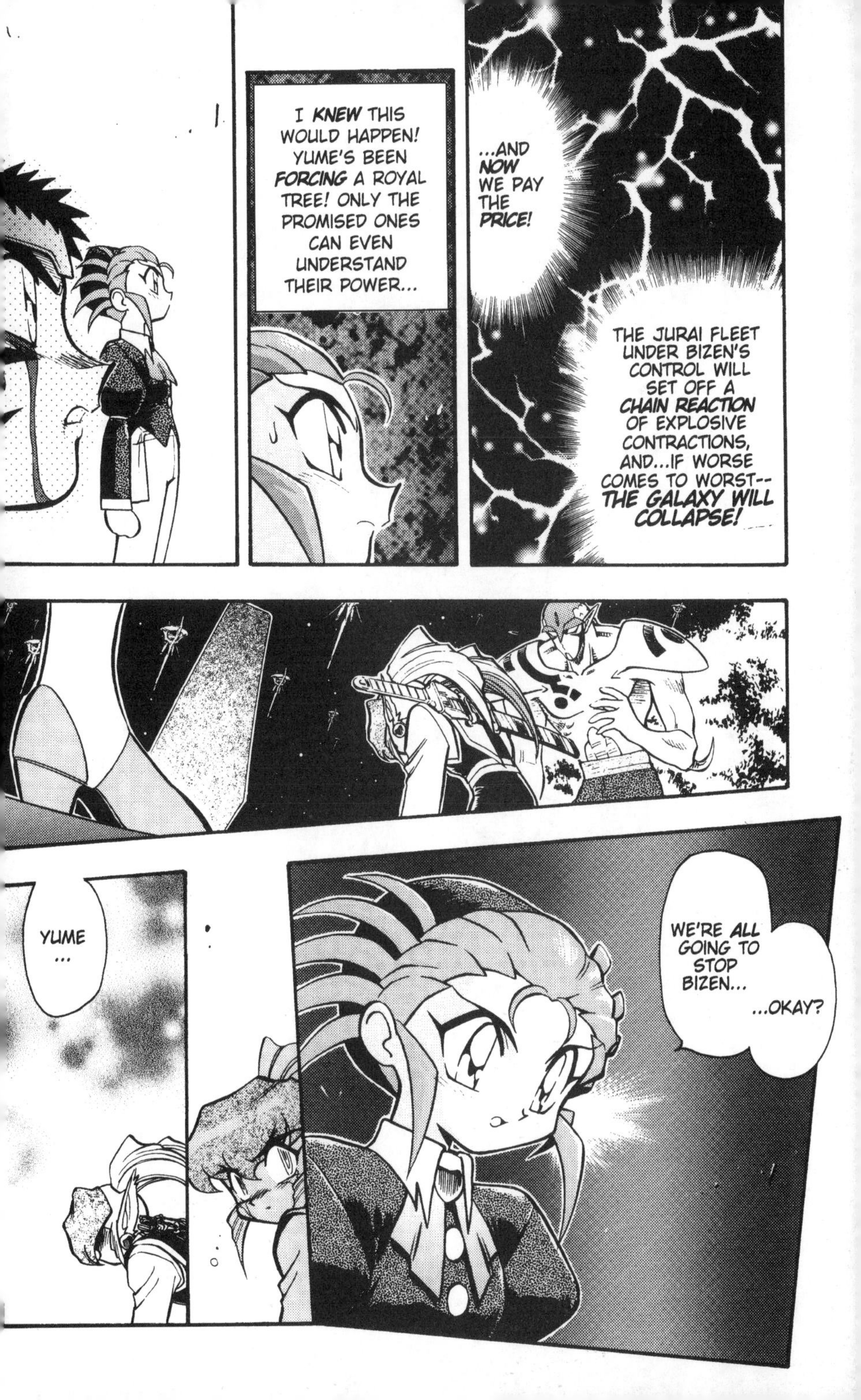
I KNEW THIS WOULD HAPPEN! YUME'S BEEN FORCING A ROYAL TREE! ONLY THE PROMISED ONES CAN EVEN UNDERSTAND THEIR POWER...
...AND NOW WE PAY THE PRICE!
THE JURAI FLEET UNDER BIZEN'S CONTROL WILL SET OFF A CHAIN REACTION OF EXPLOSIVE CONTRACTIONS, AND...IF WORSE COMES TO WORST--THE GALAXY WILL COLLAPSE!
YUME ...
WE'RE ALL GOING TO STOP BIZEN...
...OKAY?

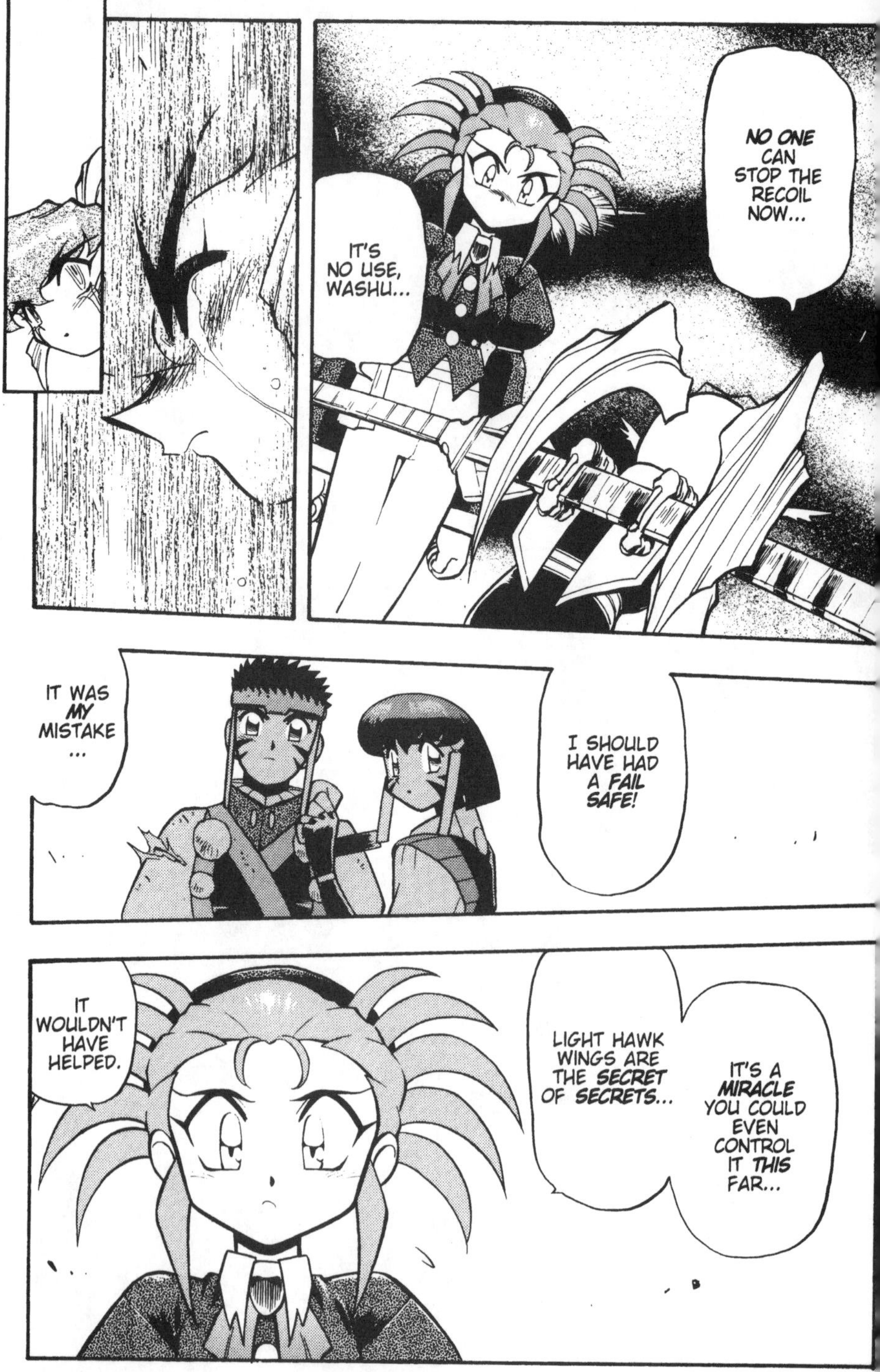
IT'S NO USE, WASHU...
NO ONE CAN STOP THE RECOIL NOW...
IT WAS MY MISTAKE ...
I SHOULD HAVE HAD A FAIL SAFE!
IT WOULDN'T HAVE HELPED.
LIGHT HAWK WINGS ARE THE SECRET OF SECRETS...
IT'S A MIRACLE YOU COULD EVEN CONTROL IT THIS FAR...

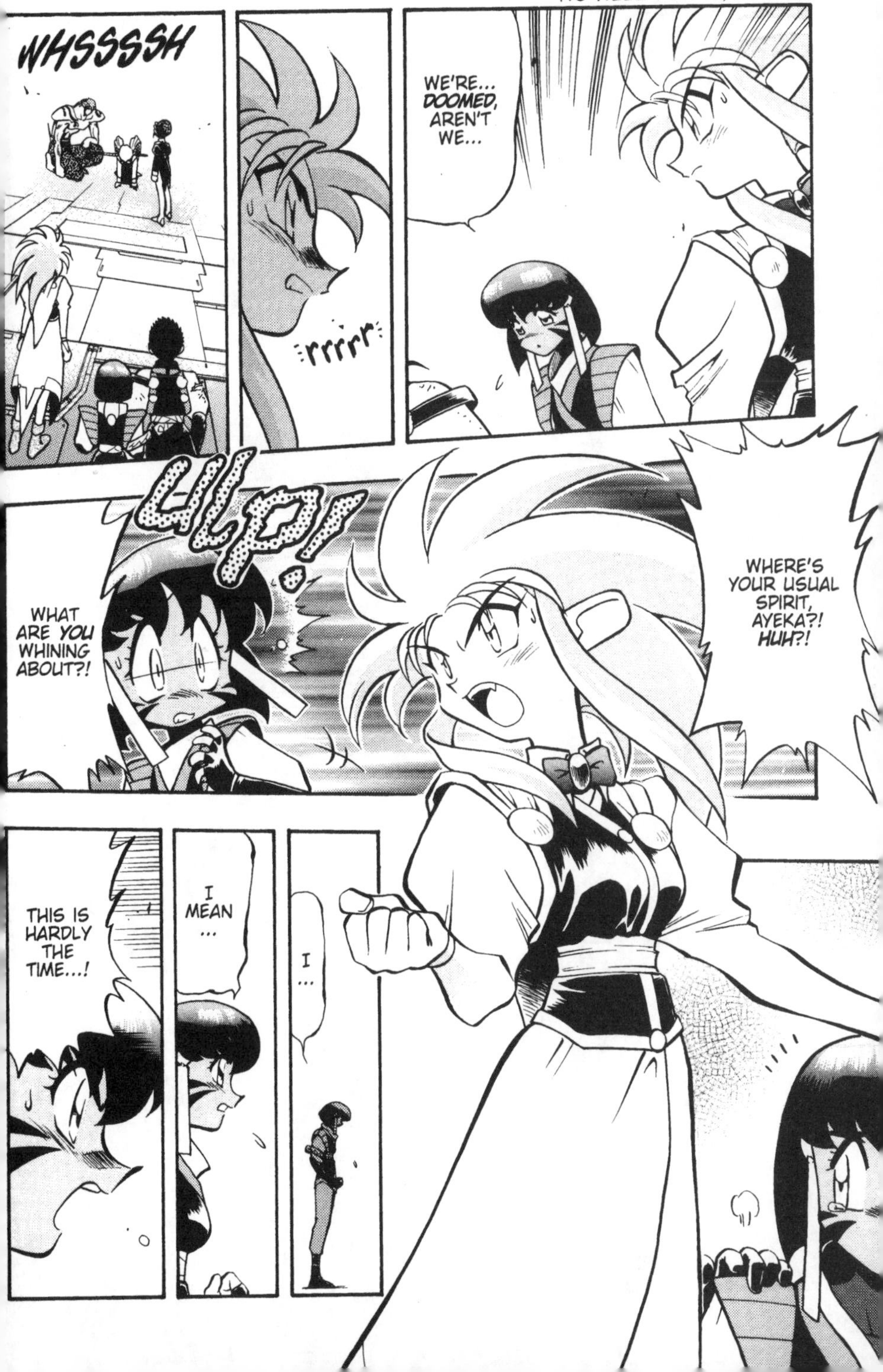
WHSSSSH
rrrrr
WE'RE... **DOOMED,** AREN'T WE...
ULP!
WHAT ARE *YOU* WHINING ABOUT?!
WHERE'S YOUR USUAL SPIRIT, AYEKA?! **HUH?!**
THIS IS HARDLY THE TIME...!
I MEAN ...
I ...

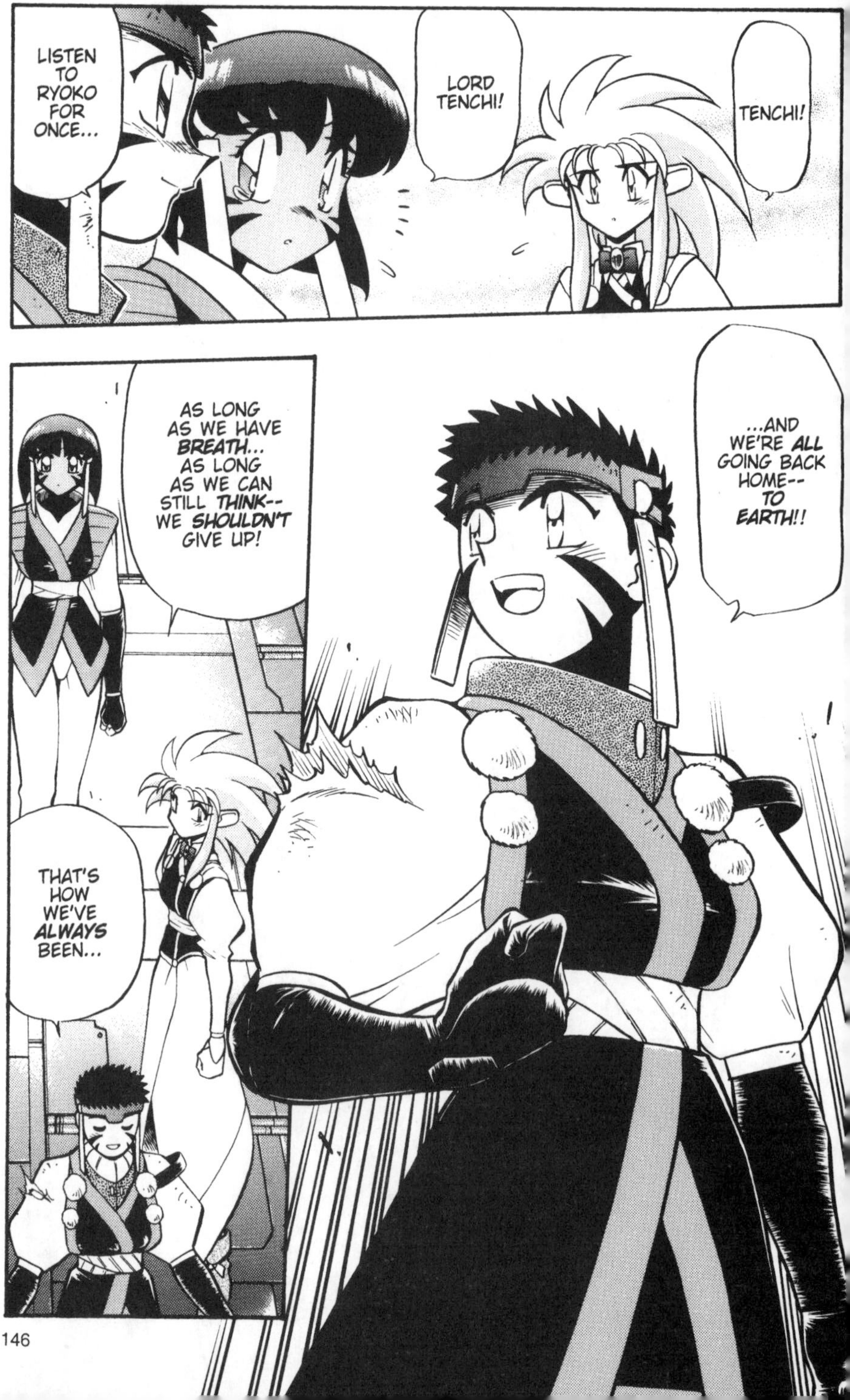
LISTEN TO RYOKO FOR ONCE...
LORD TENCHI!
TENCHI!
AS LONG AS WE HAVE BREATH... AS LONG AS WE CAN STILL THINK-- WE SHOULDN'T GIVE UP!
...AND WE'RE ALL GOING BACK HOME-- TO EARTH!!
THAT'S HOW WE'VE ALWAYS BEEN...

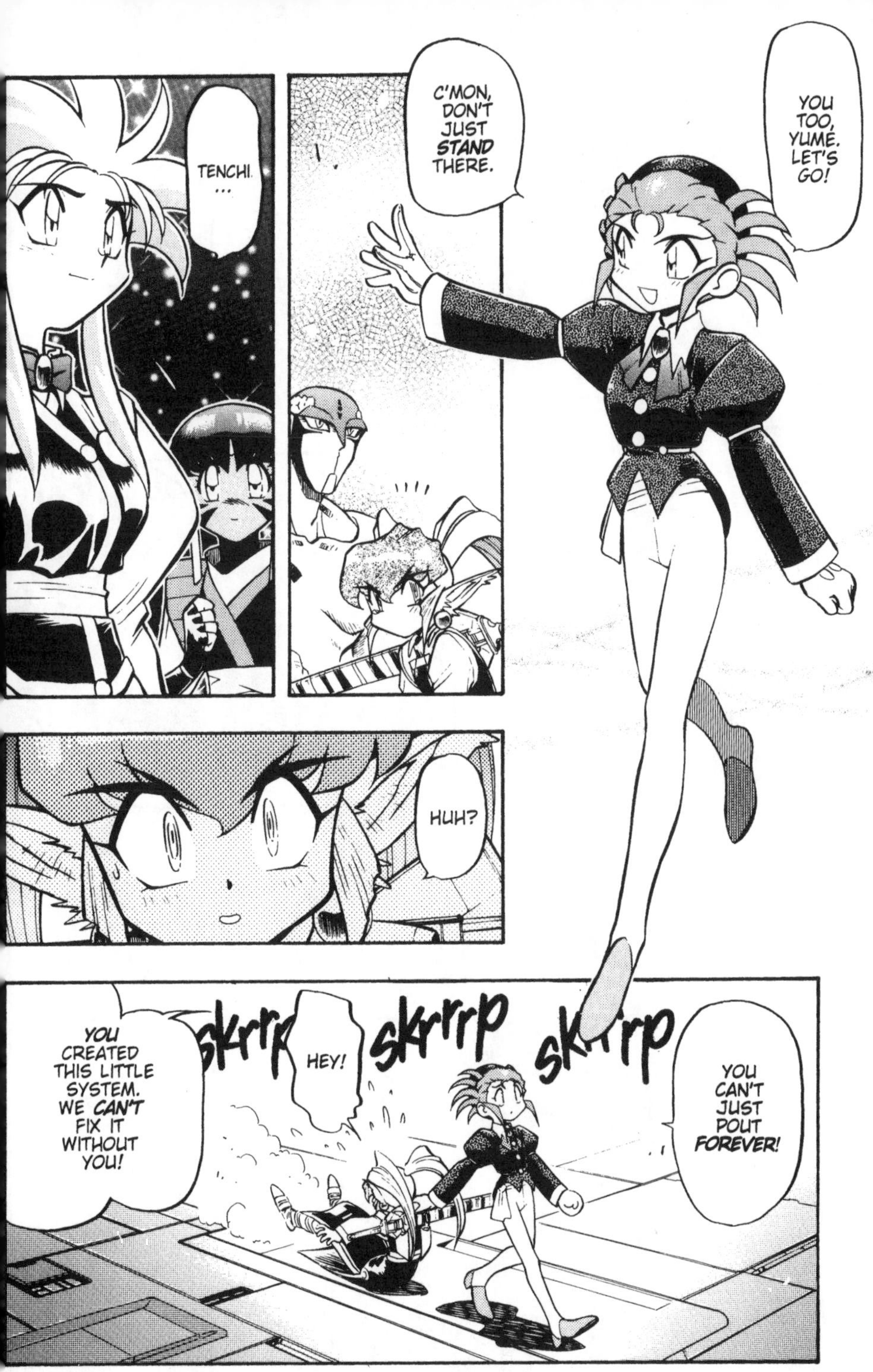

TENCHI. ...
C'MON, DON'T JUST STAND THERE.
YOU TOO, YUME. LET'S GO!
HUH?
YOU CREATED THIS LITTLE SYSTEM. WE CAN'T FIX IT WITHOUT YOU!
skrrp
HEY!
skrrrp
skrrrp
YOU CAN'T JUST POUT FOREVER!

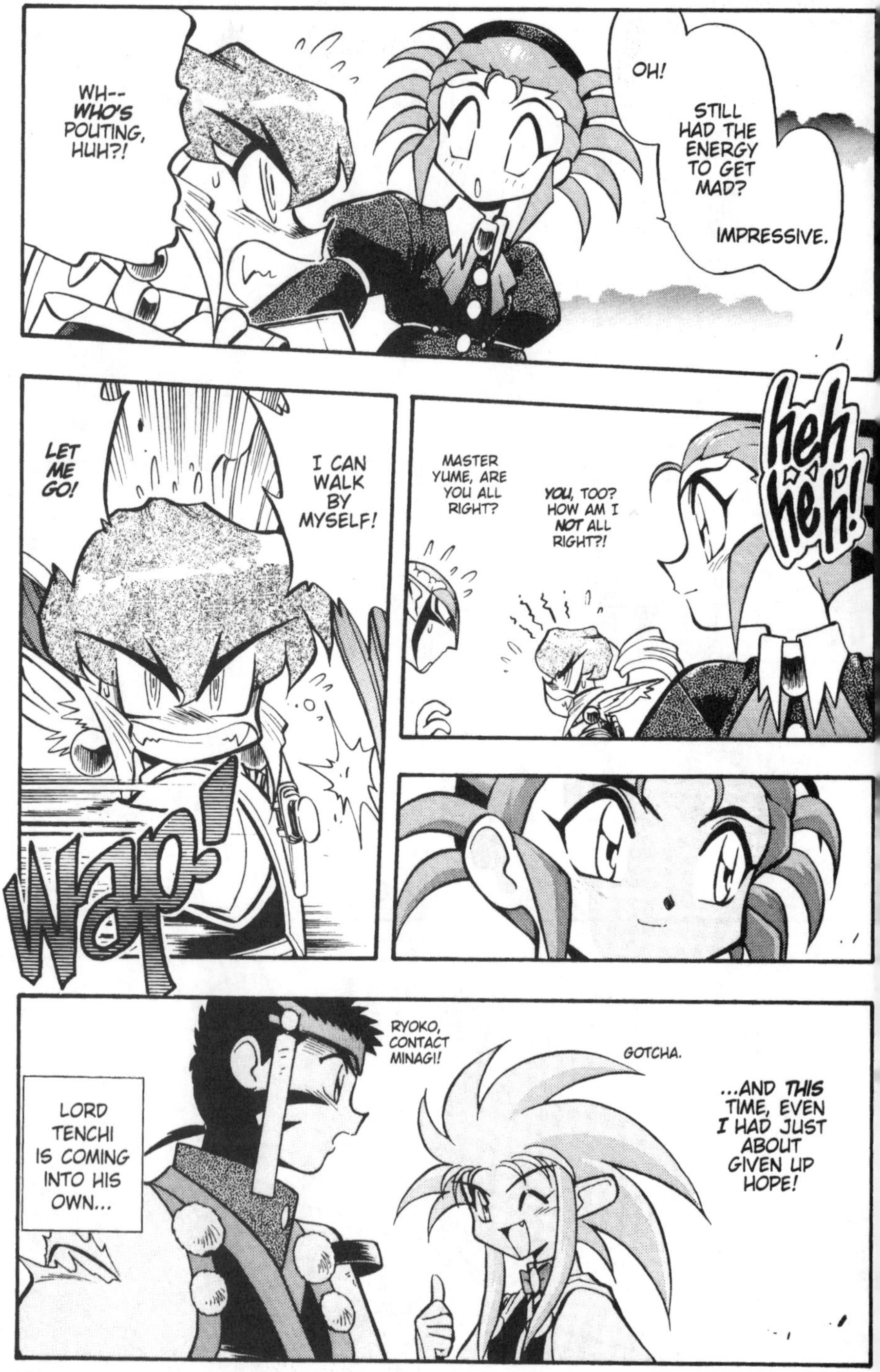
WH-- WHO'S POUTING, HUH?!
OH!
STILL HAD THE ENERGY TO GET MAD?
IMPRESSIVE.
LET ME GO!
I CAN WALK BY MYSELF!
WAP!
MASTER YUME, ARE YOU ALL RIGHT?
YOU, TOO? HOW AM I NOT ALL RIGHT?!
heh heh!
LORD TENCHI IS COMING INTO HIS OWN...
RYOKO, CONTACT MINAGI!
GOTCHA.
...AND THIS TIME, EVEN I HAD JUST ABOUT GIVEN UP HOPE!

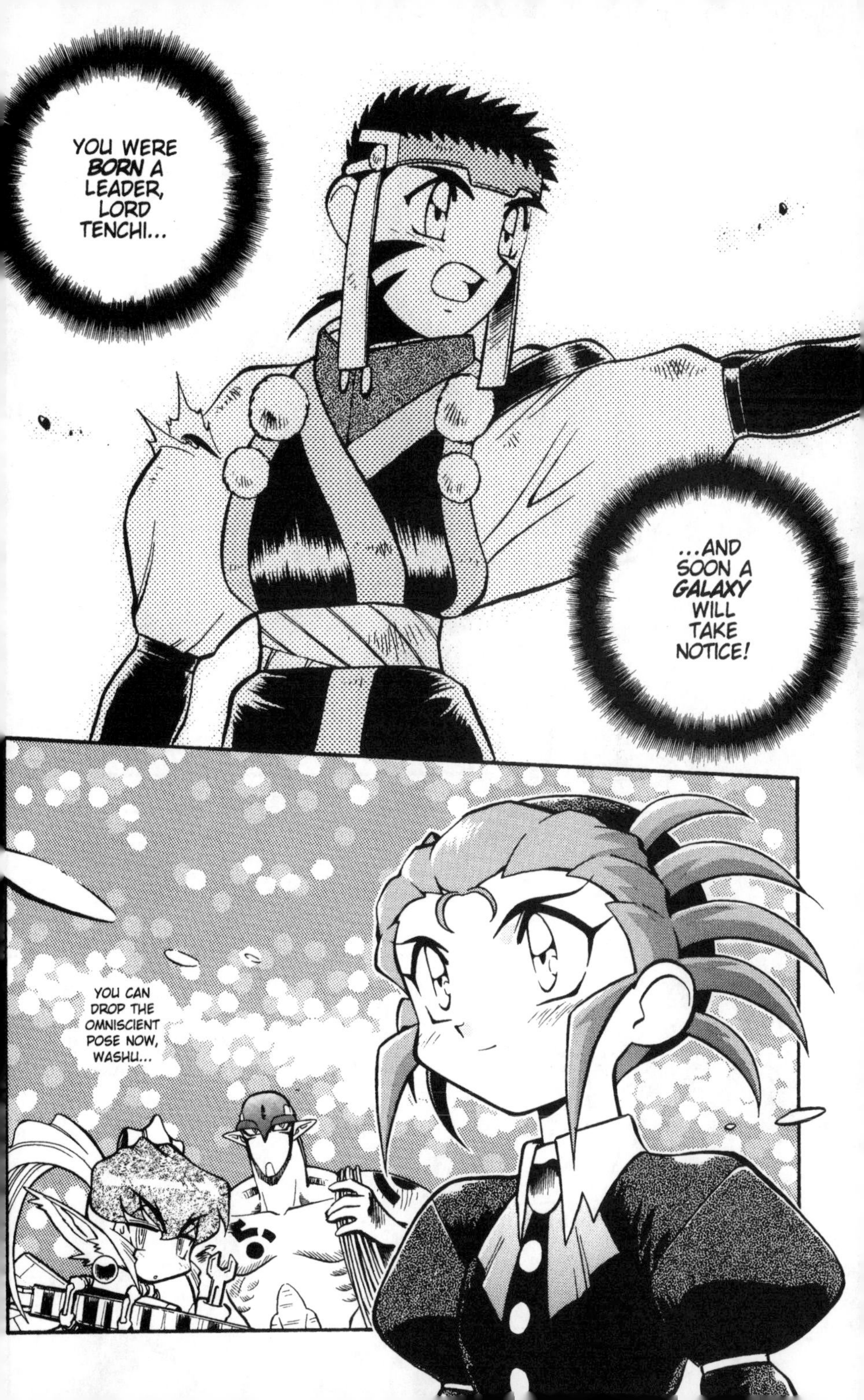
YOU WERE *BORN* A LEADER, LORD TENCHI...
...AND SOON A *GALAXY* WILL TAKE NOTICE!
YOU CAN DROP THE OMNISCIENT POSE NOW, WASHU...

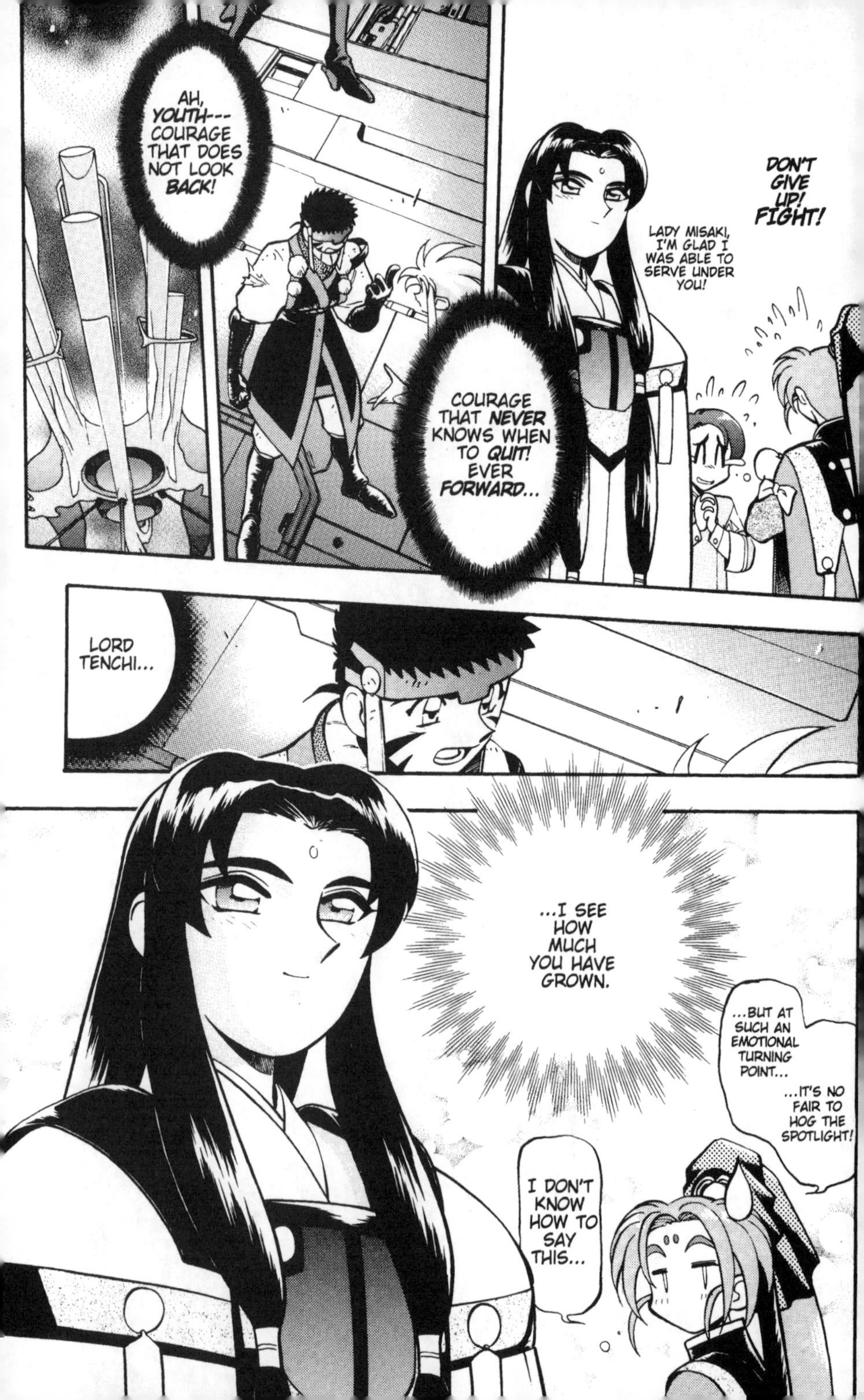
AH, YOUTH--- COURAGE THAT DOES NOT LOOK BACK!
COURAGE THAT NEVER KNOWS WHEN TO QUIT! EVER FORWARD...
LADY MISAKI, I'M GLAD I WAS ABLE TO SERVE UNDER YOU!
DON'T GIVE UP! FIGHT!
LORD TENCHI...
...I SEE HOW MUCH YOU HAVE GROWN.
I DON'T KNOW HOW TO SAY THIS...
...BUT AT SUCH AN EMOTIONAL TURNING POINT...
...IT'S NO FAIR TO HOG THE SPOTLIGHT!

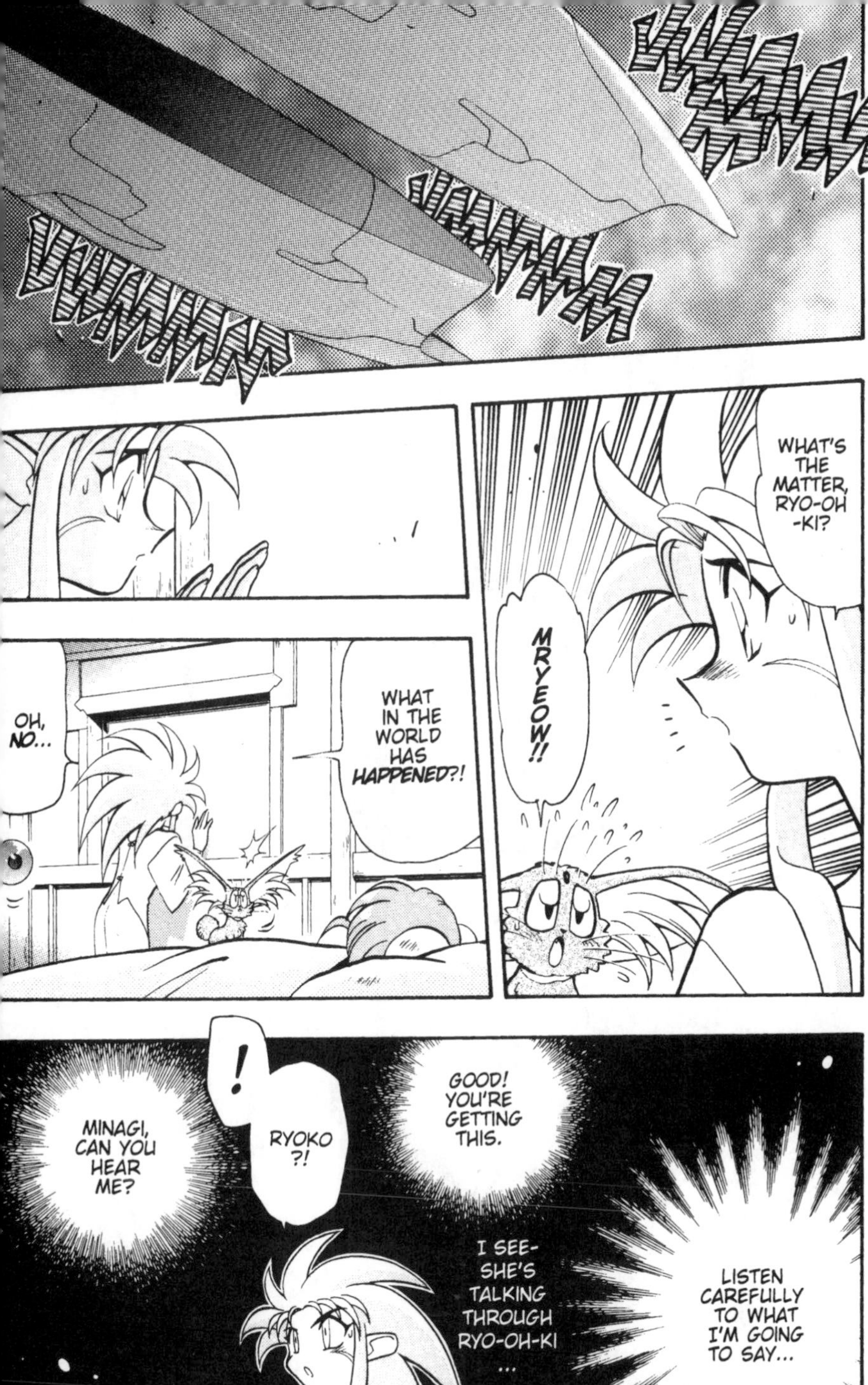
OH, NO...
WHAT IN THE WORLD HAS HAPPENED?!
WHAT'S THE MATTER, RYO-OH-KI?
MRYEOW!!
MINAGI, CAN YOU HEAR ME?
!
RYOKO?!
GOOD! YOU'RE GETTING THIS.
I SEE- SHE'S TALKING THROUGH RYO-OH-KI...
LISTEN CAREFULLY TO WHAT I'M GOING TO SAY...

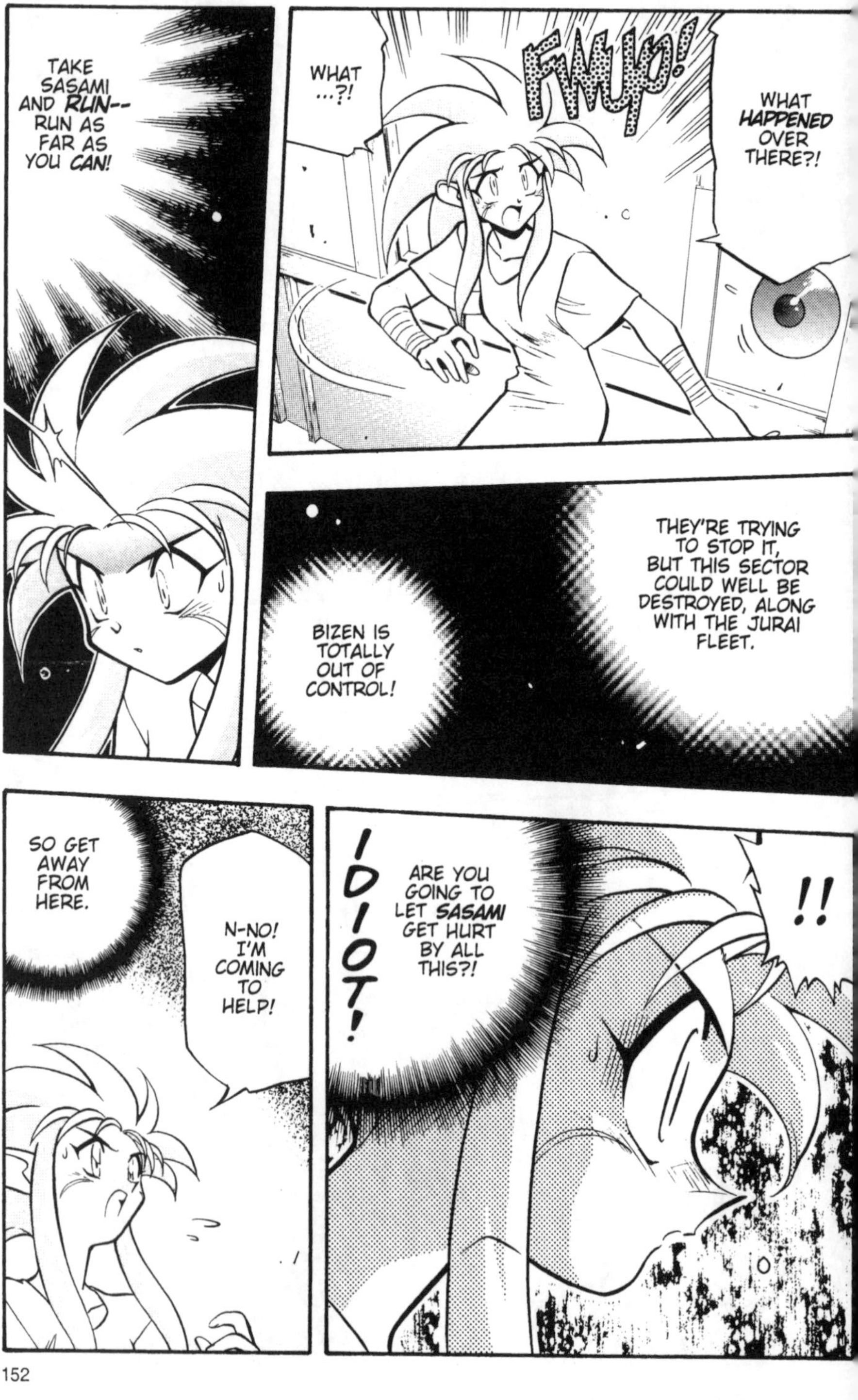
TAKE SASAMI AND RUN--RUN AS FAR AS YOU CAN!
WHAT ...?!
FWUP!
WHAT HAPPENED OVER THERE?!
BIZEN IS TOTALLY OUT OF CONTROL!
THEY'RE TRYING TO STOP IT, BUT THIS SECTOR COULD WELL BE DESTROYED, ALONG WITH THE JURAI FLEET.
SO GET AWAY FROM HERE.
N-NO! I'M COMING TO HELP!
IDIOT!
ARE YOU GOING TO LET SASAMI GET HURT BY ALL THIS?!
!!

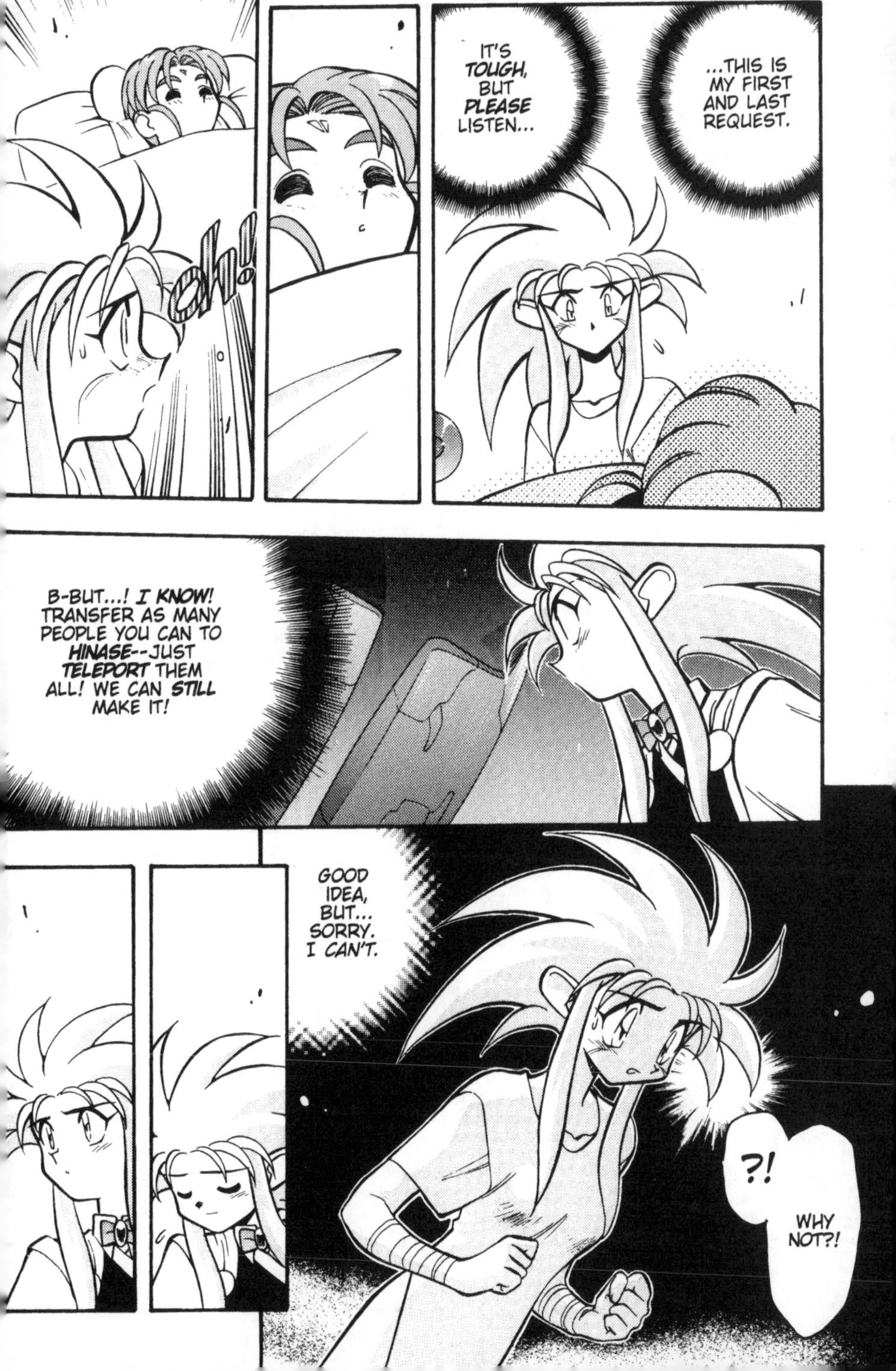
oh!
IT'S TOUGH, BUT PLEASE LISTEN...
...THIS IS MY FIRST AND LAST REQUEST.
B-BUT...! I KNOW! TRANSFER AS MANY PEOPLE YOU CAN TO HINASE--JUST TELEPORT THEM ALL! WE CAN STILL MAKE IT!
GOOD IDEA, BUT... SORRY. I CAN'T.
?!
WHY NOT?!

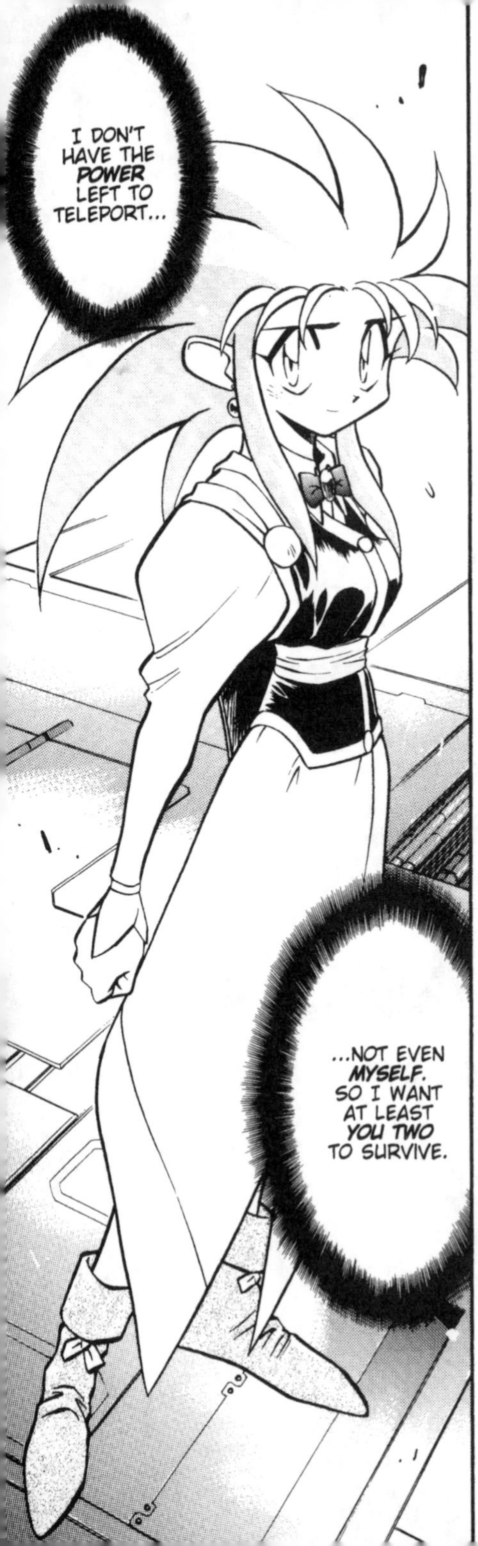
I DON'T HAVE THE POWER LEFT TO TELEPORT...
...NOT EVEN MYSELF. SO I WANT AT LEAST YOU TWO TO SURVIVE.

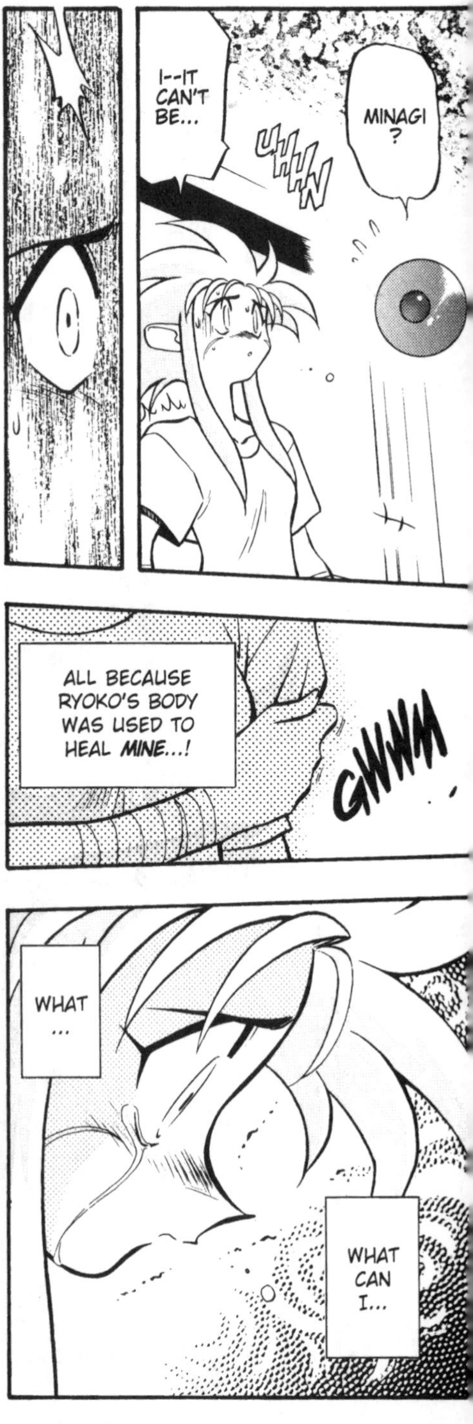
I--IT CAN'T BE...
UHHN
MINAGI ?
ALL BECAUSE RYOKO'S BODY WAS USED TO HEAL MINE...!
GWWM
WHAT ...
WHAT CAN I...

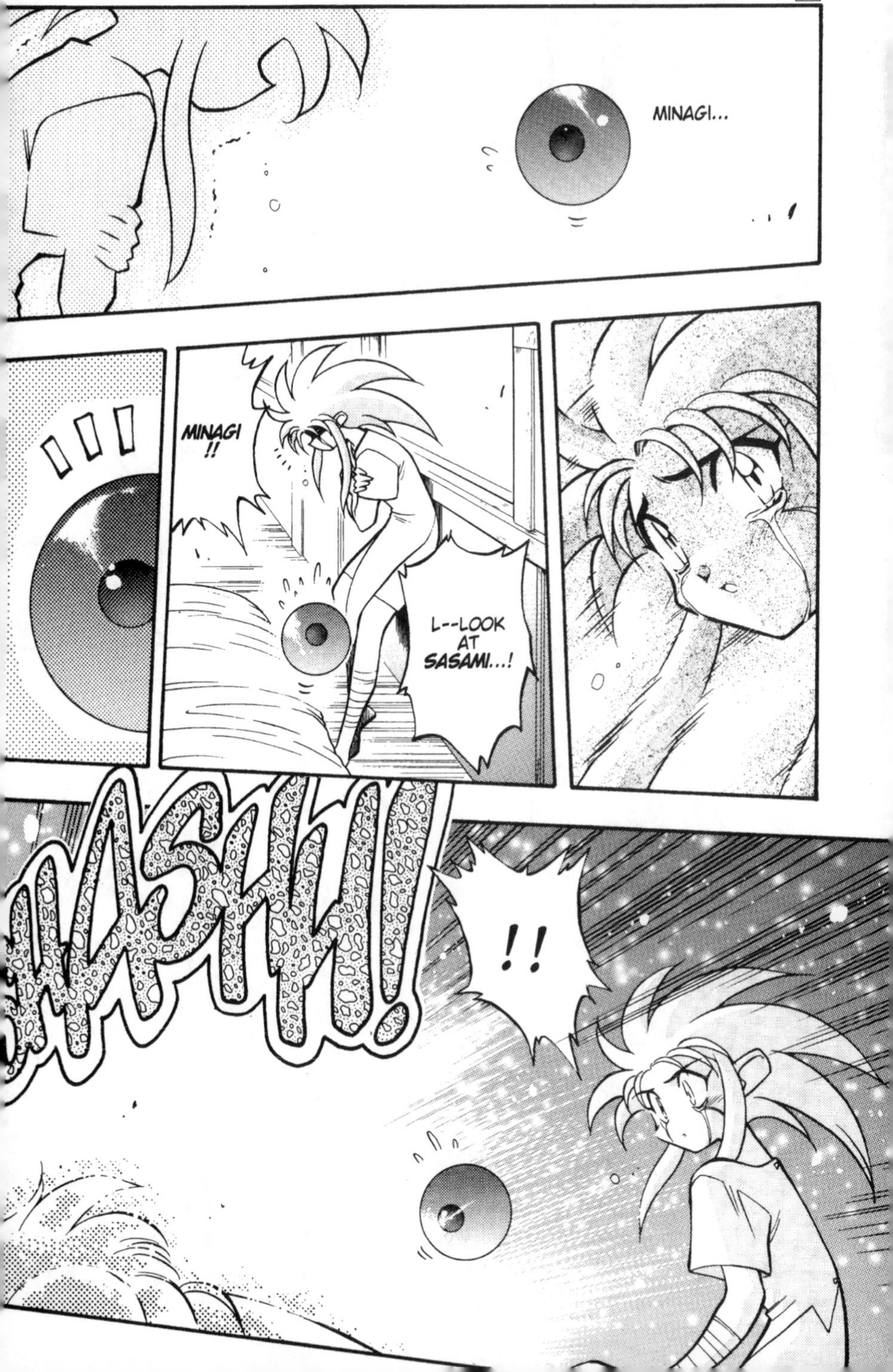
MINAGI...
MINAGI !!
L--LOOK AT SASAMI...!
!!

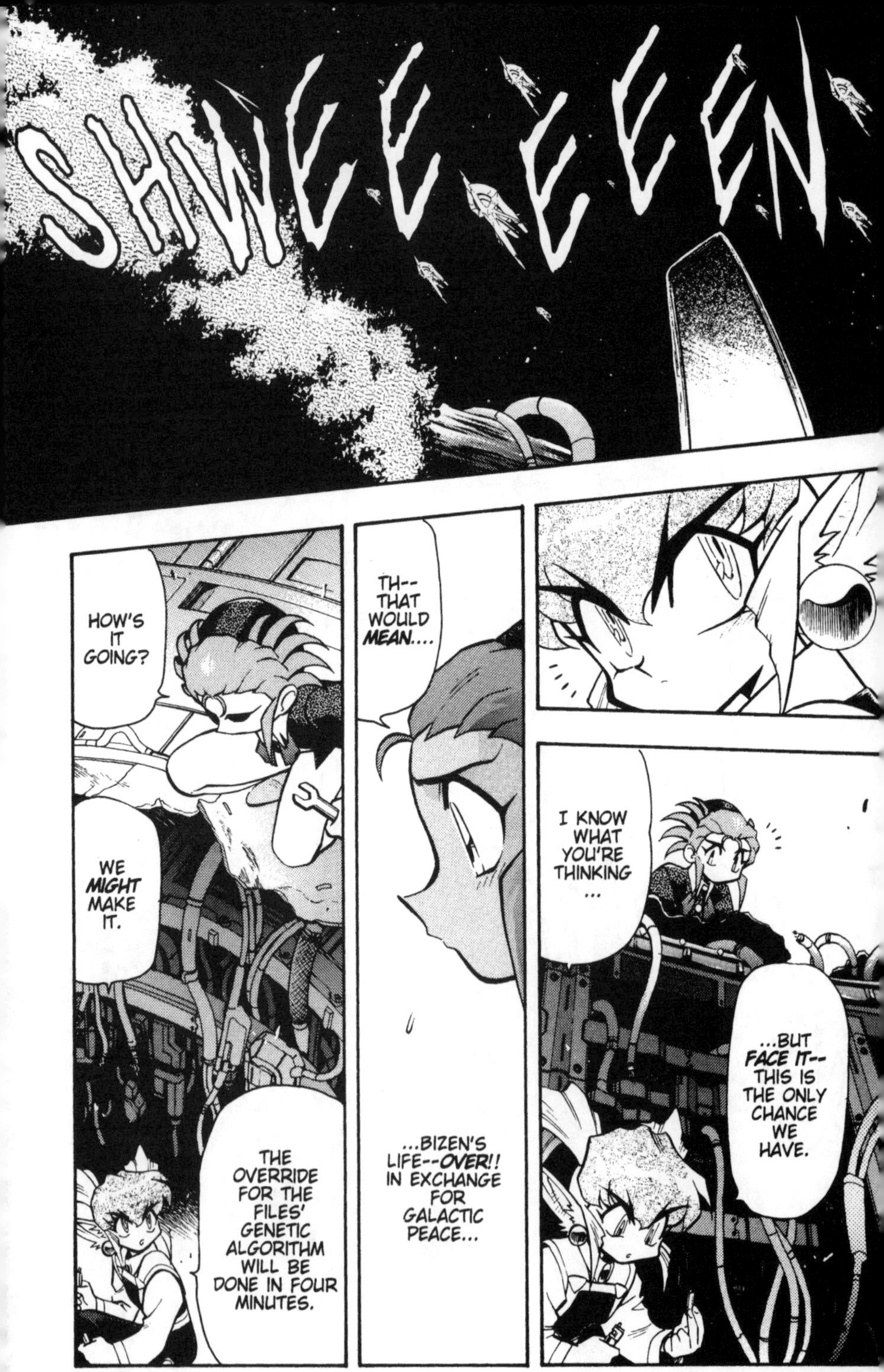
SHWEEEEN
HOW'S IT GOING?
WE MIGHT MAKE IT.
THE OVERRIDE FOR THE FILES' GENETIC ALGORITHM WILL BE DONE IN FOUR MINUTES.
TH-- THAT WOULD MEAN....
...BIZEN'S LIFE--OVER!! IN EXCHANGE FOR GALACTIC PEACE...
I KNOW WHAT YOU'RE THINKING ...
...BUT FACE IT-- THIS IS THE ONLY CHANCE WE HAVE.

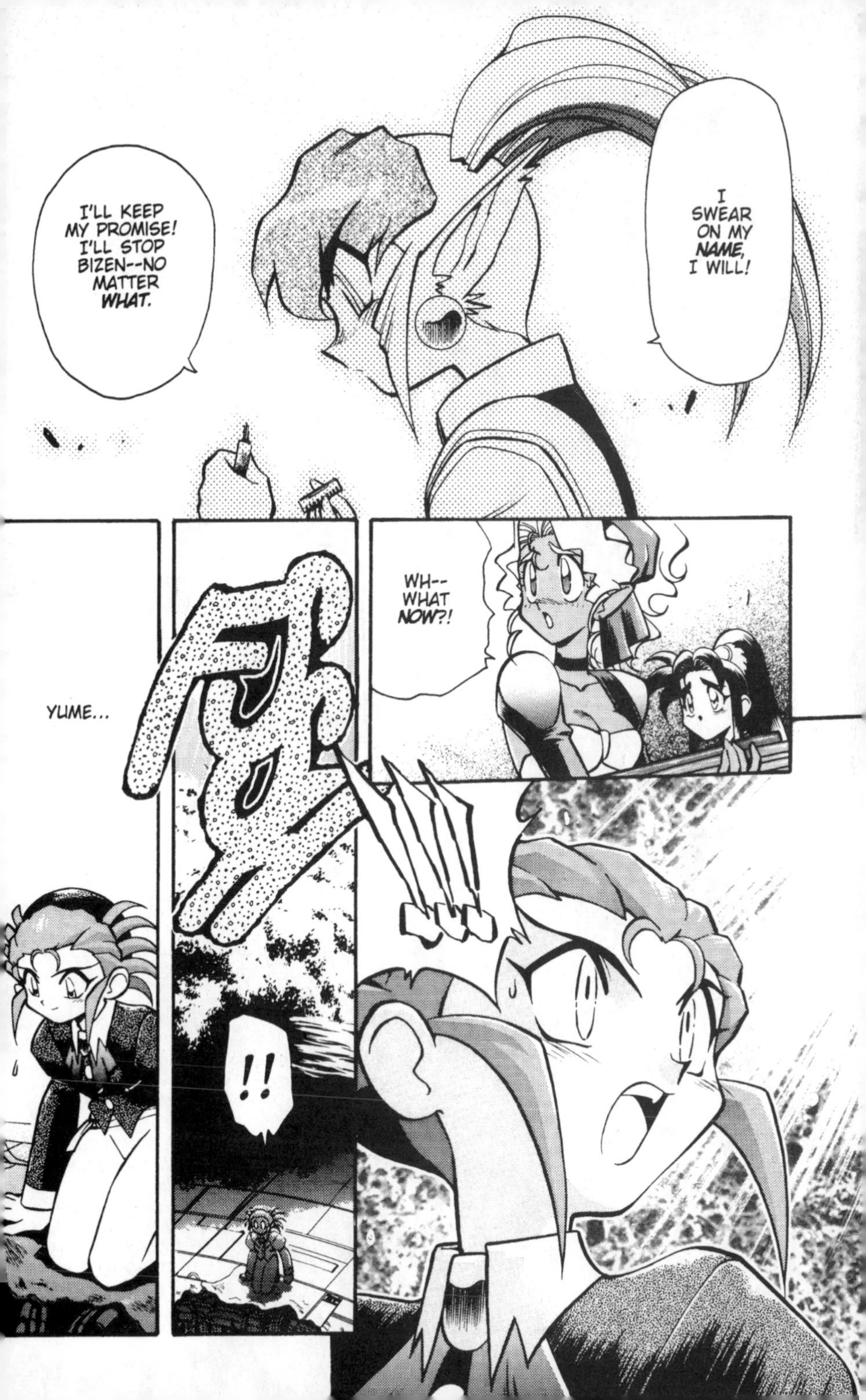
I'LL KEEP MY PROMISE! I'LL STOP BIZEN--NO MATTER WHAT.
I SWEAR ON MY NAME, I WILL!
YUME...
WH--WHAT NOW?!
!!

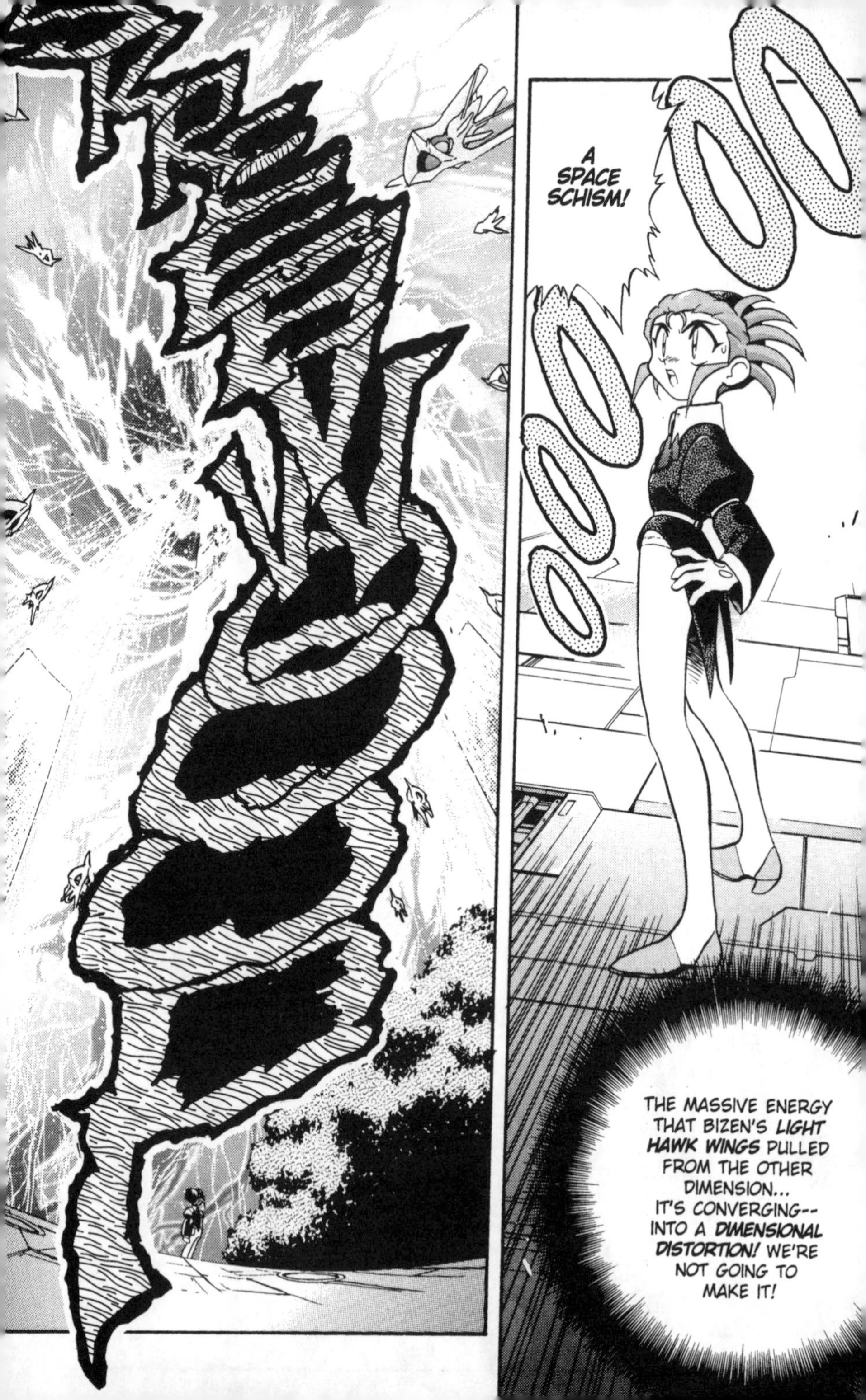
A SPACE SCHISM!
THE MASSIVE ENERGY THAT BIZEN'S **LIGHT HAWK WINGS** PULLED FROM THE OTHER DIMENSION... IT'S CONVERGING-- INTO A **DIMENSIONAL DISTORTION!** WE'RE NOT GOING TO MAKE IT!

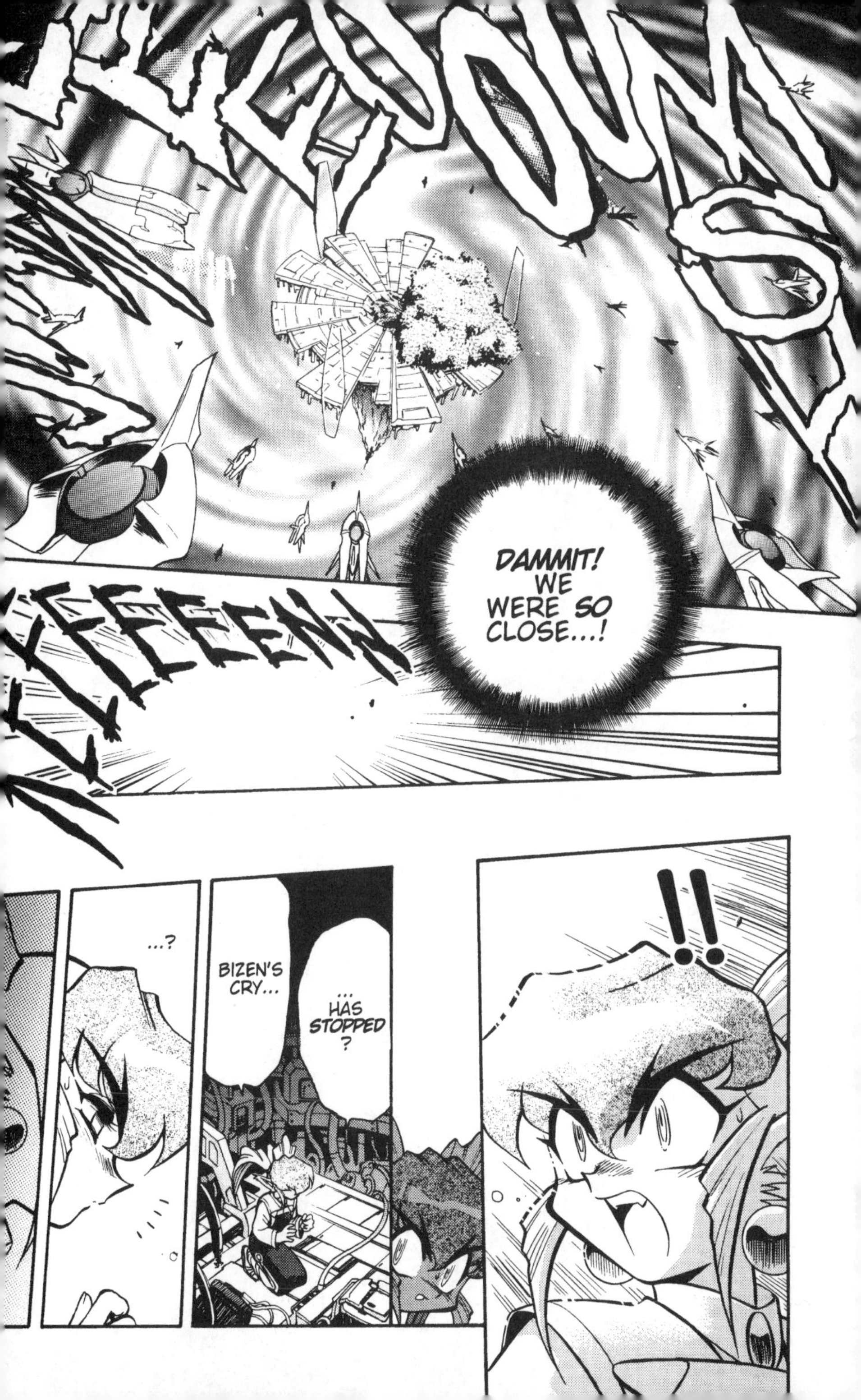
DAMMIT! WE WERE SO CLOSE...!
...?
BIZEN'S CRY...
... HAS STOPPED ?
!!

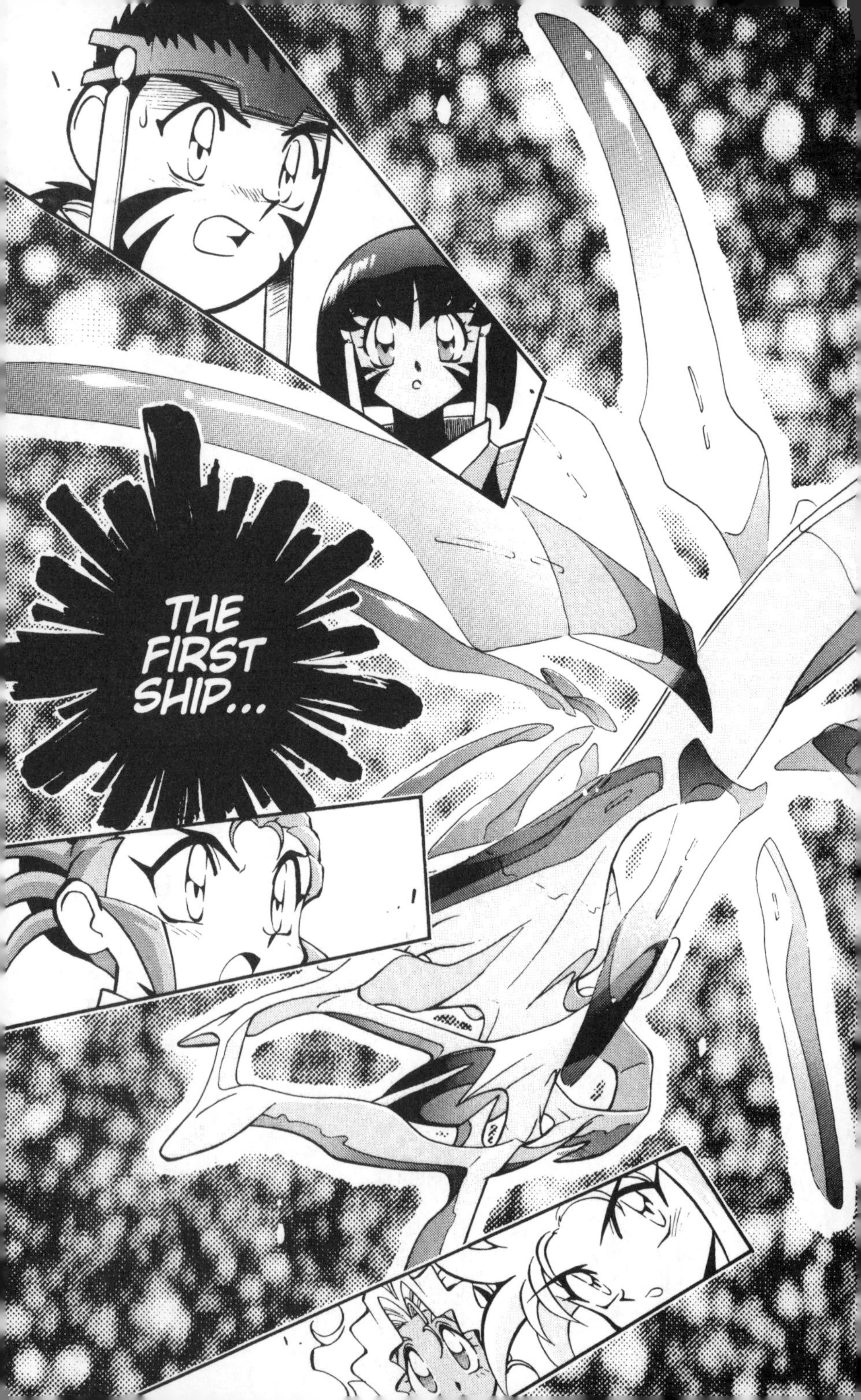
THE FIRST SHIP...

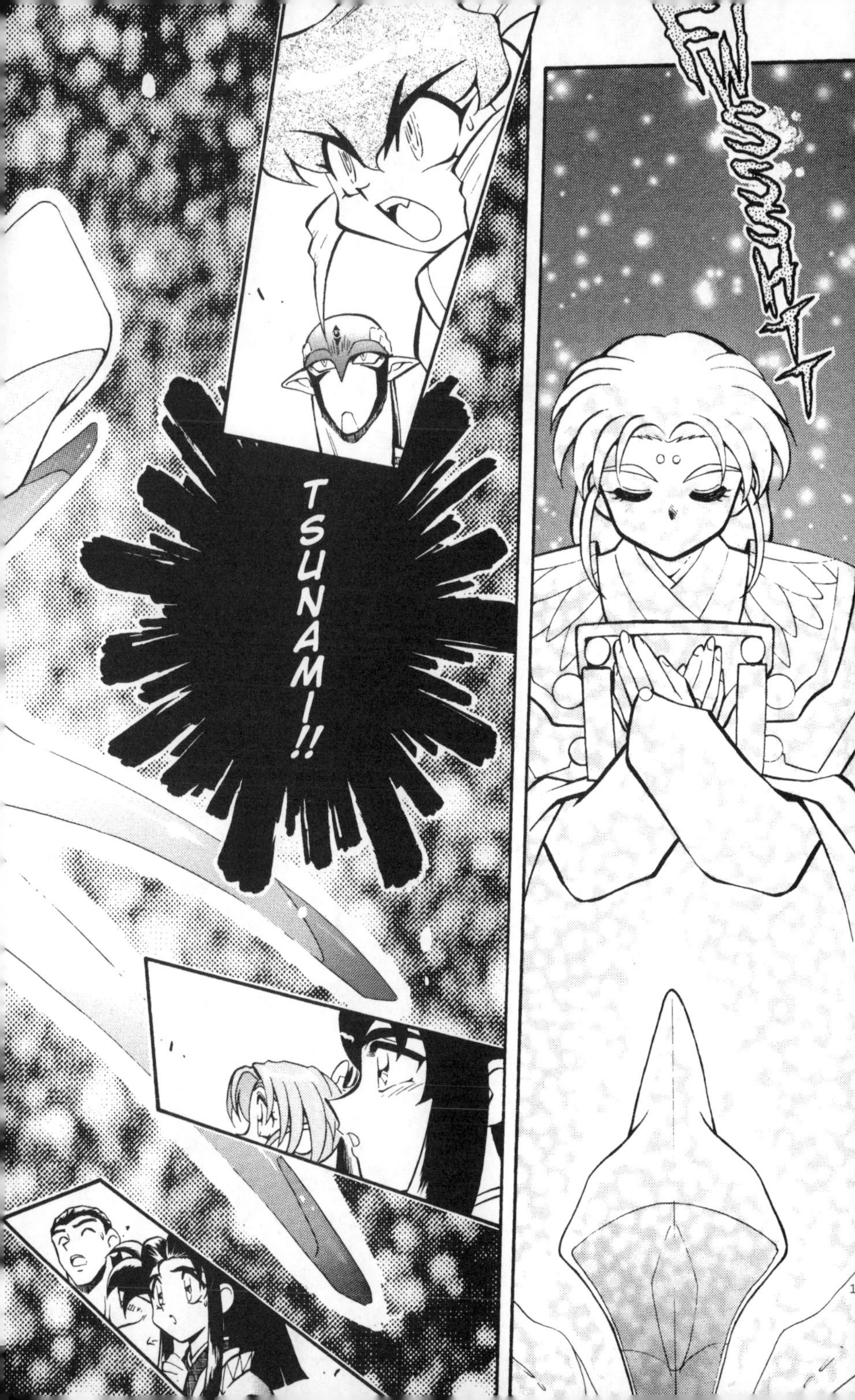
TSUNAMI!!
FWSSSSH

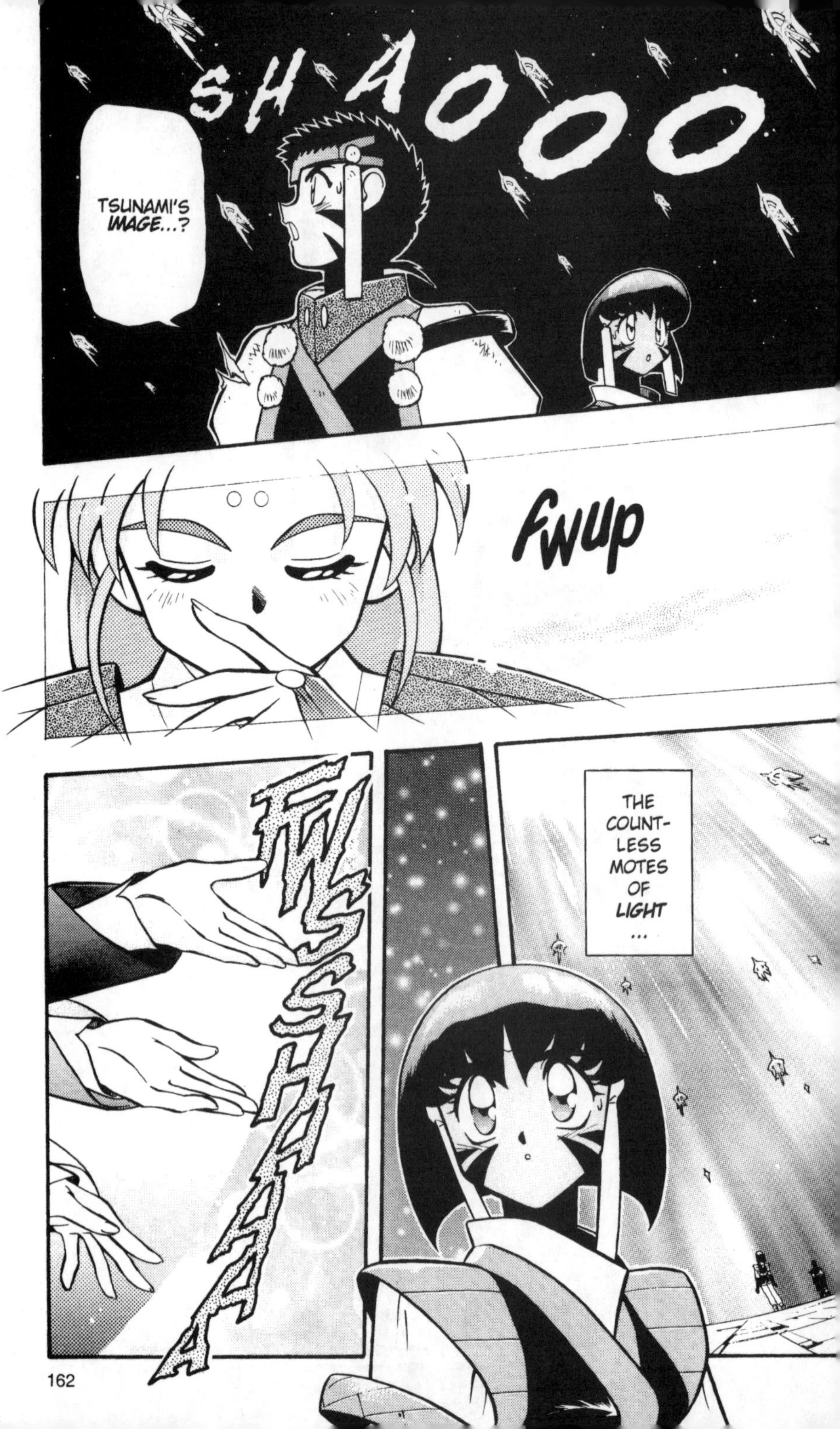
SHAOOO
TSUNAMI'S IMAGE...?
fwup
FWSSHAAA
THE COUNTLESS MOTES OF LIGHT ...

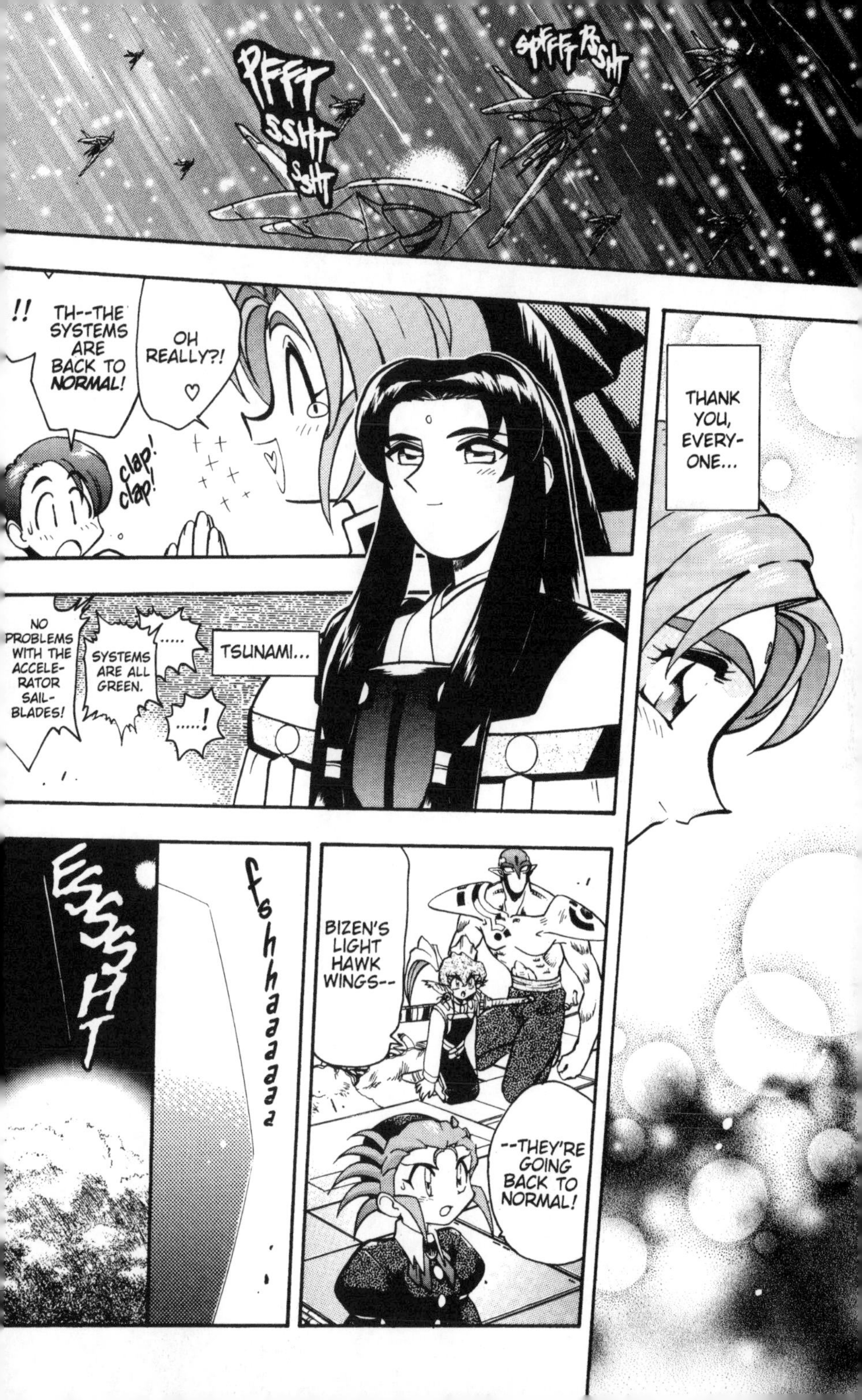
PFFT SSHT SSHT
SPFFFT PSSHT
!!
TH--THE SYSTEMS ARE BACK TO NORMAL!
OH REALLY?!
clap! clap!
THANK YOU, EVERY-ONE...
NO PROBLEMS WITH THE ACCELE-RATOR SAIL-BLADES!
SYSTEMS ARE ALL GREEN.
.....
.....!
TSUNAMI...
ESSSHT
fshhaaaaaaa
BIZEN'S LIGHT HAWK WINGS--
--THEY'RE GOING BACK TO NORMAL!

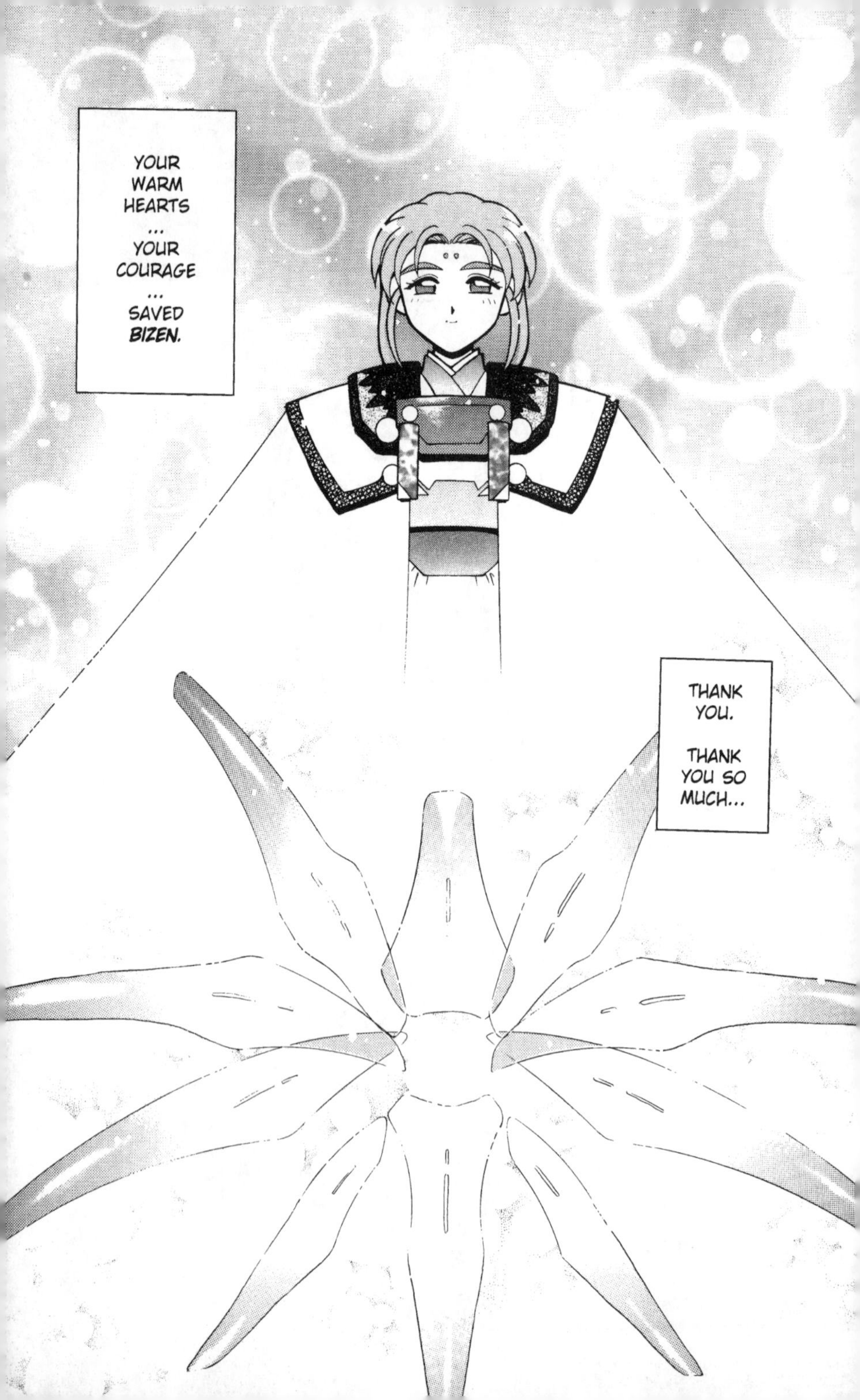
YOUR WARM HEARTS ... YOUR COURAGE ... SAVED BIZEN.
THANK YOU.
THANK YOU SO MUCH...

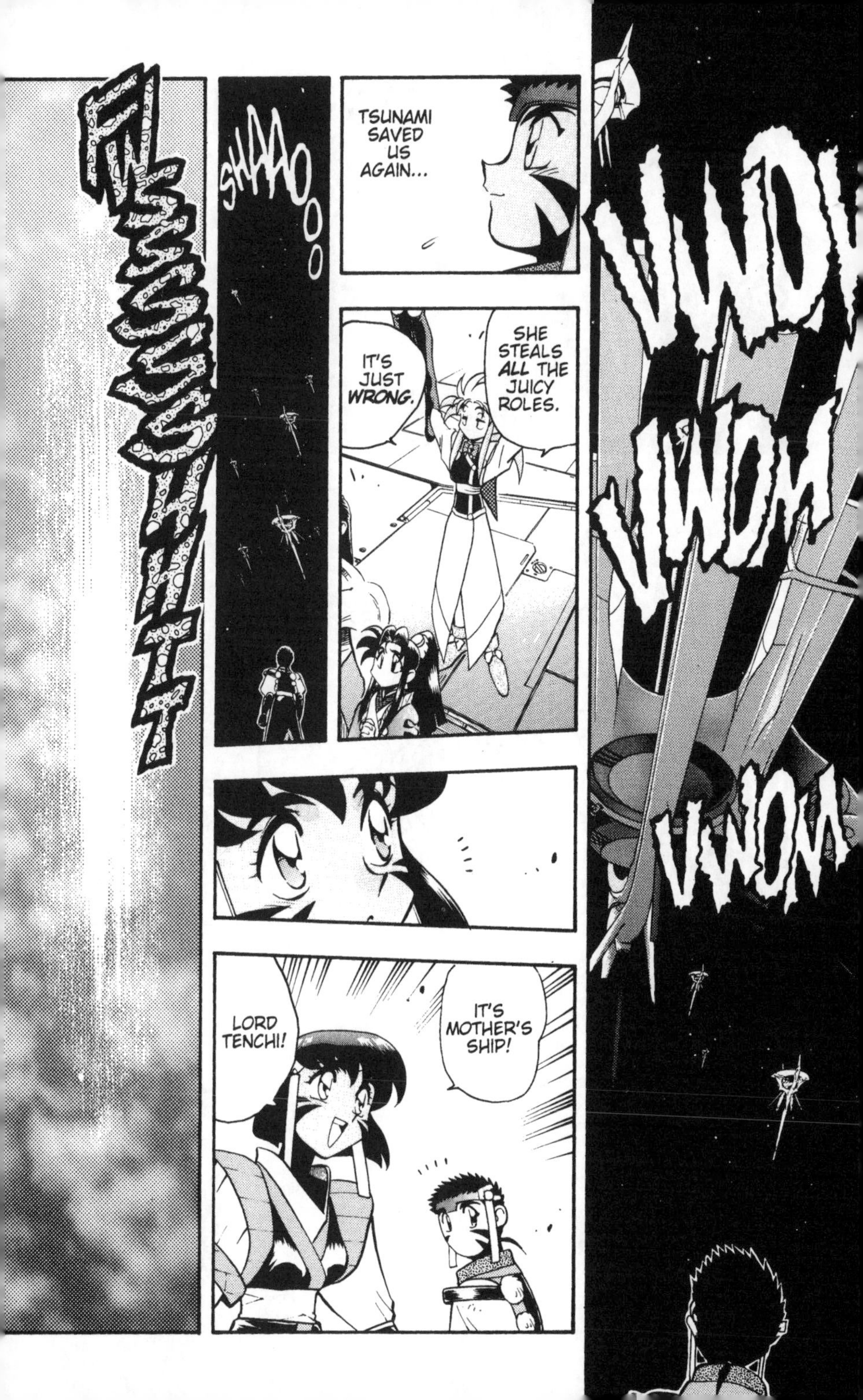

FLSSSSHHHT
SHAAAOOO
TSUNAMI SAVED US AGAIN...
IT'S JUST WRONG.
SHE STEALS ALL THE JUICY ROLES.
LORD TENCHI!
IT'S MOTHER'S SHIP!
VWOM
VWOM
VWOM

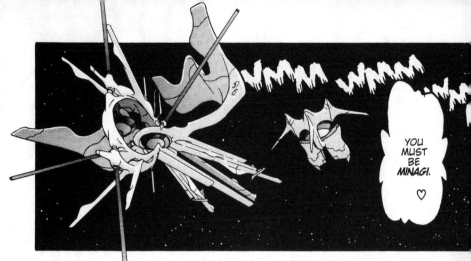

YOU MUST BE *MINAGI.* ♥

I DON'T KNOW *HOW* TO THANK YOU FOR TAKING CARE OF OUR KIDS!

OOH, SHE'S SO CUTE!

OH, NO PROB-- *REALLY* ...

THIS OLD WOMAN HASN'T CHANGED...

WAS IT *YOU* WHO SAID "OLD WOMAN"?!

LADY FUNAHO...

...YOU SEE, IT'S ABOUT *YUME...*

I DON'T *THINK* JURAI WILL BE BOTHERED ANYMORE.

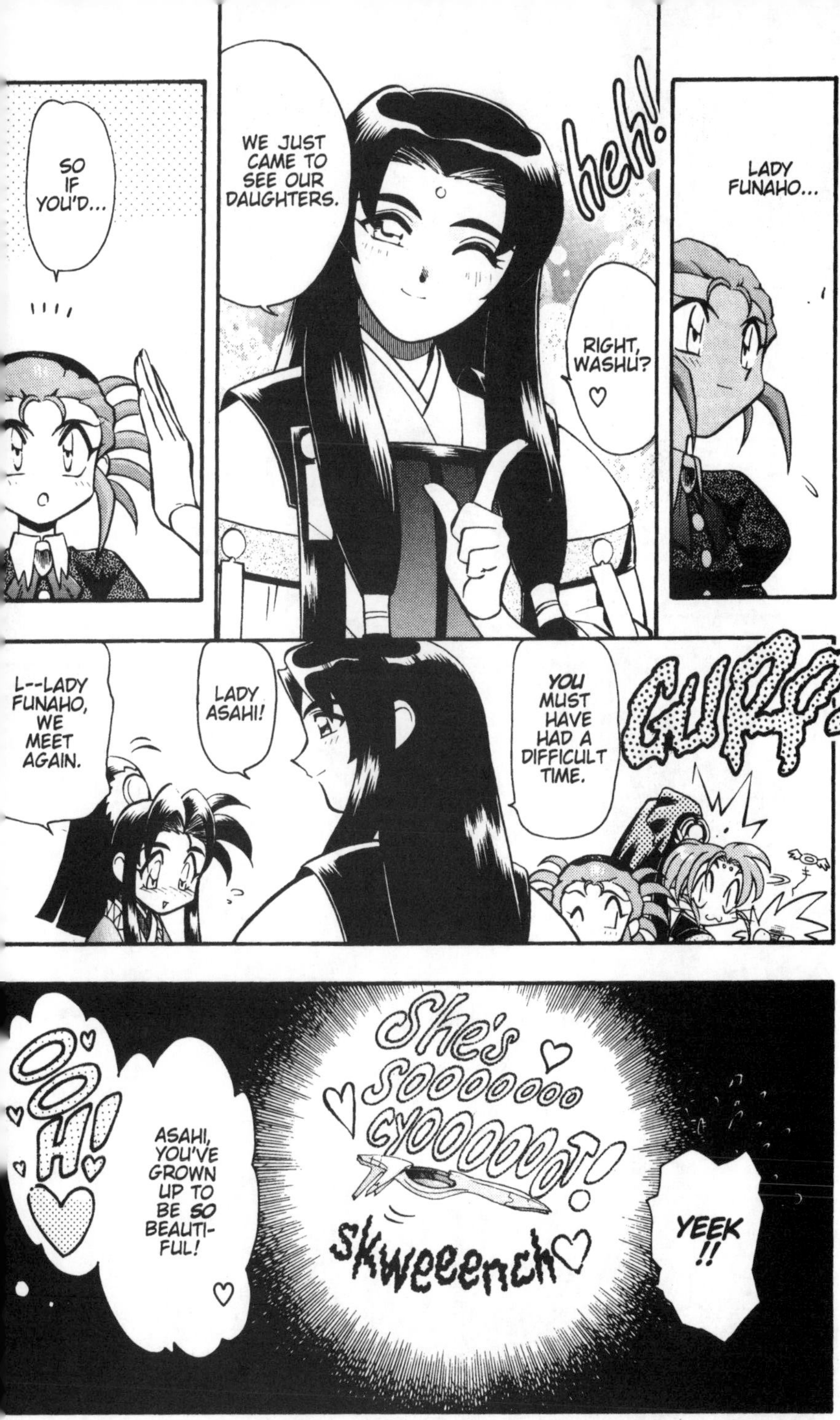

SO IF YOU'D...
WE JUST CAME TO SEE OUR DAUGHTERS.
heh!
RIGHT, WASHU? ♡
LADY FUNAHO...
L--LADY FUNAHO, WE MEET AGAIN.
LADY ASAHI!
YOU MUST HAVE HAD A DIFFICULT TIME.
GURQ!
OOOH!
ASAHI, YOU'VE GROWN UP TO BE SO BEAUTIFUL!
She's SOOOOOOO CYOOOOOOT!
skweeench
YEEK!!

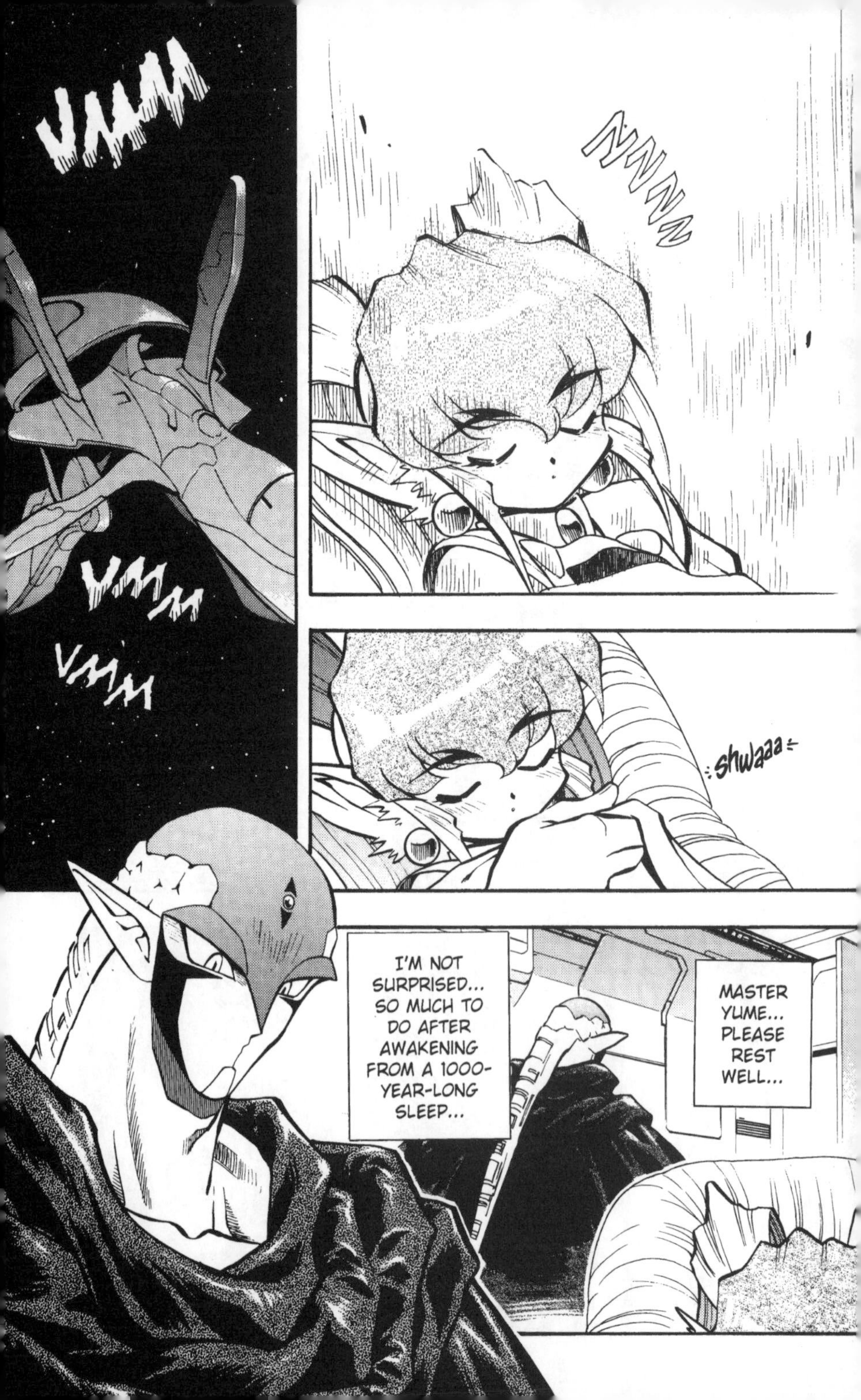
VMM
VMM
VMM
NNNN
shwaaa
I'M NOT SURPRISED... SO MUCH TO DO AFTER AWAKENING FROM A 1000-YEAR-LONG SLEEP...
MASTER YUME... PLEASE REST WELL...

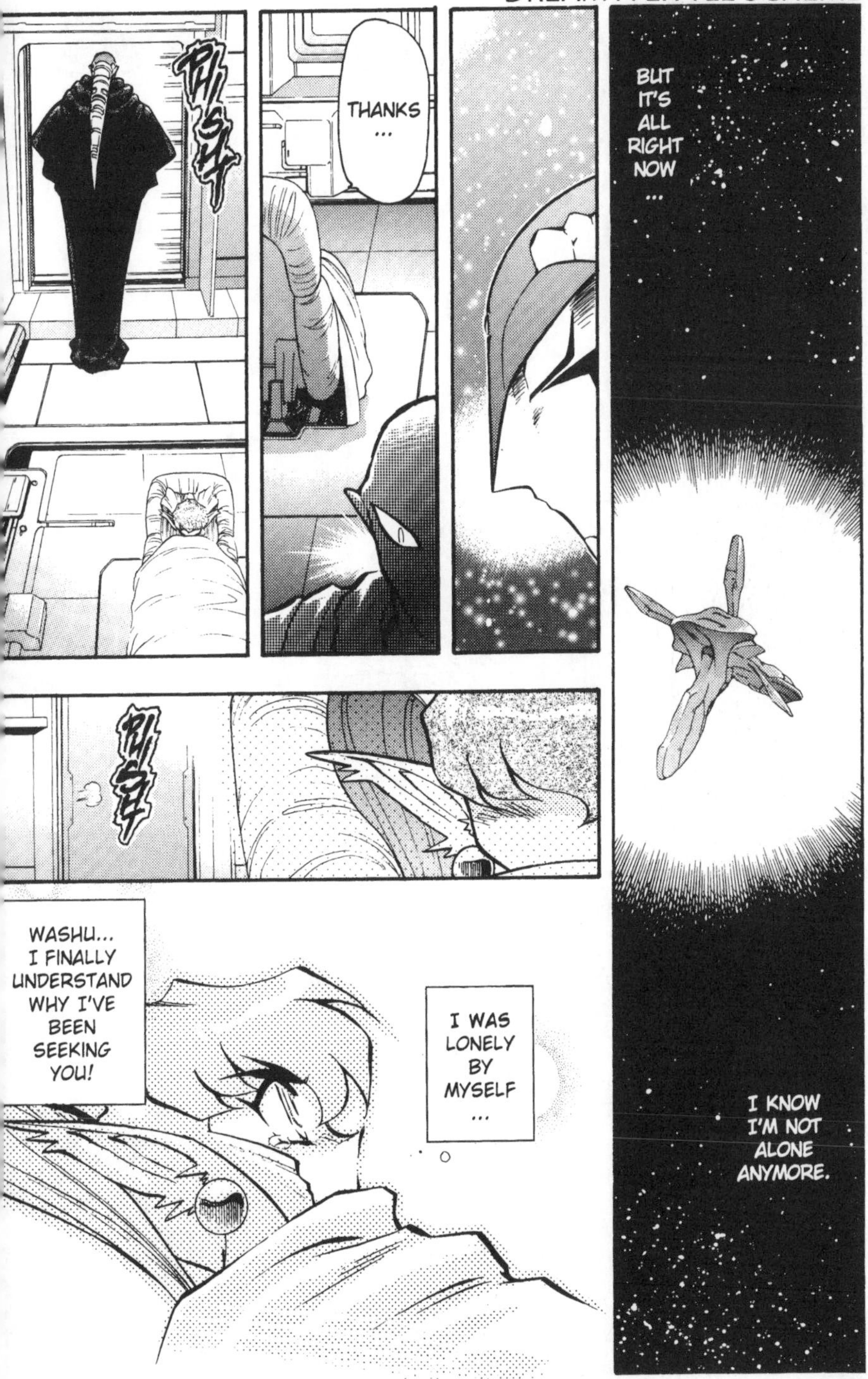
PHSH
THANKS ...
RUSH
WASHU... I FINALLY UNDERSTAND WHY I'VE BEEN SEEKING YOU!
I WAS LONELY BY MYSELF ...
BUT IT'S ALL RIGHT NOW ...
I KNOW I'M NOT ALONE ANYMORE.

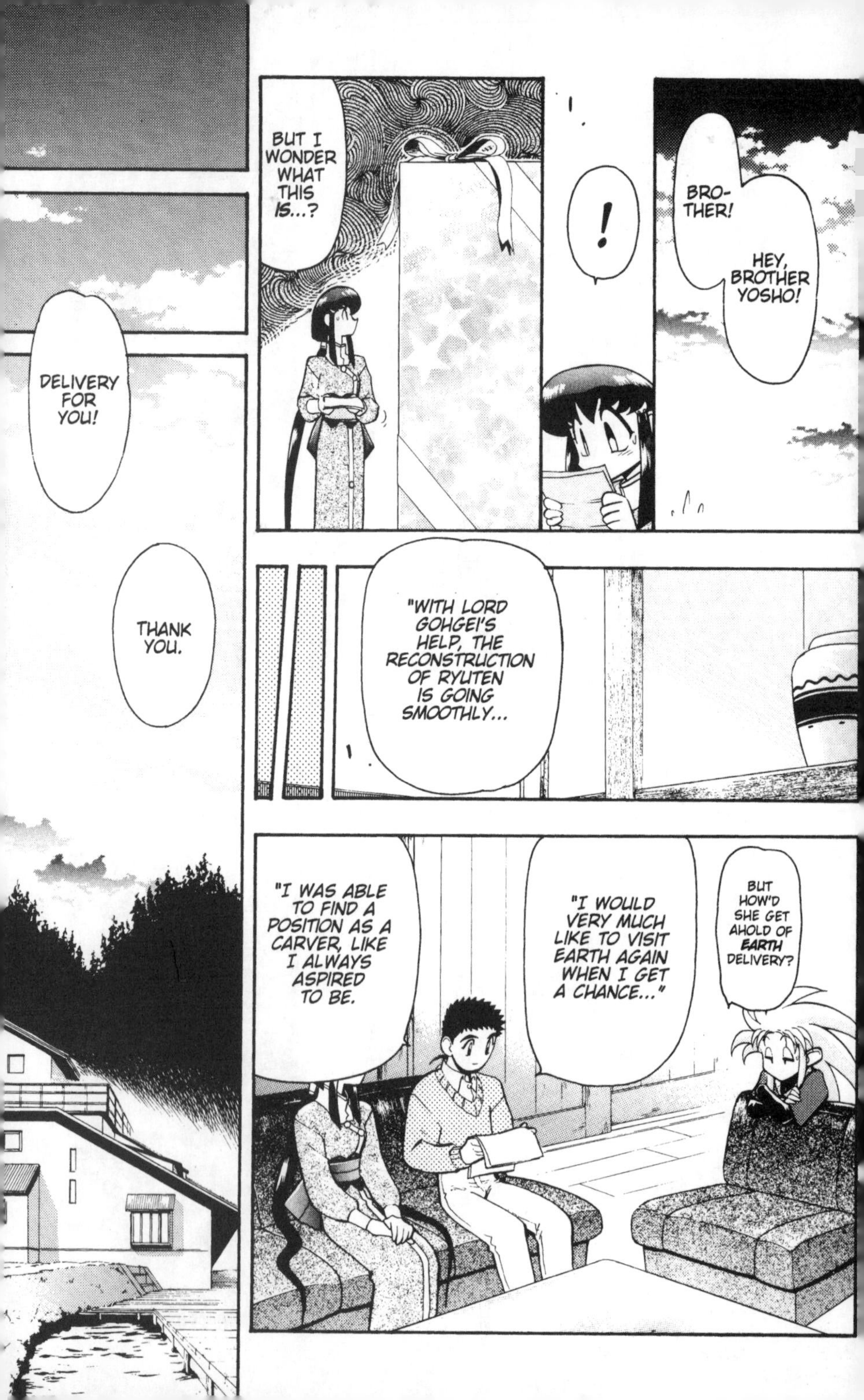
DELIVERY FOR YOU!
THANK YOU.
BUT I WONDER WHAT THIS IS...?
!
BRO-THER!
HEY, BROTHER YOSHO!
"WITH LORD GOHGEI'S HELP, THE RECONSTRUCTION OF RYUTEN IS GOING SMOOTHLY...
"I WAS ABLE TO FIND A POSITION AS A CARVER, LIKE I ALWAYS ASPIRED TO BE.
"I WOULD VERY MUCH LIKE TO VISIT EARTH AGAIN WHEN I GET A CHANCE..."
BUT HOW'D SHE GET AHOLD OF EARTH DELIVERY?

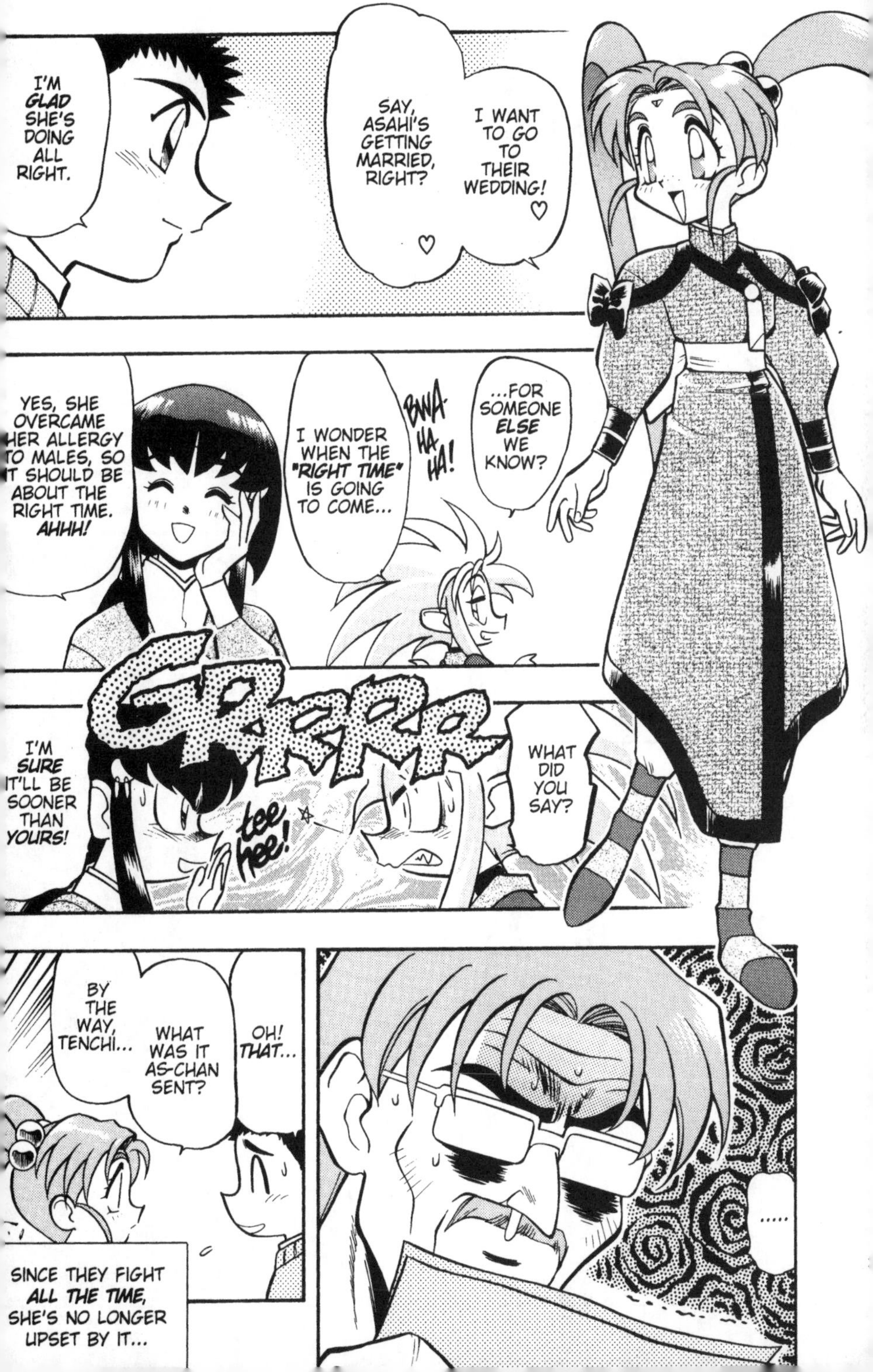

I'M GLAD SHE'S DOING ALL RIGHT.
SAY, ASAHI'S GETTING MARRIED, RIGHT? ♡
I WANT TO GO TO THEIR WEDDING! ♡
YES, SHE OVERCAME HER ALLERGY TO MALES, SO IT SHOULD BE ABOUT THE RIGHT TIME. AHHH!
I WONDER WHEN THE "RIGHT TIME" IS GOING TO COME...
BWA HA HA!
...FOR SOMEONE ELSE WE KNOW?
GRRRR
I'M SURE IT'LL BE SOONER THAN YOURS!
tee hee!
WHAT DID YOU SAY?
BY THE WAY, TENCHI...
WHAT WAS IT AS-CHAN SENT?
OH! THAT...
SINCE THEY FIGHT ALL THE TIME, SHE'S NO LONGER UPSET BY IT...
.....

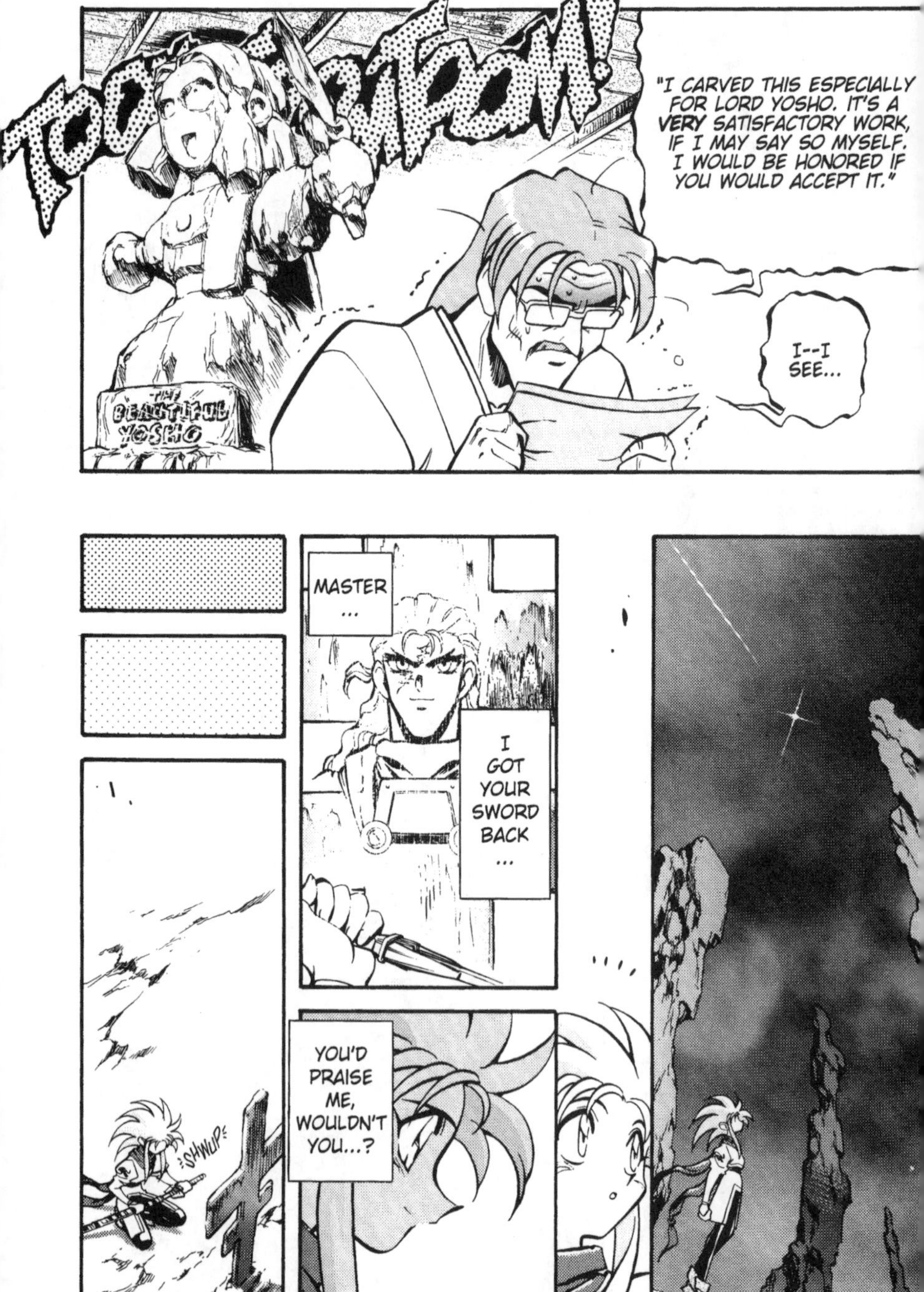
THE BEAUTIFUL YOSHO
"I CARVED THIS ESPECIALLY FOR LORD YOSHO. IT'S A **VERY** SATISFACTORY WORK, IF I MAY SAY SO MYSELF. I WOULD BE HONORED IF YOU WOULD ACCEPT IT."
I--I SEE...
SHWUP
MASTER ...
I GOT YOUR SWORD BACK ...
YOU'D PRAISE ME, WOULDN'T YOU...?

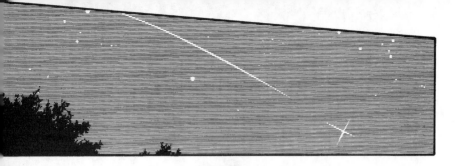

DO YOU WISH UPON A STAR ON *JURAI*, TOO?

NO...

YOUR FATHER TAUGHT US.

I WISH THAT I WILL MARRY LORD TENCHI... I WISH THAT RYOKO WOULD GO AWAY...

I WISH TO KISS SWEET TENCHI'S LIPS. I WISH THAT *ANYTHING* BAD WOULD HAPPEN TO AYEKA!

SO... WHAT DID YOU WISH FOR?

ME?

WELL, I...

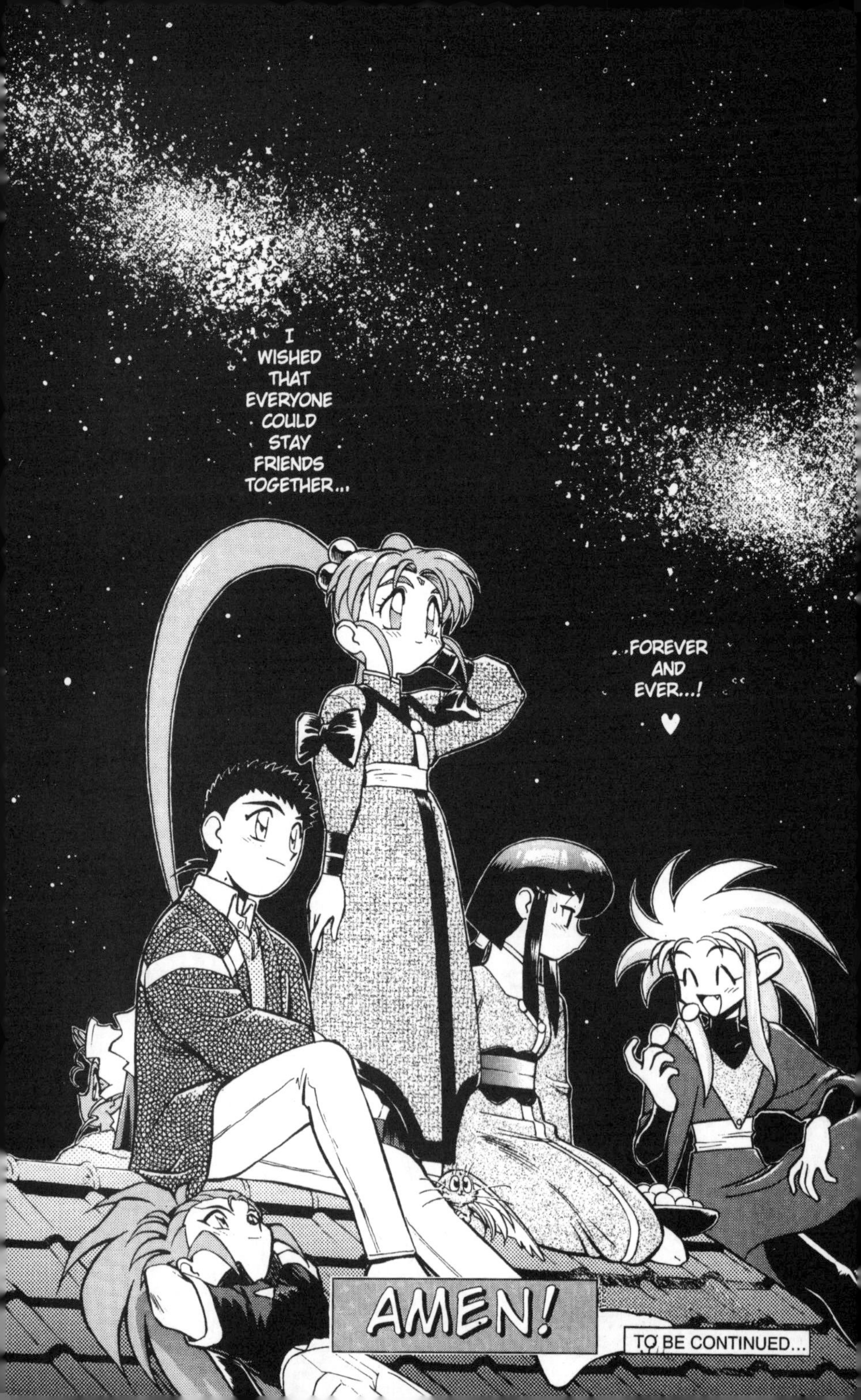
I WISHED THAT EVERYONE COULD STAY FRIENDS TOGETHER...
...FOREVER AND EVER...! ♥
AMEN!
TO BE CONTINUED...

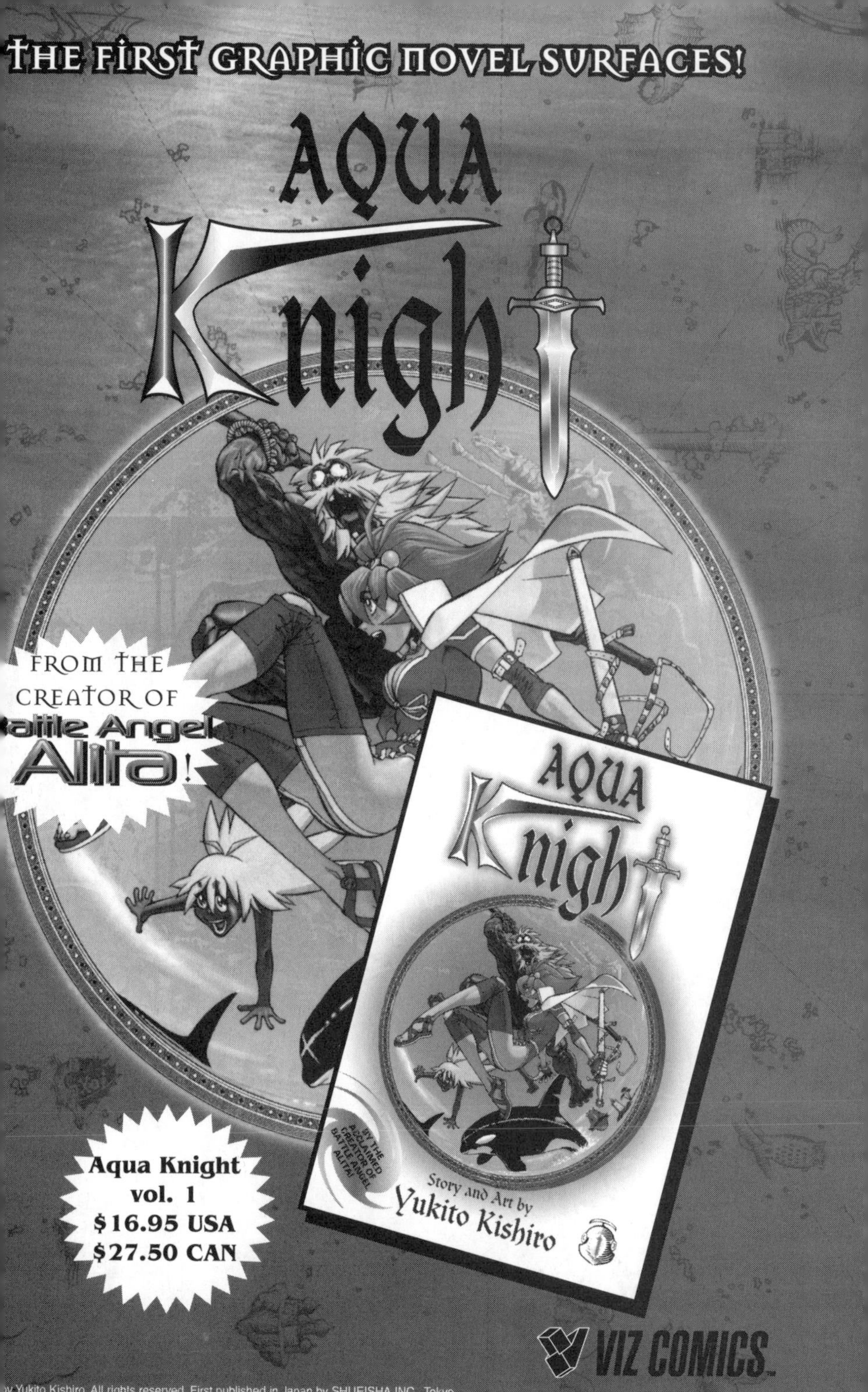
THE FIRST GRAPHIC NOVEL SURFACES!
AQUA Knight
FROM THE CREATOR OF
attle Angel
Alita!
AQUA Knight
BY THE ACCLAIMED CREATOR OF BATTLE ANGEL ALITA!
Story and Art by
Yukito Kishiro
Aqua Knight
vol. 1
$16.95 USA
$27.50 CAN
VIZ COMICS

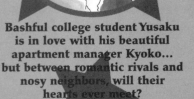